Moshe Idel
The Privileged Divine Feminine in

Perspectives on Jewish Texts and Contexts

———

Edited by
Vivian Liska

Volume 10

Moshe Idel

The Privileged Divine Feminine in Kabbalah

—

DE GRUYTER

ISBN 978-3-11-073643-4
e-ISBN (PDF) 978-3-11-059980-0
e-ISBN (EPUB) 978-3-11-059760-8
ISSN 2199-6962

Library of Congress Control Number: 2018952920

Bibliographic information published by the Deutsche Nationalbibliothek
The Deutsche Nationalbibliothek lists this publication in the Deutsche Nationalbibliografie;
detailed bibliographic data are available on the Internet at http://dnb.dnb.de.

Typesetting: Integra Software Services Pvt. Ltd.
Printing and binding: CPI books GmbH, Leck

www.degruyter.com

"[She...] is higher than all."

Zohar, Tiqqunei Zohar, R. Moshe Cordovero, R. Hayyim Vital, R. Naftali Bakharakh, R. Abraham Yehoshu'a Heschel of Apta, R. Shlomo Eliashiv

"Since whatever is done, is always done only by [means of] *Malkhut*."
R. Shlomo Eliashiv, *Leshem, Shevo ve-'Ahlemah, Sefer De'ah*, 2, fol. 158a.

"Put me under Your Wings

And by my mother and sister."

הַכְנִיסִינִי תַּחַת כְּנָפֵךְ,

וַהֲיִי לִי אֵם וְאָחוֹת

Chaim Nachman Bialik

Preface

The present study addresses a complex topic: the preeminent status of the divine feminine power, referred to also as Female, within the theosophical structures of many important Kabbalists, Sabbatean thinkers, and Hasidic masters. The complexity derives from the usual compact and allusive language of Kabbalists, whose discourse was not oriented toward analytical expositions; nor were they concerned with dealing with issues of sex and gender in the way they are conceived in modern, direct types of discourse. Their treatment of such important topics is, in many cases, oblique. The greater complexity is not only a matter of the opacity and intricacy of many Kabbalists' texts; an additional factor stems from mediation based on modern scholarly concepts in which an exploration of issues related to sex and gender has become an intrinsic part of scholarship in the humanities. At present, this approach is more than simply a tool for empowering women, part of the struggle against misogyny, or the striving for social changes in the present – indubitably very laudable developments. The problem arises upon attempts to apply this methodology for an understanding the past, including texts that do not subscribe to the ideals forged in some circles during the last century, and to judge them by these standards. Analyzing the past with the use of modern techniques has become a way of unmasking its darker sides; in many cases, this does not represent an effort toward a new understanding of a different culture but, unfortunately and preeminently, a critique of ancient or medieval cultures, which, naturally, do not comply with the requirements of political correctness with regard to attitudes toward sex and gender. Frequently, critiques precede a sustained effort at understanding, and scholars' neglect of most of the texts analyzed below, constitutes just one example of this approach.

Despite the two main theses of this study as to the relatively privileged status of the divine Feminine and the importance of what I call the three phases gender theory, this is by no means an attempt to defend Kabbalah or Kabbalists, or even less Judaism, from criticism of their androcentric attitudes, which, indeed, exist there substantially. Nor do I intend to emulate the Kabbalists' more positive approaches to the divine Feminine, mainly ignored in scholarship in the field. My aim is to highlight the existence of other attitudes that have been ignored or neglected in scholarship. I therefore do not recommend viewing my conclusions as any recommendation for a new understanding of Judaism as a whole or as a source of inspiration for a spiritual reform of Judaism or its theology. Nor are the texts addressed below helpful in formulating a "feminine character" as Kabbalists envisioned it. My primary aim here, as in my other studies, is to gain a better understanding of some aspects of a vast literature by pointing to the richness and diversity found in Kabbalistic literature. Such a project requires a

https://doi.org/10.1515/9783110599800-201

non-ideological attitude that differentiates among diverse voices, not only within the broad spectrum of Kabbalistic literature as a whole but also in the writings of individual authors. In fact, I postulate that one can discern diverse types of theosophical thought in Kabbalah that shaped the understanding of the divine feminine powers. Occasionally, a careful inspection of the diapason of voices reveals isolated theosophical theories, and I shall deal with various discussions that constitute what I call circular theosophy in Kabbalah. In this work, I advance beyond my earlier studies in which I dealt with the many cases of equality between the divine Male and Female, of reciprocity in their relationship, and of what I call two distinct categories: "feminine theurgy" and "Female's theurgy." Scholarship has overlooked so many quintessential discussions concerning gender in Kabbalah; moreover, my analysis of these debates, presented here for the first time, offers a totally innovative picture.

I wish to emphasize that I am not attempting here or elsewhere merely to rescue a few marginal voices from oblivion or to contribute to an archeology of the suppressed, although those are worthy undertakings. Rather, I want to highlight a major topic that has been ignored or suppressed, sometimes by scholarly misinterpretation of Kabbalistic thought, despite and perhaps even because of the recent wave of interest in feminism as an ideology. From this point of view, this is an unfashionable study. The extent of this trend's impact on other modern developments outside Judaism is a separate matter. Nevertheless, I believe that it is possible to lay the groundwork for a tentative understanding of the transition of a particularistic, ethnocentric, approach such as that which most of Kabbalah embraced, though in a modest manner, to the thought of some Renaissance and subsequent modern thinkers, which, in turn, probably influenced modern feminism.

Many thanks are due to the Matanel Foundation for establishing and supporting the Matanel Chair for Kabbalah at the Safed Academic College, and to the Kogut Institute for Advanced Studies at the Hartman Institute in Jerusalem. They enabled me to spend time on the research and writing of the present study, which is part of a broader project.

Last but not least: thanks to the editor of the series, Prof. Vivian Liska of the series, who kindly accepted this book for publication and to Dr. Stefani Hoffman for her excellent editing.

Jerusalem, January 2018

Contents

1 Introduction – Theosophical Kabbalah: Complexity and Dynamism

The claim that a divine feminine power may occupy a privileged place in a series of Jewish theologies may come as surprise to some scholars. This is not a reiteration of the common assumption as to the existence of a divine feminine power, known generally by the name of *Shekhinah*, by now a well-known assumption in scholarship and broader circles. Neither is it a feminine theological approach, attempting to strike a new balance in Jewish thought. I emphasize the term "privileged," as the texts that I analyze deal with the eminent status of the feminine power within the complex Kabbalistic theosophy that posits ten divine powers. A variety of readers may contest this claim. These include: those who believe in or assume an exclusive monotheism, implicitly of a masculine character, that is allegedly characteristic of Judaism; some scholars of Kabbalah, who attribute a humble role to a feminine power in the various theosophical systems, viewing it as the last and subordinated entity; and, finally, some adherents of a simplistic feminist approach to the question of gender topics in traditional societies as invariably androcentric.

The contents of this work may seem strange, marginal, or counter to clichéd ideas about Judaism that have been circulating in recent generations in scholarly and intellectual circles. Indeed, the ideas addressed below are not in consonance with the rational claims of "Enlightened" Jews or the all-encompassing vision of an androcentric *imaginaire* in put forth recent decades by scholarly followers of some sort of feminism.

This work may evoke disagreement among those who adhere to what I call exclusivist approaches. Some scholars embrace very broad pictures that, although dramatically different from one academic circle to another, envision some form of conceptual coherence, that is allegedly underlying one mode of Jewish thinking, whether rabbinic or Kabbalistic. Although no serious scholars, to be sure, will subscribe today to a monolithic reading of Judaism, they would, nevertheless, depict some of its religious schools as monolithic or homogeneous, especially with regard to the place and role of the divine Female.[1] This is part of modern scholars' search for unity in the topics they investigate. They hope to enhance their scholarly authority by discovering and critically analyzing undiscovered

---

[1] Although it is plausible to distinguish between Female as an entity, human and divine, and Feminine, as the latter can reflect a feature that is not necessarily related to a female, in the following, I use them interchangeably as Kabbalists also did not always distinguish between them. See also below n. 7. For more on this issue, see "Concluding Remarks."

https://doi.org/10.1515/9783110599800-001

coherences and thus advance their role in academic, intellectual and social circles. The scholar may feel that he or she is fulfilling a task that is conceptually novel and even contributes to society.

Although scholars often employ sophisticated methods – and discussions about methodological issues abound in recent scholarship – their results, in many cases, are much less sophisticated. In many cases, they posit generalizations, which, they allege, are applicable uniformly to significant types of Jewish literatures. A new, academic Jewish elite thus ensures a scholarly career and eventually a place in society. By forging grand historical narratives or fascinating general or essentialist phenomenologies, some of them marginalize what I see as core aspects of Jewish religious life as imagined or as actually reflected in the literary corpora that scholars analyze. Let me distinguish between the anthropological approach and my own: I contend that by using the same tools, namely the philological, historical, and phenomenological, one may emphasize in a given literature the importance of ritual, namely, performative aspects more than the importance of the ideitic ones. Although observing the behavior of Kabbalists may facilitate an understanding of their literature, one does not need field research in order to discern the centrality attributed to rituals and customs in certain literature.[2] In my opinion, the failure to ascribe a more significant role to the divine feminine power is correlated with an essentialist vision that also neglects the centrality of performance, as in many cases, religious rituals were supposedly devoted to the Female. This is the reason for a certain emphasis in this study not only on theosophical Kabbalists but also on rabbinic Judaism.

My work rests on the assumption that one can discern multiple voices not only in the religion that developed over millennia but also in writings of specific schools of thought such as theosophical Kabbalah. Those authors' main concern was to strengthen a specific mode of religious behavior, one with which scholars often were unfamiliar. The new academic elites in Judaism offer a series of biased visions of this religion, as if they are representative, by dramatically shifting the focus. The performative religious life was subordinated to speculative preoccupations; the image of the corporate personality of the Jewish nation was diminished in favor of the individual one. Many scholars ignored an emphasis on "modest" ideals such as procreation or communal life of the past based on particularistic rituals in order to prioritize a mental or imaginal approach, which is more

---

2 See, e.g., Maurizio Mottolese, *Bodily Rituals in Jewish Mysticism, the Intensification of Cultic Hand Gestures by Medieval Kabbalists* or M. Idel, *Enchanted Chains, Techniques and Rituals in Jewish Mysticism*, and notes 400, 940, 944.

universal than particularistic. Seeking the "genius" and centrality of Judaism in the domain of abstract forms of thought, the advocates of these approaches forgot the human body and the role played by the community, and to a great extent, also the women. In a performative and communal religious modality, however, women can play a greater role than has been generally acknowledged thus far in scholarship. If the main issue is not multiplication of knowledge but procreation of bodies – and for the Kabbalists also of the corresponding souls – the balance between the roles of men and women, or the divine attributes of Male and Female, necessarily changes. The meaning of a basic theosophical aspect of Kabbalah changes dramatically depending on whether the ideal of Kabbalistic theosophy is the perfection of the divine system, which, as Gershom Scholem claimed, intrinsically contains both male and female in the structure, or it is procreation. He declared that the divine includes the "female as companion to the male, since both together are needed to constitute a perfect man."[3] It is the state of perfection of the theosophical system or of the supernal man that concerns some scholars.[4]

The picture becomes more complex when we add the national significance of the Female in theosophical Kabbalah, as She represents both the vicissitudes of the people of Israel and their redemption, thus introducing the *imaginaire* of national perfection, in addition to an interest in systemic perfection and procreation. Last but not least: being a median entity, She is often considered instrumental in revelations of secrets to Kabbalists, as we shall see at the beginning of chapter 7.

This work strives to contribute a complex picture that does justice to the multiple types of relationships among powers within the divine sphere. My methodology, less dependent on certain modern intellectual fashions, tries to shed light on the plurality of voices that informed Kabbalistic and Hasidic material, without ignoring the weird ones or harmonizing them by simplifications that betray stereotypes. In a search for theologies and intellectual systems that can be highlighted and categorized in scholarly terms, academics have marginalized many aspects of the prevalent mundane, concrete, performative, and thus particularistic dimensions of religious life in Judaism, which were also the concerns of most Kabbalists. Most traditional forms of Judaism situate performative religiosity at the center of attention, considering it more important in shaping religious

---

3 Scholem, *Kabbalah*, 107. Compare also to idem, *On the Mystical Shape of the Godhead*, 34, where he describes the *Shekhinah* as "complementing" the Male.

4 See also, *mutatis mutandis* in Elliot Wolfson's theory of gender, which is a shift from Scholem's androcentric approach, as exemplified in the foregoing short quote, to a phallocentric one. For his studies on this topic, see the references below in n. 28.

identity than the theological aspects, which were more fluid, and secondary in this religion. A study of Judaism including Kabbalah that is theosologically oriented thus treats only a secondary dimension.

Even in the theosophical-theurgical main school of Kabbalah, a particular school and even an individual Kabbalist may adhere to several different theologies. As depictions of divine female elements represented a figment of human religious imagination – unlike the performative aspects of their life and relatively freer of theological inhibitions – Kabbalists could imagine them in diverse ways. The centrality of the feminine images in the main Kabbalistic schools is the result of the importance of the social-national unit and a search for continuity, attained by performative religious acts; it is less a matter of intellectual coherence, such as dominates Greek thought, for example, or later forms of philosophical religions. The evident multiple roles played by women evoked a more dynamic treatment than that of men; this was reflected also in the theosophical elaborations, which went far beyond the concrete data of social reality.

Human life, especially in more "developed" societies, entails complex relations with external factors: not only family, religious groups, and clans but also multiple professional engagements and participation in civil affairs. In each of these relationships, the individual plays different roles and displays different aspects of his or her personality. Women are naturally multifunctional. They regularly give birth, raise and nourish, and educate; a woman may earn money for the household, especially in a traditional Jewish society where the ideal was for the males to be scholars, all this in addition to being a sexual object. The masculine attitude toward her should certainly be more complex than reducing the male gaze to only one of her activities. On the most basic level, everyone is a daughter or a son, and most people are also husband and wife, father or mother, sister or brother, sometimes simultaneously, other times diachronically. Most people, males and females, thus encounter a variety of persons of the opposite sex, with whom they have diverse relationships, and, subsequently, they embrace more than one attitude to the opposite sex. In other words, an individual woman's roles change over time and accrue a variety of functions with age; an appropriate understanding of the way they are conceived by others should admit this complexity. Complex situations may generate complex personalities, which have multiple perceptions of the eventually complex other, whether a man or a woman.

Prima facie, this is a commonplace, which need not be addressed in a scholarly discourse; yet, such observations are not totally superfluous. When dealing with the concept of the feminine components in a certain society and literature, or in a vast mystical literature, such as Kabbalistic literature, it is advisable to address very complex constellations of different ideas that vary even in the same culture from one generation to another. The diverse roles played by a mother, a wife, a daughter, or a grandmother are among the most basic experiences and situations in most human societies; although these roles differ, some of them may nevertheless coexist for some segments of a woman's life. In reality, human identities shift with the years, as do others' perceptions of them; for example, the perception of the other sex by an adolescent differs from that of a mature or an old person. This commonsense observation thus requires a more sophisticated scholarly approach that is dynamic and less fixed than in recent stereotypes. Kabbalists have been sensitive to this variety, sometime highlighting them by using different terms to account for those diverse functions.[5]

A concept of the feminine, as with many other general terms, includes a variety of aspects and attitudes, which preclude simplistic generalizations. Using multiple descriptions of the woman, as sister and mother, diachronically and synchronically, reflect her special roles, as is the case with some rabbinic depictions mentioned below or in Chaim Nachman Bialik's famous poem, cited as an epigraph. Various, and sometimes disparate types of imagery, have been combined to depict the *Shekhinah* as consoling the poet. Moreover, in this case, Mother and Sister represent not only genetic family affinities but also the imagined role of the affective feminine in her consoling capacity.

Although some of those functions are part of the social *imaginaire*, known in scholarship as gender, many of them are biological facts, related to giving birth or sex. A given, for the time being, is that men and women are born from women. Because of this complexity, any unilateral depiction by scholars that focuses on only one attribute of femininity, in an effort to rationalize a less family- and nation-oriented modern situation, will thus be at best only partial and potentially misleading, as it will ignore, suppress, neglect or marginalize most of the diverse roles played by women. Religious documents that scholars utilize to reconstruct a particular culture's approach to women reflect the variety of interpersonal affinities that constitute part of complex social structures. In addition, written documents, which encompass a variety of views found in Jewish culture, sometimes conflicting, and sometimes including conceptual schemes found in other cultures, are occasionally even more complex than social reality.

By taking in consideration the variety of her/Her functions, acts, positions, and perceptions in Kabbalah, in some cases including creative misunderstandings

---

5 See, e.g., in *Zohar* 3, fol. 75a, R. Menahem Recanati, as discussed in Idel, *R. Menahem Recanati, the Kabbalist* (Hebrew), 1: 225–226; R. Moshe Cordovero, *'Or Yaqar*, to *Tiqqunim*, 2: 1, discussed in Idel, *"Male and Female": Equality, Female's Theurgy and Eros, R. Moshe Cordovero's Dual Ontology*, ch. 2; R. Jacob Ifargan, *Sefer Minhat Yehudah*, 2: 474, 475, and the editor's preface. 23–24, and below n. 806.

of the past, an alternate history of the feminine will emerge that is not static, monolithic, mono-causal or unilinear but multifunctional.[6] Comprehensive characterizations of human nature, masculine or feminine, or of other human categories, of vast literatures, and nomadic cultures that developed for millennia cannot be simple or one-sided and must include the variety of human experiences as a fundamental fact, in literature and in life. As in many other cases, facts – in our case the various discussions – do not easily submit to simple, abstract theories and any attempt at building an image of a "feminine character" that is allegedly representative of the views of all male Kabbalists, or even a significant majority, is as problematic as what has been done by some philosophers and psychologists who attempted to define such a topic.[7] Is someone's image of the femininity of one's mother identical to that of his spouse, or of his daughter? The act of forging a masculine character, if scholars characterize it as appropriate to all Kabbalists, is, intellectually speaking, an equally precarious enterprise.

Not only in human society, but also in various mythologies, goddesses represent not just one major quality or attribute, natural or divine, but also many and sometimes conflicting ones. The famous goddess Athena, to take one example salient for our discussions, is not just the daughter of Zeus and Metis but also the goddess of wisdom, the goddess of war and, simultaneously, she represents the virtue of virginity. In the Hebrew Bible, the Hymn of Wisdom in Proverbs, ch. 8, and its parallels, demonstrates the rather unique status of the feminine entity, probably a hypostasis; subsequently, Jewish thinkers drew on the verses in this chapter. In some rabbinic texts, the roles of Daughter, Bride or Spouse are attributed to the figure of the Mother that was mentioned in the Song of Songs 3:11.[8] Those multiple

---

6 Compare to what I wrote in my *Saturn's Jews, On the Witches' Sabbat and Sabbateanism*, 102, and see also my emphasis on the existence of different Kabbalistic schools, centers, trajectories of transmission, modes of transition of Kabbalistic knowledge from one center to another in some of my studies, e.g., *Kabbalah in Italy, 1280–1510, a Survey*, 1–5; idem, "Kabbalah in Byzantium: A Preliminary Inquiry" (Hebrew), *Kabbalah*, 18 (2008); idem, *Ben, Sonship and Jewish Mysticism*, 50–57; idem, "'In a Whisper': On Transmission of *Shi'ur Qomah* and Kabbalistic Secrets in Jewish Mysticism, 477–522. See also n. 4. In a series of studies, I emphasized the role played by the mobility of Kabbalists. See, e.g., my "On Mobility, Individuals and Groups: Prolegomenon for a Sociological Approach to Sixteenth-Century Kabbalah," and "The Kabbalah's 'Window of Opportunities,' 1279–1290," 171–208.

7 See the critical surveys of various theories as to an alleged "feminine character" in Simone de Beauvoir, *The Second Sex*; Viola Klein, *The Feminine Character, History of an Ideology* and Judith Butler, *Gender Trouble: Feminism and the Subversion of Identity*. For some later cases of troubled identities, sexual and gender, in Kabbalah, see Charles Mopsik, *Sex of the Soul, The Vicissitudes of Sexual Difference in Kabbalah*, 5–52.

8 Arthur Green, "Bride, Spouse, Daughter: Images of the Feminine in Classical Jewish Sources," 248–260, and my *Kabbalah & Eros*, 39–40. See also in the *Book of Bahir*, where different positions

characterizations are important because they evoke the natural complexities and multi-functionality, which are sometimes simultaneous and cannot and should not be reduced to just one form of relationship as if it was solely representative. Neither the archetypal approach that accentuates the so-called "Great Mother" archetype in Jungianism, nor the phallocentric picture in feminism, which drastically limits the feminine to a few of the actual functions, can encompass the whole picture. Although each may facilitate an investigation of one of a woman's functions, they are inadequate if one assumes that they exhaust the much richer gamut of a woman's sex and gender.

Social, biological, psychological, and conceptual traditional components are essential for understanding documents on the topics under consideration here; none of these components is homogenous nor do scholars accord them equal weight. I would, nevertheless, like to highlight the importance of the exegetical and the systemic dimensions for the development of the discourse in Kabbalah and Hasidism. The two latter components amalgamate those different dimensions and enable some creativity. The exegetical dimension is evident in allusions to a variety of biblical verses as prooftexts, such as verses from Proverbs, Jeremiah, or Song of Songs, and of rabbinic dicta, as well as material stemming from non-Jewish sources. Each of these verses and themes have been interpreted in more than one way by different Kabbalists, and sometimes by the same Kabbalist, in some cases even with opposing meanings, and those interpretations reflect the diverse opinions on the nature and role of the divine Feminine. In many cases, radical types of exegesis have been invoked in order to elicit new meanings.

First and foremost, much of the interpreted material has been transposed from the non-divine to the divine realm, by means of what scholars call symbolic interpretations of the lower texts and themes, which are seen as referring to the various divine hypostases. This telescoping dramatically changed the exegetical practices in the theosophical-theurgical Kabbalah. Other exegetical techniques, such as gematria, some of them quite radical, were used to establish a relationship between words and themes of otherwise unrelated entities.[9] The theosophical systems, namely the complex structures of ten *sefirot*, were, however, far from identical even among the exponents of this school of Kabbalah, as the different diagrams of ten *sefirot* easily demonstrate, and they changed with time. For example, anthropomorphic symbolism, which is negligible in early Kabbalah,

---

in the sefirotic hierarchy of a certain entity, possessing feminine features, occur, as discussed in ch. 5 below and in n. 806.

9 See my *Absorbing Perfections: Kabbalah and Interpretation*, 250–271.

became essential in some parts of the Zoharic literature and turned out to be even more important later on in Safedian Kabbalah. Kabbalistic theosophy can be vertical or circular, as we shall see below, and the two models may coexist on the same page of major Kabbalists.

Last but not least: Kabbalistic theosophy displays a growing tendency to atomization of its hypostatic entities, which means that each of the ten hypostatic divine powers is understood later on, from the end of the thirteenth century, as comprising another ten, or even more aspects. The exegetical enterprise thus became more complex because of the need to take into account the multiplicity of relevant divine powers for understanding texts and rituals. In the case of the divine Feminine, the shift from being just one hypostasis to a conglomerate of several "aspects" has repercussions on the functions She may fulfill in the dynamic theosophical system. In short, in line with the increasingly complex development of Kabbalistic theosophy since the high Middle Ages, Kabbalistic theosophy developed into an increasingly complex way of thought, and one of its major components, the Female, has also changed and been enriched dramatically by various systemic developments. Those components, their division, and their continuous interactions and changes, generate a picture that is reminiscent of a kaleidoscope. It is important to keep in mind, however, that despite its kaleidoscopic aspect, theosophical thought is generally anchored in a strict mode of behavior – the rabbinic commandments common to all the Jews and some customs that differ from one community to another, whose performance is explained by means of various theosophical speculations.

To be sure, rabbinic literature already portrays the *Shekhinah* as dynamic – ascending and descending upon the various layers of reality and participating in the exile of the Jews. In this capacity, She has been associated in the sefirotic system with the last sefirah, the sefirah of *Malkhut*, and this is also the case, *mutatis mutandis*, with the *'Atarah* (diadem). Especially interesting is a rabbinic view as to the ten ascents of the *Shekhinah* caused by the sins of various persons, which provoke Her increasing separation from this world, and subsequently, the ten descents due to the good deeds of ten other people, although in those discussions, the feminine aspects of this power are not evident.[10] According to this myth,

---

10 *Midrash 'Eikhah Rabbah,* Introduction, par. 25, ch. 6–7, 19–21; Arnold L. Goldberg, *Untersuchungen ueber die Vorstellun von der Scheckhinah in der Fruehen Rabbinischen Literatur,* 125–130; Georges Vajda, *Le commentaire d'Ezra of Gérone sur le Cantique des cantiques,* 327–328, 331–332 n. 29, M. Idel, "Hermeticism and Judaism," 60–62. For the dynamic vision of the *Shekhinah,* which is, however, interpreted metaphorically, see Abraham Abulafia's epistle *Matzref la-Kesef,* 18–19. For a Kabbalistic interpretation that includes also the concept of her return to Her source on high, from where She was emanated, see R. Moshe of Kiev, *Shushan Sodot* and see also the

the ideal state of the *Shekhinah* is below in Paradise or in the Israelite Temple; the question of Her ontological origin is not addressed in rabbinic sources, whereas many other Kabbalistic texts to be discussed below affirm that She originates from on high and is destined to return there. Here one sees clear a dissonance between the rabbinic myth and the Kabbalists' theosophical speculations.

In dealing with the meanings of the divine Feminine in Kabbalah, I assume that a wider spectrum of methodologies is by far superior to any single one, an approach that I call perspectivism.[11] From the perspective of Her contact with lower realms, the divine Feminine may include characteristics of the demonic one, assuming uncanny, negative features, but when imagined as ascending to higher realms, She adopts, according to some interpretations, more merciful features.[12] The wide-ranging images used in order to reflect pictures of the feminine may differ and even contradict one another. In my opinion, however, one must be open to this diversity in order to avoid simplistic conclusions. This type of study entails mastering complex and vast literary corpora in their variety and complexity; this is particularly relevant when dealing with a religion that persisted for such a long period, changed continuously, and operated in a variety of religious and social contexts as Judaism did. There is thus no pristine form of "Jewish mysticism" or a homogeneous Kabbalah but a variety of different, often divergent, trends that sometimes overlap and sometimes contradict each other. Given this variety, there is no definitive way of determining a unifying approach to imaginary universes that Kabbalistic literature hosted or to reconstruct a pristine "original" one that split over time. Nor is it possible to demythologize such a diverse corpus, in the manner that Rudolf Bultmann – following Martin Heidegger – did for early Christianity, by decoding the New Testament as containing a religious "message" which, allegedly, transcends the ancient historical events.

In fact, even when focusing on the Kabbalistic constellation of expressions related to woman and to feminine hypostases, one finds a plethora of differing general pictures, themes, and models, sometimes even in the writings of a single

---

discussion of Abraham Michael Cardoso in the text printed by Gershom Scholem, *Studies and Texts Concerning the History of Sabbateanism and Its Metamorphoses* (Hebrew), 346.

11 See my *Ascensions on High in Jewish Mysticism: Pillars, Ladders, Lines*, 11–13. See also below, "Concluding Remarks."

12 See Neta Sobol, *Transgression of the Torah and the Rectification of God: The Theosophy of Idra Rabba' in the Zohar, and Its Unique Status in Thirteenth-Century Kabbalah*, 91–94; Shifra Asulin, "The Double Construct of the Image of the *Shekhinah* in *Ma'ayan 'Eyn Ya'aqov* and its Relation to the *'Idra'* Literature," (Hebrew), 99–101 or Sharon Faye Koren, *Forsaken, The Menstruant in Medieval Jewish Mysticism.*

Kabbalist.[13] This scholarly orientation toward a variety of models is inherently not consonant with grand historical narratives with comprehensive phenomenologies or simplistic anthropologies but requires forging diverse histories of smaller units of Kabbalistic literature, schools, centers or models, each to be understood first in itself.

Of primary importance for understanding most of the following discussions is the fact that the main claim as to the privileged status of the Female[14] within the theosophical systems is not a matter of the personal opinion of a certain Kabbalist or even of a certain Kabbalistic school. Nor is it the message of a revelation from a feminine entity, as is the case of Diotima's role in Plato's *Symposium*[15]; of some mystics such as Ibn 'Arabi, who had a revelation at Meccan from a feminine figure[16]; the famous story of the "Maiden that has no eyes" in the book of

---

13 On the two proposals: to see clusters of different treatments of the same topics on the one hand, and conceptual fluidity and incoherence in the same Kabbalistic literatures, on the other hand, see Idel, *Messianic Mystics*, 16, 233, 254, 274; idem, *Absorbing Perfections*, 8, 75, 92, 103, 107, 126, 127, 234, 255, 292, 331–332, 357, 366, 419, 420, 427, 480; idem, *Kabbalah & Eros*, 130, 213–223; idem, "Androgyny and Equality in the Theosophico-Theurgical Kabbalah," 38; idem, *Ben: Sonship and Jewish Mysticism*, 341, 343, 587, 603, and idem, "The Triple Family: Sources for the Feminine Perception of Deity in Early Kabbalah" (Hebrew), 91–110. Conceptual fluidity informs my approach to the figure of the founder of Hasidism, R. Israel Ba'al Shem Tov. See, e.g., my "Mystical Redemption and Messianism in R. Israel Ba'al Shem Tov's Teachings," 7–121, and "Prayer, Ecstasy and Alien Thoughts in the Besht's Religious World" (Hebrew), 57–120 or "'Adonay Sefatay Tiftah: Models of Understanding Prayer in Early Hasidism," 7–111.

For terminological fluidity in Hasidism, see my "The Land of a Divine Vitality: Eretz Israel in Hasidic Thought" (Hebrew), 256–275. See also my "Ascensions, Gender and Pillars in Safedian Kabbalah," 103 n. 123; idem, *Hasidism: Between Ecstasy and Magic*, 50–51, and idem, *Il male primordiale nella Qabbalah*, 350–357, and below next to n. 868. It should be mentioned that conceptual fluidity is not only the result of convergence of the mythical and philosophical tendencies, which is certainly the case in some Kabbalists such as Cordovero, but also of other factors, especially the basic associative bias of Kabbalists, following the Midrashic tendency. On gender fluidity see, e.g., Wolfson, *Language, Eros, Being*, 49, 94, idem, "Tiqqun ha-Shekhinah," 291; Ruth Kara-Ivanov Kaniel, *Holiness and Transgression: Mothers of the Messiah in the Jewish Myth*, 265–273 (Hebrew), and for quite a different position see the passage of Cordovero cited below in ch. 7 from *'Or Yaqar*, to *Tiqqunim*, vol. 6. See also below n. 903.

14 I shall use the capital letter for Female, She, Her, to refer to feminine hypostatic powers found in or stemming from the sefirotic world, not the feminine human being, and so, too, in the case of the references to the divine Male. For a survey of scholarship dealing with gender theories in Kabbalah, see Hava Tirosh-Samuelson, "Gender in Jewish Mysticism," 191–30. See also Biti Roi, "Women and Femininity: Images from the Kabbalistic Literature" (Hebrew), 131–155, especially 145–146.

15 See, e.g., David M. Halperin, "Why is Diotima a Woman?" 276.

16 Ibn 'Arabi, *L'interprète des desirs*, especially the introduction, 29–34. On the entire issue see Henry Corbin, *Alone with the Alone, Creative Imagination in the Sufism of Ibn 'Arabi*, 157–175.

the *Zohar*[17]; Ramon Llull, the famous story transmitted by R. Isaac of Acre; or, later on, in the mid-sixteenth century, Guillaume Postel's venerated historical figure Sister Juana of Venice.[18] In the thirteenth century, eminent women were conceived of as elevated figures as in troubadour literature or they were portrayed as guides, in mystical and other literature, as was the case of Beatrice in Dante's *Divine Comedy*.

In the case of theosophical Kabbalah, the special status of the Female, in fact two or more *sefirot* in the theosophical Kabbalah, is envisioned as part of a wider structure, the sefirotic systems in its different avatars, which facilitates a better understanding of Her nature and functions. In the discussions below, She is presented in the framework of more elaborated and inclusive modes of Kabbalistic thought that could be understood by other Kabbalists, although in a few cases, personal revelations of the Females are also known in this sort of literature and in Hasidism.[19] In other words, theosophy with its complex structure of many divine powers that maps the divine realm enables new considerations as to the types of relationship between the masculine and feminine entities populating the hierarchical map. Rather than the theosophical structures allocating a place for the Female, the existence of such a hypostasis in earlier Jewish sources contributed to the specific form of Kabbalistic theosophies: the higher entity in these structures is deemed more important, and when the Feminine is described as stemming from higher ontological sources and returning there, She will be considered here as privileged in comparison to the Male. I use the term "privilege" not as a translation of a Hebrew term but in relation to the attributes allegedly possessed by the divine Feminine and the various acts in which She participates.

---

17 See *Zohar,* II, fol. 99b , Idel, *Kabbalah: New Perspectives*, 227–229; idem, *Kabbalah & Eros*, 176–177, and for the wider context, ibidem, 153–178. See also my "Revelation and the 'Crisis' of Tradition in Kabbalah: 1475–1575," 255–261. This interesting Zoharic episode attracted the attention of many scholars. See, e.g., the secondary literature referred in Tzahi Weiss, *Cutting the Shoots, The Perception of the Shekhinah in the World of Early Kabbalah* (Hebrew), 110–124.

18 On Postel and Sister Juana, see e.g., Marion Leathers Kuntz, *Guillaume Postel: The Prophet of the Restitution of All Things, His Life and Thought*, 69–142; idem, "Lodovico Domenichi, Guillaume Postel and the Biography of Giovanna Veronese," 33–44; idem, "Guglielmo Postello e la 'Virgine Veneziana.' Appunti storici sulla vita spiritual dell'Ospedaletto nel Cinquecento," 3–24; Barbara Newman, *From Virile Woman to WomanChrist*, 218–223; Jean-Pierre Brach, "Son of the Son of God: The Feminine Messiah and Her progeny according to Guillaume Postel (1510–1581)," 113–130; and Judith Weiss, *A Kabbalistic Christian Messiah in the Renaissance, Guillaume Postel and the Book of the Zohar* (Hebrew).

19 See Scholem, *On the Mystical Shape of the Godhead*, 192–193, or Idel, *Kabbalah: New Perspectives*, 80–86.

In the field of Kabbalistic systems, this status is explicated by the two main theosophies – the vertical and circular sefirotic structures. In this study, I shall initiate a scholarly examination of the latter structures in the context of gender issues.[20] I contend that the circular theosophy is not necessarily related to gender issues. As the last *sefirah* in the hierarchical structure, which was commonly envisioned as feminine, is located in the circular structure close to the first *sefirah*, it is easily understood as privileged and feminine.

By the term "privileged," which is the main thesis of the present study, I refer to three major, sometimes intertwined themes: first and most importantly, the elevated ontological status of the source of the Feminine within the theosophical system in comparison to the classical masculine hypostases, *Tiferet* or *Yesod*; second, the dynamic perception of Female in the theosophical realm in comparison to the two main divine masculine powers mentioned above, as She is conceived of as supplying power to other *sefirot*, including the masculine ones; and third, this divine power's ruling role over the lower worlds, which is overwhelmingly more conspicuous than the Male's role, despite His being designated as the King and Her being the ultimate aim of the ritual.[21] One reason for the surge of interest in the divine Female in Kabbalistic literatures is the link between the cult dedicated to Her and Her representing the Jewish nation and its future redemption, two different but intertwined functions. The ritual weight and the historical role attributed to Her, corroborate each other.[22]

---

20 This model differs from Mandala types of discussions in Jewish mysticism, as analyzed in Idel, *The Mystical Experience in Abraham Abulafia*, 109–112; idem, "Visualization of Colors, 1: David ben Yehudah he-Hasid's Kabbalistic Diagram," 31–54; idem, "Visualization of Colors, 2: Implications of David ben Yehudah he-Hasid's Diagram for the History of Kabbalah," 39–51; or Alexandra Mandelbom *'Torat Ha-Mekifim.' The Circular Model in Likutey Moharan of Rabbi Nachman of Breslov*. Neither is the view of the *Shekhinah* in the *Book of Bahir*, 201 n. 116, as found both below and above, and, at the same time, encircling everything, מסובב הכל, part of what I see as the circular theosophy, as the "below" stands for the lower world. Nevertheless the dynamic aspect of the *Shekhinah* is quite evident in this paragraph. See also below nn. 56, 58. Interesting aspects of circular theology, although not connected to the status of the Feminine, are discussed in Sandra Valabregue-Perry, *Concealed and Revealed, 'Ein Sof' in Theosophic Kabbalah*, 160, 167, 177, 186, 258, 262, 272–273.

21 I shall omit here hundreds of discussions of mutuality and equality between Males and Females related to sexual intercourse, found especially in R. Moshe Cordovero's influential writings, which I discussed in detail in my "*Male and Female*," ch. 14; see also the sources referred in my *Kabbalah & Eros*, p. 272 n. 33.

22 The topic of the affinities between the performance of the commandments and the Female is central for theosophical-theurgical Kabbalah. See, e.g., *Zohar*, III, fol. 239a (*RM*). For the view of emendation of the *Shekhinah* in the Zoharic literature, see Isaiah Tishby, *The Wisdom of the Zohar, An Anthology of Texts*, 3:957; R. Moshe Cordovero, *'Or Yaqar*, on

Certain figures explicitly mention worship of a divine Feminine, especially the unknown author of *Tiqqunei Zohar,* R. Moshe Cordovero, the Moroccan Kabbalist R. Yehudah ben Jacob, and R. Moshe Ḥayyim Luzzatto. As is well known, Kabbalistic writings are replete with images of the supernal hypostases that possess feminine characteristics, some envisioned as mother, some as daughters, and others as spouses. Those images are generally correlated with various divine powers, mainly the *sefirot,* which are almost always depicted in relation to masculine divine powers, and often as a dynamic entity, fulfilling various functions in the imaginary supernal realm and in the lower world. In some cases, the Female, is depicted in Her relationship to the divine Male, either as equal[23] or subordinated to Him, in other cases in Her contacts with demonic powers.[24] The term 'female' is a literal translation of *neqeivah,* a term used by Kabbalists, but I adopted it in a wider context, in order to describe additional terms such as *Shekhinah, 'Atarah,* or *Knesset Yisra'el,* in most cases, symbols for the last *sefirah, Malkhut.* Especially significant for my discussions is the rabbinic concept of *Knesset Yisra'el,* literally the Assembly of Israel, a term that reflects the linkage between the people of Israel and its divine representation, envisioned as the consort of God and the Mother of Israel.[25] This represents part of what I call the ethno-narcissistic approach of many Kabbalists.

As I discuss in chapter 12, each of these terms has a slightly different connotation, and in some cases different meaning. The grammatical feminine gender of

---

Ra'ya' Meheimna, 16: 12; idem, *The Palm Tree of Deborah,* 177; idem, *'Or Yaqar,* to *Tiqqunim,* 5:17: "כל מעשה המצות- תיקון השבינה למעלה." which means that "All the performance of the commandments, is [intended] to amend the *Shekhinah* on high," as well as ibidem, p. 209: "כל מעשה המצות במלכות שהיא מצוה ודאי" "All the deeds of the commandments are [found or situated] in *Malkhut,* since She is Commandment indeed." See also Cardoso's sermon on the *Shekhinah,* printed by Elliot R. Wolfson, "Constructions of the *Shekhinah* in the Messianic Theosophy of Abraham Cardoso, with an Annotated Edition of *Derush ha-Shekhinah,*" 101–102, or the anonymous *Hemdat Yamim,* Mishmeret ha-Hodesh, ch. 1, vol. 2, fols. 4ab, 6d–7a, and Shifra Asulin, "The Flaw and Its Correction: Impurity, the Moon and the *Shekhinah* – A Broad Inquiry into *Zohar* 3: 79 (*Aharei Mot*) (Hebrew)," *Kabbalah,* 193–236, and my forthcoming "On Gender Theories in R. Moshe Hayyim Luzzatto," n. 3. In eighteenth century Hasidism, the focus of the ritual on the *Shekhinah* is evident already in the Besht and his students. See also below nn. 332, 600.
23 See my "Androgyny and Equality in the Theosophico-Theurgical Kabbalah," 27–38, and *Male and Female,* and more recently and independently, Julia Schwartzman, "From Mystical Vision to Gender Equality Aspirations: A Hermeneutical Journey of Two Biblical Verses," 138–149.
24 See, e.g., Scholem, *On the Mystical Shape of the Godhead,* 189–192, idem, *On Kabbalah and Its Symbolism,* 107; Tishby, *The Wisdom of the Zohar,* 1: 370–422; Vajda, *Le commentaire d'Ezra of Gérone,* 320–332.
25 See BT., *Berakhot,* fol. 35b, Scholem, *On the Mystical Shape of the Godhead,* 145–146; Idel, *Kabbalah & Eros,* 27–28, 139–140, Idel, "The Triple Family."

those words, together with the theories about hypostatic feminine in much earlier Jewish texts, contributed to the emergence of a dynamic and complex feminine hypostasis that is part of the theosophical structure. The dynamic nature of the entity, which an individual Kabbalist may designate as Daughter, Mother, or Wife in his writings, is a major reason for referring to Her in the following analyses as the divine Feminine or the Female, without qualifying precisely Her status.

The apotheosis of the divine Feminine is basically also a matter of statistics, namely the number of discussions, and does not necessarily coincide with Her portrayal in positive terms. The topic attracted the attention of many scholars, who addressed different aspects of this hypostasis. Erich Neumann described some discussions in Kabbalah dealing with the *Shekhinah* in his monograph on the Great Mother.[26] It is worth noting some of Charles Mopsik's studies that deal with the supernal couples.[27] Other scholars, most prominently Elliot R. Wolfson, insisted on the importance, in many cases even the exclusive status, of a phallocentric approach when depicting the role of the divine Feminine in the supernal world.[28] In these cases, the strong selectivity in engaging the vast amount of material is the main reason for the uni-dimensional pictures these studies provide.

---

[26] Erich Neumann, *The Great Mother*, 80, 246, 330. For the application of Neumann's views on some Kabbalistic texts, see Idel, *Kabbalah & Eros*, 63, 130, 143, 144, 146; Haviva Pedaya, "The Great Mother: The Struggle between Nahmanides and the Zohar Circle," 311–328, who duly emphasized especially the destructive role of the supernal mother, *Binah*, as the place of the return of the lower sefirotic powers, as part of the cosmic cyclical eschaton.

[27] See, especially, Mopsik's voluminous Ph. D. thesis, *Recherches autour de la lettre sur la sainteté, sources, textes, influences*, in two volumes, and the many other subsequent French studies, some of them translated into English as *Sex of the Soul*. Some of his findings in the thesis were printed as early as 1986. See his *Lettre sur la sainteté: Le secret de la relation entre l'homme et la femme dans la Cabbale*, and for later discussions see his "The Body of Engenderment in the Hebrew Bible, the Rabbinic Tradition and the Kabbalah,"1: 49–74.

[28] See, especially, in his many studies, e.g., Wolfson, *Through a Speculum that Shines, Vision and Imagination in Medieval Jewish Mysticism*; *Circle in the Square, Studies in the Use of Gender in Kabbalistic Symbolism*; *Language, Eros, Being, Kabbalistic Hermeneutics and Poetic Imagination*, passim; "Coronation of the Sabbath Bride: Kabbalistic Myth and the Ritual of Androgynisation," 301–343: "Patriarchy and the Motherhood of God in Zoharic Kabbalah and Meister Eckhart," 2: 1049–1088; "*Tiqqun Ha-Shekhinah*: Redemption and the Overcoming of Gender Dimorphism in the Messianic Kabbalah of Moses Hayyim Luzatto," *History of Religions*, 289–332, "Woman: The Feminine as Other in Theosophic Kabbalah: Some Philosophical Observations on the Divine Androgyne," 166–204; "Gender and Heresy in the Study of Kabbalah" (Hebrew), 231–262, or "Occultation of the Feminine and the Body of Secrecy in Medieval Kabbalah," 113–154; "Constructions of the *Shekhinah*," and below nn. 39, 542, and more recently in the interview in *Elliot R. Wolfson, Poetic Thinking*, and our discussions of the exclusivist nature of his approach below in "Concluding Remarks."

In the following pages, I shall refer to Kabbalistic texts dealing with the privileged status of the Female in the divine world, many of which have been ignored in scholarship.[29] They relate to images dealing mainly with the sublime status of the Female in the upper divine levels, Her origin there, and sometimes Her return. In the following discussions, "privileged" refers to Her higher position in comparison to the Male, mainly the *sefirah* of *Tiferet* that refers to the masculine body, or in some other cases of *Yesod*, the divine power corresponding to the phallus, as well as Her more dynamic role in comparison to these two masculine divine powers. One of the main manifestations of the privileged status lies in the assumption of a direct link between the last *sefirah* and the first one, sometimes represented by the locution *Keter Malkhut*, the crown of royalty, but understood as the connection between the first and the last *sefirah*. This privileged status is not representative of the entire gamut of the functions and status of the Female in Kabbalah in general, or even in theosophical Kabbalah or Hasidism. It constitutes, however, a major approach in a long series of texts authored by major Kabbalists, Sabbateans, and Hasidic masters. The existence of affinities between the first and the last power is evident in a long series of texts, whereas antipodal relationships between the two extremes of the theosophical structure are relatively rare.

Refraining from generalizations, in the following discussions, I do not make any claims about the status of women in Judaism or in Kabbalah, as my approach has little to do with sociology. I am focusing on a history of some ideas concerning the feminine hypostasis, the divine Feminine, as it was privileged in some major forms of theosophical Kabbalah, in the context of its possible sources, mainly in some texts in ancient Judaism and in the pivotal Neoplatonist concepts of cosmic descent and ascent.[30] An acquaintance with the different affinities to the Males in the theosophical system and even on the human plane is imperative, however,

---

29 This means that other cognate issues in Kabbalah or in Jewish philosophy do not concern me here. For a survey of the views of Jewish thinkers in the Middle Ages, including some Kabbalists, concerning women, see Avraham Grossman, *He Shall Rule over You? Medieval Jewish Sages on Women*, (Hebrew), which contains an updated bibliography. Unlike other meaning of the word in English, the privileged status has nothing to do with secrecy.

30 For some academic discussions of the theme of celestial ladies in a variety of cultures, see Elemire Zola, "The Archetype of the Supernal Lady from Ancient Arabia to Edwardian England," 183–208; Ioan Petru Culianu, "La "passion" di Sophia nello Gnosticismo in Prospetiva storico-comparativa," and "La femme celeste et son ombre," 1: 1–14, 77–95, and in a variety of Gnostic discussions; see Jorunn Jacobsen Buckley, *Female Fault and Fulfillment in Gnosticism*, or Rosemary Radford Ruether, *Goddess and the Divine Feminine, A Western Religious History*. See also below in "Concluding Remarks." For Neoplatonism, see below n. 847. For some phenomena of feminization of the divinity in Christian mysticism in the Middle Ages see Barbara Newman,

in order to understand Her status and function. It is unproductive to isolate the divine Feminine from the various functions She supposedly plays in the supernal and the lower worlds and speak only about one of them; rather, She ought to be portrayed within the complex systems in which She occurs – not just the ten *sefirot* but also couples and family structures that vary in the different Kabbalistic theosophies.[31]

The nature of each of the Kabbalistic systems, however, especially the later ones, is quite complex. Theosophical Kabbalah is concerned not only with offering complex maps of the divine realms,[32] namely, descriptions of the increasingly complex hypostatic powers – what is called theosophy – but also with the processes taking place among them, some triggered by human activities, namely, the performance of the commandments, which I call theurgy. The Female, therefore, refers not only to a certain entity, or many entities on the theosophical map, in certain fixed locations; it also, quite eminently, encompasses Her functions and interactions with other divine powers and with the extra-divine entities.

The multiplicity of Her tasks, not just Her subordinated position is characteristic. If the map constitutes some form of anatomy of the divine, theurgy is concerned more with physiology, or in more recent terms, with sex and gender respectively. Theurgy should be understood in many cases in theosophical Kabbalah as related to the ritual activities of both men and women.

The image of the divine Feminine is, therefore, the sum of the interactions between the status, names, symbols or appellations of some entities in theosophy, the third and the tenth *sefirah*, and functions and processes related to Her. The many pictures of the divine Feminine in theosophical-theurgical literature renders it almost impossible to offer a reliable picture of the Female. This similarly applies to the following descriptions of the Female, which address just one aspect of the divine Feminine: Her portrayal in some cases as superior to Her Husband, or in theosophical-Kabbalistic terms: the last *sefirah* as higher than the *sefirot* of *Tiferet* and *Yesod,* the masculine divine potencies.

As scholars have pointed out, the "words of Wisdom," _Hokhmah_, in the famous speech in Proverbs 8: 22–31, reflect some form of hypostatic figure, probably revealing the impact of and a reaction to a Mesopotamian deity.[33] The traces of

---

"Gender," 48–54 and Caroline Walker Bynum, *Jesus as Mother, Studies in the Spirituality of the High Middle Ages*, 139–140.

31 See Idel, *Kabbalah & Eros*, 105, 131–134.

32 See idem, *Kabbalah: New Perspectives*, 29.

33 See, e.g., Victor Avigdor Hurowitz, "Nursling, Advisor, Architect? אמון and the Role of Wisdom in Proverbs 8, 22–31," 391–400; Alan Lenzi, "Proverbs 8: 22–31, Three Perspectives on its Composition," 687–714; Bernhard Lang, *Wisdom and the Book of Proverbs: A Hebrew Goddess Redefined;*

this feminine hypostasis can be discerned also in Philo of Alexandria's theory of the Logos[34] and the important praise of Wisdom in the *Wisdom of Sirach* as created at the beginning, מראש from the mouth of God.[35] In theosophical Kabbalah, one of the highest hypostases is the second *sefirah,* called *Ḥokhmah.*[36] Proverbs displays, however, in addition to the hypostatic approach, praise of the human feminine person in the second part of the book; these have been also exploited in the theosophical Kabbalah in many cases when transposed to the sefirotic realm. The various verses in this book play a prominent role as prooftexts in many of the discussions below.

Scholars in this field, especially Gershom G. Scholem, preferred a Gnostic explanation for the Kabbalistic discussions of the topic.[37] To this day, more than eighty-five years after his conjecture, however, little has been added in this direction. Moreover, the feminine images of the Israelite nation as the consort of God,

---

Tikva Frymer-Kensky, *In the Wake of the Goddess: Women, Culture and the Biblical Transformation of Pagan Myth,* 79–183; Ronald Murphy, *The Tree of Life: An Exploration of Biblical Wisdom Literature,*; idem, "The Personification of Wisdom," 222–233. See also the more general exposition of the antiquity of the feminine divine hypostases in Judaism in Raphael Patai, *The Hebrew Goddess,* (Avon Books, New York 1978), and his analyses of the later Kabbalistic literature. Scholarship, however, still evinces reluctance to attribute feminine features to God in early forms of Judaism, especially in the biblical texts. See, e.g., Elaine Pagels, *The Gnostic Gospels,* 56–57, or the introduction of Binah Gupta, to ed. B. Gupta, *Sexual Archetypes, East and West,* 7, and even in some formulations in Scholem, *On the Mystical Shape of the Godhead,* 140–142.

34 Scholem, *On the Mystical Shape,* 143–144; David Winston, *Logos and Mystical Theology in Philo of Alexandria,* 15–16; or Émile Bréhier, *Les idées philosophiques et religieuses de Philon d'Alexandrie,* 116–117.

35 See ch. 24: 3–22. See Maurice Gilbert, "L'éloge de la Sagesse (*Siracide* 24)," 326–348; Ruether, *Goddess and the Divine Feminine,* 90–97; Helmer Ringgren, *Word and Wisdom: Studies in the Hypostatization of Divine Qualities and Functions in the Ancient Near East*; Jane R. Webster, "*Sophia*: Engendering Wisdom in Proverbs, Ben Sira and Wisdom of Solomon," 63–79, who pointed out the variety of feminine figures and their different functions in ancient Israel; Bynum, *Jesus as Mother,* 125–139, and Newman, *God and Goddesses,* 190–192. See also Peter Schäfer, *Mirror of His Beauty: Feminine Images of God from the Bible to the Early Kabbala,* and for the medieval period. the views of Newman, "Gender," 47–48, and Elliot R. Wolfson, "Conceptions of Wisdom in *Sefer ha-Bahir,*" 147–176.

36 See my *Kabbalah & Eros,* 66. Only rarely in Jewish medieval philosophy are there hypostatic images of Wisdom. See Aviezer Ravitzky, *Al Da'at ha-Maqom, Studies in the History of Jewish Philosophy* (Hebrew), 212–243.

37 Scholem, *Origins of the Kabbalah,* 70, 131–132, and compare to his *On the Mystical Shape of the Godhead,* 160–161, speaking in this context about "Jewish Gnostics," and see also his remarks in *Kabbalah,* 22. For convenient expositions of the Gnostic discussions of the hypostatic feminine figures see e.g., Pagels, *The Gnostic Gospels,* 57–83, Gedaliahu G. Stroumsa, *Another Seed, Studies in Gnostic Mythology* or Ruether, *Goddess and the Divine Feminine,* 110–120.

evident in the prophets, and of the existence of a consort to God in general, found in ancient Israel, supply another seminal source that fertilized the images of femininity in later phases of Judaism, especially theosophical Kabbalah.[38] The image of the *Shekhinah* as the consort of God, often described in feminine terms, which is taken to represent the Jewish nation, plays a conspicuous role in the history of Jewish mysticism, as we shall see below.

Different images of the supernal Feminine thus arose from various sources, which were subsequently adopted, adapted, misunderstood, and combined in different ways in the various schools of theosophical Kabbalah. Although some of the above-mentioned post-biblical authors whose works reflect feminine hypostases wrote texts unfamiliar to Kabbalists, the poetry of R. Eleazar ha-Qallir in the sixth century in the land of Israel and that of R. Shimeon bar Isaac the Great, in Ashkenaz contained hypostatic visions of the Torah, sometimes conceived in feminine terms, long before the emergence of Kabbalah.[39] A male and a female couple constituting angels of gigantic size is known from late antiquity, most probably stemming from Jewish sources.[40] Together with some views regarding the feminine, sometimes sexual aspects of the *Shekhinah*, *Knesset Yisra'el*, or the supernal Jerusalem, they could contribute the theological underpinning for the artificial imposition of a sexual polarity on earlier Hebrew texts, which is evident

---

38 Mark S. Smith, "God Male and Female in the Old Testament: Yahveh and His 'Asherah,'" 333–340; Moshe Weinfeld, "Feminine Features in the Imagery of God in Israel; the Sacred Marriage and the Sacred Tree," 515–529; James A. Emerton, "Yahweh and his 'Asherah': The Goddess or Her Symbol?, 315–337; Mayer I. Gruber, *The Motherhood of God and Other Studies*, 3–16; Patai, *The Hebrew Goddess*, 16–58; Athalya Brenner, "The Hebrew God and His Female Complements," 56–71, and the recent definitive edition of the inscription in *To YHWH of Teman and His ashera* (Hebrew), ed. Sh. Ahituv and E. Eshel; and Israel Knohl, *The Bible's Genetic Code* (Hebrew), 136–138. See also Barbara Newman, *God and the Goddesses, Vision, Poetry and Belief in the Middle Ages*, 320–321; Newman, *Sister of Wisdom, St. Hildegard's Theology of the Feminine*, 73–74. For later discussions of the status of the Female in Judaism see my *Kabbalah & Eros*, 26–36, and 258 n. 39, "The Triple Family," 91–110, and "Kabbalism and Rabbinism; on G. Scholem's Phenomenology of Judaism," 281–296; and Weiss, *Cutting the Shoots*, 2–4, 12–13, 17–18.

39 Isaac Seligman Baer, ed. *Seder 'Avodat Yisra'el*, 653–656, and *Liturgical Poems of R. Shime'on bar Yitzhaq* (Hebrew), 42–44. See also M. Idel, "The Concept of the Torah in Heikhalot Literature and its Metamorphoses in Kabbalah" (Hebrew), 41–44; idem, *Absorbing Perfections*, 28–30; and Elliot R. Wolfson, "Female Imaging of the Torah: From Literary Metaphor to Religious Symbol," 278–279; Wolfson, "Images of God's Feet," in *People of the Body, Jews and Judaism from an Embodied Perspective*, 153–154.

40 See Moses Gaster, "Das Shiur Komah," (1893), repr in Gaster, *Studies and Texts in Folk-Lore, Magic, Medieval Romance, Hebrew Apocrypha and Samaritan Archeology*, 2: 1330–1345; Idel, "The Angelic World in a Human Shape," repr. in my *The Angelic World – Apotheosis and Theophany* (Hebrew), 19–29 for some Jewish parallels, or *Kabbalah: New Perspectives*, 5–6, and Stroumsa, *Savoir et Salut*, 23–41.

at the beginning of Kabbalah. In any case, the existence of the variety of feminine hypostases in late antiquity and in early medieval forms of Judaism may serve as a solid background for later speculations about hypostatic Females in theosophical Kabbalah.[41]

I am concerned here with only with one aspect of this important issue for the history of Judaism: the question of the privileged status of the hypostatic feminine figure in the divine realm, as illustrated in some images, interpretations, and dicta in theosophical Kabbalah. A similar type of argument concerning a supernal couple that includes a feminine and masculine power has been advanced recently in some studies of mine.[42] In a recent monograph, Tzahi Weiss has suggested that traces of discussions of early Kabbalists show resistance or even a critique of an earlier cult of the *Shekhinah*.[43] My emphasis here, however, differs from those studies, as I shall dwell on the existence of a more comprehensive scheme, which I call the three-phases gender model. This scheme includes the paramount moment of the emergence of the divine Feminine from a very elevated entity in the theosophical systems; Her descent – or more rarely fall; and Her return to the initial place in privileged moments, such as the Sabbath and in the eschaton. To the best of my knowledge, none of the scholars that dealt with the divine Feminine have yet recognized the existence, not to mention the importance, of such a complex model.[44] The theme of the Sabbath represents an important dimension of some of the processes described below, as it combines on the one hand, the ritualist aspects, i.e., the observance of the biblical and rabbinic rituals connected to this day and its cyclical nature, and on the other hand, the historical ones, as some form of adumbration of the eschatological development,

---

41 This tendency toward a hypostatic vision of the feminine is comparable to what is found in the writings of the twelfth-century mystic Hildegard of Bingen. See Newman, *Sister of Wisdom*, 181–211 and her *God and the Goddesses,* especially 291–327.

42 For the status of the Feminine in pre-Kabbalistic and early Kabbalistic thought, see the English version of a much earlier Hebrew study, Idel, "On Jerusalem as a Feminine and Sexual Hypostasis: from Late Antiquity Sources to Medieval Kabbalah," 65–110, and in n. 38. I shall not address again Scholem's assumption as to the Gnostic sources of the Kabbalistic hypostatic vision of the Female, which I already discussed in my studies mentioned here and in the preceding footnote, see also above, n. 37.

43 Weiss, *Cutting the Shoots.*

44 For the first fuller description of this model, see Idel, "The Divine Female and the Mystique of the Moon." The closest discussion is found in the recent study of Cristina Ciucu, "Messie au fèminin: Mystique juive et messianisme aux XVIIe et XVIIe siecles," 68–69, where she mentions, independently, three phases of a model, the first being that of equality between Male and Female. I am dealing here with a model in which one of its phases is understood as the privileged status of the Female. For the possibly Neoplatonic sources of this model, see below n. 847. See, also e.g., Nil Menussi, "'Arise from Dust': Feminist Theology in the Light of Hasidism" (Hebrew), 123–127.

both related to the Female. This convergence of the ritual-cyclical and the historical-linear is of paramount importance, in my opinion, for understanding the outstanding role that the divine Female played. Both the historical and ritual dimensions are related to specific moments in time and thus particularistic, differing dramatically from the more universalistic, a-temporal and mental modes of thought that are ideals of Greek philosophies and of their medieval echoes, including some forms of Judaism.

The proposed model is close, although certainly not identical, to the rabbinic myth of the ascents and descents of the *Shekhinah* mentioned above and much closer to the three phases of the well-known rabbinic myth dealing with the diminution of the moon, which has been addressed by many scholars and other writers.[45] This myth posits a primordial equality of moon and sun, whereas here I am concerned mainly with the superiority of the Female versus the Male as found in the Kabbalistic theosophical systems.

In a kaleidoscopic type of speculation such as the theosophical Kabbalistic,[46] close to what is known as process-theology, it is nevertheless possible to discern some recurrent patterns that I call models. In this work I offer the first comprehensive description of one of them. In my opinion, the three phases gender model serves as a framework for certain theosophical discussions, and I intend to highlight its existence and its most significant occurrences that are known to me. I wish to emphasize, however, that the privileged vision of the divine feminine

---

45 Gershom Scholem, *On the Kabbalah and its Symbolism*, 151–153; Efraim Gottlieb, *Studies in Kabbalah Literature* (Hebrew), 324–328; Liebes, *Studies in Jewish Myth*, 42–54; Liebes, *The Cult of the Dawn*, 25–26; Kushnir-Oron, ed., *Sha'ar Ha-Razim, Todros ben Joseph Abulafia*, 49 n. 19, 51, 63–64; Charles Mopsik, *Le secret du marriage de David et Betsabée*, 68, 78–79; Mopsik, *Sex of the Soul*, 100–102, 106–108, 118, 189–190 n. 69; Weiss, *Cutting the Shoots*, 60–90, especially 63–65 n. 4, and 66–74; Haviva Pedaya, "Sabbath, Sabbatai, and the Diminution of Moon, – The Holy Conjunction, Sign and Image" (Hebrew), 143–191, Pedaya, *Nahmanides*, 359–364, Pedaya, *Vision and Speech, Models of Revelatory Experience in Jewish Mysticism* (Hebrew), 234–236; Melila Hellner-Eshed, "Of What Use is a Candle in Broad Daylight?" The Reinvention of a Myth, https://hartman.org.il/Fck_Uploads/file/havrutavol3LR.55–62.pdf; Idel, *Kabbalah & Eros*, 69, 91, 261 n. 72. See also Wolfson, *Language, Eros, Being*, pp. 144–148, 177, Moshe Halbertal, *By Way of Truth, Nahmanides and the Creation of Tradition* (Hebrew), 144–146; Bracha Sack, *The Kabbalah of R. Moshe Cordovero* (Hebrew), 232, 246, 284 n. 27, 346, 357, 359, 365, and more recently, Asulin, "The Flaw and its Correction," 193–251. See also Daniel Abrams, "The Virgin Mary as the Moon that Lacks the Sun: A Zoharic Polemic against the Veneration of Mary 7–52; Menussi, "Arise from Dust," 123–127; Sarah Yehudit Schneider, *Kabbalistic Writings on the Nature of Masculine & Feminine*.

46 See Idel, *Il male primordiale*, 53–54. For problems related to atomization of discourse in Jewish mystical literatures, see my *Hasidism: Between Ecstasy and Magic*, 15, 18–20.

may and, indeed, does appear also in cases when this model cannot be discerned.[47] The Kabbalists' focusing of discussions on the Female, who is deemed worthy of special attention, even when a hierarchical or gender issue is not evident, is also relevant to my contention.

I shall concentrate on interpretations given to two main types of imagery: that of closely intertwined thought and action and that of the Father and the Daughter, depicted in anthropomorphic terms. The former image can be described as axial, stemming as it does from Greek philosophy – Aristotelian and Neoplatonic; the latter can be depicted as pre-axial, to use Karl Jaspers' terminology. When referring to the end or the telos as the divine Feminine, both instances are suggesting the existence of strong affinities between the beginning and the end of processes within the divine sphere. Those interpretations appear in many Kabbalistic passages, spanning from the book of *Bahir* until the early twentieth century, namely, for a millennium.

The first type of imagery is probably earlier, and it occurs in a rather long series of medieval texts, Hellenistic, Persian and Arabic, and it is a statement related to Aristotle's thought as understood in late antiquity that says: "The first in thought is the last in action."[48] The statement deals with human thought; the primary recurring example in those contexts is the plan to build a house for a certain purpose. That purpose appears the last to unfold into action, although it is an implementation of the anteceding thought.[49] In other words, the final cause, considered as the highest of the four causes in Aristotelian terminology, occurs first in thought, although its implementation in action, that is, its realization, occurs later. According to this mode of thought, later may also mean better. In a much longer series of discussions, it has been applied, however, to the relationship between divine thought and action.[50] I am concerned here with some occurrences in Kabbalistic literature that followed this turn while adding, however, an unexpected interpretation related to anthropomorphism and gender issues, or

---

47 See, e.g., below n. 466.
48 See the fundamental study of this dictum, as found mainly in Arabic and Jewish philosophical sources, by Samuel Stern, "'The First in Thought is the Last in Action': the History of a Saying attributed to Aristotle," 235–252. Stern's interest in the reverberations in Kabbalah was minimal.
49 See, e.g., the recurring resort to this dictum in R. Bahya ben Asher Halewah in the late thirteenth century, in his commentary to the Pentateuch, to Leviticus 12:2. In some cases, the concept of building as the final cause has been attributed to the divine creation of heaven and earth. See, e.g., *Sefer ha-Peliyah*, (Premislany, 1883), 1, fol. 39a, or David Zori, *Not in the Hands of Heaven, The Limit of Human Action in the Teachings of Early Hasidic Masters* (Hebrew). 27 n. 79.
50 This transition is evident in some Arabic speculative sources in the eleventh and twelfth centuries. See Stern, 'The First in Thought," 245–246 and in Jewish speculative ones, mainly from the twelfth century, analyzed in Stern, 247–251.

in more general terms, with pre-axial issues.[51] In order better to understand this interpretation, let me survey some of the earliest Kabbalistic treatments that have been neglected in the scholarship on this dictum.

In the first generations of Kabbalists, we may discern efforts to connect the last divine power, *Malkhut*, understood as "deed" or "action" – *ma'aseh* – to the first divine one, referred to as Thought, designated as such because of the origin of both speech and action, without engaging the possible gender issue. It is more an ontological discourse, which is important for some aspects of the later treatments, but it is not intrinsically concerned with sex or gender differentiation, despite the interest in those issues among Kabbalists in the same period. This is true, too, of the Neoplatonic sources, which deal with the emergence and return of entities that became part of the three-phase Kabbalistic model.[52] Only later, the ontological affinity between the first and the last divine power incorporated the question of the ontological extraction of the feminine in the theosophical realms that are higher than the divine Male, *Tiferet* or *Yesod,* and even from higher levels; this will be one of the main topics of this study, following some hints found in the earlier *Book of Bahir*. In short, in a long series of Kabbalistic discussions, the divine Feminine is considered to be the teleological cause for the emanational process, an approach that sometimes transvaluates Her lowest position in the vertical systems of ten divine powers.

Although commonly considered as the last among those powers, She certainly was not regarded as the least of them; this is the significance of Her privileged status, as She was depicted as the telos of the entire divine activity. Although the biblical account of the creation of the woman does not include the explicit motif of her being the telos, it nevertheless contains the assumption that she was created last, as she was described as having been derived from Adam. This inference became a starting point for later deliberations about woman as telos, being understood as the last but not the least.[53]

This later development should be seen as part of a broader phenomenon of Her ascent to Her original sublime source and of the positive roles played by

---

51 See the two important footnotes by Yehuda Liebes, *On Sabbateanism and its Kabbalah* (Hebrew), 307–309 nn. 65, 71 and his discussion in *Sections of the Zoharic Lexicon* (Hebrew), 260. David Ariel, *The Mystic Quest,* 106–109; Reuven Kimelman, *The Mystical Meaning of Lekhah Dodi and Kabbalat Shabbat* (Hebrew), 24, 47–48, 53, 80; Idel, *Kabbalah: New Perspectives,* 196–197, Wolfson, *Language, Eros, Being,* 112–113 n. 210, 506 n. 207, Wolfson, "Constructions of the *Shekhinah*," 93–94, or Daniel Abrams, *The Female Body of God in Kabbalistic Literature* (Hebrew), 112–113 n. 210.
52 See below n. 847.
53 See, especially, the passage of Cornelius Agrippa of Nettesheim, to be discussed at the end of ch. 6 below.

divine feminine powers in Kabbalistic theosophical literatures, which are related in many cases to what I term the three-phase gender theory.[54] Given the blatantly alien origin of the pseudo-Aristotelian dictum and its obvious content, its dramatic vicissitudes in Kabbalistic literature's various receptions of it are instructive in terms of the conceptual structures that serve as exegetical grids in this literature. The theosophical structure contains two main matrixes of interpretation: the dominant one, which I call the vertical, mainly neo-platonically oriented theosophy, on the one hand, and the uroboric, circular theosophy, stemming from an interpretation of *Sefer Yetzirah*, on the other hand.[55] According to a statement in this book, the end of each of the ten *sefirot* is inserted in its beginning, and its beginning in its end.[56] I take this statement to mean that ten different entities emerged out of the divine body that sits at the center, and they encircle the divinity, each of them returning to its original source. This is clearly theological as God is the source and the locus of the return of the *sefirot*. It is not, however, theosophical because the doctrine of the divinity is not complex, as has been the case since early Kabbalists.

It is important to note that this does not imply that one *sefirah*, whatever meaning this word may have in this book, is connected to the nine others in a circular manner. This statement should be understood as dealing with ten different

---

54 On this model in other conceptual contexts, see my "The Divine Female and the Mystique of the Moon: Three-Phases Gender-Theory in Theosophical Kabbalah," 151–182 and *Male and Female*, appendix K. Needless to say, I do not assume that this is the only model of gender in Kabbalah. On this issue, see my "The Divine Female and the Mystique of the Moon," 156 and n. 19, and especially in *Kabbalah & Eros*, 125–134 as well as n. 893 below.

55 Again, although the uroboric vision of the *sefirot* in this book and the vertical one in theosophical Kabbalah had ultimately been conjugated in the Lurianic vision of the circular image of the *sefirot* and the straightforward one, the development from early to later Kabbalah is quite complex. See my "Visualization of Colors, 1, 50–54.

56 *Sefer Yetzirah* I:7:

עשר ספירות בלימה מדתן עשר שאין להם סוף, נעוץ סופן בתחילתן ותחילתן בסופן כשלהבת קשורה בגחלת, שאדן
יחיד הוא ואין שני לו. ולפני אחד מה אתה סופר.

On this passage, see Yehuda Liebes, *Ars Poetica in Sefer Yetsirah* (Hebrew), 142–148. For a remarkable parallel to this statement in the pseudo-Clementine material, see Shlomo Pines, "Points of Similarity between the Exposition of the Doctrine of the Sephirot in the *Sepher Yetzirah* and a Text of the Pseudo Clementine Homilies: the Implications of this Ressemblance," 67–68. On this late antiquity book as a ring composition, see Marla Segol, "Genre as Argument in the *Sefer Yetsirah*: A New Look at Its Literary Structure," 961–990. For the theme of Teli, a cosmic serpent mentioned in this booklet, as an uroboros, see ibidem, 981. However, the content of the passage discussed here is absent in her otherwise interesting analyses. I shall not discuss the possible affinities between this theosophy and Carl G. Jung's famous theory of mandala as referring to the state of inner perfection and totality. See above n. 20.

spheres or circles, probably related to the term *sefeirah,* in Greek. In other words, the ten *sefirot* are not concatenated to each other, neither are they concentric; rather, they are conceived of as, independently of each other, connected to the divine body, each perhaps converging at a certain point, although departing from it separately and returning to the same place in this body. From this point of view, let me emphasize, *Sefer Yetzirah* differs dramatically from the theosophical interpretations we shall survey in the following pages, even though they use the statement in this book as one of the major prooftexts for their views. As in many other cases, medieval interpretations are no more than creative misunderstandings, in this case of a metaphysical approach in terms closer to national identity.

In addition to the uroboric vision of the *sefirot* in 1:7, also the view of *ratzo wa-shov,* the perpetual movement back and forth contributed to the circular structure.[57] Although the book includes discussions of male and female, this aspect does not affect the circular approach. Thus far, there has not been a serious effort to examine the details, the implications, or the history of uroboric theosophy, which used *Sefer Yetzirah* as a prooftext for the ramifications in Kabbalistic theosophical speculations.[58] Those two main theosophical structures, whose weight in the vast economy of theosophical literature is quite different, constituted codes for interpreting various Jewish and non-Jewish texts; here we shall focus on certain aspects of understanding the status of the Feminine in the supernal world, in relation to the misunderstandings, creative as they sometimes may be, of the pseudo-Aristotelian dictum. Discerning those creative misunderstandings may facilitate an understanding of the underlying concerns that triggered them. In some cases, speculative concerns were thus more important than the plain sense of canonical texts or of articulated sentences.

Although neither the discussions in *Sefer Yetzirah* about circularity of the *sefirot,* nor the dictum, nor the Neoplatonic scheme of descent and return by ascent[59] have anything to do with the status of the feminine, human or divine, they have been interpreted, actually misinterpreted, as such because of the content and the authority of other traditions that dealt with issues of sex and

---

57 *Sefer Yetzirah* 2:7. See Scholem, *Origins of the Kabbalah,* 27–28.
58 See, e.g., Wolfson, *Language, Eros, Being,* 271, 550 n. 65, and above n. 20, and more recently in some observations about circular thinking in *Sefer Yetzirah* and R. Isaac the Blind and the Circle of the *Book of Contemplation* in the Ph.D. dissertation of Oded Porat, "'Founding of the Circle': Rudiments of Esse and the Linguistic Creation in the Book 'Fountain of Wisdom' and its Related Treatises" (Hebrew), but his discussions have nothing to do with the question of gender that concerns us here, as the topic, indeed, is absent in the texts he explored. Neither is Mary Douglas's more recent book, *Thinking in Circles* concerned with issues to be discussed below.
59 See below n. 705.

gender. A similar process occurred with the term '*Atarah*, – diadem – in pre-Kabbalistic material, which deals with the transverse of a sonorous entity generated by human prayer, in the divine world, in particular to be placed on the head of God, but without a significant sex or gender label. In all three cases we may speak of Kabbalists' delineating a process of feminization in line with other traditions as to the special place of the divine Feminine. In this study, I shall address the hermeneutical moves that contributed to an understanding of special affinities between the highest *sefirah* and the lowest one, affinities that endowed a privileged status on the lowest, feminine divine power, to be designated in the following also by the term Female, just as the divine masculine power will be referred by the form Male. Such recurrent discussions are not found in such an explicit manner in relation to any of the other lower seven *sefirot,* or even of the three higher ones.

In some of the following discussions, I shall adopt a double strategy of interrogating explicit statements as to the high status of the divine Feminine in Kabbalistic literature and Her dynamic functions, especially in the case of the three-phase gender-theory but also of attempting to discern the implicit mode of thought as found in interpretations of topics that have nothing to do with the divine Feminine or gender theory, as if they actually do so. This latter strategy can reveal inherent assumptions that inspired some of the Kabbalists' exegesis. Given the exegetical nature of much of Kabbalistic literature, and its minor preoccupation with systematic theology *per se*, but a mode of thought that is coupled by a strong mythical propensity, we can learn much about the details of theological categories from the modes of interpretation that many Kabbalists adopted. This is particularly true of Kabbalah in its initial stages. Kabbalists did not compose lengthy theological treatises until much later, mainly since the mid-sixteenth century. This does not mean, however, that those theological treatises, whether Cordoverian or Lurianic, are coherently systematic, in the manner of theological treatments in philosophically-oriented authors such as St. Thomas of Aquinas.

In other words, I shall address some instances where the sexual polarity of hypostatic entities was used in order to interpret statements that do not contain such polarities, in order to accentuate the existence of such a grid that facilitated phenomena of eisegesis.[60] To put it differently, in most cases, Kabbalistic theosophies are not an intrinsic realm, a transcendental object of contemplation, in basically Platonic terms, but intricate and dynamic systems, used mainly as

---

60 See, e.g., my *Kabbalah: New Perspectives*, 132–133, 223–225, and "Leviathan and Its Consort: From Talmudic to Kabbalistic Myth" (Hebrew), 145–187.

a grid to comprehend canonical texts, national identities, and rabbinic rituals.[61] The greater the discrepancy between the plain sense of the interpreted texts and their Kabbalistic interpretations, the greater the importance that should be attributed to theological codes that continue some earlier traditions.[62] Occasionally, those theosophical codes have similar structures, triggered by the cognitive processes that nourished their emergence, such as the tendency to find polarities, binitarian structures, imaginary symmetries, median entities, and occult correspondences between various cosmic levels.[63] They enable a few sexually differentiated concepts to attain a more balanced type of relationship than in other types of religious discourse, especially when they are conceived of as essential principles of reality, as part of what I call the dual ontology. These strong propensities toward schematic thinking, on the one hand, and associative leaps on the other, together with repetitions and the integration of some earlier traditions about the hypostatic Female mentioned above, combined to allocate to a Female a more preeminent role in theosophical speculations than in earlier forms of Judaism or in theories contemporary with Kabbalah.

Positioned at the intersection of Jewish and of other intellectual modes of thought, most of the Kabbalists borrowed selectively, often misinterpreting the plain sense of more than one source, including classical Jewish texts. In my opinion, any scholarly attempt at extracting a more unified picture is inevitably an act of a belated harmonization, which reduces wide diversity, found in a continuous flux, to uniformity, and the prevailing multivocality and multifunctionalism, to monochromatic or monolithic schemes, and it is doomed to fail.[64] The construction of several different models represents a methodological attempt to find repetitive clusters of themes in a kaleidoscopic literature and to ascertain from those repetitions which elements were most important for the Kabbalists. In other words, theosophical Kabbalists created "fugitive truths," to resort to Clifford Geertz's phrase, especially by interpreting canonical texts by means of

---

61 For a nexus between *Knesset Yisra'el* as a feminine entity and the ritual of blessing after meals, see in *BT., Berakhot*, fol. 35b. For an emphasis on the dynamic nature of theosophical Kabbalah, see e.g., my *Kabbalah: New Perspectives*, xiii, 55, 112, 139–141, 144, 153, 166, 176, 182, 203–204, 222–226, 230–233, 248; *Absorbing Perfections*, 8, 51, 54, 92–94, 228, 248–249. For an emphasis on dynamism in Jewish theology generally, as opposed to Christian theology, see Jaroslav Pelikan, *The Christian Tradition*, 1: 22.

62 See Idel, *Absorbing Perfections*, pp. 301–302.

63 See my "Symbols and Symbolopoiesis in Kabbalah," 197–247.

64 For more on this issue see, in "Concluding Remarks." This essentialist approach to Kabbalah is the application of Luce Irigaray's approach to masculine thought as "the economy of the same"; in the context of philosophers, it is itself an essentialist project. See her Postface *to A Sex that is not One*, 74.

earlier speculative predilections and theosophical structures. Late interpretation can help reveal the intellectual biases of interpreters.

I decided to arrange this study in a historical rather than topical manner. I therefore tried to elucidate the various conceptions of the Female presented by a particular school or author, rather than arranging my analysis in accordance with major topics on the divine Feminine in Kabbalah. I thus try to avoid the so-called "oblique fallacy" of attempting to formulate some comprehensive over-arching theory based on isolated hints found in different authors. In my opinion, views that do not belong to the same Kabbalistic school, should not be conflated with those in other schools without reason, as such a practice is very selective and sometimes even arbitrary. The historical approach seems better suited to the topics discussed here, especially at the initial stage of the analyses. Following such a type of analysis, namely a "scholastic" one, I strive to show the differences between the various manifestations of the general model that was mentioned above, as it was shaped by different Kabbalists in some cases, or the different ways in which the divine Feminine has been privileged, in some other cases. I shall arrange the discussions of those schools in historical order as much as possible, although more than one type of history is necessary in order to do justice to the different themes and their specific developments.

In my opinion, the gender model proposed here properly addresses most of the Kabbalists' major inclinations: an attempt to deal with national identity and continuation and an emphasis on the significance of rituals, especially those of the Sabbath, by means of reflections about entities imagined to populate the dynamic theosophies.[65]

---

[65] Some of the discussions below are parallel to additional material found especially in R. Moshe Cordovero's writings, elaborated in my "*Male and Female*".

2 Reification and the Ontological Status of Thought and Action in Early Kabbalah

Although the *imaginaire* of sexually distinguished couple[s] in the divine world abounds in Kabbalistic literature, several Kabbalists do not subscribe to such a view. Subsequently, there are no privileged or other specific attitudes to the divine Feminine. This applies to Kabbalists such as Abraham Abulafia, R. Isaac ibn Latif, or R. David ben Abraham ha-Lavan, and, to a great extent, also to an earlier Kabbalist, R. Azriel of Gerona. The hypostatic Female is, therefore, not uniformly found in Kabbalistic literature, even many decades after She appears, for example in the *Book of Bahir*, as we shall see in chapter 5. For example, Abraham Abulafia uses the terms *Malkhut*, and *Shekhinah*, – identified in many cases as a reference to a feminine hypostasis in theosophical Kabbalah – to designate a non-sexual entity such as the cosmic Agent Intellect. He thus follows certain philosophical antecedents that were indifferent to gender issues or delineated some masculine features.[66]

I shall start with an interesting passage of R. Azriel of Gerona that exemplifies processes of reification and hypostatic transformation of the concepts of thought and action found in the echoes of the pseudo-Aristotelian dictum mentioned above, without any reference at this stage in the history of Kabbalah to topics concerning sex or gender. My analysis will demonstrate the indifference to those issues in the thought of an important Kabbalist, whose approach is typical of the early Kabbalistic school to which he belongs. In one of the most lucid statements related to the theory of emanation, R. Azriel of Gerona portrays the process of emanation as an explication of what is found within the divine thought in a compact manner.[67] Divine Thought, and Will, identical to the first *sefirah*, is conceived of as including everything; later developments only make explicit what is originally implicit:

> All that is immersed and hidden within the depth of the Will of Thought, and is revealed in action, and wants to reveal secrets so that everything will be revealed and known to His creatures in visible action ... And all these sages agree that all was immersed within

---

66 See my *Ben: Sonship and Jewish Mysticism*, 279–280.

67 On this Kabbalist and some of the topics found in the following passage, see, e.g., Scholem, *Origins of the Kabbalah*, 343–344, 370–378; Isaiah Tishby's various discussions in his edition of R. Azriel's *Commentary on the Talmudic Aggadot*; Mordechai Pachter, "The Root of Faith is the Root of Heresy," 13–51; Gabrielle Sed-Rajna, *Azriel de Gerone, Commentaire sur la Liturgie Quotidienne*; Valabregue-Perry, *Concealed and Revealed,* 66–82; Lawrence Kaplan, "Faith, Rebellion, and Heresy in the Writings of Rabbi Azriel of Gerona," 278–301.

https://doi.org/10.1515/9783110599800-002

Thought, but the paths of Thought were revealed in speech and action, and nothing stopped from being one thing from another to the end of the Will of Thought that there is no change or shift, and addition or diminution .... All the visible attributes are stored within Thought without any separation [between them], and in any case, action emerges in accordance with the conceptualization of Thought, and there is no distinction between the end of the Action and the beginning of Thought, as everything that is immersed within Thought will reverse from its root, and it will be prominent in the action, 'as the material is inversed in the seal,'[68] the immersed is prominent and the prominent is immersed in its concept, right turns into left and left into right, and this is why it is said[69] that within Thought, the fire is on the right [side] and the light is on the left, and their inverse in [matters of] action and speech. And Thought is like a mirror that whoever sees his shape in it thinks that there are two [different] shapes but they are just one ... as there is the action and the speech that is visible and distinguishable but [only] what there was there within the potential [state] of the Will of Thought, which is the cause of everything."[70]

The Kabbalist refers to the explicit aspects as action and speech, as distinguished from thought, as part of a well-known triad in the Middle Ages: thought, speech, and deed or action.[71] Although distinct, those three are also conceived of as being identical: despite their different natures, they are nevertheless one. If the main topic of the passage is not the human manner of action, but the divine one, it poses the question: what is the identity of the "end of action" that is equal to "the beginning of thought"? These two syntagms are part of another well-known dictum in the Middle Ages "the first in thought is the last in action," whose reverberations have been studied in

---

68 Job 28:14.

69 Tishby proposed in *Perush ha-'Aggadot le-R. Azriel of Gerona*, 94, n. 18, that the source may be the relatively late composition *Midrash Konen*.

70 *Perush ha-'Aggadot*, ed. Tishby, 92–94:

וכל השקוע והנסתר בעומק רצון המחשבה בולט ומתגלה ונראה במעשה ורצה לגלות הנסתרות כדי שיהיה הכל גלוי וידוע לבריותיו במעשה נראה...כל אלו החכמי' מסכימים שהכל היה גנוז במחשבה ונתיבות המחשבה נתגלו בדבור ובמעשה ולא סר מהיות דבר מדבר עד תכלית רצון המחשבה שאין בה שינוי וחלוף ותוספת ומיעוט...וכל המדות הנראות הן גנוזות במחשבה בלי הפסק, ועל כל פנים המעשה יוצא כפי ציור המחשבה. ואין הפרש בין סוף המעשה לתחלת המחשבה כי כל השקוע במחשבה נתהפך משרשו להיות בולט במעשה 'כהתהפך כחומר חותם' השקוע בולט והבולט שקוע בציורו והימין נעשה שמאל והשמאל נעשה ימין. ולכך אמ' כי האש מימין והאור משמאל במחשבה וחלופיהם במעשה אצל סדרי הדבור והמעשה. והמחשבה כמראה שהרואה בה רואה צורתו בתוכה וסבור שהם ב' צורות ואינן אלא אחת, מפני שהמראה מקפת אותו והוא בתוכה ולכך רואה בה צורתו בולטת כאשר הוא והימין ימין והשמאל שמאל... כי אין מעשה וד[י]ב[ו]ר נראה וניכר אלא מה שהיה בכח רצון המחשבה שהיא סבת הכל.

Compare also to discussions found in *Perush ha-'Aggadot*, 42, 47, 110. As Tishby pointed out (13, n. 17), this text could have influenced the anonymous fourteenth century Kabbalist who authored the classical *Ma'arekhet ha-'Elohut*, ch. 12, identified later by Efraim Gottlieb as R. Reuven Tzarfati. See below, n. 278.

71 On this topic in early Kabbalah, see Mottolese, *Bodily Rituals in Jewish Mysticism*, 37, n. 172.

Samuel Stern's erudite essay.[72] From the lengthy passage translated earlier, it is hard to discern what is "the last in action" when speaking in theosophical terms. Isaiah Tishby, the erudite editor of R. Azriel's text, however, speculates correctly, in my opinion, that the last *sefirah*, *Malkhut*, is the referent of "the last in action." He bases his conclusion on two parallels that he adduces from the Kabbalistic writings of R. Azriel's Geronese contemporaries, R. Jacob ben Sheshet and R. Joseph ben Shmuel, where the "last in action" is mentioned in this context.[73] In the following, we shall examine the theosophical interpretations of this dictum to the extent that a feminine dimension is inserted into its interpretation. In many other cases, the Kabbalists allude to this dictum in reference to divine activity.

R. Azriel's passage, as well as many others to be discussed below, reify the two terms in the dictum: thought and action. By elevating them into the divine realm, they treat both as forms of action but also as hypostases, a shift that introduced a totally different type of problem than in the Aristotelian sources. In other words, this presents a fascinating example of filling old wineskins with new wine: an attempt to map the supernal world by means of terms, dicta, and biblical verses conceived as hinting at various divine powers.[74] The Gerona Kabbalists were acquainted with the pseudo-Aristotelian dictum and with the famous Neoplatonic cyclical activity of descent and ascent to the source, but it seems that the association between the two occurred elsewhere in the history of Kabbalah.[75] The references to the dictum can be easily understood if we remember that the earliest Kabbalistic documents, such as the *Book of Bahir* and R. Isaac the Blind, already adopted the term *Mahashavah*, Thought, in order to refer to one of the highest divine powers, the first or the second *sefirah*. Although the source of this apotheosis of thought is not clear, and there are also some rabbinic parallels to the status of the divine thought, I shall not discuss that topic here.

Neither R. Azriel nor his Geronese contemporaries from the Kabbalistic school to which he belonged, however, were concerned with the potential gender implications of the statement that distinguishes between the hypostases of thought and

---

72 Stern was not acquainted with the thirteenth century Kabbalistic discussions translated or referred to here, but he mentioned two texts from the beginning of the fourteenth century and mid-sixteenth century.

73 *Perush ha-'Aggadot*, 93, n. 15. See, especially, the passage from R. Joseph ben Shmuel's commentary on *Ma'aseh Bereshit*, quoted by, Jacob ben Sheshet Gerondi in *Meshiv Devarim Nehokhim*, 193.

74 See Idel, *Enchanted Chains*, 215–220.

75 See Scholem, *Origins of the Kabbalah*, 299–300 and 136.

action.[76] Although *Malkhut* was definitely considered a feminine divine power in that period in the book of *Bahir* and in Nahmanides, the above discussion does not engage the feminine dimension of this hypostasis and I would prefer not to engage in unnecessary speculations, especially as the imagery of בולט versus שוקע – that is, of prominent versus immersed, or convex versus concave, does not work with the gender issue as the highest is concave and the lower, *Malkhut,* is the convex. This does not mean that later Kabbalists could not derive such a nexus between the feminine that is both the end and the beginning.

R. Azriel's main preoccupation was to negate the concept of change in divine action. Similarly, in a discussion written one generation later, R. Isaac Todros, a disciple of Nahmanides, wrote (probably in Barcelona) in his *Commentary on the Maḥzor,* that unlike creatures, whose thought comes first and action occurs later, in the case of God, thought and action take place simultaneously.[77] This theme recurs also in the work of R. Isaac Todros's student, R. Shem Tov ben Abraham ibn Gaon, the author of an influential commentary on Nahmanides's secrets. He hints at this idea in his commentary to the Pentateuch, entitled *Keter Shem Tov.*[78] In general, by inserting the coupling of the first and last *sefirot* within the framework of the pseudo-Aristotelian dictum, the author bestows a certain dignity on a divine power conceived of as the last by emphasizing its direct connection to the first one.

I shall next turn to what an important Kabbalist, R. Isaac of Acre, who was well-acquainted with many aspects of Nahmanidean Kabbalah, wrote sometime at the beginning of the fourteenth century:

> One of the qualities of the [divine] unity is that each of the ten *sefirot* comprises all [of the others] and is united with all. You should know that 'A[tarah] is the first in thought and last

---

76 See R. Ezra of Gerona's view of the ascent of *sefirot* to *Keter* and the affinity of *'Ateret* and *Keter* as discussed in Idel, *Kabbalah: New Perspectives*, 196–197, and R. Azriel of Gerona in the name of R. Isaac the Blind, as discussed in idem, *Kabbalah & Eros*, 40, 311 n. 45. See also the view, most probably of R. Azriel, as to the gradual ascent of the *Shekhinah* up to the *Causa Causarum*, in his *Commentary on the Secret of the Sacrifice*, copied in R. Menahem Recanati, *Commentary to the Pentateuch*, fol. 51d and below n. 168. See also the view of R. Jacob ben Sheshet, *Sefer ha-'Emunah ve-ha-Bitaḥon*, 2: 379, where the dictum is quoted in a different context. Neither of these two Kabbalists operated with an explicit feminine feature of the last *sefirah* in this specific context, although they were cognizant of such a feminine view of the last *sefirah*.
77 Ms. Paris BN 839, fol. 222b:

אבל הבורא אינו כן אין מחשבתו קודמת לפעולתם אלא תחילת המחשבה סוף המעשה.

78 *Keter Shem Tov*, ms. Paris BN 774, fol. 75b:

אין צריך למחשבה תחלת המעשה רק מחשבתו היא גמר המעשה.

See also my R. *Menahem Recanati, the Kabbalist*, 1: 180 (Hebrew).

in emanation, namely that when in the thought of *'Ein Sof*,[79]… ascended [the intention] to emanate the [realm of] emanation, *'A[tarah]* was first in thought and last in emanation. And a person that is a last being, when he conceptualizes this issue, *'A[tarah]* is the first in action and last in thought, and the illuminated one will understand [the secret].[80]

The term "emanation" here is not the description of an act of emerging or a flow from the divinity, as in most cases in theosophical Kabbalah, but a reference to a special ontological realm or world, which is identified with the concept of action that follows after what ascends in the divine thought, namely the divine Feminine, which is the final cause, or the telos. It stands for the ten divine powers, and as such, the *'Atarah* was conceived as emerging in divine thought before the highest of the sefirotic powers.[81] Unlike the divine vertical order that allocates the last position to the *'Atarah* in the realm of emanation, which is described as "action," for the human understanding of the divine system, the *sefirah* that is last on the ontological hierarchy is the first that human thought understands. The first thought for the human, namely, what is first perceived from the divine realm, namely the lowest divine manifestation, is for the divine the last action, an implementation of the divine thought. The vertical order relates to a noetic observation that assumes that the last *sefirot* can be better known.[82] Here, as in the earlier sources mentioned in this chapter, the Kabbalist focuses on ontological and theosophical topics and a certain epistemological reflection, without attributing to the last *sefirah* a conspicuous gender-related role, despite the grammatical feminine gender of *'Atarah*. In a strongly hierarchical system such as the sefirotic one is in most of its manifestations, attributing a profound connection between the last and first *sefirah* represents an attempt to preserve some form of unity in this diversified realm of divine powers.[83]

---

79 Following is a series of designations for God.

80 R. Isaac of Acre, *Me'irat 'Einayyim*, 118:

אחת מדרכי הייחוד שכל אחת מעשר ספירו' כלולה מכלם ומיוחדת בכלם ויש לך לדעת כי הע' ראשון למחשבה
ואחרון לאצילות ר"ל כי כשעלה במחשבה אין סוף ממציא ראשון סבת הסבות עלת כל העלות ית' ויר' להאציל
האצילות היתה הע' ראשון למחשבה ואחרון לאצילות והאדם שהוא אחרון נמצא כשבא לציור העניין תהיה הע' ראשון
למעשה אחרון למחשבה והמשכיל יבין.

81 For the importance of this term in Kabbalah, see the interesting remarks, often overlooked in scholarship, of David Neumark, *Toledot ha-Filosofia be-Yisrael* (Hebrew), 1: 191–196, 311 334–346. For its eschatological valence and its parallel in ancient Christianity, see Avi Elqayam, "'The Burden of Silence': Queen Esther as a Messianic Prototype of Fluid Identity in Sabbatean Mythopoesis (Hebrew)," 208 n. 106.

82 This is an issue that deserves a separate study, as it appears in the late thirteenth century among disciples of ibn Adret, and later on several times in *Sefer ha-Peliy'ah*. See e.g., 2, fol. 53b.

83 See the views of R. Meir ibn Gabbai, in the texts referred to below in nn. 297, 300.

The connection of the last *sefirah* to the highest aspect in the theosophical world is summarized in an anonymous, perhaps fourteenth-century text: "in spite of the fact that it is beneath [the other *sefirot*], sometimes it ascends to *'Ein Sof* and becomes an *'Atarah* on their head,[84] and for this reason, it is called *'Atarah*."[85] Thus, sometimes *'Atarah* is just another name for *Keter*, which is not so complex semantically.[86] This is a development of a widespread tradition found in a variety of earlier Jewish literatures, mainly late Midrashim, which deal with the ascent of the words of prayer and their transformation into a diadem that angels place on the head of God.[87] In short, early theosophical Kabbalists had adopted the concept of the ascent of the *'Atarah* to the highest place in the divine world, the head of God, from even earlier sources, but they adapted it to the pleromatic structure that they developed. In theosophical systems where the feminine aspects are important, such a return sometimes had a gender dimension.

Those earlier sources were not necessarily concerned with gender issues related to the grammatically feminine diadem. *'Atarah* may serve as a classical symbol for *Malkhut*, the lowest *sefirah* in this type of Kabbalah, but in my cases, it is portrayed as ascending to *Keter* or to *'Ein Sof*, in accord with later rabbinic sources about the ascent of the liturgical, vocal diadem.[88] Although the gender aspects of these affinities may be negligible, the theory of the ascent of the diadem, *'Atarah* – a grammatically feminine term and one used in the book of Proverbs in the context of the wife – to the highest divine realm contributed, nevertheless, to some of the discussions to be analyzed below, where gender issues play a role. The amalgamation of the ascending *'Atarah* – which is generated by human oral ritual activity and ascends on high – and the dynamic vision of

---

84 Namely, the head of the lower *sefirot*.

85 See the anonymous "Commentary on a Kabbalistic Song," printed in the compilation of various Kabbalistic texts by R. Yehudah Qoriat, *Ma'or va-Shemesh*, fol. 3a. Although this commentary is a relatively late work, it also includes many passages of earlier Kabbalistic material. See the discussion in Idel, "Kabbalistic Material from R. David ben Jehudah he-Hasid's School" (Hebrew), 170–173. See also below at the end of ch. 8, in one of the passages of Nathan of Gaza.

86 The association between *Keter* and *'Atarah* is found also in some of R. Abraham Abulafia's writings: *Hayyei ha-Nefesh*, 92, *Shomer Mitzwah*, 38, *'Imrei Shefer*, 104, and *Sefer ha-'Ot*, as printed in *Matzref ha-Sekhel*, 9. His mentioning such an affinity in the eighties shows that it was already known by mid-thirteenth century Kabbalists. See also below in ch. 5, the texts of R. Todros ha-Levi Abulafia and the various Zoharic passages. See also below n. 459.

87 See, especially, Assi Farber-Ginat, *The Concept of the Merkabah in the Thirteenth-Century Jewish Esotericism - 'Sod Ha-'Egoz and its Development* (Hebrew), 231–244, my *Kabbalah: New Perspectives*, 191–197; and Arthur I. Green, *Keter: The Crown of God in Early Jewish Mysticism*, 20–41, 94–96.

88 See Mopsik, *Recherches autour de la lettre sur la sainteté*, 209–213, Idel, *Kabbalah: New Perspectives*, pp. 196–197 and many discussions in the following pages.

the sefirotic realm, have conspired to produce a new elaborated understanding of the already existing concepts of divine Feminine, which have not been sufficiently taken into consideration in the recent burgeoning discussions of gender in Kabbalah.

Semiotically speaking, the combination of the ancient theory of the investiture of the king by means of the '*Atarah* – itself in the feminine case – as a diadem, has been combined with the Proverbs' discussion of the "diadem of her husband," and thus the diadem acquired a feminine overtone. In fact, already in a Midrashic discussion, the Diadem, apparently, has been equated to the *Shekhinah*.[89]

---

89 See Idel, *Kabbalah: New Perspectives*, 372, n. 149.

3 The Gender Addition to "Action"

The Geronese Kabbalists from the school of R. Isaac the Blind were not particularly concerned with gender issues within the divine realm.[90] This concern appears more strongly, however, among the members of Nahmanides's school active in Catalunia and even more so among Castilian Kabbalists, most of whom were writing in the thirteenth century. The two Kabbalistic schools active in the same Catalan town, Gerona, thus diverge significantly on this and other important topics.[91] Immediately after the short discussion quoted in the previous chapter from R. Shem Tov ibn Gaon's book, this Kabbalist elaborates as follows:

> This is the intention of our sages, blessed be their memory,[92] when they said that to Him, blessed be He, the beginning of thought is the end of the action. And according to his attributes that are linked to each other as "a flame that is linked to the coal,"[93] and everything is called [by the name] "the Holy One Blessed be He"[94] ... In any case, when the sages, blessed be their memory, said[95]: "*Knesset Yisra'el* said in front of the Holy One blessed be He, as a

---

90 See, however, Vajda, *Le commentaire d'Ezra of Gérone*, 320–332, the text of R. Ezra, translated in Wolfson, *Language, Eros, Being*, 376. The Christotropic assumption of some scholars that the Provencal Kabbalah shows the influence of the Marian cult in its attribution of feminine qualities to a divine power, based especially on the *Book of Bahir*, is unrelated to the Provencal Kabbalah from the school of R. Isaac the Blind. Neither is the *Bahir* necessarily a Provencal book; although he was, perhaps, known there, this has not yet been proven. See more below, ch. 5. To be sure, my rejection of the Marian explanation for the emergence of the divine female in early Kabbalah does not apply to later phenomena in Kabbalah such as the literature related to the book of *Meshiv*, and in Sabbatean instances. See, e.g., Idel, "The Attitude to Christianity in *Sefer ha-Meshiv*"; Idel, *Kabbalah & Eros*, 47–49, or Wolfson, "Construction of the *Shekhinah* in the Messianic Theosophy of Abraham Cardoso." See also below, n. 666.
91 This relative indifference as to the gender of the divine attributes is evident in R. Isaac the Blind's *Commentary on Sefer Yetzirah*. For many other divergences between those two schools, see the material and the earlier bibliography in my M. Idel, "Commentaries on the Secret of Impregnation in the Kabbalahs of Catalunia and their Significance for Understanding of the Beginning of Kabbalah and its Development" (Hebrew). The enigmatic nature of Nahmanides's Kabbalah still requires clarifications in a meticulous study of manuscripts, as to the many details hidden by him and his followers.
92 This is a misunderstanding of the reference in Jewish philosophers' attribution of the statement to "sages," namely Greek philosophers, as if they refer to the rabbinic sages. See also below n. 299.
93 Cf. *Sefer Yetzirah* 1: 4.
94 Each of the ten *sefirot* is called by this name as they are considered in this theosophical system as part of the divine essence.
95 *Genesis Rabba'*, 11: 8, *Pesiqta' Rabbati*, section 23. It should be mentioned that already more than one century ago, the hypothesis that Gnostic theories of syzygies had an impact on Midrashic material was proposed by Manuel Joel, *Blicke in die Religionsgeschichte*, 1: 107, 160–161.

https://doi.org/10.1515/9783110599800-003

supplication, " it refers to the "world" that is the "equal line"[96] and it is [also] the first preponderant [power], and it is called also the *Yesod*. And this attribute is supplicating to it and
it is referred by the majuscule *Dalet*[97] in the word *'EḥaD*, despite the fact that what is found
in it is poor[98] as its name, and it is the tenth in number[99] and the first in the building[100]
and in meaning, as I wrote "the flame that is linked to the coal," and the beginning of the
thought is the end of action.[101]

This passage, more so than selections in the preceding chapter, emphasizes divine
unity, given the acceptance of the existence of ten divine attributes. Accordingly,
the last and the first are described as identical. The theosophical narrative is
explicit: the first *sefirah* and the last one are referred to as the first and the tenth
digit; more importantly from my point of view, the last *sefirah*, is identified with
Knesset Yisra'el, a feminine power, in the context of the latter's supplication to
receive a partner. The rabbinic prooftext is somewhat problematic: It mentions
the Sabbath's complaint to God that it does not have a partner, and God gives
it *Knesset Yisra'el* as a partner.[102] This complaint is related to the fact that the
Sabbath is the seventh day, and as such, it does not have a partner as do the
other three days: the first, the third and the fifth, have the second, the fourth
and the sixth day. The question of gender in the rabbinic story is tricky: both
Sabbath and *Knesset Yisra'el* are feminine nouns, and the term *ben zug*, partner,
is masculine. The rabbinic story, however, clearly indicates that it is Sabbath that
asks for a partner, not *Knesset Yisra'el*. Here, however, it is the latter that is given
as a partner to the Sabbath, which is symbolized by *Yesod*. In other words, the
rabbinic story has been interpreted as the complaint of the last *sefirah*, the feminine one, addressed to the *sefirah* of *Tiferet*, and, consequently, the ninth *sefirah*,
Yesod, has been given to Her as a partner.

---

96 'World' just as the 'equal line' and the 'preponderant power', refers to the *sefirah* of *Tiferet*.
97 In many Kabbalistic sources, this is a letter that refers to the last *sefirah*.
98 This is a pseudo-etymology of *Dalet* as *Dalah*, poor. The last *sefirah* was commonly depicted
in theosophical Kabbalah as being poor.
99 *Minya*n. The ten is considered as the repetition of one.
100 *Binyan*, namely the structure of the last seven *sefirot*, of which the Feminine power is a part.
101 *Keter Shem Tov*, Ms. Paris BN 774, fol. 75b:

לכן נתכוונו ז"ל באמרם כי ראשית המחשבה הוא סוף המעשה מאתו ב"ה וכפי מידותיו הקשורות זו בזו כשלהבת
קשורה בגחלת והוא הכל נקרא קב"ה...מכל מקום כשא' ז"ל אמרה כנסת ישראל לפני הקב"ה בדרך תחנה הוא רומז
לעולם שהוא הקו השוה והוא המכריע ראשון ואף גם כן נקרא היסוד ומדה זו היא המתחננת לו והיא רמוזה בדלת
רבתי שבאחד אף על שמה יש בה רמז לפי שהיא דלה כשהיא העשירית והיא העשירית למנין ואחד לבנין ולעניין כמו שכתבתי
בשלהבת קשורה לגחלת ותחילת המחשבה הוא סוף המעשה.

102 *Genesis Rabbah*, 11: 8.

The meaning of this inversion is that the two divine powers involved in R. Shem Tov's passage are the first one, the divine thought, and the last one, the divine feminine, the action. The gender connotation of the last *sefirah*, the action, is very noticeable here. In fact, this entails a structural mode of thinking: according to the Biblical account, the woman was created last, after Adam[103]; the Sabbath is the last day of the week; the last *sefirah* in the vertical theosophy is feminine, and the action is considered to be last; the four different entities "naturally" are read together, in order to "reveal" a profound correlation that is not evident from reading the different traditions separately. This gender connotation is more prominent when compared to an early thirteenth century interpretation of the same rabbinic myth. R. Yehudah ben Yaqar, who was most probably Nahmanides's teacher in matters of Kabbalah, wrote as follows: "The commandment of union which concerns us is connected also to what God said to the Sabbath: *Knesset Yisra'el* will be your partner and it [the Sabbath] is the Righteous, the foundation of the word and therefrom all the spirits and souls come ... this is the reason why people are accustomed to celebrate [the event of marriage on the day of] Sabbath."[104]

The couple here is constituted by the hypostasis called Sabbath, identified as righteous and as foundation, namely the ninth *sefirah*, the male hypostasis, while *Knesset Yisra'el* serves as the feminine hypostasis. The understanding of the Sabbath as the supernal Male that is the source of souls is evidently a sexual one, and it implies a sexual understanding also of *Knesset Yisra'el* as the divine Feminine, especially in the context of the treatment of the *sefirah* of *Yesod* as Righteous in the book of *Bahir*.[105] Ben Yaqar's sexualized way of thought is found also in an anonymous Kabbalistic passage that links itself to Nahmanides's school. The text was printed in mid-sixteenth century, and it is extant also in manuscripts, together with short commentaries on Nahmanides's secrets:

> Sabbath said to the Holy One blessed be He: You gave to all a partner, but you did not give me a partner[106]; it means that each of them has one [additional entity], emanated and

---

103 This point has not been emphasized in Jewish exegesis. See, however, the fifteenth century Italian Jewish commentator R. Ovadiah of Bertinoro, on Leviticus 12: 2. See also below at the end of ch. 6.

104 *The Commentary to Prayers and Blessings*, ed. Sh. Ashkenazi, (Jerusalem, 1979), 2: 42, and see the English translation and discussion of this text in Scholem, *Origins of the Kabbalah*, 158–160; Elliot Ginsburg, *Sabbath in Classical Kabbalah*, 102–103, 109, 110, 111, 167, n. 179, 190; Wolfson, *Language, Eros, Being*, 445, n. 104; Idel, *Ben: Sonship and Jewish Mysticism*, 390–391; and *Kabbalah & Eros*, 50–51.

105 See Scholem, *Origins of the Kabbalah*, 155–156; idem, *On the Mystical Shape of the Godhead*, 94–95, and Idel, *Ascensions on High in Jewish Mysticism*, 81–82.

106 In Hebrew *bat zug*, namely a feminine partner as in other versions of the rabbinic myth and in other early Kabbalistic versions. See, e.g., ms. Oxford, Bodleiana 1646, fol. 108b, ms. Milano-Ambrosiana 57, fol. 23b, ms. Jerusalem, NLI, 8° 1073, fol. 30a.

enumerated, which is emanated from them. And He created *Malkhut*, that receives and is emanated from it, and She is governing over the world, and She is called *'Atarah*, since She is encrowning all [the *sefirot*] and encompasses them,[107] and She is called a recipient, and *Yesod* is called *Z* that is receiving ... and *Malkhut* is called the "angel of 'Elohim," as She is ruling over the world, and She is called *Shekhinah* and *Knesset Yisra'el*.[108]

The description of the last *sefirah* contains an image of Her comprehensiveness in comparison to the other *sefirot*, and the use of the verb *mesavvevan* [which is translated as "encompasses them" above] is, indeed, rather exceptional, as it implies a vision of concentric circles whose circumference is the *'Atarah*, a picture that does not conflict with the encompassing nature of a diadem. It may stem from an interpretation of the verse from Jeremiah 31: 21, understood in cosmic terms. Another reading, according to which this verb would mean that "She caused them" is, conceptually speaking, less plausible, although grammatically not impossible. Less explicit is the meaning of the other verb *me'atteret* [translated as "encrowning"], which is widespread in the Aramaic terminology of the Zoharic literature, and whose meaning is not always evident. Nevertheless, the special nature of the divine Feminine in comparison to other *sefirot* is quite clear. The view of the divine Feminine as recipient is connected to Her being the Ruler, namely of allocating power, and the understanding of Her nature solely as recipient would be a distortion.[109] Nota bene: the combination of the receptive imagery, on the one hand, and Her active function of governing, occurring together in the same passage, is part of the complexity characteristic of the Kabbalistic mode of thought. Moreover, *Knesset Yisra'el* appears as a link between the theosophical and the national thought, as the hypostatic *imaginaire* conveys, as a representative remotely connected to the divine realm.

Elsewhere in R. Shem Tov ibn Gaon's book that was quoted above, he writes:

> ... and in the days of the Messiah, the *Shekhinah* will ascend and the womb laden[110] will be renewed, and Her light was like the role of the sun at the beginning, [while] in[111] the

---

107 מעטרת כלן ומסבבתן See also above n. 283. Compare also to the recent similar reading cited in Schwartzman, "From Mystical Vision to Gender Equality Aspirations," 153.

108 See *Liqqutei Shikhehah u-Fe'ah*. On the anonymous Kabbalistic material in those pages, see M. Idel, "An Unknown Commentary on Nahmanides's Secrets" (Hebrew), 121–126, especially 122 n. 9.

109 See the pertinent discussions of Jonathan Garb, "Gender and Power in Kabbalah, A Theoretical Investigation," 86–91 that put in relief the function of the Female as a source of power in a substantial series of Kabbalistic texts.

110 *'ammusei baten*, a phrase referring to the people of Israel, used in the monthly ritual of the blessing over the new moon.

111 Or, according to another reading, "as."

primordial light.[112] And the name of Esau and 'Amaleq will be erased because of the power of Israel,[113] which will have the kingdom [*ha-Malkhut*] ... as it was at the beginning ... and God and His Name will be one,[114] in an explicit and adequate manner, if you will merit, despite the fact that the connection of *du-partzufin*[115] is not absolute as it was in the primordial days, and even if this connection will be, what was [in the past] will not repaired.[116]

This statement contradicts what R. Shem Tov ibn Gaon wrote earlier about the return to the primordial equality. The three phases model is, nevertheless, found here: the state of initial equality between Sun and Moon in the past is evident, but it has been disrupted by sin and exile, reflecting the state in the present, while the third phase is reflected in the possibility of atonement in the future. As in some other cases in Kabbalah, the national element and the divine Feminine are entwined. Kabbalists, all males without exception, were more concerned about their national identity than their sexual one. This was also the case, I suspect, with regard to Jewish women, at least until recently, when the split between the individual-feminist pole and the national-social pole, became prominent in some feminist circles. In attributing certain abstractions to Kabbalists, scholars ignore contradictions among the different views of Kabbalists that are meaningful in a society that derived its identity to a large degree from observing commandments, i.e., performing certain specific deeds. Different views were considered legitimate if they served to reinforce the rabbinic *modus vivendi*, to which Kabbalists contributed customs and poems. Identity was conceived to be secured not by what someone thinks but by what someone does. Kabbalists considered those deeds as barriers between Jews and others, whereas the scholarly celebration of the alleged cerebral Judaism based on ideas represents a desire to be "universal" and "philosophical" by diminishing the national aspects of Kabbalah and the centrality of the performative orientation.[117]

Last but not least insofar as the above passage is concerned: the term *Malkhut* has been translated as kingdom, according to the context. Though grammatically feminine, *Malkhut* as kingdom does not necessarily reflect in this context a gender

---

112 In several instances, the primordial light is identified with the *sefirah* of *Tiferet*. See *Keter Shem Tov*, in *'Amudei ha-Qabbalah* (Jerusalem, 2001), 11 twice, 27.

113 Here, as in the previous quote where the term *Knesset Yisra'el* is used, the nexus between the nation and the Female power on high is evident. See more on this issue in Concluding Remarks.

114 Zekhariah 14: 9.

115 The intention is not so clear, but it seems, nevertheless, evident that even in the future, the sexual divide will not be overcome.

116 Ms. Paris BN 774, fol. 91a, and in ed. *'Amudei ha-Qabbalah*, 33. This passage in found in a paraphrastic version in R. Menahem Recanati's *Commentary to the Pentateuch*, fol. 44c.

117 Compare what I wrote in 1998 in *Messianic Mystics*, 293.

issue as the subject matter is national supremacy. Associatively, however, it has been connected to the gender implied in the technical phrase *du-partzufin*, which implies the existence of a feminine power. This shift is part of the complex *imaginaire* that plays on the existence of more than one meaning of a certain word, even when this duality occurs in the same context.

Although written late in the thirteenth or early fourteenth century, Shem Tov ibn Gaon's passages reflect earlier views, connected to Nahmanides's Kabbalistic thought, as we shall see in the following chapter.[118] Hermeneutically speaking, the first stage of Kabbalah in Europe includes some modest earlier tendencies of hypostatization related either to interpreting a myth or creating one, and some tentative beginnings of feminization. Both processes will be enhanced as part of the developments of Kabbalah since the late thirteenth century and will culminate in mid-sixteenth century in Safed, as we shall see in chapters 7 and 8. In the later phases, however, the mythic aspects became less evident, given the mechanization or the stereotyping of many of the Safedian types of discourse, as pointed out by Yehuda Liebes.[119]

---

118 See also Mopsik, *Recherches autour de la lettre sur la sainteté*, 78–86; Idel, "The Divine Female and the Mystique of the Moon," 171–172; and *R. Menahem Recanati, the Kabbalist*, 1: 223–224.

119 Yehuda Liebes, "Myth vs. Symbol in the Zohar and Lurianic Kabbalah," 212–242 and Liebes, "Shablonization and its Revival of Jewish Myth" (forthcoming) (Hebrew).

4 On the Elevated Status of the Divine Feminine in Theosophical Kabbalah

The understanding of the status of the divine Feminine in theosophical Kabbalah depends on the more comprehensive sefirotic schemes. Indubitably, diverse as they may be, they are maps charted by men for making sense of a basically androcentric society. In the common descriptions and diagrams of the ten *sefirot, Malkhut* or *'Atarah*, is situated at the lower end of the sefirotic pleroma, below the *sefirot* of *Tiferet* and *Yesod*, which represent the paramount masculine powers, and, as such, She was considered by some scholars to be created out of the body of the Male, and subsequently also subordinated to Him. This rather static picture, however, is not the only way of depicting the relations between those powers. I shall address some examples that attribute a higher status to the Feminine than that of most of the lower *sefirot*. R. Shem Tov ibn Gaon, who has been mentioned several times above, wrote in *Keter Shem Tov*:

> [T]he correspondence of the [seven] days[120] is so and so in our true Kabbalah,[121] and if you will understand the [world of] emanation and the secret of the two luminaries that was told to you concerning the two kings that wear one crown, you should know that this is a very occult secret, and I was not permitted to hint at it more. And as to the correspondence of this seventh day, our sages, blessed be their memory, said in the 'Aggadah[122]: "Sabbath told to the Holy One, blessed be He, 'Lord of the World, you gave a partner to all but to me you did not give one, etc., Behold, He gave to him His Name.'"[123]

This is a very cryptic statement that centers around an alleged secret hidden in a rabbinic myth. It is not always possible to penetrate the cloud of esotericism this Kabbalist built around Nahmanides's thought, but in this specific case, he writes more explicitly elsewhere in his book: "the first and the second days refer to the sun and to the moon ... and they are called *du-partzufin* and the third and the

---

120 To the lower seven *sefirot*.
121 On this topic see Efraim Gottlieb, *The Kabbalah in the Writings of R. Bahya ben Asher ibn Halawa* (Hebrew), 250 and Haviva Pedaya, *Nahmanides, Cyclical Time and Holy Text* (Hebrew), 217–221.
122 *Genesis Rabbah* 11: 8.
123 Ms. Paris BN 774, fol. 74a, in ed. *'Amudei ha-Qabbalah*; 3; R. Menahem Recanati, *Commentary to the Pentateuch*, fol. 8b; and the fourteenth century Catalan Kabbalist R. Yehoshu'a ben Shmuel Nahmias, 73–74, where he refers several times to Nahmanides and connects the discussions about the luminaries to the assumption that "all is one and the end is the beginning." שהכל אחד והסוף הוא הראש a statement that implies some form of circular theosophy.

https://doi.org/10.1515/9783110599800-004

fourth to the two crowns that are the arms of the world ... and the seventh day is Sabbath and it corresponds to the Righteous."[124]

The seventh day corresponds to the ninth *sefirah*, the phallus, which is considered to be therefore later in time in comparison to the divine Feminine, emanated in the second day. As pointed out by Gottlieb, this view has been copied in *Ma'arekhet ha-'Elohut*,[125] which adds that the two *sefirot* are the essence of the operators or the agents, *ha-po'alim*, a technical term in Nahmanidean Kabbalah, just as is the two-faced structure *du-partzufin*.[126] The two arms are the *sefirot* of *Hesed* and *Gevurah*, which are higher than *Tiferet* in the regular diagrams of the ten *sefirot*. In any case, per ibn Gaon, it is possible to elevate the *Shekhinah* to the level of *Tiferet*[127] and, per another text, perhaps even to the Infinite,[128] a view that does not depend solely on eschatological situations.

Let me turn to another Kabbalist, the nomadic R. Isaac ben Samuel of Acre, who was acquainted with R. Shem Tov's book, which he sometimes criticized. He sees the antecedence of the Diadem to *Tiferet* in terms taken from the pseudo-Aristotelian dictum, writing as follows:

> Behold, you should understand from what the Rabbi,[129] blessed be his memory, said as to the verse "And the Lord said, let be light"[130] that the 'A[tarah] preceded *Tiferet* in thought, and *Tiferet* preceded 'A[tarah] in [the realm of] action, namely in the [realm of] emanation, as the entire building,[131] that is the last one, was first in thought, behold that Adam was created the last of all the creatures, but the world was created for his sake, and this is what the sages, blessed be their memory, said that the thought of Israel preceded everything,[132] and this is what the verse hinted at [about] the 'A[tarah]: "I am the first and I am the last,"[133]

---

124 Ms. Paris BN 774, fol. 74a:

יום ראשון ושיני מתיחסין לשמש ולירח...הנק' ד"פ והשלישי והרביעי לב' כתרים שהם זרועות עולם...יום שביעי הוא שבת נתייחס לצדיק.

125 *The Kabbalah in the Writings of R. Bahya ben Asher*, 250.

126 *The Kabbalah in the Writings of R. Bahya ben Asher*, 256.

127 See *'Amudei ha-Qabbalah*, 27, 63.

128 Ibid., 71.

129 Namely, Nahmanides.

130 Genesis 1:3.

131 *Binyan*, namely, the lower seven *sefirot*, whereas the pseudo-Aristotelian dictum refers to the example of the intention of building a building.

132 See e.g., *Zohar* I, fol. 24a, II, fol. 108b, 119ab, III, fol. 306b. This is an example where the theme of the nation is parallel to that of the Female.

133 Isaiah 44: 6. This is another recurring prooftext for uroboric interpretations, when understood in theosophical terms. Whether R. Isaac's recurring phrase מאין סוף לאין סוף namely, from the Infinite to the Infinite should be understood as part of the circular theosophy is a difficult question to answer. See Valabregue-Perry, *Concealed and Revealed*, 166–176.

I am the first in thought and the last in action This is what I ... [134] have understood from what I received.[135]

The attribution of the interpretation of the Genesis verse to Nahmanides is very important. Indeed, it is possible to confirm that R. Isaac received such a tradition in the name of Nahmanides, or at least that such a tradition existed. Further on in the same book, he refers to what he heard from the mouth of a certain *RShNR*, probably a Castilian Kabbalist whose precise identity is not known,[136] concerning a parable that illustrates the end of the last sentence in the previous passage.[137] The gist of the parable is that God created the lower world as a palace and placed the *'Atarah* on top of it in order to illuminate the world. This means that the Diadem is the last in the divine action, which means the lowest in the world of emanation that contains ten *sefirot*, although She was the first intention in the divine thought, and the world was created solely to allow Her to shine.[138] The story is an interesting case of referring to the pseudo-Aristotelian dictum, whose major illustration is the process of building a house that emerges first in the architect's thought as the telos of his operation.[139]

Evidently, R. Isaac of Acre is not the first Kabbalist who employed the dictum in the service of allocating a significant role to the feminine power, the *'Atarah*, as "first in Thought," which means higher than *Tiferet* and *Yesod*, the two masculine powers in the "Building." Elsewhere, this Kabbalist describes the emergence of *Tiferet* and *Malkhut* as the first and second day of the week, namely, that the latter two are higher than the other five lower *sefirot*, including the *sefirah* of *Yesod*, which refers in many cases to the phallus, a view echoed in Cordovero's

---

134 Here there are some acronyms referring to the name of R. Isaac of Acre himself.

135 *Me'irat Einayyim*, 15:

הרי יש לך להבין מתוך מה שאמ'' הרב ז''ל בפסוק ''ויאמר אלהים יהי אור וגו', שהע' קדמה לתפארת במחשבה, והתפ' קדמה לע' במעשה כלומ' באצילות כי כל בנין שהיא אחרון למעשה הוא היה הראשון במחשבה והנה האדם לא נברא אלא אחרון לכל הנבראי' ובעבורו נעשה העולם. וזהו שאמ' חז''ל מחשבתן של ישראל קדמה לכל, וזהו שרמז הכתו' על הע' 'אני ראשון ואני אחרון' אני ראשון למחשבה ואחרון למעשה כך הבנתי אני יה''ב שב''ר דעת''ו מתוך מה שקבלתי .

See also Mopsik, *Recherches autour de la lettre sur la sainteté*, 213–218.

136 He is mentioned again in *Me'irat 'Einayyim*, 64, 137, 157, 204, and see especially Goldreich's discussions on 390–391, 417, 433.

137 *Me'irat 'Einayyim*, 243–244.

138 For an interesting parallel see the anonymous *Ma'arekhet ha-'Elohut*, ch. 10, 185, whose views will be discussed below in ch. 6.

139 See Stern, "The First in Thought."

Kabbalah.[140] As Paul Fenton has already pointed out in the context of another text by R. Isaac of Acre, the second day's connection to *'Atarah* and the Moon may be related to the designation of the second day of the week as the day of the Moon – *Luna, Lunes, Luni, Lundi,* in Romance languages and *Montag* and *Monday* in German and English.[141]

The formulation used in the last passage indicates an attempt to account for the more common vertical theosophy, with the divine Feminine at the end, namely lower than *Tiferet,* and Her privileged status as found on a level higher than Him. This reading misinterprets the pseudo-Aristotelian dictum, by assuming that thought and action do not coincide, but coexist at different ontological levels, as the result of a divine decision to create. It is important to note that many of the discussions in chapters 3 and 4 are related to the Nahmanidean type of Kabbalah, as is the treatment of other topics related to the status of the divine Feminine.[142] Nahmanides's Kabbalah differs, as mentioned above, on this crucial issue from the other Kabbalists in Gerona.[143]

Another instance showing the importance of Nahmanides's Kabbalah concerns a mid-thirteenth century work by Jacob ben Jacob ha-Kohen in Castile. A passage mentions a tradition from an unidentified source dealing with the supremacy of the Moon, a symbol of the divine Feminine, over the Sun, a symbol of the Male.[144] R. Jacob reports that it was said that the moon "understands the knowledge of our Creator" more than the Sun does,[145] and the light of the Moon is more beneficial to eyes than that of the sun.[146] The Moon is the luminary that is connected to the Jewish nation, and to redemption.[147] This text connects the

---

140 *Me'irat 'Einayim,* 8, translated and discussed in a different manner by Wolfson, *Language, Eros, Being,* 61– 62; see also Idel, "The Divine Female and the Mystique of the Moon," 173–174.

141 See *Judah b. Nissim ibn Malka, Judeo-Arabic Commentary on the Pirqey Rabbi Eli'ezer,* 32 n. 46.

142 See Idel, "The Divine Female and the Mystique of the Moon," and my discussions of the status of the Female in Nahmanides's school in *R. Menahem Recanati, the Kabbalist,* 1: 215–219.

143 See also "The Divine Female and the Mystique of the Moon," 163–175.

144 First printed by Gershom Scholem, *The Kabbalot of R. Jacob and R. Isaac, the sons of R. Jacob ha-Kohen* (Hebrew), 240–241; Daniel Abrams, "*The Book of Illumination*" of R. Jacob ben Jacob ha-Kohen, A Synoptic edition (Hebrew), 330– 38. The passage has been printed in part and discussed also in Kushnir-Oron, ed., *Todros ben Joseph Abulafia, Sha'ar Ha-Razim,* 49 n. 19, who pointed to a possible connection to R. Jacob ha-Kohen's brother, R. Isaac ha-Kohen; see more recently Pedaya, *Vision and Speech,* 223; Shifra Asulin, "The Flaw and its Correction," 195–196, n. 12; Yehuda Liebes, *The Cult of the Dawn, The Attitude of the Zohar toward Idolatry* (Hebrew), 25–26; and Weiss, *Cutting the Shoots,* 83–87.

145 Abrams, "*The Book of Illumination,*" 331, 336.

146 "*The Book of Illumination,*" 332.

147 "*The Book of Illumination,*" 335, 332–333, 337–338.

Moon to the *Shekhinah*[148] while the sun is related to the wicked people.[149] This short text is based on a different type of Kabbalah than the theosophical one, a combination of linguistic and philosophical speculations.

A few decades later, however, R. Isaac of Acre interpreted it in new ways: one is the assumption that God told Abraham to listen to the voice of Sarah,[150] Moses to Miriam, Elkanah to Hannah, and Barak to Deborah, implying that although the men may be more intelligent, on the human level, women of valor have more understanding, profound knowledge, and capacity to give counsel than men do.[151] This has a corollary on the theosophical level, and R. Isaac hints at the "secret" of ʿ*Ateret* and *Tiferet* that are described as *du-partzufin*, namely in a theosophical manner, as in traditions adduced above.[152] In my opinion, this is a clear case of imposing the Nahmanidean Kabbalah on the tradition that R. Jacob reported. Kabbalists such as R. Isaac who were acquainted with most of the existing schools of Kabbalah sometimes offered syntheses of them, although R. Isaac himself once warned against such a practice – another example of conceptual fluidity.

The correspondences between the two astral bodies, man and woman, and the two lower *sefirot* as found in R. Isaac's elaboration, are not new in Kabbalah: they are found in the late twelfth century,[153] but at that time, the feminine entities were not accorded a privileged status. This passage is an example of the privileged status of the divine Feminine, as envisioned as moon and *Shekhinah*, which is not part of the three-phases model. Moreover, it deals with the superiority of specific women in the biblical accounts, without transforming them into symbols of supernal Females. It is noteworthy that a parable about the contemplation of a feminine entity, of Platonic origin, which was transmitted and influenced Jewish mysticism, derived from a lost book of R. Isaac of Acre.[154] At least three different traditions about women and the divine Feminine thus made their way into this Kabbalist's writings, without his attempting to incorporate them into a harmonious picture.

Following the Nahmanidean tradition, a major concern of the Kabbalists discussed in this chapter, in chapter 6, and in the writings of R. Moshe Cordovero

---

148 "*The Book of Illumination,*" 336–337.

149 "*The Book of Illumination,*" 338.

150 Cf. Genesis 22: 12.

151 *'Otzar Ḥayyim,* ms. Moscow-Ginzburg, 775, fol. 95b–96a, Abrams, "*The Book of Illumination,*" 339.

152 *'Otzar Ḥayyim.* For a late antiquity list of wise women, some of them biblical figures, see Clemens of Alexandria, discussed in Pagels, *The Gnostic Gospels,* 84.

153 See the passage on *du-partzufin* by R. Abraham ben David of Posquieres, analyzed in Idel, *Kabbalah & Eros,* 61–73.

154 See Idel, *Kabbalah & Eros,* 153–178.

and R. Isaac Luria was to depict the relationship between the sefirot of *Tiferet* and *Malkhut*, often in terms of equality. Earlier Kabbalists, however, were less concerned about the ascent of the latter to the highest levels of the theosophical system, as we shall see in the next chapter, than Kabbalists in some other theosophical traditions. This is also true of several later Kabbalistic books, such as *Sefer ha-Peliy'ah* in the late fourteenth century, and R. Moshe of Kiev's *Sefer Shushan Sodot* in the late fifteenth century, both in circulation, at least for a while, in the Byzantine empire.

As we shall see at the end of ch. 6, the sixteenth century occult magician Cornelius Agrippa of Nettesheim presented a view as to the superiority of women in the context of the pseudo-Aristotelian dictum, mentioning, inter alia, as R. Isaac did, certain specific biblical women.

5 The Father, the Head, and the Daughter

The vision of the divine Feminine as a daughter, in the context of her special relationship to the divine Father, conceived of as the second *sefirah*, *Hokhmah*, represents another theme worthy of consideration in an analysis of the privileged aspects of the divine Feminine in theosophical Kabbalah. The *Book of Bahir* provides evidence that Jewish thinkers, most probably somewhere in the East, spoke about a supernal daughter long before the emergence of Kabbalah in Europe.[155] This seminal book describes various attitudes of the divinity toward an entity sometimes referred to in the work as a daughter[156] and sometimes as a cherished entity that He puts on His head.[157] I regard this act, which corresponds in this book to some actions in connection with a precious stone, gem, or a precious vessel,[158] and the phylacteries[159] as conferring a privileged status in comparison to the other divine powers described in this book. This is also the case in another paragraph in this work, when the anonymous Kabbalist elaborates

---

155 Ronit Meroz, "The Middle Eastern Origins of Kabbalah," 39–56; Meroz, "A Journey of Initiation in the Babylonian Layer of *Sefer ha-Bahir*," 17–33; Meroz, "On the Time and Place of Some Paragraphs of *Sefer Ha-Bahir*," 137–180; see also Israel Knohl's "From the Birth of the Bible to the Birth of Theosophical Kabbalah," 193–225, and his "The Chariot, the Righteous Man and Satan: Towards Resolving the Puzzle of *Sefer ha-Bahir*" (Hebrew), *World Union of Jewish Studies* 52, (2017): 47–76. See Haviva Pedaya, "The Provencal Stratum in the Redaction of *Sefer ha-Bahir*" (Hebrew). I do not address here the Christotropic explanation of the emergence of the hypostatic Daughter that some scholars attribute to this book. See my remarks in "The Divine Female and the Mystique of the Moon."
156 *The Book Bahir*, ed. D. Abrams, par. 137, 221. See also Scholem, *Origins of the Kabbalah*, 88, 91–92, 157–158, and Green, *Keter*, 134–150. Compare to the opening poetic paragraph of R. Abraham Axelrod of Cologne's treatise written in the earlier part of the second half of the thirteenth century, entitled *Keter Shem Tov*, 29–39. The subject is a "daughter" who knows the source she was hewn from and returns to it after she has been purified. Though this is a hint at the soul, the image of the daughter is nevertheless interesting. For the soul as hewn from the cosmic intellect, see the many discussions in Abraham Abulafia's works and in some cases in Jewish philosophy.
157 *The Book Bahir*, par. 101, 187. See also Adam Afterman, "The Phylacteries Knot, The History of a Jewish Icon" (Hebrew), 466–467 . Putting different things on different limbs in the *Bahir* is paralleled by a discussion that I attribute to the twelfth century R. Jacob the Nazirite, one of the earliest known Kabbalists; cf. my "Prayer in Provencal Kabbalah" (Hebrew), 285–286.
158 *The Book Bahir*, par. 101, and Green, *Keter*, 139–141, who subscribes to Scholem's Gnostic theory of the source of this image. The various syntagms found in this book for the privileged entity, occurred, however already in rabbinic literature. See also the different analyses of the Bahiric discussions in Wolfson, "Woman, The Feminine as Other in Theosophic Kabbalah," 171–173.
159 *The Book of Bahir*, par. 101, 187, and Afterman, "The Phylacteries Knot," 466–468.

https://doi.org/10.1515/9783110599800-005

on the term *Zarqa'*, a sign for a certain type of cantillation or intonation of the Hebrew Pentateuch, a tittle found on the top of letters located at the end of a word. The translation of this seminal passage, whose impact on the *imaginaire* of the Female was paramount, reads:

> What is *Zarqa'*...[it] is a tittle and comes to the head of the creator[160] as it is written, "He creates heaven and earth."[161] And when it goes, it is like a *zarqa'* and a special dear feature after it, and it is on the head[162] of all the letters. And why is it only at the end of a word and not at its beginning? This is done in order to teach you that this tittle ascends higher and higher. What does it teach? That this tittle is a precious stone that is perfect and embellished, as it is written: "a stone rejected by builders became a cornerstone."[163] And it ascends to the place from which it was hewn, as it is written:[164]: "from thence is the shepherd, the stone of Israel."[165]

The images that inform this passage are "precious stone," Israel, and the tittle, which are perfect, on the one hand; the entity discussed here, however, is conceived as hewn from a high source, to which it returns, on the other hand. It is quite plausible from some contexts in this book that this source is the head of the creator. Based on earlier-mentioned parallels in this book, the stone – in Hebrew

---

160 Cf. *BT., Hagigah*, fol. 15a and several times in the following discussions in this chapter.
161 Genesis 14: 19.
162 Namely, on the top of letters.
163 Psalms 118: 22. This verse, used many times in the Zoharic literature, occurs in several Kabbalistic texts to be discussed below, especially Lurianic ones, and served as a prooftext for the privileged status of the Female. See, e.g., below nn. 292, 457, 461, 476 and the discussion of the teaching of R. Nahman of Bratzlav in ch. 11.
164 Genesis 49: 24. On the image of the stone, see Ithamar Gruenwald, "God the "stone-rock": myth, idolatry, and cultic fetishism in ancient Israel," 428–449.
165 *The Book Bahir*, par. 61, 153–155:

ומ"ט זרקא... שם אתגא ואתיא לראש קונה, דכתיב (בראשית יד:יט) 'קונה שמים וארץ', וכד אזלא הוי כזרקא וסגולה אבתריה והוי בראש כל אותיות. ומאי טעמא היא בסוף התיבה ואינה בראשה? ללמדך שאותה תגא עולה עד למעלה למעלה. ומאי משמע דהאי תגא? אבן יקרה היא מכוללת ומעוטרת דכתיב (תהלים קיח:כב) 'אבן מאסו הבונים היתה לראש פנה' ועולה עד המקום אשר נחצבה ממנו דכתיב (בראשית מט:כד) 'משם רועה אבן ישראל'.

Compare also to Scholem, *Origins of the Kabbalah*, 174–175, the fuller text translated in Green, *Keter*, 137–138, and see Jordan S. Penkower, *The Dates of Composition of the Zohar and the Book of Bahir, The History of Biblical Vocalization and Accentuation as a Tool for Dating Kabbalistic Works*, 139–141. This passage had a long history in Kabbalah, as is evident, for example, in a passage from *Tiqqunei Zohar*, to be discussed immediately below, in R. Menahem Recanati, *Commentary to the Torah*, fols. 14a, 37b, 93a; R. Menahem Zioni, *Commentary on the Pentateuch*, fol. 34bc, and in R. Moshe Cordovero's writings. See, e.g., *Pardes Rimmonim*, 29: 1, and more in the following chapters. The theme of having "been hewn" from a source, which is essential for the three-phases model, is found both in the Hebrew Bible, especially in the context of the divine voice, in *Sefer Yetzirah* in the context of the letters, and in some Midrashim in various contexts.

a feminine noun – parallels a feminine entity on high. No doubt this entity is privileged, as the imagery of the cantillation sign of *zarqa'* as a sign placed on the top of the end of a word in the Pentateuch indicates.[166] This cantillation sign was designed in the Middle Ages in Europe in a serpentine shape and, later on in the book of the *Zohar*, it was perceived as referring to an uroboros. Perhaps the uroboric form is related to the return of the stone to the original source.[167] The organic understanding of the stone, not only as hewn but also as striving to return to the source by means of ascent, is based on Neoplatonic assumptions regarding the origin and nature of the human soul in the world-soul and its eventual return to it. In any case, many Kabbalists adopted this vision of the soul, and, apparently, the divine Feminine was conceived as operating in such a manner.[168]

This imagery means that despite Her being, according to this anonymous Kabbalist, lower than the other divine powers, because of the King's love, She is elevated to another status, higher than theirs. Elsewhere, this Kabbalist mentions the bride who is also the "Fiancée of the Holy One blessed be He."[169] For our present discussion, the elevation of a feminine entity to the divine head, as an act of special affection, is paramount. It does not matter for this purpose whether those phrases allude to paternal love, eroticism, sexuality, or incest, as, in any case, they refer to a very special form of attention, greater than that accorded to other divine powers, who are called sons. It is not clear whether the ascent of the lowest to the highest is an attempt to operate within the frame work of an

---

166 On the various forms of this cantillation sign in early and high Middle Ages, see Penkower, *The Dates of Composition*, 133.

167 See also below, in ch. 12.

168 For a discussion of the ascent of the *'Atarah* to the head, referred as the first *sefirah*, *Keter*, in the context of the return of the soul to the source, see the anonymous "Twenty-Four Secrets," a short, rather eclectic Kabbalistic composition, authored, in my opinion, by the early fourteenth-century Kabbalist, R. Joseph Angelet, which is found in several manuscripts, e.g., ms. Oxford-Bodleiana 1663, fol. 95b. The discussion in this treatise deserves a more detailed analysis in the context of the topics discussed here. As to its possible authorship, see M. Idel, "Types of Redemptive Activities in Middle Ages" (Hebrew), 264, n. 46. See also R. Meir ibn Sahulah or R. Joshu'a ibn Shu'aib's supercommentary on Nahmanides's secrets in the Pentateuch, on pericope Leviticus (Warsaw, 1875), fol. 14bc, similar to the view of R. Azriel, cf. n. 76 above; R. Meir ibn Gabbai, *'Avodat ha-Qodesh*, 3: 18, fol. 81a, 3: 61, fol. 107d; and R. Moshe Cordovero, *'Or Yaqar*, 3: 184.

169 ארוסתו של הקב"ה ibidem, par. 137, 221, and see Afterman, "The Phylacteries Knot," 466. See also the *Book Bahir*, ed. Abrams, no. 104, 187, as well as Daniel Abrams, "The Condensation of the Symbol 'Shekhinah' in the Manuscripts of the *Book Bahir*," 7–82, and the many discussions of the different feminine aspects of the Female found in this book, in his *The Female Body of God*, passim, especially 74–78, and Scholem, *On the Mystical Shape of the Godhead*, 161–170, 173–174. See also below the secondary literature mentioned in n. 847.

uroboric theosophy; moreover, the impact of *Sefer Yetzirah* 1: 7 seems unlikely. Given the lasting impact of this book on Kabbalistic literature, however, we may consider it a major source that served as a prooftext for some later discussions. It is worth noting that the *Book of Bahir* resorts to the symbolism of *Maḥashavah* – Thought – as a very high entity in the divine pleroma, thus also adopting an axial type of thought.[170] The views of the book of *Bahir* on the topics under scrutiny here are thus much closer to the Nahmanidean Kabbalah as discussed above, than to the Kabbalistic school of R. Isaac the Blind. Finally, in a paragraph from this book, the *Shekhinah*, in parallel to the daughter, is described as stemming from the second *sefirah, Ḥokhmah*, a view that will have a strong impact on Kabbalistic literature.[171]

I shall start, however, with a text that does not show the impact of this influential book. A short composition that I assume was written around 1260, in the circle of R. Nehemiah ben Shlomo, the prophet of Erfurt, synthesizes Ashkenazi material and themes stemming from early theosophical Kabbalah in Provence or Catalunia.[172] Scholars, including myself in my earlier studies, regarded some of the theosophical themes as part of what Gershom Scholem has called "proto-Kabbalistic" elements, preserved in a treatise that they regarded as the work of R. Eleazar of Worms, from early in the thirteenth century or earlier.[173] Later findings, described first in an important study by David Matatiahu ha-Levi Siegel[174],

---

170 See Scholem, *Origins of the Kabbalah*, 85, 115, 116, 126–130, 152, 158.

171 *The Book Bahir*, 201, n. 116.

172 On this figure, his writings and his circle see, e.g., M. Idel, "Some Forlorn Writings of a Forgotten Ashkenazi Prophet: R. Nehemiah ben Shlomo ha-Navi'," 188–196, Idel, *Ascensions on High in Jewish Mysticism*, 63, 86, 88, Idel, "From Italy to Germany and Back, On the Circulation of Jewish Esoteric Traditions," 47–94; Idel, "The Anonymous Commentary on the Alfabet of Metatron – An Additional Treatise of R. Nehemiah ben Shlomo the Prophet" (Hebrew); Idel, *Ben: Sonship and Jewish Mysticism*, 218–235; Idel, "On R. Nehemiah ben Shlomo the Prophet's 'Commentaries on the Name of Forty-Two' and *Sefer ha-Hokhmah* Attributed to R. Eleazar of Worms" (Hebrew), 157–261; and M. Idel, "On Angels in Biblical Exegesis in Thirteenth-Century Ashkenaz," 211–244; Idel, "On the Identity of the Authors of the Ashkenazi Commentaries to the Poem *Ha-'Aderet ve-ha-'Emunah*, and on the Concepts of Theurgy and Glory in R. Eleazar of Worms" (Hebrew), 67–208; Idel, "R. Nehemiah ben Shelomo the Prophet's Commentary on Seventy Names of God and the Threefold Discourse" (Hebrew), 801–848; and Na'ama ben Shahar, "MS Nurenberg, Stadtbibliotek Cenr. V. App. 5: A Fresh Window on Mid-Thirteenth-Century Ashkenazi and French Tradition" (Hebrew), 73–123, as well as below n. 191.

173 Cf. Scholem, *Origins of the Kabbalah*, 184–185; Joseph Dan, *The Esoteric Theology of Ashkenazi Hasidism* (Hebrew), 118–129; Dan, "The Emergence of Mystical Prayer," 112–115; Farber-Ginat, *The Concept of the Merkabah*, 236–238; Green, *Keter*, 94–96, 125–130; Elliot R. Wolfson, *Along the Path*, 40–43, 158–160; Idel, *Kabbalah, New Perspectives*, 195.

174 *Sefer Sodei Razei Semukhim* (Hebrew).

and then in one of mine,[175] convinced me, however, that the treatise which pre-served these themes, *Sefer ha-Hokhmah*, was not written by R. Eleazar of Worms, although it may contain some of his views. I consider, however, that is possible to determine at least some of the sources of the theosophical themes in manuscripts related to the school of R. Nehemiah ben Shlomo, which flowered somewhat later, in texts found in manuscripts.[176] In *Sefer ha-Hokhmah* we read:

> *Bereshit* ... *Roshi Bat*[177] as the *Shekhinah* of the Creator is called *Bat*, as it is written[178] "And I shall be Dwelled at Him," and the translation[179] is *W-MTRBYH*, which are the same conso-nants as *BRTYH* [His daughter] and it is the tenth *sefirah* and *Malkhut*, as *Keter Malkhut* is on his head.... "And I was to him as a nurseling"[180] and She was coveting[181] Him on high, and She was ascending and sitting in His Bosom as His Daughter[182] ... and then the prayer was ascending to be a crown [*keter*] on the head of the Holy One, blessed be He,[183] and the Holy One blessed be He tells Her: "Sit on my right."[184] And the world has been created for Her.[185]

---

175 See "On R. Nehemiah ben Shlomo the Prophet's Commentaries on the Name of Forty-Two," 157–261.

176 See Idel, On R. Nehemiah ben Shlomo the Prophet's Commentaries, 202–205.

177 Although this way of deconstructing and reconstructing the word *Bereshit* is very simple, it does not appear in *Tiqqunei Zohar*, or in any early Kabbalistic writing before the eighteenth century, and even then it has nothing to do with *Sefer ha-Hokhmah*.

178 See R. Shimeon ben Isaac's *Yotzer* to the first Day of Shavu'ot, printed in *Liturgical Poems of R. Shime'on bar Yitzhaq*, 43–44.

179 Unknown. See Scholem, *Origins of the Kabbalah*, 185, n. 213.

180 Proverbs 8: 30.

181 *Mefa'emet*. For the meaning of this verb as referring to arousing and seducing, see in the early medieval liturgical poems printed by Joseph Yahalom, *Priestly Palestinian Poetry, A Narrative Liturgy for the Day of Atonement* (Hebrew), 96, 124, and in *Genesis Rabba'* 18: 23, 164, and the footnotes of the editors there, as well as in *BT., Sotah*, fol. 9b, describing the *Shekhinah* as triggering or coveting.

182 See Scholem, *Origins of the Kabbalah*, 184–187.

183 On the "Head of the Creator"; see also note 191.

184 Psalms 110: 1.

185 Ms. Oxford-Bodleiana 1568, fol. 25a–25b, printed as the introduction to the *Commentary on the Torah* attributed to R. Eleazar of Worms, *Perush ha-Roqeah 'al ha-Torah*, 1: 15, quoted below as *Sefer ha-Hokhmah*. This introduction is not always connected to the commentary. I corrected the text according to the manuscript:

בראשית....ראשי בת, לפי ששכינת הבורא נקראת בת שנאמר 'ואהיה אצלו שכונה' ומתרגמין ומתרבי"ה אותיות ברתיה והיא נקראת ספירה עשירית והמלכות, לפי שכתר מלכות בראשו... 'ואהיה אצלו אמון', והיתה מפעמת עליו במרום והיתה עולה ויושבת בחיקו כבתו,... ואז עולה התפילה לכתר על ראש הקב"ה, והקב"ה אומר לה: שב בימיני, ובשבילה נברא העולם.

The passage and its parallel have been discussed several times in scholarship. See Joseph Dan, *The Esoteric Theology of Ashkenazi Hasidism*, 120; Farber-Ginnat, *The Concept of the Merkavah*, 241–242, 609, Green, *Keter*, 94–96, Wolfson, *Along the Path*, pp. 41–43, and my *Kabbalah & Eros*, 39–40, 262, n. 86.

The consonants of the word *Bereshit,* which means "at the beginning," when transposed, are the same as *Roshi Bat,* which can be understood as "My head [is/touched/approached by a] daughter." In any case, the special affinity of the head and the daughter is undoubtedly the starting point of the passage, and most of the quotation adduced here explicates the significance of the relations between the two terms. One of these imagesrelates to the ascent of the *'Atarah* and its position on the "head of the Creator," a phrase that occurs elsewhere in the writings belonging to this group of texts, and in a somewhat different manner in the *Book of Bahir,* as seen earlier. In this text, the head plays an important role in the religious outlook, as is the case in another text to be discussed below, which continues a series of discussion found in books written in Ashkenaz to this effect.[186] It is not clear whether the meaning of the biblical word "at the beginning" is relevant to this text, in connection with a primordial event. In any case, She is regarded as the telos of the creation, in the way that some Kabbalists saw the Female in the context of the pseudo-Aristotelian dictum.

This ascent of prayer and the coronation of the divine head follow a long tradition found in later Midrashim and in Ashkenazi liturgical poems and their commentaries.[187] The other image, dealing with ascent and sitting together with the Creator has more erotic overtones that are reminiscent of the relationship between God and the Torah.[188] Although the emergence of the hypostatic prayer by the human liturgy is well-known, rabbinic texts did not describe it as being or becoming a daughter, and the sitting beside God or in his bosom are unmatched in the Ashkenazi material or earlier sources.

What is the nature of the daughter in comparison to the Creator? We may learn from the Aramaic and Hebrew grammatical forms translated above as "His daughter" that She is the daughter of God and not just the entity that emerges from the humans' performance of the oral rituals.[189] The syntagm the "*Shekhinah*

---

186 Green, *Keter,* passim, M. Idel, "Gazing at the Head in Ashkenazi Hasidism," 265–300. For the importance of the face in ancient Judaism from a religious point of view, see Samuel E. Balentine, *The Hidden God, The Hiding of the Face of God in the Old Testament*; Walter Eichrodt, *Theology of the Old Testament,* 2: 35–40; Yohanan Muffs, *Love & Joy, Law, Language and Religion in Ancient Israel,* 104–105, 113, 124, 146, 178, 190; Shmuel Ahituv, "The Countenance of YHWV" (Hebrew), 3–11, and for discussions in later Jewish literatures, see my two studies "*Panim* – On Facial Re-Presentations in Jewish Thought," and "The Changing Faces of God and Human Dignity in Judaism," 71–121.

187 See Green, *Keter,* passim.

188 See *Sefer ha-Hokhmah,* 29.

189 See the syntagm בתו של האל the daughter of God, as the explanation of the biblical name Bethuel, in *Sefer ha-Hokhmah,* 28 and compare to Philo's etymology adduced in a text dealt with by Scholem, *On the Mystical Shape of the Godhead,* 144.

of the Creator" points in the direction of a linkage between the two, in which each entity is independent of human activity, and it suggests a more organic connection between them. I assume that two different traditions have been juxtaposed, and it is hard to offer a unified view of the text. This is the case also in another passage belonging to the same synthetic Ashkenazi-theosophical traditions:

> The place of the 'Atarah [diadem] is on the "head of the Creator," in [or by the means of] the [divine] name of forty-two letters[190] ... and when the 'Atarah is on the head of the Creator,[191] then the 'Atarah is called 'Akatriel.... Of it, David said:[192] "He that dwells in the secret [place] of the most High, shall abide in the shadow of the Almighty" – that is: "in [or by the means of] the prayer of the Almighty we shall abide" ... since the prayer is Tzelota' to God,[193] and it sits on the left side of God,[194] like a bride and [her] bridegroom. And it is called Bat Melekh [the daughter of the King], and sometimes it is called Bat Kol, after the name of its mission. Of it, Solomon said:[195] "and 'eHYeH, –Shekhinah – 'eTzLW" and the name of the Shekhinah is 'eHYeH, and the [Aramaic] translation of 'eTzLW is TRBYH,[196] derived from BRTYH[197] as it is called Daughter of the King, for the name of the Shekhinah [means] that She is with Him – 'eTzLW – in this house.... He has a Tzelot[198] named 'eTzLW, that is the tenth,[199] Malkhut [the Kingdom].[200]

---

190 In this group of texts, this name was sometimes conceived as facilitating the ascent on high.
191 Rosh ha-Bore'. On this term, see also R. Nehemiah ben Shlomo, Commentary on the Seventy Names of the Angel of Presence, printed as Sefer ha-Hesheq, fols.6a, 8b, no. 65 and the additional sources in my "R. Nehemiah ben Shlomo, the Prophet from Erfurt's Commentary on the Poem 'El Na' le-'Olam Tu'aratz" (Hebrew), 25 and n. 132, 73 and n. 44, 74; Idel, "On the Identity of the Authors," 57, 65, 83, 84–85, n. 148, 88, n. 162, 89, n. 165, 100, n. 189, 101, 105, n. 217, 113, 115–116, 117, n. 271, and in Afterman, "The Phylacteries Knot," 461 and n. 80 and in n. 183 above.
192 Psalms 91: 1.
193 Tzelota' le-QBH.
194 In a treatise of R. Eleazar of Worms, Hilkhot Tefillah, he indicates that the 'Atarah is tantamount to the divine phylacteries; see ms. New York JTS 1885, fol. 19b. Phylacteries are donned on both the head and the left hand. See the explicit nexus between Keter and phylacteries of the head in the same text, reproduced in Dan, The Esoteric Theology, 121–122, and see Afterman, "The Phylacteries Knot," 441–480. On phylacteries and 'Atarah see also the late thirteenth century theosophical treatise Sefer ha-Yihud, ms. Milano-Ambrosiana 62, fol. 114b, where the commandment of donning phylacteries is described as crowning the King with an 'Atarah.
195 Probably a reference to Proverbs 8: 30.
196 On the problem connected to this translation, see Scholem, Origins of the Kabbalah, 185, n. 13.
197 That is, 'His daughter' in Aramaic.
198 Prayer, together with the mentioning of Akatriel, seems to be an indication of the impact of the passage from BT, Berakhot, fol. 7a. See also Green, Keter, 62–65.
199 Or, perhaps, "the tenth, which is also Kingdom," viewing tenth and kingdom as two independent epithets for the last sefirah.
200 Ms. Oxford-Bodleiana 1822, fols. 60b–61a. See also my "On R. Nehemiah ben Shlomo the Prophet's Commentaries," 181–183 and Dan, The Esoteric Theology, 120.

Here, too, the theme of the Daughter is conspicuous. The passage describes the same relationships between *Keter, 'Atarah, Akatriel,* and the motif of secrecy.[201] Moreover, the anonymous author interprets this term, in Hebrew *be-Seter*, as referring to a daughter – *Bat Sar*, the daughter of an appointed power, angelic or otherwise, as the two words are an anagram containing exactly the same consonants.[202] Apparently, in a few cases, the Daughter functioned in a manner reminiscent of the divine Son, *Ben*, as part of the exegetical code used by this anonymous author.[203] The *Ben* code most probably stems from earlier sources, and I cannot speculate here whether such sources are involved in the case of the *Bat*. This latter code may depend to a certain extent on the theory of the book of *Bahir*, or on the concepts of Feminine in the Nahmanidean type of Kabbalah, although in addition, it is possible that there were also other sources. The other term "head" also recurs frequently, and in this case, the earlier sources are evident.

In the translated passage directly above, the dynamic ascent of the *'Atarah* and its transformation into a Crown – *Keter* – is a central topic. This text also deals, however, with three different transformations of prayer in the supernal world: first, it stands, at least implicitly, for prayer as the spouse of God, referring to a vision of the spouse as the diadem of her husband.[204] The second feminine manifestation defines the 'prayer of God' as His bride, and this description is quite explicit. The third transformation of prayer is alluded to by the term *Shekhinah*, designated here as the daughter of God. Human vocal prayer – one of the major ritual activities in Ashkenazi culture – thus ascends on high and adopts three different feminine forms, starting with the youngest, the daughter, then the bride, and finally the spouse, presumably, the oldest among them. In other words, prayer undergoes a maturing process while ascending and forming a relationship to God. In Ashkenazi Hasidism, a concept describes the ascending prayer also as expanding in size.[205]

---

201 Compare also the motif of God's residence in a place named *setarim*, Secrecy, cf. *BT, Hagigah*, fol. 5b, which is attributed to the *Shekhinah* in the much later *Alphabet of R. Akivah* (Hebrew), 2: 360, 428.

202 See *Sefer ha-Hokhmah*, 25. The specific way this correspondence between two words is indicated, by resorting to the word אותיות, is found in R. Nehemiah's writings. See Idel, "On Angels in Biblical Exegesis," 217, 219, 236, n. 31.

203 See Idel, *Ben, Sonship and Jewish Mysticism*, 194–275.

204 Proverbs 12: 4. On this verse, which became part of some ritual recitation, see the literature mentioned in Roni Weinstein, "Abraham Yagel Gallico's Commentary on Woman of Valor," 118–135. See also below nn. 226, 239, 462, 471, 589.

205 See the first quotation in this paragraph, and Idel, *Kabbalah: New Perspectives*, 160–161; Wolfson, *Along the Path*, 170–171, n. 307; Green, *Keter*, 122, and R. Eleazar of Worms, *Commentary on Prayerbook*, 1: 148–149.

In another discussion in this text, the *Shekhinah* is understood as being an emanated entity, as the term *ne'etzelet* occurs explicitly in this treatise, in a manner that is reminiscent of Catalonian Kabbalah.[206] These two feminine expansions may represent a permutation: the human reaches the divine while the divine reaches the lowest stage in the divine realm through prayer, the daughter, and fulfills a mission, presumably in the lower world.

Elsewhere in this small literary corpus, we find stronger erotic imagery, when the *sefirah* of *Malkhut* is depicted as a bride: "As it is called *Malkhut*, the tenth, *N*[207] as She is a Female, as a bride that sits with the Bridegroom, and this is why She is called *Shekhinah*, which her [name] is the acronym of [the words] ***Sham Kallah Yoshevet neged he-Hatan*** [There the bride sits in front of the bridegroom]."[208]

From the formulations used here, it seems that the bride, *Kallah*, alias, *Malkhut*, alias, *Shekhinah* as Female, refers to the tenth *sefirah* in relationship to the divine Male, the bridegroom, although in this context, the Male has not been described symbolically as related to a particular *sefirah*. *Knesset Yisra'el* is portrayed in a certain passage as a daughter,[209] whereas elsewhere in this modest literary corpus, it seems that the *Shekhinah* is identical to *Keter*.[210] This inconsistency is not accidental: the material preserved in *Sefer ha-Hokhmah* stems from a variety of divergent sources, from R. Nehemiah and from theosophical Kabbalah; the book also includes several later glosses, and it is not worth attempting to harmonize the different discussions. In principle, the concept of a "bride of God" is found in the same period in Ashkenaz, namely in the mid-thirteenth century – not necessarily as the result of a theosophical treatment stemming from Provence or Catalunia, as we learn from a short but explicit syntagm of R. Eleazar

---

206 See Dan, *The Esoteric Theology*, 121, where it is said that crowns of royalty, *Kitrei Malkhut* are situated alongside the *Shekhinah*.
207 N is the shorthand reference to *Neqeivah*, mentioned immediately afterwards, as part of an esoteric language, found already in Nahmanides's circle. See Daniel Abrams, "New Manuscripts to the 'Book of Secrets' Compiled by R. Shem Tov bar Simha and the Sources He Possessed" (Hebrew), 63.
208 Ms. London, British Library 752, fols. 40b–41a:

לפי שהוא מלכות, עשירית, נ' היא נקיבה, ככלה היושבת אצל החתן, ולכך נקראת שכינה. שכינה - נוטריקון שם כלה יושבת נגד החתן.

For the fuller text and a discussion of its context, see Idel, "On R. Nehemiah ben Shlomo the Prophet's Commentaries," 202–203. On the affinities between some of the material found in this manuscript and views to be found in R. Nehemiah ben Shlomo's circle, see also, e.g., M. Idel, *The Angelic World: Apotheosis and Theophany*, 135–147.
209 *Sefer ha-Hokhmah*, 25.
210 See the text printed in Dan, *Esoteric Theology*, 122.

ha-Darshan, the grandson of R. Yehudah he-Ḥasid.[211] In any case, I assume that
the theme of the Daughter and Father in *Sefer ha-Ḥokhmah* does not derive explicitly from the passages from the book of *Bahir* that were analyzed at the beginning
of this chapter.

The impact of the pseudo-Aristotelian dictum can be discerned also in the
main body of Zoharic literature.[212] In another context, a serpent, probably the
same as the primordial one that caused Adam's death, was described in terms of
uroboros, where the shape of the *zarqa'* is mentioned.[213] In the latter discussion,
however, there are no theosophical implications to the uroboros. Those two discussions are, most probably, unrelated. Elsewhere, in a dense anthropomorphic
treatise, *Sifra' di-Tzeni'uta'*, the image of the uroboric serpent is quite evident.[214]
Zoharic literature explains that the term *'Ateret* is "called by the name of the
supernal *Keter* that is hidden more than all [others] in order to unite the beginning with the end, and comprise them in one name."[215] This means that the first
letter of the Tetragrammaton refers to the beginning, the first or second *sefirah*,
whereas the last letter *He'*, refers to the end, *Malkhut*. This is one of the beginnings of the circular theosophy that unites the beginning with the end, based on
the special affinity of the names of the first *sefirah* and the last one – *Keter* and
'Atarah.[216] Some hints at such theosophy appear at the beginning of the second

---

211 See his Collectanea on the Pentateuch, ms. Munchen 221, fol. 137b:

כלתו של הקב"ה

On this Ashkenazi figure see Daniel Abrams, "The Boundaries of the Divine Ontology: The
Inclusion and Exclusion of Metatron in the Godhead," 304ff.
212 See *Zohar*, II, fol. 239a, III, fol. 26b, as well as III, fol. 6a, as pointed out by Liebes, *Sections
of the Zohar Lexicon*, 260.
213 See *Zohar*, III, fols. 205b–206a, translated into English in Daniel C. Matt, *The Zohar, Pritzker
Edition*, 9: 329–330, and discussed in detail by Penkower, *The Dates of Compositions*, 120–123.
About this seminal treatise in Zoharic theosophy, see Ronit Meroz, "The Archaeology of the
Zohar – *Sifra Ditseni'uta* as a Sample Text," 10–85.
214 *Zohar*, II, fol. 176b; English tr, Matt, *The Zohar*, 5: 536. For the profound impact of this treatise on Lurianic Kabbalah see below ch. 8.
215 *Zohar Hadash*, fol. 45d:

עטרת, בשמא דכתרא עילאה, טמירא דכולא, ליחדא רישא בסופא, ובחד שמא אתכלילת

This is a rather rare view in the Zoharic literature; see Tishby, The Wisdom of the Zohar, 3: 987.
This passage inspired R. Tzadoq ha-Kohen, as will be discussed in ch. 11 below. At the time of the
writing of Zoharic literature in the 1380s, diagrams depicting a circular theosophy were already
known. See n. 403 below.
216 See also the diagram in ms. Vatican 441, fol. 116a. Another drawing, to which Dr. Menachem
Kallus kindly drew my attention, is found in ms. Vatican 598; there, too, the *sefirot* are depicted in
counterclockwise direction. This is also the case of the diagram found in R. Abraham Abulafia's
book *Gan Na'ul*, 15. See also in *Gan Na'ul*, 14, on the affinity between *Keter* and *Tzedeq*, the latter
standing in his symbolism for the last *sefirah*. See also his diagram in *'Imrei Shefer*, 18. Abulafia's

part of the thirteenth-century booklet, *Keter Shem Tov,* by R. Abraham Axelrod of Cologne, which combines theosophical speculations of Catalan origins and Ashkenazi material.[217]

The writings of a contemporary of the Zoharic literature, R. Todros ben Joseph ha-Levi Abulafia, a leading figure in Castilian Jewry, whose name has been mentioned in the context of the emergence of Zoharic literature,[218] display some form of circular theosophy in relation to the concept of the divine Female. In the context of the statement found in the book of *Bahir,* as to the presence of the

---

diagram allows us to date the terminus ante-quem datation, which is the 1380s. In my opinion, his view probably reflects an even earlier type of diagram, as those two books, written in Sicily in the 1380s, reflect what was found in the early seventies, when he left Spain. See also two diagrams in R. Naftali Bakharakh, *Sefer 'Emeq ha-Melekh,* fols. 14c, 15d, to be discussed in ch. 8 below.

The emergence of such diagrams may be connected to a diagram of the structure of the entire reality in Neoplatonic terms, found in the influential twelfth century Neopythagorean/ Neoplatonic treatise by Muhamad ibn Sid Al-Bataliausi, known as *Sefer ha-'Aggulot ha-Ra'yon-iyyot,* that was translated into Hebrew at least three times; see ed. D. Kaufmann, 25 and below n. 310. For other, more astral oriented similar circular diagrams of the heavens, especially the zodiacal signs, see Elèmire Zola, *I mistici dell'Occidente,* between pages 104 and 109, and in the Kabbalistic manuscript, ms. Vatican 441, fol. 115b.

It should, however, be mentioned that not all the circular depictions of the ten sefirot assume the contact of *Keter* and *Malkhut.* See, e.g., the drawing printed in Giulio Busi, *Qabbalah Visiva,* 131 or Cordovero's *'Or Yaqar,* 11: 218. The traces of pleromatic or uroboric theosophy are sometimes represented by the phrase *Keter Malkhut.* See also the drawings found on the very last page of R. Shabbatai Sheftel Horowitz's *Shefa' Tal.* See, e.g., *Tiqqunei Zohar,* fol. 17a as discussed in chapter 6 below.

Let me emphasize that the circular theosophy differs from the theory of ten concentric circles that correspond to the ten sefirotic powers, which is more widespread in Kabbalistic diagrams. Compare also to the discussion found in R. David ben Yehudah he-Hasid, *The Book of Mirrors: Sefer Mar'ot ha-Zove'ot,* 87, where *Keter* is described as the husband of *Malkhut,* as wife. See also in this work, 27–29, and Roi, *Love of the Shekhinah,* 96, n. 22. For the theme of the circle in the context of theology, see e.g., Clemens Baumkehr, ed. *Das pseudo-hermetische Buch der XXIV Philosophorum,* 208; Dietrich Mahnke, *Unendliche Sphaere und Allmittelpunkt;* Chaim Wirszubski, "Francesco Giorgio's Commentary on Giovanni Pico's Kabbalistic Theses," 154; Georges Poulet, *Les Metamorphoses du cercle,* 25–69; Frances A. Yates, *Giordano Bruno and the Hermetic Tradition,* 247 and note 2; Alexander Koyre, *From the Closed World to the Infinite Universe,* 18, 279, n. 19; and Edgar Wind, *Pagan Mysteries in the Renaissance,* 227–228; Karsten Harries, "The Infinite Sphere: Comments on the History of a Metaphor," 5–15; and for some Jewish uses of this theme, see M. Idel, "The Magical and Neoplatonic Interpretations of the Kabbalah in the Renaissance," 169, nn. 239–240 and Idel, "Judah Muscato. A Late Renaissance Jewish Preacher," 41–66.

217 See ed. Jellinek, *Auswahl Kabbalistischer Mystik,* 36–37.

218 See e.g., Yehuda Liebes, *Studies in the Zohar,* 130, 135–138, 168, n. 46.

Shekhinah above and below,[219] the latter term referring not to the lower sefirotic realm but to this world, he wrote:

> It reveals to us the great secret of the ten utterances that the world has been created by [means of] them,[220] that six of them correspond to the six days of creation, "and the seventh is Sabbath to God,"[221] and to the three[other], no name can be applied to them, and, accordingly, all are a resplendent light, a pure light and a polished light, to the Infinite[222] ... that the seven that remain, when you will draw a circle that has no beginning and no end, where there are seven points and all are on one rank, each of them is the seventh when he will start [to count] with the last, it is the seventh and so also with the second and the third, and so all [the other].[223]

The context of this discussion is a directive found in the Talmud as to what happens to someone who is in a desert and has lost track of when the Sabbath starts. The recommendation is that he should count six days and then observe the seventh as if it is the Sabbath day.[224] Todros ha-Levi Abulafia applies this teaching to the structure of the seven lower *sefirot*: if they are depicted on a circle, the first will be next to the seventh after all the other points will be displayed on the circumference. As he refers immediately afterwards to the passage about the *Shekhinah* in the *Book of Bahir*, evidently, he assumes the proximity of the last *sefirah* to the first of the seventh, *Ḥesed*, thus introducing a feminine aspect. In any case, the circularity is very evident, and some mitigation of the centrality of hierarchy is clear, even if only the seven lower *sefirot* are involved.

---

219 *The Book Bahir*, no. 116, 201; Scholem, *Origins of the Kabbalah*, 133, n. 143, 137, 161, 180.

220 For the reverberations of the ten creative utterances – found already in rabbinic sources – in Jewish mysticism, see Idel, *Kabbalah: New Perspectives*, 112–122.

221 Exodus 20: 10.

222 Or in an infinite manner. On the sources of the doctrine of the three lights and their presence in the Infinite, see Scholem, *Origins of the Kabbalah*, 347–364.

223 Todros ben Joseph ha-Levi Abulafia, *'Otzar ha-Kavod*, fol. 11a:

גלה לנו סוד גדול בסדר עשרה מאמרות שבהם נברא העולם שהששה מהם כנגד ששת ימי בראשית ושביעית שבת לה' והשלושה אין שם תופס בהם לפיכך כולם אור בהיר צח ומצוחצח עד אין סוף ... אולם השבעה הנותרים כשתצייר עגול שאין לו ראשו וסוף שיש בו שבע נקודות וכולם במעלה אחד נמצא בכל אחד מהם הוא שביעי כשיתחיל מזה האחרון הוא שביעי וכן מן השני וכן מן השלישי וכן כולם.

Let me point out that there are some discussions and diagrams of the seven lower *sefirot* in a circle that include six of them on the circumference and the seventh as the center; this approach differs from R. Todros Abulafia's passage.

224 The rabbinic statement in *BT. Sabbath*, fol. 69b and R. Todros Abulafia's book are commentaries on the Talmudic legends. Compare also to the early thirteenth-century Catalan Kabbalist R. Yehudah ben Yaqar, who discusses Sabbath in the context of the head and the end in his *Commentary on Prayers and Blessings*, part I, 24: לעשות הסוף ראש.

Some significant affinities between the Female and the first *sefirah* are prominent, however, in discussions found in another early fourteenth-century classic of Kabbalah, *Tiqqunei Zohar* and *Ra'aya' Meheimna'* [RM], which belongs to the later layer of Zoharic literature. This distinct layer played a crucial role in the further developments of the image of the Female in theosophical Kabbalah, especially in R. Moshe Cordovero's works. This affinity is evident in statements found in the two introductions to this book.[225] The first one says:

> *Bereshit*: this is the Torah, about which it is said, "The Lord created me at the beginning of His ways."[226] This is the lower *Shekhinah* that is the beginning of the creatures. And She is the end of the supernal *Hokhmah* and because of Her it is said, "He tells the end from the beginning."[227] When She [the Torah] is taken from [the *sefirah* of] *Keter*, She is called 'Ateret Tiferet, 'Atarah on the head of all the *Tzaddiqim*, the tittle of the book of Torah[228] ... and when She [the Torah] is taken from the supernal *Hokhmah*, She is called *Reshit*.[229]

The main topic here is the variety of supernal sources of the Torah in the sefirotic pleroma. Ontologically speaking, in the wider context of the passage, the Torah is depicted as taken from all the *sefirot*, as is evident from the sequel to this passage. I am concerned here, however, mainly with the theme of the beginning of this lower *sefirah*, depicted as *Shekhinah*. The anonymous Kabbalist insists that She is called "beginning," even though She is portrayed as the end of the pleromatic structure and as being, nevertheless, the head of the lower creatures. Elsewhere in this book, in Her quality as the end, the Torah is called *Malkhut* in a very

225 On this literature, see Pinchas Giller, *The Enlightened will Shine. Symbolization and Theurgy in the Later Strata of the Zohar*; Amos Goldreich, "Investigations in the Self-Understanding of the Author of *Tiqqunei Zohar*," 459–496; Biti Roi, *Love of the Shekhina: Mysticism and Poetics in Tiqqunei ha-Zohar* (Hebrew), especially 90–130 about the affinities between the *Shekhinah* and the highest aspects of the supernal world; see also Ruth Kara-Ivanov Kaniel, *Holiness and Transgression, Mothers of the Messiah in the Jewish Myth*, 192–203.
226 Proverbs 5: 22.
227 Isaiah 46: 10. I consider the use of the verse here as referring to the superior status of the Female in comparison to the Males.
228 See also *Tiqqunei Zohar*, fol. 61b, to be discussed toward the end of this chapter.
229 *Tiqqunei Zohar*, fol. 11b:
בראשית, דא אורייתא, דאתמר בה ה' קנני ראשית דרכו, ודא שכינתא תתאה, דאיהי ראשית לנבראים, ואיהי אחרית לחכמה עלאה, ובגינה אתמר מגיד מראשית אחרית. כד אתנטילת מכתר אתקריאת עטרת תפארת, עטרה בראש כל צדיק, תגא דספר תורה.
For an interesting association between the diadem and the tittle, see also the discussion found in the anonymous *Sefer ha-Tzeruf*, from Abraham Abulafia's circle, 6, and see also *Zohar*, II, fol. 158a. For an interpretation of this passage, see Cordovero's *'Or Yaqar*, to *Tiqqunei Zohar Hadash*, 3: 46.

similar context.[230] The phrase "end of _Hokhmah_" should be understood as part of the symbolism that refers in this _sefirah_ to a representation of the Father, '_Abba_'.

For our purpose here, I would suggest regarding Her also as representing the Torah and its different avatars: as lower _Shekhinah_ and _Malkhut_, as the Oral Torah, as is the case in numerous instances in Kabbalah, and on the other hand, as stemming from the higher _sefirot_ up to the moment She reveals Herself to prophets. Those different identifications enable a vision of Her as being at the beginning and at the end, although part of a more complex and detailed emanational process[231 In this context, it is worth noting the dictum that occurs several times in this Kabbalistic literature: "_Hokhmah_ at the beginning and _Hokhmah_ at the end,"[232] an interesting formulation that possibly epitomizes another type of circular approach in Kabbalistic theosophy, against the background of the special relationship of the last _sefirah_ to _Hokhmah_.

The nexus between the first and last _sefirah_ is reiterated elsewhere in this remarkable book, for example, when interpreting the meaning of the syntagm _Keter Malkhut_, which is connected to the verse from Isaiah 46: 10, as if referring to the beginning and to the end, as seen earlier.[233] Interestingly, in another instance, this verse again brought together with the uroboric view of the _sefirot_ as found in _Sefer Yetzirah_ 1: 7.[234] There are no signs here of androgyny, of splits of the alleged supernal male androgyne, or of absorption of the Female: the Diadem is taken from _Keter_, which means the presence of the Female in that zone.[235] Attempts to clarify Her subordinate status on that supreme level are mere scholarly speculations aimed at proposing a certain theory on the basis of elusive and fragmentary hints. The best we can do is to explore discussions found in this layer of the Zoharic literature related to the existence of a decad of inner or supernal _sefirot_, which include, to be sure, also a feminine power.[236] In any case, in the circular diagrams of ten _sefirot_, the vicinity of the first and last _sefirah_ does not include the absorption of the latter.[237]

---

230 _Tiqqunei Zohar_, fol. 11a.

231 _Tiqqunei Zohar_, fol. 11b.

232 _Tiqqunei Zohar_, no. XL, fol. 80b, _Zohar_, I, fol. 26b, [_RM_] III, 238a, [_RM_] and in the writings of R. Joseph Gikatilla. See also below n. 346.

233 _Tiqqunei Zohar_, fol. 17a and compare also to _Tiqqunei Zohar_, fol. 61b. As is well known, Ibn Gabirol's famous poem _Keter Malkhut_ had a strong impact on the introduction to _Tiqqunei Zohar_.

234 _Tiqqunei Zohar_, fol. 61b. On this passage, see Roi, _Love of the Shekhinah_, 104–105.

235 See also _Zohar_, III, fol. 71a [_RM_], discussed in Roi, _Love of the Shekhinah_, 161–162, n. 89.

236 M. Idel, "The Image of Man above the _Sefirot_: R. David ben Yehuda he-Hasid's Theosophy of the Ten Supernal _Sahsahot_ and its Reverberations, 181–212; Idel, "Sefirot above Sefirot" (Hebrew), 239–280; Idel, "Kabbalistic Materials from the School of R. David ben Yehuda he-Hasid" (Hebrew), 169–207.

237 See above n. 216.

In the context of the texts quoted at the beginning of this chapter, let me address some discussions of the special relationship between the Father and the Daughter. This special affinity is part of a wider structure, the fourfold divine family, which includes also a Mother and a Son.[238] A passage belonging to this later layer of Zoharic literature states: "The secret of the issue of 'By [means of the] *Hokhmah* He founded the earth,'[239] *Hokhmah* is 'Abba,' earth is the Daughter."[240] The verb *yasad* – translated above as "founded" – in the biblical verse, became part of a dictum that recurs several times in the literature close to *Tiqqunei Zohar* in the context of the direct relationship of Father and Daughter. For example, the same anonymous Kabbalist wrote: "She is *Bat* from *Bereshit*, who is comprised from ten sayings, from the side of *Hokhmah, Bat Y*,[241] 'by [means of] *Hokhmah* He founded the earth,' 'by means of the Father He[242] founded the Daughter.'"[243]

It is not clear whether this verb *YSD* has some sexual connotation related to the *sefirah* of *Yesod*. The initial foundation of the Daughter is indubitably the reason for Her later ascent to the Father[244] as part of the three-phases model mentioned earlier. Elsewhere in the same book, we read: "The Daughter ... ascends higher than all the supernal ranks, as it is written 'Many daughters are valorous but you surpassed them all' and Her ascendance will be to the Father."[245] The ascent to a position higher than all the other *sefirot* – or ranks – is a clear indication of the preeminence of the Female. My impression is that the Aramaic formula

---

238 See Idel, *Ben, Sonship and Jewish Mysticism*, 380–385, 420, 471–472; Idel, *Male and Female*, ch. 2.

239 Proverbs 3: 19.

240 *Zohar* III, fol. 248a [*Ra'aya' Meheimna'*]: ,רזא דמלה (משלי ג:יט) בחכמה יסד ארץ, חכמה אבא, ארץ ברתא. See also Roi, *Love of the Shekhinah*,. 23, 69, 97–98, 101, 338, 347, 368. See also below, the passage from Cornelius Agrippa, to be adduced at the end of ch. 6.

241 Those three consonants occur in the word *Bereshit*. On *Y* in a similar context, see below the passage from *Tiqqunei Zohar*, fol. 61b.

242 Either *Keter* or the Cause of the Causes.

243 *Zohar* III, fol. 256b [RM]:
ואיהי ב"ת מן בראשית, דכלילא עשר אמירן, מסטרא דחכמה בת י', (משלי ג יט) בחכמה יסד ארץ, באבא יסד ברתא
See also below n. 260, as well as *Zohar*, fol. 258a (where also the *'Atarah* is mentioned), and in *Tiqqunei Zohar*, fols. 35a, and 61b, to be discussed below in the chapter. For the attention accorded to the divine head in this Zoharic layer, see Roi, *Love of the Shekhinah*, 338.

244 *Tiqqunei Zohar*, fol. 26b:
ברתא סלקא לגבי אבא and see also *Tiqqunei Zohar*, fol. 35a.

245 See *Ra'aya' Meheimna'* in *Zohar*, III, fol. 28a:
ברתא... סליקת על כל דרגין דלעילא, הדא הוא דכתיב (משלי לא:כט) רבות בנות עשו חיל ואת עלית על כלנה, וסליקו דילה תהא לאבא.
For the ascent to the Father in an ancient Gnostic tradition, most probably of Jewish origin, see Idel, *Kabbalah: New Perspectives*, 192–193.

'Abba' Yasad Barta', is reminiscent of the Talmudic formula *Rabba' bara' Gavra'*, related, perhaps later on, to the creation of the Golem.[246] Given the existence of two couples, the Daughter's rapprochement to the Father is hardly a sexual one; nor can we speak about the absorption of the Daughter by the Father or of Her masculinization because of Her ascent.

It is necessary to address the historical-philological issue of the relationship between the two bodies of Kabbalistic writings cited in this chapter: the Askenazi and the Spanish. Although written by different authors, anonymous for the time being, they share not only the concern with the head/daughter relationship but also an additional detail. The starting point of the discussion in the first quote – *Bereshit* [= *Roshi Bat*] and other many discussions in *Sefer ha-Hokhmah*[247] are reminiscent of the main exegetical strategy in *Tiqqunei Zohar*: this is a book dedicated entirely to seventy different interpretations of the various words produced by the permutation of the consonants of *Bereshit* – those are the amendments or *Tiqqunim* – and one more example for this type of exegesis is found in the last quote.[248]

In my opinion, it would be an interesting scholarly desideratum to examine the possible infiltrations of Ashkenazi themes into the layer of *Tiqqunei Zohar*, especially some themes found in writings from the circle of R. Nehemiah ben Shlomo the prophet.[249] Additional research is required to establish whether the

---

246 See *BT, Sanhedrin*, fol. 65b.

247 *Sefer ha-Hokhmah*, passim.

248 See also the discussion found in what I assume are the earlier Hebrew fragments of this author, which have been printed in Efraim Gottlieb, *The Hebrew Writings of the Author of Tiqqunei Zohar and Ra'aya Mehemna* (Hebrew), 94.

249 See Farber-Ginat, *The Concept of the Merkavah*, 244, n. 40, 255, 301, n. 43, 418, 587; Daniel Abrams, *Sexual Symbolism and Merkavah Speculation in Medieval Germany*, 69–73; Abrams, "The Book of Illumination," 111; Abrams, "Traces of the Lost Commentary to the Book of Creation by R. Jacob ben Jacob ha-Kohen" (Hebrew), 327, n. 8; for the affinity between R. Jacob ha-Kohen and *Sefer ha-Hokhmah*, see my introduction to Gottlieb's *The Hebrew Writings of the Author of Tiqqunei Zohar and Ra'aya Mehemna*, 13–17; Israel M. Ta-Shma, *Ha-Nigle She-Ba-nistar, The Halakhic Residue in the Zohar* (Hebrew), passim; and Roi, *Love of the Shekhina*, 27–28, 67, n. 3. See also my discussion in "The Anonymous Commentary on the Alphabet of Metatron," 1–10, where I refer also to Israel Weinstock's insight as to the impact of this commentary on *Tiqqunei Zohar*. See also my study "Prophets and Their Impact in the High Middle Ages: A Subculture of Franco-German Jewry."

For an acquaintance with the views of R. Nehemiah and his circle of Kabbalistic authors active in late thirteenth-century Castile, see also my "On *Magen David* and the Name *Taftafiah*: from Jewish Magic to Practical and Theoretical Kabbalah" (Hebrew), 18–32, and "Incantations, Lists, and 'Gates of Sermons' in the Circle of Rabbi Nehemiah ben Shlomo the Prophet, and their Influences," 489–490; Amos Goldreich, *Automatic Writing in Zoharic Literature and Modernism* (Hebrew). In more general terms, the impact of Ashkenazi themes in Castilian Kabbalah, including the *Zohar*, has been pointed out by Israel M. Ta-Shma, "Rabbeinu Dan Ashkenazi" (Hebrew), 386; Idel, "Ashkenazi Esotericism and Kabbalah in Barcelona," 69–113; Idel, "*Sefer*

theories about the divine heads, which are an important aspect of a major component of the Zoharic theosophy, are also a result of the influence of Ashkenazi anthropomorphism[250] or, to use Franz Rosenzweig's term, "theomorphism." We may also question whether it is possible to speak of common sources nourishing the two types of speculation, which would, therefore, be independent of each other. We may thus consider the views found in *Tiqqunei Zohar* as an additional, very important source of what I call the uroboric theosophy, namely of attempting to anchor the beginning of the last *sefirah* continuously in the first one as part of the supernal pleroma conceived in a circular manner.

Another passage from the *Tiqqunim* explicitly reflects basic elements of the three-phases gender model mentioned above:

> The perfect and embellished stone[251] is like the stone on the head of the ring,[252] and when Israel are studying the wisdom [*Hokhmah*], that is *Y*,[253] the supernal thought, they know how to throw[254] that stone that is a single Daughter, to the place She was hewn from, as the Daughter was made by the Father ... *Hokhmah*, namely the Father founded the Daughter ... as the stone is the tittle, a diadem on His head, the diadem of the book of the Torah.[255]

Yetzirah and its Commentaries in the Writings of R. Abraham Abulafia, and the Remnants of R. Isaac Bedershi's Commentary and Their Impact" (Hebrew), 485. See also Adam Afterman, *The Intention of Prayers in Early Ecstatic Kabbalah* (Hebrew), 115–117.

250 On anthropomorphism in Judaism in this period, see Ephraim Kanarfogel, "Varieties of Belief in Medieval Ashkenaz: the Case of Anthropomorphism," 117–159; Carlos Fraenkel, "The Problem of Anthropomorphism in a Hitherto Unknown Passage from Samuel ibn Tibbon's *Ma'amar Yiqqawu ha-Mayim* and in a Newly-discovered Letter by David ben Saul," 83–126; Wolfson, *Through a Speculum that Shines*, 192–195; Idel, "In a Whisper: On Transmission of *Shi'ur Qomah*," 477–522.

251 Although the Aramaic term *'Avna'* means the stone, here the meaning is a precious stone, or a gem, as the context of the ring shows. This sentence follows the imagery of *Sefer ha-Bahir*, where the term 'precious stone' is used. See par. 61 of this book, translated earlier in this chapter, and Roi, *Love of the Shekhinah*, 405–409.

252 This image occurs elsewhere in *Tiqqunei Zohar*, no. LXX, fol. 133b:

אבנא בריש עזקא.

Whether or not the seal or the ring is connected to *Keter*, crown, because of the similar shape, is not clear to me. Compare also to the view found in R. Isaac of Acre as to the divine Feminine found on the top of a building, beside n. 138 above.

253 I speculate that this is the wisdom of Kabbalah that deals with the ten *sefirot*, represented by the letter *Y* = ten. In many cases in theosophical Kabbalah, however, *Y* is a symbol for the second *sefirah*, *Hokhmah*.

254 The verb "to throw" relates to the etymology of *Zarqa'*, whose consonants are identical to ZRQ. See Green, *Keter*, 137, n. 13.

255 *Tiqqunei Zohar*, no. XXI, fol. 61b:

אבנא כלילא ומתעטרא כאבנא בריש עזקא, וכד אית בישראל משכילים בחכמה דאיהי י' מחשבה עלאה, ידעין לזרקא לה להאי אבנא דאיהי בת יחידה, להההוא אתר דאתגזרת, בגין דברתא באבא אתעבידת... בחכמה דאיהו אבא יסד ברתא...דאבנא דאיהי תגא עטרה על רישיה, עטרה דספר תורה.

It is important to emphasize the image of the ring, which may be part of the urob-oric theosophy, which does not occur in the matrix of this passage in the *Book of Bahir* that was discussed earlier. Although the term *'izqa'* for a ring appears often in Zoharic literature, its precise meaning is far from clear. Although a ring is sometimes a clearly feminine term, and, eventually, also a sexual symbol in this literature, in this specific context, it does not seem to be the case. Nevertheless, a uroboric understanding is corroborated by the assumption that the Daughter comes from a supernal source to which She returns, again a circular move. Here, unlike other discussions in this book, the association of the Father and his head on the one hand, and the Daughter on the other, is very evident. In my opinion, there is no reconstruction of a primeval androgynous by a split between the two components, but some form of creation of one entity – the Female – by the other – the Father, and Her return to Him does not restore or reconstitute a hypothetical, implicit androgyne structure.

The Daughter's return to the place from which She was originally hewn is but the last stage of the three-phases model, whose first phase is depicted as the derivation of the Female from Her highest source. The second stage is implied in the assumption that only the Kabbalists know how to cause the Daughter's return; this appears in a passage before the cited passage, which describes the *Shekhinah* as the stone to be thrown upwards and the *zarqa*,'[256] which means that by now She is in Her low position, roughly corresponding to the second stage in the three-phases model. Most importantly, this passage portrays the "scholars," namely the Kabbalists, as capable of bringing about the Female's ascent to Her original source – the third stage – namely, by the study of the Torah, conceived as a theurgical operation. Given the relationship mentioned between the Father and the Daughter, I cannot see how such a passage could be interpreted in a phallo-centric manner.

This model appears elsewhere in the late layer of Zoharic literature, where the *Shekhinah* is described as ascending on high. When asked to where She ascends, the answer is: "to the place She was hewn from there that is the Infinite, that is higher than all the *sefirot*,[257] and this is the reason why it has been written:

---

256 *Tiqqunei Zohar*. For the list of the occurrences of the term *zarqa'* in *Tiqqunei Zohar*, see Penkower, *The Dates of Composition*, 136–137 and Roi, *Love of the Zohar*, 107–108.

257 For a parallel, see *Tiqqunei Zohar*, fol. 25a: "She is ascending higher than all, up to the Infinite."

איהי סלקא על כלהו עד אין סוף.

This ascent to the Infinite is found also in many Zoharic sources, e.g., *Zohar* I, fol. 84b, II, fol. 51b, and in Cordoverian discussions.

the holocaust[258] in its entirety ascends to God,[259], and when She ascends, all the *sefirot* grasp Her and they ascend with Her."[260]

The ascent to the Infinite, and her role as a vehicle drawing all the other *sefirot* upward is certainly a sign of Her privileged status. Moreover, Her active role here is accentuated in comparison to all the other *sefirot*. In this context, we should mention another Zoharic text, which also belongs to the later layer although it was printed together with the earlier stage of this literature, where the ascent of the *Shekhinah* employs the image of the stone thrown on high, and depicts Her as reaching the "head of all the heads," a statement that adumbrates some developments in Lurianic Kabbalah.[261]

The passages discussed in the previous pages are quintessential for an understanding of theosophical Kabbalah as a peak of the early phase of this lore in Spain, but also as the starting point of many more elaborated discussions in Safedian forms of Kabbalah that gravitate around the different aspects of Zoharic theosophies. Though easily available in printed texts, they have thus far been neglected in analyses dealing with gender theories in Kabbalah.[262]

It should be noted that <u>Hokhmah</u>, a paramount feminine noun, which refers to a feminine entity in some texts in ancient Jewish literature, has become a term for a *sefirah* that functions as masculine, as part of the sefirotic scheme that already situated it as such, independent of the question of the Father-Daughter

---

258 The Holocaust sacrifice, עולה is understood here as ascending on high, because of the identical spelling in Hebrew. The word here refers to a Jewish sacrificial offering that is burned completely on an altar.

259 This statement is cited in the name of the ancient authorities, מתניתין in *Zohar,* III, fol. 27a [*RM*].

260 *Zohar* III, fol. 256b [*RM*]:

ולאן סליקת? לאתר דאתגזרת מתמן, דאיהו אין סוף, ואיהו גבוה מכל ספיראן, ובגין דא אוקמוה, עולה כלה לגבוה סלקא, וכד איהי סליקת, אחידן בה כל ספירן, ואינון סלקין עמה.

See also above, n. 243, a reference to a discussion on the same page. See also *Tiqqunei Zohar*, Tiqqun LXIII, fol. 94b:

זכאה איהו מאן דתב לגבי בעלה דידה איהו רזא דתיובתא, דיחזיר ויתוב ההוא דרגא דרחיק ליה מאתריה, דיחזיר לה לאתרה ויקרב לה תמן, בההוא זמנא דשכינתא מרחקא מבעלה.

Compare also to *'Or Yaqar*, to *Tiqqunim*, 3: 46 and the view of R. Naftali Bakharakh, cited below in n. 524.

261 See *Zohar* I, fol. 24a:

וכד איהי סליקת לעילא, ברישא דכל רישין סלקא.

In my opinion, this passage is the plausible source of a verse in R. Isaac Luria's famous hymn, to be discussed in the following chapters. For more on this issue, see below in chs. 7, 8 and 11.

262 See also the passage, which is indubitably related to the later Zoharic layer, quoted in the name of the sages, by the early eighteenth century Hasidic figure R. Moshe of Kobrin, as printed in R. Abraham Weinberg of Slonim, *Yesod ha-'Avodah*, epistle 10, 2: 24:

דמלכות אזדריקת ועלתה לכתר לאתר דאתנטלת מתמן.

relation. Interestingly enough, in those Kabbalistic writings, inclined as they are to a mythical approach, the pseudo-Aristotelian dictum is absent or negligible. Moreover, the nexus between the head, most probably of the Father, and the divine Daughter is reminiscent of the myth of the goddess Athena as emerging from the head or the forehead of her father, Zeus.[263]

---

263 See Hesiodos, *Theogonia*, line 929. I could not find any trace of this Greek myth in Jewish literature, not even in the writings of Itzhak Baer and A. A. ha-Levi, the two scholars in modern studies who championed the idea of a significant Greek influence on early rabbinic literatures. See, however, the important discussion in Yehuda Liebes, *God's Story, Collected Essays on the Jewish Myth* (Hebrew), 262–263, which deals with one of the reverberations of the earlier Greek myth in the image of Helena, the female companion of the ancient figure Simon Magus, and then in Jewish literatures. See also Roi, *Love of Shekhinah*, p. 105 and n. 63 for the reverberation of this theme in *Tiqqunei Zohar*, Tiqqun XXI.

6 *Sefer Ma'arekhet ha-'Elohut* and its Reverberations

Let me now turn to another anonymous Kabbalist, a contemporary of the author of *Tiqqunei Zohar*, who wrote another influential classic of Kabbalah, most probably in Barcelona in the first third of the fourteenth century.[264] Written in the circle of the followers of Nahmanides's disciples, the anonymous *Sefer Ma'arekhet ha-'Elohut* widely employed the Pseudo-Aristotelian dictum. This treatise became a classic in Kabbalah, and various Kabbalists commented on it in the fourteenth and fifteenth centuries, explicitly disseminating a certain Nahmanidean approach to much wider audiences.[265] It is difficult, however, to offer a unified account because the book contains differing understandings of the dictum. According to some discussions, the dictum refers to the assumption that God's initial thought did not change but it was realized only at the end because various changes in the middle were conducive to the primordial intention.[266] This is exemplified, among other things,[267] by the creation of the first couple initially as a unified entity; its subsequent separation; and then the reunion of the couple, which was conceived to be the initial divine intention.[268]

However, in other instances in this book, the interpretation of the pseudo-Aristotelian dictum as referring to divine immutability assumes a more ontological approach, in the vein of the earlier Kabbalists in Gerona discussed in ch. 2 above. This is related to the assumption that in the first divine thought, the perfection of creation and the changes described in the Genesis stories, were intended or premeditated.[269] As Efraim Gottlieb pointed out, the anonymous author was significantly influenced by R. Shem Tov ibn Gaon's *Keter Shem Tov*.[270] In my opinion, there is also a similarity between the parable used by *RShNR*, and quoted

---

264 On this book, see Gershom Scholem, "On the Problems of *Sefer Ma'arekhet ha-'Elohut* and its Commentators," 284–295; Isaiah Tishby, "Passages from *Sefer Ma'arekhet ha-'Elohut* in *Sefer Tzioni*" (Hebrew), 55–57; Efraim Gottlieb, *Studies in Kabbalah Literature* (Hebrew), 324–328; Avraham Elqayam, "Between Referentialism and Performativism: Two Approaches in Understanding Symbol in *Maarekhet ha-Elohut*" (Hebrew), 5–40; and Weiss, *Cutting the Shoots*, passim.

265 See Scholem, "On the Problems of *Sefer Ma'arekhet ha-'Elohut* and its Commentators." The impact of this book's discussions of the pseudo-Aristotelian dictum is discernable in a series of Kabbalistic writings, which include R. Menahem Zioni's *Commentary on the Torah* and the anonymous *Sefer has-Peliy'ah*.

266 *Ma'arekhet ha-'Elohut*, ch. 10, 185.

267 *Ma'arekhet ha-'Elohut*, ch. 8, 108, 111, 113.

268 *Ma'arekhet ha-'Elohut*, ch. 8, 113. See also Wolfson, *Language, Eros, Being*, 173.

269 *Ma'arekhet ha-'Elohut*, ch. 8, 257–258.

270 Efraim Gottlieb, *The Kabbalah in the Writings of R. Bahya*, 249–259.

https://doi.org/10.1515/9783110599800-006

in R Isaac of Acre's *Me'irat 'Einayyim*, about the *'Atarah* as the initial intention and the perfection of the lower world, mentioned toward the end of chapter 4.[271]

In connection with the gender theory in this book, we may distinguish between a phallocentric discussion, which conspicuously subordinates the Female to Her husband, articulated in the context of the present, and Her position in the hoary past and in the future.[272] However, an anonymous gloss in this book in the context of the Midrash about the Sabbath and *Knesset Yisra'el* that was discussed above, states:

> Sabbath is a hint at the seventh millennium, and in that millennium, *'Atarah* will ascend to the place of the first cooperation [*shittuf rishon*],[273] and "two kings will wear the same crown of kingship" [*Keter Malkhut*][274] as it was at the end of the action, and then She will not be under the dominion Her husband, as it is now, She will not need to do anything She [already] did, while She was in [the period of] Her diminution below.[275]

The first cooperation seems to refer to the existence of the *'Atarah* together with *Tiferet* in a primordial time that preceded the diminution of Her size and light, in accordance to another rabbinic myth that had a lasting impact on theosophical Kabbalah.[276] The gloss is undoubtedly part of the wider conceptualization that reflects a theory reminiscent of the three-phases gender-theory. The time of the diminution represents the second stage, while the first and the last are part of the cyclical theory of time, the doctrine of the *shemitot* that recurs in Nahmanidean

---

271 *Ma'arekhet ha-'Elohut*, ch. 10, 185. There is no contradiction between Goldreich's view that RShNR – one of the many acronyms used by R. Isaac in his writings – may have been a Castilian Kabbalist and the Catalan extraction of the anonymous Kabbalist who authored this book, as the latter contains traces of Castilian Kabbalah. See Michal Oron, "Did R. Todros Abulafia ha-Levi write *Sefer Ma'arekhet ha-'Elohut*?" (Hebrew), 697–704.

272 *Ma'arekhet ha-'Elohut*, ch. 10, 186 and ch. 8, 110.

273 *Shittuf* stands here for sexual union, and the first shittuf stands for the relationship between the divine Female and Male before the diminution of the former. See *Ma'arekhet ha-'Elohut*, ch. 8, 107, 108, 110, 111. See in this same work the term *Hibbur rishon*, 113; for its Platonic background, see Idel, *Kabbalah & Eros*, 59–77.

274 See especially, *BT.*, *Ḥulin*, fol. 60b, *Genesis Rabba*, VI:3, and *Pirqei de-Rabbi Eliezer*, ch. 53, and Idel, "Divine Female."

275 *Ma'arekhet ha-'Elohut*, ch. 10, 187. See also Mopsik, *Lettre sur la sainteté*, 135–136, who extrapolated from this statement that this is a case of "feminism" that preceded Sabbateanism. See below n. 595. The anonymous discussion, however, deals on the one hand with the supernal Feminine, and on the other hand, with the era of cosmic *Shemittah*, namely an eschatological time when the world as it is known now will be obliterated. Little change is envisioned for women at present or in the immediate future.

276 *Ma'arekhet ha-'Elohut*, ch. 8, 133–134.

Kabbalah.[277] The very syntagm "period of diminution" reflects an awareness of the temporality of this second stage, not its basic essence. Sabbath is conceived of as the time of repose and return to the initial source and connection. Unfortunately, we do not know who is the author of the gloss. In my opinion, however, he does not distort the view of the book upon which he commented . The term *shittuf rishon*, for example, which is a rare term, is understood appropriately. This also applies to R. Reuven Tzarfati, a mid-fourteenth century commentator on *Ma'arekhet ha-'Elohut*[278] active in Italy, who writes: "The Sabbath day hints at the seventh millennium, 'and the night will shine like the day'[279] and two kings wear the same crown and all will depend on the spring,[280] and the slave that is the moon, will be as its master[281] that is the sun and there will be no donor nor recipient."[282]

Moreover, in another discussion in *Ma'arekhet ha-'Elohut*, a special affinity is established between the *'Atarah* and the higher *sefirot*:

> ... behold, "the female encompasses the male,"[283] as the [letter] *W* in the middle of the [divine] name refers to *Tiferet*, and in the case of the two [divine] names I have mentioned and explained,[284] you will find "its end is fixed in its beginning, and its beginning in its end"[285] and the *W* in the name *YHWH* refers to the six extremities[286] that emerge from the three first [*sefirot*] ... the third [*sefirah*] innovated the six extremities by the dint of a supernal power. And the last *H* from the name refers to *'Atarah*, which is operating together[287]

---

277 Pedaya, *Nahmanides*.

278 For the authorship of this commentary, see Gottlieb, *Studies in Kabbalah Literature*, 357–369. See also above n. 70. On this Kabbalist, see also Charles Mopsik, *Les grands textes de la cabale, Les rites qui font Dieu*, 287–292 and Avraham Elqayam, "Topics in the Commentary of Reuven Tzarfati to the *Book of Ma'arekhet ha-'Elohut*, (M.A. Thesis, Hebrew University, Jerusalem, 1987) (Hebrew).

279 Psalms 139: 12.

280 Namely, from the *sefirah* of *Binah*, as it is in the text that that contains the comment.

281 *BT., Berakhot*, fol. 58b.

282 Printed in *Ma'arekhet ha-'Elohut*, ch. 10, 176–177.

283 Jeremiah 31: 21. See also, above n. 107 and below n. 737. This is one example where this biblical verse was not understood by a Kabbalist phallocentrically. Compare to Wolfson, *Language, Eros, Being*, 376–377, who, in my opinion, unjustifiably interprets the ascent to *Keter* and surrounding the Male as part of the phallocentric approach. On this verse, see also Schwartzman, "From Mystical Vision to Gender Equality Aspirations," 149–151.

284 *Ma'arekhet ha-'Elohut*, ch. 14, 279.

285 Cf., *Sefer Yetzirah*, 1: 7. This ancient treatment of the concept *sefirot* served as an important prooftext for the circular or the uroboric theosophy that will be discussed below in more detail in the context of R. Moshe Cordovero's theosophy. See the "Commentary to *Sefer Yetzirah*" by R. Joseph ben Shalom Ashkenazi, *ad locum*, in *Sefer Yetzirah*, fol. 28ab.

286 The numerical value of *W* in Hebrew is six.

287 מתגלגלת The precise meaning of this verb here is not so clear. In some other cases in the book, it refers to transmigration of souls, but in a few cases, it seems to refer to cooperation. It may also have something to do with the theory about cosmic cycles that return in a certain rhythm.

with the first [*sefirah*] and the second[288] and the third, as I mentioned. And the principle is "the beginning of the thought is the end of action" and "its end is fixed to its beginning and its beginning is fixed to its end."[289]

Unlike the six extremities, namely, the six *sefirot* that were emanated by the third *sefirah*, the *'Atarah*, clearly, is related to the higher *sefirot*, thus skipping over the Male, *Tiferet*, which is part of the six extremities, and behaving as if She belongs to the highest realm. This superiority may be reflected also by the quotation of the biblical verse dealing with the female as encompassing the male. Interestingly, the pseudo-Aristotelian dictum is presented here as a principle, relatively early, in a classical book of Kabbalah, not just the opinion of a specific Kabbalist.

The anonymous Kabbalist possibly drew upon an important passage of the mysterious Kabbalist R. Joseph of Hamadan, who wrote sometime near the end of the thirteenth century in Castile and amalgamated the uroboric views of the *sefirot* in *Sefer Yetzirah* with the theme of *Keter* and *Malkhut*: "When the attribute of *Keter* was revealed, [also] the attribute of *Malkhut* was revealed."[290] We may speak here about an uroboric theology or, to use Erich Neumann's term, "pleromatic" view,[291] which found its expression also somewhat later in the fourteenth century, perhaps in Italy, in an interesting passage that deals with the enumeration of the ten *sefirot* as part of a reversible move which may began with "'*Atarah*, to let you know that it is also *Keter;* and if you will reverse the [order of the] *sefirot*, then *Malkhut* will be the first ... as they have neither beginning nor end, the beginning of thought being the end of the action."[292]

---

288 The letter *H* is described as referring to both the second and the tenth *sefirah*. See *Ma'arekhet ha-'Elohut*, ch. 14, 279.

289 *Ma'arekhet ha-'Elohut,* ch. 14, 280:

הנה 'נק' תסובב גבר' כי הו' שבאמצע השם רמז לתפ' והנה בשני השמו' שזכרתי ובארתי תמצא 'נעוץ סופו בתחלתו ותחלתו בסופו' והו' שבשם יקוק מורה על שש קצוו' הנמשכו' משלש ראשונו' הנכללות בשש אותיות הנזכרות בשלש שמות ונכללות בשלישי המתחיל בו' ורומז לשלישית והיא אשר המציאה השש קצוות בכח עליון. והה' אחרונה שבשם רומזת לעטרה המתגלגלת עם הראשונה והשניה והשלישית כמו שזכרתי. וכללו' של דבר 'תחלת המחשבה הוא סוף המעשה ונעוץ סופו בתחלתו ותחלתו בסופו'.

290 See *Sefer Toledot 'Adam,* printed in J. Toledano, ed., *Sefer ha-Malkhut,* fol. 96b, cited by Abrams, *The Female Body of God,* 112, n. 210. For the authorship of this Kabbalistic treatise, which was printed anonymously, see Gottlieb's discussion of, *Studies in Kabbalah Literature,* 251–253. At least in one case, R. Joseph identifies *Malkhut* with the feminine. See the passage translated in Idel, *Absorbing Perfections,* 70–71.

291 See Erich Neumann, *The Origins and History of Consciousness,* 1: 276–277.

292 Ms. Vatican 441, fol. 114a. See also ibid., fol. 114b, where *'Ateret* is twice referred to as the "cornerstone" *rosh pinnah*, cf. Psalms 118: 22, and the image found in the *Book of Bahir*. See also above n. 163, and below nn. 457, 461, 476. Compare to the view found in R. Moshe of Kiev, *Sefer Shushan Sodot,* no. 248, fol. 52b:

Although the anonymous Kabbalist is dealing with a term, '*Atarah*, that is, grammatically speaking, feminine, it is not self-evident that he was concerned with the question of gender. Based on the passage from *Ma'arekhet ha-'Elohut*, such a reading is quite plausible, however, as is also the case of the earlier cited text from *Tiqqunei Zohar*. The association of the second and the last *sefirah*, namely, *Hokhmah* and *Malkhut*, is evident elsewhere in this book: "when you will inquire and examine deeply, you will find that there is the same status to the second [*sefirah*] and to the last one, if you will fix their end in their beginning ... as the second and the last are equal insofar as all the names[293] are concerned, if you will fix its end in its beginning, this is *Hokhmah* and this is *Hokhmah*."[294]

Whereas the fifth chapter of this book aims at pointing to the various lexical similarities of terms related to more than one *sefirah* – which can be understood also as polisemy – this passage reveals an additional dimension. It adopts a theological position rarely found in Nahmanides's school, seeing the beginning of the *sefirah* as connected to the end, under the impact of the formulation in *Sefer Yetzirah*.

Another influential Kabbalist, who flourished in the first half of the sixteenth century, R. Meir ibn Gabbai,[295] paraphrased a passage from this work, writing[296]:

"You should know that the diadem and the crown are synonymous nouns, so that this name is not part of the nouns of the crown, but from the names of the diadem, as this name enters the innermost part [of the temple] in order to worship, and this is why it is called by this name [Akatriel], namely *Keter*, namely the diadem."

דע כי עטרה והכתר שמות נרדפים א"כ זה השם איננו משמות הכתר אך הן משמות העטרה לפי שהשם הזה נכנס לפני ולפנים לשמש לכן נקרא בשם הזה דהיינו כת"ר והיינו עטרה.

This passage is an interpretation of the rabbinic legend from *BT., Berakhot*, fol. 7a.

293 Namely, the terms that are attributed to each of the *sefirot*; following this passage, the Kabbalist enumerates additional instances of the same terms attributed to these two *sefirot*. Compare to n. 298 below.

294 *Ma'arekhet ha-'Elohut*, ch. 5, 84:

וכאשר תדרוש ותחקור היטב תמצא כי לשניה ולאחרונה מעמד אחד אם תנעוץ סופן בתחלתן...כי השניה והאחרונה שוים בכל השמות אם תנעוץ סופו בתחילתו זו חכמה וזו חכמה.

295 On the theosophical-theurgic system of this Kabbalist see Roland Goetschel, *R. Meir Ibn Gabbay*; *Le Discours de la Kabbale espagnol*, and Mopsik, *Les grands textes de la cabale*, 364–383.

296 See *Ma'arekhet ha-'Elohut*, ch. 3, 37–38, which was influenced by Nahmanides's authentic *Commentary to Sefer Yetzirah* 1: 7; cf. the edition of Gershom Scholem, *Studies in Kabbalah* (1) (Hebrew), 94. This commentary elaborates a theory of emanation and return, understood as expiration and inspiration, stemming from one of the highest sefirot and returning there. See Scholem, *Studies in Kabbalah*, 71, 87; see also Idel, "On the Concept of Zimzum in Kabbalah and Its Research" (Hebrew), 69, n. 60. On the theory of cosmic elevation in Nahmanides's Kabbalah and in his school, see Pedaya, *Nahmanides*.

On the theosophical-theurgic system of this Kabbalist see Goetschel, *R. Meir Ibn Gabbay* and Mopsik, *Les grands textes de la cabale*, 364–383.

As the aspect of union is equal insofar as all [the *sefirot*] [are concerned] because all are united to the essence of the root,[297] as it is said in another treatment, "ten *sefirot* of *Belimah*, their end is fixed in their beginning," as from the end of a thing the beginning is found, and from its beginning its end is found, and there is no end without beginning nor a beginning without an end, as the beginning of a thing and its end are equal,[298] as one is not found without another, as the sages, blessed be their memory, said[299]: "the beginning of the thought is the end of the action."[300]

This represents another instance of the circular conception of the *sefirot* joined with the pseudo-Aristotelian dictum, although the latter is absent in what may be the kernel of this discussion, a passage from Nahmanides's much earlier *Commentary to Sefer Yetzirah*. This is by no mean an isolated discussion in ibn Gabbai's writings.[301] Although ibn Gabbai does not explicitly discuss the gender aspect, it seems plausible that it is inherent in his version of circular theosophy, as presented in earlier Kabbalistic sources discussed above. Elsewhere ibn Gabbai speaks about *'Atarah* as another name for *Keter*[302]; he mentions *'Atarah* several times as found on the head of a person, in many cases as a metaphor for the knowledge of God, in the vein of Maimonides's thought, in clearly non-sexual contexts.[303] In one case, he speaks about the return of the *'Atarah* to Her former status, when Her light will be equal to that of the Sun,[304] basically reaffirming

---

297 Namely, all the ten *sefirot* are conceived of as united with the Infinite in an equal manner, part of ibn Gabbai's vision of the *sefirot* as the essence of God.

298 This is a rare instance of which I am aware when equality of the two extremities is mentioned explicitly. See also above, n. 293 and below n. 304.

299 See above, n. 92.

300 R. Meir ibn Gabbai's *'Avodat ha-Qodesh*, 1:3, fol. 9cd:

כי צד הייחוד שוה בכולן כי כולן מתאחדות בעצם השרש, וכמו שאמר שם בבבא אחרת עשר ספירות בלימה נעוץ סופן בתחלתן, כי מסוף דבר נמצא ראשו ומראשו נמצא סופו, ואין סוף בלתי ראש, ולא ראש בלתי סוף, כי ראש דבר וסופו שוים במציאותו ובאחדותו, כי לא ימצא זה זולת זה, הוא מה שאמרו חז"ל תחלת המחשבה הוא סוף המעשה.

301 See also Meir ibn Gabbai's *'Avodat ha-Qodesh*, 3: 32, fol. 91d, and in this author's other book *Derekh 'Emunah*, 108–109. The source is most probably Zoharic. See *Zohar*, I, fol. 99b, (*Midrash ha-Ne'elam*), and Cordovero, *'Or Yaqar* (Jerusalem, 1986), 14: 114.

302 *'Avodat ha-Qodesh*, 1: 16, fol. 17a. Such a view is found also in other instances. See, e.g., below in the text of Yalish beside n. 679. Compare also the discussion in *Sefer ha-Peliy'ah*, 1, fol. 73b, which contained, perhaps, a diagram that is not found in the printed version. See also 2, fol. 19c. On the very same page, 1, fol. 73b, there is also a discussion of *'Atarah* and *Yesod*, though two are nevertheless being one entity, but only when the latter descents to the former. Many of the discussions of the diadem in this book are concerned solely with the lower couple that includes the diadem, following the Nahmanidean school; they are thus less concerned with the ascent to the higher levels of divinity. For the descending mode, see also *Sefer ha-Peliy'ah*, 2, fols. 16b and 22a.

303 *'Avodat ha-Qodesh* 2: 20, fol. 39d, 2: 23, fol. 43c, 2: 25, fol. 44d, 2: 41 fol. 55b, 2:43, fol. 57d.

304 *'Avodat ha-Qodesh*, 4: 8, fol. 119b, and see also Idel, "The Divine Female and the Mystique of the Moon," 178–180 and in n. 298 above.

the connection between the last *sefirah* and the supernal Male, a situation that corresponds to the dwelling of the *Shekhinah* in the Temple. This dwelling below is a recurring leitmotif in his book. Although less concerned than other Kabbalists about the ascent of the *Shekhinah* to the highest levels of the divine pleroma, ibn Gabbai subscribes to the rabbinic axiology.

A contemporary of ibn Gabbai, the notorious Christian Kabbalist and magician Heinrich Cornelius Agrippa of Nettesheim, was acquainted with one or more of the Kabbalistic texts dealt with in the preceding chapters, and he formulated a view as to the preeminence of the woman, not of Female, on the basis of the above arguments. As this text was well-known in later literature about the excellence of women, I shall quote it at length and analyze some of its details. I am using mainly the English translations of Barbara Newman and Albert Rabil Jr., combined with the seventeenth century one,[305] of the passage from his Latin booklet *Declamatio de nobilitate et praecellentia foeminei sexus*.[306] In dealing with this text Newman alluded duly to a possible Kabbalistic influence, which she regards as part of its "esoteric theology":

> .... dignity was to Woman above Man, by order of Creation ... Then [God] created two humans in his likeness, first the male and then the female, in whom "the heavens and the earth were finished, and all their embellishment."[307] For the Creator, coming to the creation of woman, rested in her,[308] as he had nothing more noble at the hand to create, and in her were enclosed and consummated all the wisdom and power of the Creator.[309] Beyond her no other creature exists, nor can be imagined. Since woman, therefore, is the last of the creatures and the goal, the most perfect completion of all the works of God, and the perfecting of the universe itself, who will deny that she is the most worthy of preeminence over all crea-

---

305 *Declamatio de nobilitate et praecellentia foeminei sexus, Female Pre-eminence or the Dignity and the Excellency of That Sex above Male.*

306 See Albert Rabil, Jr., *Henricus Cornelius Agrippa, Declamation on the Nobility and Preeminence of the Female Sex*, English translation on 47–48; Roland Antonioli's *Préface*, to *Heinrich Cornelius Agrippa, De nobilitate et praecellentia foeminei sexus*, 7–38, and the pertinent text on 53–54. See also Wolfson, *Language, Eros, Being*, 594, n. 40. However, he did not see the importance of the final statement of the quote dealing with thought and action as male and female, which depends on the Kabbalistic tradition, as it has not been quoted and translated by Newman. He thus was not interested in the Kabbalistic source of the gender issue found in this passage, which does not fit his theory.

307 Genesis 2: 3. The theme of female and male as symbols for earth and heaven, symbolized also as Female and Male, or *Malkhut* and *Tiferet* respectively, is found in many Kabbalistic theosophical writings.

308 *The Wisdom of Sirach*, 24: 12. This is part of the famous chapter praising Wisdom. See also the text from the later layer of the *Zohar*, beside n. 240 above.

309 This sentence may reflect a hypostatic vision of the woman rather than solely a human being.

tion? ... for the whole Universe being created by God, as an entire and perfect circle,[310] it was requisite the same should be made up, and finished in such an exact and absolute particle, as might with a most strict tye, unite and glew together the first of all things with the last. When the world was created, woman was the last in time among all created things,[311] but in authority and dignity she was the first of all in the conception of the divine mind, as it is written in the prophet: "before the heavens were created God chose her and foreordained her"[312] ... it is a commonsense among the philosophers,[313] I cite their own words, being ever first in intention, though last in execution.[314]

This is the first argument adduced to support the thesis of woman's nobility. Two main points are reminiscent of the Kabbalistic discussions above: the woman was first in the divine mind, and this is the reason why she was the last in time, as in the pseudo-Aristotelian dictum, which is explicitly quoted, as it was understood by Kabbalists. She is also described as the telos of creation, and thus as the noblest of the creatures. This is, to be sure, a rare view. Rabil refers in this context (as in many others), to the Spanish mid-fifteenth century author Juan Rodriguez del Padrón, who wrote a book on the *Triumph of the Women* (1445), as Agrippa's source for this statement.[315] Rodriguez's book, which no doubt influ-

---

310 This view is found in twelfth century Muhamad ibn Sid al-Bataliusi's *Sefer ha-'Aggulot ha-Ra'yoniot*, which had a significant impact in the late fifteenth and early sixteenth century, on the writings of Agrippa's older contemporaries active in Italy, R. Yohanan Alemanno, R. Isaac Abravanel, his son Leone Ebreo, and perhaps also on Giovanni Pico della Mirandola's vision of the dignity of man as a fluid concept on the great chain of being. See below n. 403 and M. Idel, "The Sources of the Circle Images in *Dialoghi d'Amore*," 162–166; Idel, "The Anthropology of Yohanan Alemanno: Sources and influences," 93–112; *Ascensions on High*, passim, or *Kabbalah in Italy*, 204–205. See also the association of beauty and the circle in Rabil, *Henricus Cornelius Agrippa*, 50–51, n. 42.

311 This is an uncommon argument in Jewish texts. See, nevertheless, above n. 103, in the late fifteenth century of R. 'Ovadia of Bertinoro and below, in ch. 8, the passage from Abraham Michael Cardoso. It is not clear whether the Sabbatean thinker, who was well-acquainted with Christian thought, was influenced by Agrippa.

312 *Wisdom of Sirach* 24: 5,14. In the French translation of Béné, *Heinrich Cornelius Agrippa*, 53–54, he proposes to see the Wisdom as a reference to the *Shekhinah*. This is an interesting proposal that, if proved, would support my understanding of Agrippa as dependent on Kabbalah on this issue, which is pertinent to our discussions here.

313 The Latin text of this sentence, which has not been properly evaluated by the scholars who dealt with Agrippa's text, is: "Ea siquidem est pervulgata philosophantium (ut illorum verbis utar) sententia finem semper priorem esse in intentione & in executione postremum." See below, n. 315.

314 I used elements from different English translations. See Rabil, *Henricus Cornelius Agrippa*, 47–48. Newman also translated part of the text in, *From Virile Woman to WomanChrist*, 230–231; see also her accompanying endnotes. Part of the Latin original has been reproduced on 306, n. 24.

315 Rabil, *Henricus Cornelius Agrippa*, 48, n. 30. This note is rather confusing as it is attached to the end of the dictum, giving the impression that Rabil claims that it is found in Rodriguez. Rabil

enced Agrippa, does not, however, refer to the dictum or to the philosophers. I therefore regard the Kabbalists as a more plausible source of inspiration for this Christian Kabbalist.

As pointed out by Grossman, he seems to follow a principle found in a Midrashic statement stating, "What has been created after his companion, is ruling over him,"[316] although in its original context it is a cosmogonic issue, unrelated to the rank of the woman. The passage hints at circular theology although it relates it here to the world and to woman, not to the divine realm. Agrippa applied the theosophical speculations about the divine Female to the creation of the woman, using also the verse from the *Wisdom of Sirach,* with which Jewish Kabbalists were unfamiliar. It is noteworthy that in this small booklet, Agrippa referred twice to Kabbalists, although not in the specific context of this passage. In one case, he declares that the Hebrew name of Eve, <u>H</u>avah, according to Kabbalists, is close to the Tetragrammaton.[317] Surprisingly, this linguistically weird observation, appears later on, in Guillaume Postel's work.[318]

The Latin booklet was first printed in Antwerp in 1529, although Agrippa delivered it twenty years earlier.[319] It was reprinted many times, translated, and the arguments of the Christian Kabbalist had a huge impact on further discussions about the privileged status of woman, especially in England.[320] Interestingly, ibn Gabbai in the Ottoman Empire and Cornelius Agrippa in Germany adduced the pseudo-Aristotelian dictum and some form of circular thinking in the very same period, together with the privileged status of the woman/Female, although I do not see any possible direct contact between those texts or authors. In my opinion,

---

confesses that he did not find the source of the dictum. Nevertheless, I consider that Rodriguez influenced some other aspects of Agrippa's arguments.

316 This is the saying of the authority from late antiquity, R. Yehudah ben Shime'on, found in a widespread Midrash, *Genesis Rabbah,* 19: 3, 173. See also *Yalqut Shime'oni* on Genesis ch. 3, no. 27. I did not find this Midrash used in order to praise women except in the work of a mid-sixteenth century historian who wrote a book on the supremacy of women, R. Gedalyah ibn Yehia'. See Grossman, *He Shall Rule over You?* 523. In this work (531), Grossman is inclined to see Agrippa's booklet as the source for ibn Yehia's views.

317 Rabil, *Henricus Cornelius Agrippa,* 46 and n. 25. My assumption is that the letter *H* in *Havah* has been misperceived as *He',* generating HWH, which is reminiscent of the Tetragrammaton.

318 See Weiss, *A Kabbalistic Christian Messiah,* 255.

319 Rabil, *Henricus Cornelius Agrippa,* 39.

320 See the introduction of Rabil, *Henricus Cornelius Agrippa,* 3–4, 27–29. In addition to Newman's analysis, see, e.g., Grossman, *He Shall Rule over You?,* 529–532, especially 529, where he points to the parallel to Gedaliah. See also the study of Sarah Apetrei, *Women, Feminism and Religion in Early Enlightenment England,* 52–53.

we may assume, therefore, the existence of an earlier, Hebrew text that influenced them separately, but so far, I have been unable to identify it. This assumption is reinforced by a Kabbalistic discussion by R. Isaac of Acre that was cited at the end of chapter 4. The two authors used examples of the wisdom of women from the Hebrew Bible in order to make their case.

7 R. Moshe Cordovero and
R. Shlomo ha-Levi Alqabetz

א״כ בבתר תחלת המחשבה המלכות קודמת.

"Therefore, [with]in *Keter,* at the beginning of the thought, *Malkhut* precedes."
(R. Moshe Cordovero, *'Or Yaqar,* on *Tiqqunim,* 4: 96)

עטרת בעלה מצד הכתר ... שמתעטרת על ת״ת
אפי׳ מקום שאין הת״ת יכול לעלות- היא עולה ונקשרת ...
וכן עלתה בזריקה שאין שום ספירה עולה שם ...
זרקא...כאלו נזרק ענין ממטה למעלה עד א״ס.

"She is the diadem of Her Husband from the side of *Keter* ... that She encrowns onto *Tiferet*
Even in the place where *Tiferet* cannot ascend, She ascends and unites with [Him]...
and so She ascends by being thrown [to a place] that no *sefirah* ascends there
Zarqa ... as if it was thrown from beneath to on high, up to the Infinite."
(R. Moshe Cordovero, in Sack, ed., *From the Fountains of Sefer Elimah,* 122–123)

At the beginning of the second part of the sixteenth century, Safed, a small town
in the Galilee, became the most active, creative, and productive center in the
history of Kabbalah. After some decades of wandering in various Mediterranean
countries, a few Spanish Kabbalists, refugees from the expulsion from the Iberian
peninsula, decided to settle in the town and to study Kabbalah in groups, in
the close vicinity of the tomb of the alleged author of the *Zohar,* R. Shimeon bar
Yohai, in the village of Meron.[321] The few Kabbalists that flourished there were
familiar with much of the earlier Kabbalistic literature in this field, and they
introduced a variety of the topics discussed above into their impressive and voluminous writings. This and the following chapters will deal with the development
of some of the earlier discussed themes in the works of the two major Kabbalistic
schools that emerged in this town. As the Safedian Kabbalists and their many
disciples wrote extensively, the number of pertinent texts in this chapter and in
the next one far exceeds that found in earlier forms of Kabbalah, and in some
cases, they are longer and thus more explicit than the earlier discussions. This
exegetical elaboration is indubitably part of a systemic development, generated
by the canonization of the *Zohar* on the one hand,[322] and by the need to confront

---

321 See Boaz Huss, "Holy Place, Holy Time, Holy Book: The Influence of the *Zohar* on Pilgrimage
Rituals to Meron and the Lag-BaOmer Festival" (Hebrew); Idel, "On Mobility, Individuals and
Groups," 145–176.
322 See Boaz Huss, "Zoharic Communities in Safed" (Hebrew), 149–169.

https://doi.org/10.1515/9783110599800-007

the claims of the emerging Christian Kabbalah, especially in Italy, on the other hand.[323] The encounters and even the friction among the Spanish, Italian, and Ashkenazi figures, undoubtedly, contributed to the flowering of Kabbalistic literature. The main clue to understanding the creative aspects of the Safedian unparalleled productivity lies in the Kabbalists' feeling of returning to the most creative place in rabbinic Judaism, the province of Galilee, which had hosted the compiling of the *Mishnah* – and for the Kabbalists – also the *Zohar*.[324] They viewed it as a very remarkable Renaissance, which generated a more intense mode of life in Safed and later on in many other centers of Jewish culture, by recovering what the Kabbalists regarded as an ancient esoteric corpus.

The beginning of the Safedian period concludes a longer period of what I call the "crisis of tradition" in Kabbalah, meaning the decline of the oral transmission of secrets from teacher to student – indubitably a paramount masculine affair – and the ascent of the importance of revelations as the source of Kabbalah, a process that originated in the last decades of the thirteenth century.[325] As part of this turn toward a vertical type of communication of receiving secrets from on high, the lowest *sefirah*, the *Shekhinah*, the entity between the two worlds *par excellence*, acquired a greater role than it had earlier. This means that Kabbalists not only accorded Her a greater role in their understanding of the past but also attributed a more important role to Her in the present. Whereas the ecstatic Kabbalists saw the Agent Intellect as playing the role of the intermediary, as the source for receiving a special type of information, now, the theosophical Kabbalists accorded the *Shekhinah* a structurally similar role. In the Galilee, one could heal the rupture – temporal, spatial, and spiritual – by studying the reputed ancient texts and communicating with the souls of the deceased religious heroes.

R. Moshe Cordovero, one of the pillars of the mid-sixteenth century Kabbalah in Safed, and one of the greatest Kabbalists ever,[326] became part of a small group of Kabbalists to whom the *Shekhinah* revealed Herself while the group was still

---

323 See Idel, "Italy in Safed, Safed in Italy, Toward an Interactive History of Sixteenth-Century Kabbalah," 239–269, and in more general terms, Idel, "On European Cultural Renaissances and Jewish Mysticism," 43–64; and Idel, "Jewish Thinkers versus Christian Kabbalah," 49–65.

324 I have lectured on this thesis on various occasions and I hope to dedicate a separate study to it.

325 See my "Revelation and the 'Crisis' of Tradition in Kabbalah," and Jonathan Garb, *Modern Kabbalah, as an Autonomous Domain of Research* (Hebrew), 35.

326 On the Kabbalistic thought of this Kabbalist see, e.g., Joseph ben-Shlomo, *The Mystical Theology of Moses Cordovero* (Hebrew); Bracha Sack, *The Kabbalah of Rabbi Moses Cordovero* (Hebrew); Yoed Kadary, *The Angelology of R. Moses Cordovero* (Hebrew); and Idel, *"Male and Female,"* and in n. 339.

in the Ottoman Empire, before they arrived in Safed and met Cordovero there. This group, which played a major role in the Safedian Renaissance, included R. Shlomo ha-Levi Alqabetz and R. Joseph Karo, Cordovero's two main teachers, and Cordovero himself.[327] In his voluminous writings, Cordovero, more than any earlier Kabbalist, amplified the role of the Female, following the lead of the various Zoharic layers.[328] For example, Cordovero describes the Daughter of the King, namely the last *sefirah*, as flowing and innovating secrets all the time, namely, also in the present, as we learn from the tense of the verbs.[329] This continuous emanation of secrets is one of the reasons prompting these Kabbalists to roam in fields near Safed. This became almost a ritual, designed to lead them to identify with the plight of the Female. Moreover, this was perceived as the moment of receiving some minor revelations, which, in some cases, the Kabbalist uttered involuntarily.[330] Cordovero was also interested in the ecstatic Kabbalah of Abraham Abulafia, where mystical experiences were the aim of Kabbalah.[331] In addition to viewing revelations as an important mode of receiving Kabbalistic secrets, Cordovero also envisioned Jewish worship as directed toward the Female, as we learn from an important passage in his commentary on the *Zohar*:

---

327 See my "R. Joseph Karo and His Revelations: On the Apotheosis of the Feminine in Safedian Kabbalah," *Kabbalah & Eros*, 137–147, and "Revelations and 'Crisis of Tradition,'" 278–281.

328 For the *Shekhinah* in Cordovero, see, e.g., Sack, *The Kabbalah of Rabbi Moses Cordovero*, 249–266; Sack, "The Secret of Thight, the Struggle between Good and Evil," 148–160; Abrams, *The Female Body of God*, 122–123; Wolfson, "Gender and Heresy," 249–251; and especially now the very detailed analysis of Asulin, "The Double Construct of the Image of the *Shekhinah*," 61–111. A belated Kabbalist, Cordovero had to account for the existence of different views that accrued in Kabbalistic literature.

329 *'Or Yaqar*, on *Tiqqunim*, vol.15, n. 90: ברתא דמלכא נובעת ומחדשת תמיד סודות See also in the same place, מלכות בסודותיה that may be translated as "*Malkhut* in Her secrets." It is reasonable to assume that this is one of the echoes of the Zoharic parable of the Maiden without eyes, as initiating the Kabbalists into the secrets of the Torah; see also the sentence in the *'Idra' Zutta', Zohar*, III, fols. 287b–288a. Cordovero juxtaposes the need to guard faithfully the content of revelations on Kabbalistic issues with the very different approach of the Halakhists, who decide according to the opinion of the majority of the rabbis, without relying on revelations. See Scholem, *On the Mystical Shape of the Godhead*, 174–175, 186–187, 196, where he duly emphasizes the active role of the Female.

330 See Cordovero's *Sefer ha-Gerushin*; cf. R.J. Zwi Werblowsky, *Joseph Karo, Layer and Mystic*, 51–54; Sack, *The Kabbalah of Rabbi Moses Cordovero*, 17–21, 219–220, 226–227, 263–265; Lawrence Fine, *Physician of the Soul, Healer of the Cosmos: Isaac Luria and His Kabbalistic Fellowship*, 59–60, 272–273, 293; Haviva Pedaya, *Walking Through Trauma: Rituals of Movement in Jewish Myth, Mysticism, and History* (Hebrew), 128–142; for the background of these Safedian discussions in the later layer of the Zoharic literature, see Roi, *Love of the Shekhinah*, 137–240.

331 See M. Idel, *Studies in Ecstatic Kabbalah*, 136–140.

Whoever performs a commandment nowadays, prepares something that sustains the *Shekhinah*,[332] and draws a little bit of influx to Her … and he has notwithstanding a retribution for his toil … and the proof for it is the [parable of] the Daughter of the King, when She sits in the palace of Her father and one of Her servants performs for Her an act of worship, She will certainly pay attention to him but not as much as She would do when outside the palace in troubles in exile. And if the servant would give Her even a small thing, such as a piece of moist grass,[333] to help Her uplift her spirits, it will be more important in Her eyes then whatever She had when She was governing. Know that the main intention of Rashby,[334] blessed be his memory, when he composed the book of the *Zohar*, was for this reason, as the *Shekhinah* was in exile without any influx, without anyone to sustain and help Her.[335] And he wanted to do something [in order] to sustain Her, and to cause Her union with Her husband, [creating] a little union by [means of] the composition of the book of the *Zohar*, by [means of] what he and his companions are dealing with the secrets of the Torah, which is causing the union of the Holy One, blessed be He, and His *Shekhinah* by means of [the *sefirah* of] *Yesod*.[336]

Both the performance of the rabbinic rituals and the emergence of the Zoharic literature are conceived of as part of the Kabbalist's special attachment to the Female, which is related to the need to amend Her plight in the exilic situation, when She needs more help than ever before. In fact, we may speak about a cult

---

332 Compare also to *'Or Yaqar*, 12: 28, 16: 12, and to *'Or Yaqar*, on *Tiqqunim*, 3: 192. On the theme of sustaining the *Shekhinah*, see also Idel, *"Male and Female,"* n. 58. See also above, n. 22.

333 Compare to the content of the letter of R. Moshe Hayyim Luzzatto to his teacher R. Isaiah Bassan, in ed., Simon Ginzburg, *RaMHa"L u-Venei Doro: 'Osef 'Iggerot u-Te'udot* (Hebrew), 2: 236.

334 The acronym of *R*abbi *S*himeon *b*ar *Yo*hai, the alleged author of the *Zohar*.

335 See also the text of R. Naftali Hertz Bakharakh, an introduction to his book *Seva' Ratzon*, printed with footnotes by Yehuda Liebes, "On the Image, Writings, and the Kabbalah of the author of '*Emeq ha-Melekh*,'" (Hebrew), 130.

336 *'Or Yaqar*, 5: 219; R. Abraham Azulai, *Hesed le-'Avraham*, fol. 6c; Azulai, *'Or ha-Hammah*, vol. 1, on the last page of the unnumbered preface.

שישו כי העושה מצוה בעת הזאת הוא עושה סמך אל השכינה ומושך לה שפע קצת... ועכ"ז יש לו שכר טוב בעמלו ועז"ז נאמר אתה משמש וגו כי הוא עושה לה סמך, ואדרבה שכרו יותר גדול והעד ע"ז בת מלך בהיותה יושבת בהיכל אביה המלך, ואי מעבדיה יעשה לה איזה עבודה ודאי תשים לו שכר אבל לא שכר כ"כ כמו שאם תהי חוץ להיכל המלך בדוחק בגלות, ואם העבד יתן אז חע כי עיקר כונת. אפילו דבר קל כמו עשב לה להבריא נפשה הוא חשוב בעיניה מכל אלי נביות אשר היה בשעת הממשלה הרשב"י ע"ה בחבור ספר הזוהר היה לזה, להיות השכינה בגלות באפס שפע באין תומך ובאין עזר לה, ורצה לעשות לה סמך ליחדה בבעלה יחד מעט ע"י החיבור הזוהר, במה שהיה הוא וחביריו עוסקים בסודות התורה, שזהו גורם ליחוד קב"ה ושכינתיה ע"י היסוד.

See also the other salient passages adduced and discussed in Sack, *The Kabbalah of R. Moshe Cordovero*, 36–38, 266; *'Or Yaqar*, 9: 99, 15: 90; and *'Or Yaqar*, on *Tiqqunim*, 1: 97, and Idel, *Kabbalah & Eros*, 235–236; Idel, "Revelation and the 'Crisis of Tradition,'" 269–273. For a parallel to this parable see *'Or Yaqar*, on *Tiqqunim*, 4:14, 65–66.

For the pedigree of the various parts of the canonical Jewish writings according to the hierarchy of the theosophical scheme see *'Or Yaqar*, 22: 129, to be deal with in detail elsewhere. For additional discussion of Cordovero's views as to the exile of the *Shekhinah* and their sources, see Sack, *The Kabbalah of R. Moshe Cordovero*, 249–265 and Roi, *Love of Shekhinah*, 210–214.

of the *Shekhinah* in exile, and although Cordovero was living in Safed, namely, in the land of Israel, he considered himself still in exile. Interestingly, here the privileged status is to be sought in the eyes of the Kabbalist, who focuses his religious life on helping Her; this type of privilege differs from Her ascending on high, or Her privilege of birth derived from Her stemming from the highest divine source.

Elsewhere, Cordovero describes the feast of *Shavu'ot* as the moment of the coronation of the *Shekhinah*,[337] another instance of connecting a ritual to this *sefirah* specifically, as was the case of the famous revelation of the *Shekhinah* to R. Joseph Karo before his arrival with Alqabetz at Safed. Ornaments and the amendations of the *Shekhinah* already play an important role in the Zoharic mythology and consequently in Cordovero's commentary on this literature.[338]

This Safedian Kabbalist's writings provide the most interesting and influential treatments of the Female and of the uroboric theory in combination with the pseudo-Aristotelian dictum. He was very fond of this dictum, which recurs several times in his voluminous writings.[339] At the same time, he mentions, following *Tiqqunei Zohar*, the concept of the Father that founded the Daughter and the theory of the *Zarqa'*.[340] It should be mentioned that at least in one passage, Cordovero declares that *Malkhut* is the general soul of the people of Israel, thus establishing a patent connection between the Female and the Jewish nation.[341]

In Cordovero's earlier and most influential book, *Pardes Rimonim*, the dictum occurs at least twice. The first occurrence includes a comment on a Zoharic discussion that already contains much of the elements of the dictum[342]:

---

337 *'Or Yaqar*, 3: 102.

338 See, e.g., *'Or Yaqar*, 11: 103, 216, 217; 13: 34.

339 See Esther Liebes, "Cordovero and Luria" (Hebrew), 10, 39, n. 31, and Sack's footnote, *R. Moshe Cordovero, Ma'ayan 'Ein Ya'aqov*, 4, n. 4; and Asulin, "The Double Construct of the Image of the *Shekhinah*," 73, n. 47, and Cordovero's important discussion found in the text printed by Bracha Sack, ed., *From the Fountains of Sefer Elimah by R. Moshe Cordovero and Studies in his Kabbalah* (Hebrew), 119–120. See also Cordovero's *'Elimah Rabbati*, fol. 109b. See also Wolfson, "Woman, The Feminine as Other in Theosophic Kabbalah," 176–177, where he describes a passage from Cordovero as a noble attempt or a departure from his phallocentric theory, although he carefully qualifies it as being only "apparent." Later in this chapter, we shall see whether dozens of discussions of a major Kabbalist are just a departure or a much more substantial approach.

340 See his *Commentary to Sefer Yetzirah*, ch. 1, 70, and Sack, *R. Moshe Cordovero, Ma'ayan 'Ein Ya'aqov*, 104–130.

341 See *'Or Yaqar*, 9: 1 (Jerusalem, 1976).

342 See *Zohar* II, fol. 239a and compare to *Zohar* III, fol. 26b and Liebes's important remark in *On Sabbateanism and its Kabbalah*, 307–309, nn. 65, 71.

It is known that the revelation and the [emanative] expansion is by [means of the process of] generation of a thing at the beginning and at the end, as this is the definition of [the process of] generation, that has a beginning and an end.[343] This is why it has been said [in the *Zohar*] that the Infinite is not making the beginning and end, which is the end and the thing, namely the other extremity, and the end and thing, as from the bottom to below, the beginning of a thing is the end.... *Keter* is revealing itself, and its revelation is by means of the beginning and the end, namely *Hokhmah* and *Malkhut* ... and by its means is the revelation of *Keter,* as within *Keter* there is an aspect of *Hokhmah* that is the beginning, and an aspect of *Binah* that is the aspect of the end.[344] And its revelation is by means of *Hokhmah* and *Malkhut,* which are the beginning and the end...**What is the beginning? It is a point, etc.**[345] Namely the intention is to *Hokhmah* that is the head and the beginning of emanation ... and it is said that though it is the beginning of revelation, it is not a full revelation but somewhat of a beginning, and this is the reason why he wrote '**Setima'ah de-Qayma'** etc. and it is not comprehended but by Thought alone and as there it is the beginning of Thought, it is the beginning of the revelation of *Keter*. **"And he made the end"** etc., the meaning is that the beginning of thought is the end of action, because *Hokhmah* is at the beginning and *Hokhmah* is at the end [346]... and this is *Yod* at the beginning and *Y'* at the end. And the emanation of *Malkhut* is from there ... and this is the reason that *Hokhmah* made the end that is *Malkhut,* the end of [the world of] emanation.[347]

---

343 Cordovero is evidently influenced by the widespread Aristotelian locution of "generation and corruption" understood here as beginning and end.

344 The existence of the aspect of *Binah* within *Keter* is repeated hundreds of times in Cordovero's writings, and thus *Keter* includes one of the feminine aspects found within it. See, e.g., *'Elimah Rabbati*, fols. 86d, 88a, 91b, 92a, 106d, and in *Shi'ur Qomah* (Warsau, 1883), fol. 69c; all this is addition to the presence of *Malkhut* within the first *sefirah*. This presence is described in several instances, and it is part and parcel of Cordovero's theosophy. See my *"Male and Female,"* passim, and below, n. 375.

345 A quote from *Zohar* II, fol. 239a. A close parallel is found in *Zohar* III, fol. 26b. Compare to the English translation of Daniel Matt, *The Zohar*, 6: 383, which obfuscates the possible anthropomorphic overtone of *Reisha'*. It should be mentioned that even if the "head" means beginning, the image of the point is nevertheless referring to a locative conceptualization, not to a temporal one. See, e.g., the use of the term רישא עילאה the supernal head, in the context of end, in *Zohar Ḥadash*, fol. 87b.

346 For some earlier sources of this view, see above, n. 232.

347 *Pardes Rimmonim* 11: 5:

ונדע כי הגילוי וההתפשטות הוא ע"י התהוות הדבר בתחלה וסוף שזהו גדר ההוויה שיש לה ראש וסוף. לזה אמר שאין הא"ס עומד למעבד תחלה וסוף שזהו סוף ודבר. והכוונה סוף היינו קצהו האחד ודבר היינו קצהו השני, וזהו סו"ף ודב"ר, כי ממעלה למטה תחלת דבר הוא סוף...פי' הכתר הוא מתגלה, וגלויו הוא ע"י הראש והסוף דהיינו חכמה ומלכות כדמפרש ואזיל. ועל ידו הוא גלוי הכתר מפני שבכתר בחי' החכמה שהוא הראש ובחינת הבינה שהיא בחינת הסוף, וגלויו הוא ע"י חכמה ומלכות שהם הראש והסוף...מאן ראש דא נקודה וכו'. פי' הכוונה על החכמה כי הוא ראש וראשית לאצילות... שעם היות שהוא תחלת הגלוי לא שיתגלה גילוי עצמי אלא תחלת הגלוי קצת ולכן הפליג ואמר סתימאה דקיימא כו'. ואינה מושגת אלא במחשבה לבד. ובערך ששם תחלת המחשבה לכן הוא ראשית לגילוי הכתר. ועביד סוף וכו' פי' כי תחלת המחשבה הוא סוף המעשה כי חכמה בראש וחכמה בסוף וזהו יו"ד בראש וי' בסוף... ואצילות המלכות משם ולכן החכמה עביד סוף שהיא המלכות סוף האצילות.

In my translation, I marked the Zoharic words in bold letters.

Especially fascinating in this passage is the shift from the term "beginning," logical in the context of describing generation, to that of head, following the anthropomorphic terminology found in the Zoharic passage that was interpreted. The full form of the phrase **Setima'ah de-Qayma'**, found in the *Zohar* and in the quote from it at the beginning of ch. 5 of Cordovero's work is **Reisha' de-kulla' Setima'ah de-Qayma' go Ma</u>hashavah.** This can mean "the beginning that is entirely occult, that stands within thought," but it can be understood also as the "head that is entirely occult." In any case, the Zoharic text poses the question, "What is Head [*rosh*]? and answers "the point," etc.[348] The thought that is the beginning thus can be understood as containing a Head, which is a supernal hypostasis that is part of the Zoharic theosophy. In lieu of the regular assumption that thought is found within a head, in this case, the head is found within the thought. It is this head that **'Avid sof**, "made an end". Here, the mixture of pre-axial image of the head with the axial one – the thought – is obvious.

In a manner reminiscent of the last passage quoted from *Ma'arekhet ha-'Elohut*, the creation of the last *sefirah* is not predicated on its emergence from one of the lower, masculine *sefirot* but on one of the highest three, in the vein of the uroboric theory, and, here, Cordovero circumvents most of the *sefirot*. In this instance, too, the discussion gravitates around the pseudo-Aristotelian dictum, but here the Zoharic theosophies, especially the *Tiqqunei Zohar*, impacted on the understanding of the theosophical processes. This matching of the two different modes of thought – the Aristotelian one that privileges cognitive processes, and the theosophical/anthropomorphic one that follows the Zoharic passage and deals with anthropomorphic structures – is accompanied by a third one, namely that of gender, the special status accorded to the emergence of the divine feminine power. This triple register testifies to the complexity of Cordovero's discussions concerning the Female.[349] The two references to *Yod* relate to Cordovero's theory of two sets of *sefirot* that are related to each other: one decad proceeds in the downward direction, while the other ten proceeds in the upward direction. They are understood as having been connected to each other,[350] what Cordovero refers to in other instances as the two types of light, the direct light and the returning one.[351]

---

348 In Cordovero's commentary on the *Zohar*, *'Or Yaqar*, 11: 221 (Jerusalem, 1981); three heads are mentioned in this context.

349 See Idel, "Male and Female." For a subordinated vision of *Malkhut* as an emissary of *Tiferet*, see, e.g., Cordovero's *'Or Yaqar*, 15: 232–233.

350 See *'Or Yaqar* (Jerusalem, 1985), 13: 129–130; *'Or Yaqar*, 16: 87. See also below, n. 403.

351 On these two types of lights in Cordovero, see ben Shlomo, *The Mystical Theology in Moses Cordovero*, 268–274; Sack, *The Kabbalah of Rabbi Moshe Cordovero*, especially 143, 146, 162,

This specific and intricate context facilitates an understanding of the line from the famous poem composed by Cordovero's brother-in-law, the equally well-known R. Shlomo ha-Levi Alqabetz. Samuel Stern, the author of the erudite treatment of the pseudo-Aristotelian dictum, translated the pertinent verse at the end of his study as follows:

> "Let us go out to meet the Sabbath,
> Since it is the source of blessing
> From the beginning, of old, it had been appointed[352]:
> The end of action, in thought the first."[353]

This is a correct literal translation, dealing with the preeminent status of Sabbath, here a symbol of the feminine divine power, but it assumes that the Hebrew terms מראש and מקדם, translated as "from the beginning," are synonymous. Such an assumption is, however, not necessary. Although מראש can, indeed, be translated as "from the beginning," namely, as an adverb to be understood in a temporal manner in many instances, here it may also stand for "from the head" in the vein of Cordovero's passage translated above, namely, as an adverb related to the place. Indeed, I know *me-rosh* would better represent this understanding *me-ha-rosh*, but I assume that one must take into consideration the constraint of the poem's rhythm. As both Kabbalists were deeply immersed in Zoharic theology, one may assume that Alqabetz was acquainted with the Zoharic passage upon which his brother-in-law commented. If so, and we shall return to the plausibility of this theme in the next chapter, the Sabbath, described in the poem as the bride, and synonymous with the last *sefirah*, is a feminine entity emerging from the divine

---

169, 189, 192; Liebes, *On Sabbateanism and its Kabbalah*, 309–310, n. 77, and in several cases in authors to be discussed below.

352 *Nesukhah.* I am not sure that the translation is precise, and I would prefer the depiction of the Sabbath as emerging from the head/thought, some form of emanation. Better would be an understanding grounded in the interpretation of Isaiah 30: 1, where the very same term *nesukhah* may be understood as planned in thought: "make an alliance, but not of my Spirit." For a contemporary parallel to Alqabetz's phrase, see Kimelman, *The Mystical Meaning of Lekhah Dodi*, 53, n. 117. For the ancient background of this verb as a name of a Mesopotamian goddess of water, see the view of Hurowitz, "'Nursling, Advisor, Architext?" אמן and the Role of Wisdom in Proverbs 8: 22–31," 391–400 and Lenzi, "Proverbs 8: 22–31, Three Perspectives on its Composition," 700. See also Scholem, *On the Mystical Shape of the Godhead*, 142.

353 "First in Thought," 252. The Hebrew original is:

לִקְרַאת שַׁבָּת לְכוּ וְנֵלְכָה, כִּי הִיא מְקוֹר הַבְּרָכָה, מֵרֹאשׁ מִקֶּדֶם נְסוּכָה, סוֹף מַעֲשֶׂה בְּמַחֲשָׁבָה תְּחִלָּה.

See also Kimelman, *The Mystical Meaning of Lekhah Dodi*, 53, 78, and Patai, *The Hebrew Goddess*, 244.

head. My proposal also takes into consideration the parallelism between Thought and the supernal head as the organ where thought takes place.

Moreover, Alqabetz bases his verse on the biblical lines in Proverbs 8: 22–23, dealing with the preexistence of Wisdom,[354] which can be translated as follows: "The Lord created me [or acquired or possessed me] at the beginning of His way, before His deeds in the old days./Before all I have been emanated, from the beginning, before earth." The final phrase in Hebrew מראש מקדמי ארץ can be interpreted, although perhaps not correctly from a philological point of view, as Prof. Israel Knohl pointed out to me, as locative, namely, "out of the head, before the [creation of] the earth." Cordovero's rather cryptic phrase נסיכת הזכר מהנקבה – which may be translated as the emanation of the Male from the Female – may provide a clue to the way the verb NSKh was understood.[355] The context of Cordovero's discussion is the emergence of the *sefirah* of *Binah* and Her preparation of the lower *sefirot* for emanation. This phrase differs from Alqabetz's verse, as here the Female emanates the Male, not vice versa. In a manuscript that preserves relatively early Kabbalistic material, not later than mid-fourteenth century, however, the verse from Proverbs is understood as the emanation of *Hokhmah* from the head, namely from a place that is conceived to be higher than all the other *sefirot*.[356]

Interestingly, the second *sefirah* that emerged from the first *sefirah*, the Thought, and the head within it, according to Cordovero's passage, is called *Hokhmah*,[357] wisdom, like Athena, the goddess of wisdom, although, unlike the *Shekhinah*, she is a symbol of a virgin goddess. If my hypothesis is correct, this verse of Alqabetz's famous poem, which became an integral part of the Sabbath eve ritual very soon after its composition, comprises an encounter of the Aristotelian dictum with a Greek myth, or of an axial and pre-axial theme, respectively. The primordiality of the Sabbath, which is conceived also as a Bride, should be understood as the first phase in the model that I propose here; another verse in the poem speaks about the rising of the female from dust because the divine light dwells

---

354 יְדִיד קָנָנִי רֵאשִׁית דַּרְכּוֹ קֶדֶם מִפְעָלָיו מֵאָז: מֵעוֹלָם נִסַּכְתִּי מֵרֹאשׁ מִקַּדְמֵי אָרֶץ On this verse, see the literature mentioned in n. 33 above. For a recent translation of the entire poem, see Peter Cole, *The Poetry of Kabbalah*, 133–135.

355 *Sefer 'Elimah Rabbati*, fol. 24b as well as Cordovero's passage discussed in Asulin's "The Double Construct of the Image of the *Shekhinah*," 104, where she describes the statute of the *Shekhinah* as not stemming from the Male, in fact: שאינו מעצם הזכר ממש.

356 Ms. New York, JTS 838, fol. 53ab. Compare to the view of Wolfson, below, beside n. 885.

357 It is questionable whether this represents an echo also of the ancient Jewish myth of the pre-existing Sophia. See the view in the *Wisdom of Solomon*, 7: 26, 8: 2–3: "for she is an effulgence from everlasting light/ and an unspotted mirror of God's working and an image, eikon of his goodness," 436, and *Wisdom of Solomon*, 8: 2–3, discussed in Scholem, *On the Mystical Shape of the Godhead*, 143.

upon Her. These verses may reflect the second and the third stages of the model.[358] It should be noted that the stanza dealing with the supernal source of the Sabbath/ Bride is followed by another one that constitutes a description of Her lower position; Her redemption is then mentioned in the following stanzas, a sequence that fits the three-phases model. In this theosophical reading, which envisions Sabbath as a feminine power stemming from the highest source, the syntagm *meqor ha-Berakhah,* the source of blessing, can be understood as a supreme power in the sefirotic realm by the dint of parallels in Safedian Kabbalah.[359]

In this context, the opening of Nahmanides's famous poem deserves mention. Dealing with the descent of the soul, the Kabbalist has it declare: "from the beginning [*me-rosh*] before the world ever was, He brought me forth from nothing, and in the end, I shall be withdrawn by the King."[360] Structurally, the poem follows the pattern of the Neoplatonic sequences of procession and reversion, in the vein of Alqabetz's poem about the Female. [361] Another famous poem, a hymn written in Aramaic by R. Isaac Luria, and recited during the Sabbath, may also be pertinent to a better understanding of Alqabetz. In the second of Luria's three stanzas, Luria speaks about the ascent of "the power" "up to the Head," but it is not clear why the Aramaic verb is in the feminine. Yehuda Liebes, the editor, translator, and commentator on the hymn, following Kabbalistic commentators, attributes it to the ascent of *Malkhut.*[362] Although the head mentioned in the footnote is,

---

358 For the biblical sources, see Isaiah 51: 7, 52: 1, 60: 1. See Benjamin D. Sommer, *A Prophet Reads Scripture: Allusions in Isaiah 40–66,* 137–138. For the Kabbalistic sources of Alqabetz's verses, see Kimelman, *The Mystical Meaning of Lekhah Dodi,* 69–79. Also relevant is a passage in the famous Epistle of Alqabetz, reporting the revelatory events connected to R. Joseph Karo during the two nights of the Feast of Shavu'ot; in describing the low status of the *Shekhinah,* and then Her elevation by the Kabbalists, it states: "you have restored the diadem to his previous [glorious] status." We thus have here the three phases of Her career represented briefly. See also Wolfson, *Language, Eros, Being,* 374.

359 See *Pardes Rimonim,* 5: 4. There are many earlier references to the first and second *sefirah* as the source of blessing, from the time of early fourteenth century Kabbalists, in R. Menahem Recanati's *Commentary to the Torah* and the anonymous author of *Ma'arekhet ha-'Elohut,* for example. See, however, the different understanding of this locution in Cordovero's other book *Sefer ha-Gerushin,* ch. 19, another case of conceptual fluidity.

360 *Kitvei* מראש מקדמי עולמים נמצאתי במכמניו החתומים מאין המציאני ולקץ ימים. נשאלתי מן המלך *ha-Ramban,* 1: 392.

361 For a full English translation of the poem, see Cole, *The Poetry of Kabbalah,* 94–96. See also above, the passage from Nahmanides's younger contemporary R. Abraham Axelrod referred to above in n. 156.

362 צְרוֹרָא דִלְעֵילָא. דְּבֵיהּ חַיֵּי כֹּלָּא. וְיִתְרַבֵּי חֵילָא. וְתִיסַק עַד רֵישָׁא
See Cole, *Poetry of Kabbalah,* 155. The term חילא translated as the power, does not appear in the context of the female in Zoharic literature, although I found one example later than Luria, where

according to Liebes, that of *Ze'yir 'Anppin*, I am, nevertheless, inclined to regard it as the supernal head, known as '*Attiqa*', a configuration that was actually mentioned in line 4 of this hymn, *in tandem* with a theosophical theory to be analyzed in detail in the next chapter.[363] In my opinion, Luria follows the lead of the passage in *Tiqqunei Zohar* quoted at the end of ch. 5.[364]

Returning to Cordovero, Alqabetz's younger brother-in-law and one of the teachers of R. Isaac Luria, elsewhere in his *Pardes Rimmonim* he refers to the *sefirah* of *Malkhut* as both the beginning – when also *Binah* is mentioned – and the end, in the context of the pseudo-Aristotelian dictum.[365] He presents a somewhat different view, however, in his commentary on the *Zohar*, where he describes the perfection of all the *sefirot*, including the higher ones, as dependent on the *sefirah* of *Malkhut*, a widespread topos in his Kabbalistic theosophy. He then writes:

> It has been explained in several places that the beginning of thought is the end of action, which means that when the [divine] will and generosity[366] contemplated to create, the others, namely the entities separated from him that comprehend his essence and praise his greatness when they realize a little bit of it, and the intention of His will and generosity of His spirit when He intended to create all creatures and their adherence to Him by means of the last attribute, that is, an angel [*sar*][367] appointed to govern all the lower [entities], She was the first intention and first entity between the Emanator and *Keter*, and She is the real cause for the innovation of *Keter* and whatever emerges [later]. And out of the great closeness,[368] She emanated *Keter*, and that Thought was lowered one rank, and these are two

---

the phrase חילא דנוקבא, namely, the power of the Female, does occur. See R. Jacob Ifargan, *Minḥat Yehudah*, 1: 369.

363 Yehuda Liebes, "The Songs for the Sabbath Meals Written by the Holy Ari" (Hebrew), 551, footnote to lines 17, 20, following the commentary of R. Israel Sarug. My interpretation is consonant with that of R. Tzadoq ha-Kohen of Lublin, to be discussed at the end of ch. 11.

364 See *Zohar* I, fol. 24a.

365 *Pardes Rimmonim* 14: 3.

366 *Nedavah* the term is reminiscent of the Neoplatonic vision of creation because of the abundance descending from the First Cause. For another use of this term, see Cordovero's *Shi'ur Qomah*, fol. 10c.

367 This is an unusual reference to a *sefirah*, as Cordovero was very careful about distinguishing the sefirotic from the extra-sefirotic realms. The primary source is a discussion found in *Ma'arekhet ha-'Elohut*, ch. 8, 138. In this anonymous book, the discussion of the appointed entity is reminiscent of the pseudo-Aristotelian dictum; and the meaning is that She was appointed in the lower world from the very beginning. See above, ch. 6.

368 *Qurvah*. This term, which occurs several times in Cordovero's Kabbalah, refers to the opportunity of a certain entity to create because of an affinity to a higher cause. See, e.g., *'Or Yaqar*, 12: 49; *'Or Yaqar*, to *Tiqqunim* (Jerusalem, 1973), 2: 73, 89, 159, 161; *'Or Yaqar*, to *Tiqqunim* (Jerusalem, 2007), 5: 279, *Pardes Rimmonim*, 2: 7, 8: 15, 16: 9 and R. Shabbatai Sheftel Horowitz ha-Levi, *Shefa' Tal*, fol. 28c. The main assumption is that without a distancing from the source, there is no identity, but creativity assumes also closeness to the higher entity. In Cordovero's *'Or*

ranks from the first Thought that precedes *Keter*, the second is later than *Keter* preceding *Ḥokhmah* and out of closeness, it was lowered another rank, and She is preceding *Binah* but later than *Ḥokhmah*. And in this manner, She descended to Her place, in union with *Tiferet*, so that in their cooperation they govern the two great [astral] luminaries, and, despite their being great, they are male and female, emanator and emanated, as we have commented in *Sefer Pardes Rimmonim* in its [appropriate] place,[369] and there I elaborated in the commentary on the Sabba',[370] and behold, this is the perfection of the thought at the end of the action. And now how will the half of the action adhere to the entire, complete thought? And to the sage [it is hinted at] by a hint, that the action should be complete, *du partzufin*, and will ascend rank after rank, up to the Head of all the thoughts,[371] up to the union with the Master of the thought.[372]

This is a rich and fascinating passage, whose main framework is the creation and descent of the divine Female, as the first stage of the theogonic process, then Her gradual descent, and, ultimately, the ascent of the couple of the Male and Female to the Infinite. The pseudo-Aristotelian dictum is interpreted as dealing with the various stages of the emergence and the descent of the Female. At the beginning, She is a thought that precedes *Keter*, and the ultimate intention is that She will be the attribute that governs the lower world.[373] As shown by Shifra

---

Yaqar on *Tiqqunim*, 2: 160, *qurvah* is described in good Neoplatonic terms, as "the power of the emanator [that is found] within the emanated" and also 207, 212, 213, 218, it is again related to emanation. See also *'Or Yaqar on Tiqqunim*, 9: 7. Whether this closeness has sexual overtones, too, is not clear; see, nevertheless, the discussion in *Pardes Rimmonim*, 2: 7.

369 Probably *Pardes Rimonim*, 14: 3, 18: 1.

370 Namely, the treatise printed in *Zohar* vol. 2, pericope *Mishpatim*.

371 On the difference between thoughts and Thought in the context of the pseudo-Aristotelian dictum when dealing with the highest levels of the sefirotic realm, see Cordovero, *'Or Yaqar*, 11: 344. On the ascent to the head see more in the Lurianic texts discussed in the next chapter.

372 *'Or Yaqar*, 12, 29–30:

והוא במה שנתבאר בכמה מקומות תחלת המחשבה סוף המעשה, וירצה כי בעלות הרצון והנדבה לפניו להמציא
זולתו היה כל הכוונה בנפרדים ממנו המשיגים אמתתו ומרוממים גדולתו בהשגתם קצת מן הקצת, וזהו רצונו ונדבת
רוחו בכוונתו בהמצאת כל נמצא ודבקותם בו על ידי המדה האחרונה שהיא שר המנהגת כל השפל והרי היא
היתה כוונה ראשונה ונמצא ראשון בין המאציל והכתר שהיא הסבת האמיתית להמציא הכתר וכל הנמשך. ולרוב
קורבה האציל הכתר והוריד אותה המחשבה מדרגה אחת והם שני מדרגות אל המחשבה הראשונה קודמת אל
הכתר, השנית מאוחרת אל הכתר קודמת אל החכמה. ולרוב קורבה הורידה מדרגה אחרת, והיא קודמת אל הבינה
ומאוחרת אל החכמה, ודרך זה ירד עד היותה אל מקומה בייחוד עם התפארת, לנהל בשותפותם שני המאורות
הגדולים, ועם היותם גדולים הם בסוד זכר ונקבה, משפיע ומושפע כדפירשנו בספ״ר במקומו ושם הארכתי בביאור
הסבא והרי זהו שלימות המחשבה בסוף המעשה. ועתה איך ידבק חצי המעשה בכל המחשבה השלימה ולחכימא
ברמיזא, שצריך שיהיה המעשה שלם דיו פרצופין, ויתעלה מדרגה אחר מדרגה בראש כל המחשבות עד דבקותם
בבעל המחשבה.

373 For the expansion of the supernal Thought in the entire sefirotic realm, see also *'Or Yaqar* (Jerusalem, 1963), 2: 29.

Asulin on the basis of other Cordoverian texts, the Female has been emanated directly from *Keter*,[374] an assumption that corroborates my theory of the privileged Female.

The concept that the status of the first Thought is higher than *Keter* is not a unique treatment in Cordovero's theosophy, as he hints in some instances in the context of the discussions of the *sefirah* of *Keter*, that there is a womb most probably situated between the Infinite and the "place," first *sefirah*.[375] Though different from the Thought, both refer to a space that precedes *Keter*, and both are understood as feminine. Here the assumption is that *Keter* is produced by the supreme Feminine entity, just as the womb presumably functions as productive. Thought and Head are clearly connected, a mixture of axial and pre-axial attitudes, respectively. The interpretation of the dictum is clear: the feminine entity is the first in thought and also the last in action. Here "last" refers to the end of the sefirotic realm, namely the *sefirah* of *Malkhut*.[376] As such, it constitutes the final

---

374 "The Double Construct of the Shekhinah," 104–105.

375 See Idel, "The Womb and the Infinite in the Kabbalah of R. Moshe Cordovero" (Hebrew), 37–58. See Cordovero, *'Or Yaqar* (Jerusalem 1974), 6: 262, and also the quote in the name of Cordovero in R. Abraham Azulai's *'Or ha-Ḥammah*, 1, fol. 237a; here it is said that " his *Shekhinah* is contracted [with]in *Keter* in order to emanate [by it] all the other *sefirot*." צמצם שכינתו בכתר להאציל ע"י שאר הספירות

On *tzimtzum* in Cordovero, see Sack, *The Kabbalah of Rabbi Moses Cordovero*, 57–82. Compare, however, the general claim of Elliot R. Wolfson as to the absence of a feminine element in the first *sefirah*, in his *Language, Eros, Being*, 179–180, as part of his vision of the centrality of phallocentrism. This is an unwarranted claim that does not hold for dozens of texts in Cordovero's opus alone – see, e.g., above, n. 344 and below, n. 379 – not to mention many other Kabbalists, for example, the Lurianic ones, some of whom will be discussed in the following chapter, especially in nn. 458, 512, or later on, in R. Jacob Koppel Lipshitz, *Sha'arei Gan 'Eden*, fol. 22a. In fol. 69bc, he speaks about the elevation of the Female to *Keter*, by the deeds of the Kabbalist and the equation of Her size to the higher *sefirot* when ascending, in the vein of some Cordoverian traditions. See also below, n. 679. Wolfson confidently articulates his thesis about the absence of a feminine dimension in *Keter* – a major cornerstone in his phallocentric edifice. Although this observation pertains, perhaps, to a few passages in Kabbalah, it ignores many others where the opposite is true. I see no benefit from building a comprehensive theory that fails to take into consideration many explicit statements that belie it. Many Cordoverian texts contradict his discussion in *Language, Eros, Being*, 447, n. 118, which related to Cordovero as if the feminine aspects of *Keter* are a matter of androgynity or of *coincidentia oppositorum*, attempting to obliterate the feminine aspect. Wolfson attempts to harmonize different approaches in an artificial manner that is phallocentrically biased. See also *Language, Eros, Being*, 508, n. 244, but compare to Asulin, "The Double Construct of the Image of the *Shekhinah*," 105 and below in Concluding Remarks.

376 See also Cordovero's *'Elimah Rabbati*, fol. 145b and fol. 107b.

cause and, therefore, according to Aristotle's theories, She would be superior to the three other causes.[377]

The ascent of the divine couple, found in some form of sexual connection described as *du-partzufin*, toward the Infinite is evident in a series of Cordoverian sources.[378] It is connected to the persistence of the male-female polarity within the highest levels of the theosophical realm, part of what I call the dual ontology. E. R. Wolfson's denial of the existence of such a sexual polarity or of a significant feminine dimension in *Keter* is invalidated by a long series of Cordoverian passages that appear in all his major books that explicitly note this polarity immanent within this *sefirah*.[379] One instance states that "*Keter* comprises both male and female."[380]

In this passage, the union of the lower manifestation of the Feminine is attained by the descent of the Female to the Male, *Tiferet*. Cordovero's writings that mention "Her place" frequently refer to the initial status of the Female in the lower sefirotic realm, where She is found together with *Tiferet,* and higher than the three lower *sefirot*, namely above *Netzah, Hod* and *Yesod*, as is evident in a long series of his texts, as well as from a diagram found in *'Or Yaqar*.[381]

The description of the Female as the "half," namely, the half of the body, is another recurrent theme in Cordovero's writings, following the Zoharic term *palga' de-gufa'*, "the half of the body." The assumption is that the other half, *Tiferet*, joins Her in order to constitute a complete or perfect unity, which enables its ascent. I wonder whether this recuperation of the Male dimension in the lower

---

377 See e.g., G. E. R. Lloyd, *Aristotle: the Growth and Structure of his Thought*, 105. For the superiority of the final cause, see, e.g., Abraham Abulafia, *Sefer 'Or ha-Sekhel*, 16, 62, 102.

378 See Idel, "The Womb and the Infinite," 43 and the references found in footnotes 5 and 6 there, and the texts of Luzzatto and Eliashiv, to be discussed in chapters below.

379 See, e.g., *'Elimah Rabbati*, fols. 59a, 59b, - הנקבה שבכתר - 'the female within *Keter*" or fols. 59c, "In order to innovate something different from Itself, *Keter* needs Male and Female," הכתר להוציא זולתו צריך זכו"ן as well as *'Elimah Rabbati*, fols. 86a, 97d, 109a, *'Or Yaqar*, 14: 69, or *Pardes Rimmonim*, 13: 17. See also other texts of Cordovero discussed in Idel, "The Womb and the Infinite," 47–50 and the texts mentioned later on in this chapter. Compare, however, to Wolfson, *Language, Eros, Being*, 180, 447, n. 118, where he offers some reservations about his unqualified denial, although he nevertheless reinterpreted some of the numerous "dissenting" texts in the vein of his phallocentric theory as to the alleged absence of the distinctly feminine element in the first *sefirah*. See also below, n. 407.

380 See his *Shi'ur Qomah*, fol. 9a: שהכתר כולל זכר ונקבה

381 See the many references to this issue collected in my "Wedding Canopies for the Divine Couple in R. Moshe Cordovero's Kabbalah." See also *'Or Yaqar, 7*: 8–9; *'Or Yaqar*, to *Tiqqunim*, 5: 31, 64; Cordovero, *Tefillah le-Moshe*, fols. 352b, 345b. Compare also to *Zohar* III, fol. 77b, where the union of Male and Female is followed by an ascent of the couple, all this in an eschatological context. See also Alqabetz's text adduced by Kimelman, *The Mystical Meaning of Lekhah Dodi*, 78.

sefirotic world is a reconstruction of the primordial sexual relationship She had with the Infinite, when in the pre-sefirotic realm.[382] In any case, it is worth noting that "half" implies some form of equality between the two bodies, as, indeed, Cordovero reaffirms in his writings.[383] Plausibly, the process of descent entails diminution, rendering the Female on the level of *Tiferet* half the original size; presumably, the ascent reconstitutes the original size.[384] Evidently, the main perspective of this passage derives from the angle of the divine feminine entity; the Male is mentioned only marginally. In my opinion, the above passage encompasses the entire realm of the divine feminine from Her pre-sefirotic stage to Her status as ruling over the lower world.[385] In a discussion pertinent to the subject of this study, Cordovero mentions the ideal "to bring the *Shekhinah* and Her operations close to the Infinite ['*Ein Sof*] [and] to think that '*Ein Sof* emanates those operations by intermediaries [in order to] operate in the lower world by means of the *Shekhinah*. The end of this action, therefore, is [tantamount to] the beginning of the thought on high."[386]

The specific affinity of the *Shekhinah* to the Infinite is explicit here, both as Her source and as the place of Her return. Elsewhere, the *sefirah* of *Malkhut* is described as ascending though the sefirotic hierarchy, arriving at a place that

---

382 See above, n. 375.

383 For the concept of פלגא דגופא in the *Zohar*, see Liebes, *Sections in the Zohar Lexicon*, 277–279, where he duly pointed to the Platonic origin of this term. In any case, in a text of Cordovero's, "the half of the body" is described as completing or perfecting the Male configuration, פרצוף הזכר that is, the supernal husband, while elsewhere the two halves are regarded as compounding a perfect body. See *'Or Yaqar*, 15: 11, 186, *'Or Yaqar*, to *Tiqqunim*, 5: 84, 251, and *'Or Yaqar*, on *Ra'aya' Meheimna'*, 5: 11;and *'Or Yaqar*, 3: 198; *'Or Yaqar*, on *Tiqqunim*, 1: 83; 5: 13–14 (Jerusalem, 2007). See also below, n. 692.

384 See, e.g., *'Or Yaqar* on *Tiqqunim*, 2: 225.

385 See also Cordovero's passage cited in Asulin, "The Double Construct of the Image of the *Shekhinah*," 95.

386 *'Or Yaqar*, on *Tiqqunim*, 4: 176 (Jerusalem, 2004):

מקרב השכינה ופעולותיה בא"ס שיחשוב שא"ס ישפיע באלו האמצעים לפעול ע"י השכינה בתחתונים, א"כ סוף המעשה הזאת תחלת המחשבה למעלה.

Compare in the same work, 97, 178, 190, and especially 189:

שהיא תחלת המחשבה שהמלכות בתחלת המחשבה מציאותה למעלה, ולכך בהתפשטות האצילות יקדם מציאותם אליהם בסוד החכמה מחשבה, והיא מציאות אצילותה בבינה.

"that She is the beginning of thought, as *Malkhut* is the beginning of thought and Her existence is on high, and this is the reason why, by the expansion of emanation, Her existence precedes them, in accordance with the secret of the *Ḥokhmah* is *Maḥashavah*, and this is Her existence within *Binah*." I have corrected in my translation *Metziy'utam* to *metziy'utah*. See also the interesting discussion of the Female as linking the lower worlds to the Infinite in Sack, ed. *From the Fountains of Sefer Elimah*, 123: מאחדת כל המציאיות

is described as "higher than all."[387] She is not, therefore, depicted as absorbed, masculinized, or part of an alleged "reconstituted masculinity,"[388] or even less subservient, but most probably as maintaining Her identity. In other instances, however, Cordovero presents a different picture. It is worth noting that, in line with a long series of similar statements in Midrash and early Kabbalah, he mentions that the light of *Malkhut* is equal to that of the sun, namely *Tiferet*.[389] It goes without saying that Cordovero was acquainted with the myth of the ascent of prayer as a crown on the head, although Cordovero does not specify whose head[390]; in some cases, however, he mentions *Keter* and even the Infinite in the context of Her ascent.[391] He thus follows the view of his teacher in matters of Kabbalah, R. Joseph Karo.[392]

Let me turn to an important passage dealing with the state of the divine Feminine in the eschaton, part of what I term the three-phases gender theory. Cordovero discusses the emendation of the moon's diminution, namely, of the divine Feminine, in the future, and Her state as follows:

> In the future ... She will ascend and sit with Her Husband at His right, one in front of the other, and She will ascend face to face, head to head, the first three [*sefirot*] within Her [versus] the three first in Him, and the arms on the arms, the body on the body, the hips on the hips, and forever the Female is Female and the Male is Male, namely, She is always the recipient of the influence and He [always] influences, but She is like a wife always at the right of Her Husband, and She will enjoy the dates of Her *'Onah*[393] without

---

387 *'Or Yaqar*, to *Tiqqunim*, 5: 2:

עולה על ששה היא עולה דרך כל המדרגות, כשהיא עולה מחתמת עצמה בכל מדרגה ומדרגה, עד שהיא עולה למעלה מהכל.

See also *'Or Yaqar*, to *Tiqqunim*, 5:. 283. For the syntagm "higher than all" in the context of the divine Female, see the Aramaic locution in *Zohar*, III, fol. 74b, and Idel, *Kabbalah & Eros*, 141–142; it is plausible, however, that despite speaking about the Female as higher than all the ranks, here the intention is much more modest, namely Her ascent to *Tiferet*. In the sense of Cordovero, see also the discussions of R. Hayyim Vital and R. Shlomo Eliashiv, translated in the next chapter, and in Hasidism, in ch. 10. See also Cordovero, *'Or Yaqar*, 11: 317, 323 for additional uroboric tendencies. Or more of the ascensions of the Female, see Idel, "Ascensions, Gender and Pillars," 60–61, n. 11, and below, in ch. 12.

388 Wolfson, "Woman, The Feminine as Other in Theosophic Kabbalah," 169.

389 Cordovero, *'Or Yaqar*, to *Tiqqunim*, 5: 278.

390 *'Or Yaqar*, to *Tiqqunim*, 9: 117. In the same work see also 7: 113 and 11: 31, 383.

391 *'Or Yaqar*, to *Tiqqunim*, 15: 137, 218, 223 and 16: 35; and the passage quoted and translated in the motto to this chapter from Sack, ed., *From the Fountains of Sefer Elimah*, 122–123, and Asulin, "The Double Construct of the Image of the *Shekhinah*," 109.

392 Karo, *Maggid Meisharim*, 206.

393 Namely, the obligation of the husband to satisfy the sexual needs of the wife, according to the Hebrew Bible.

disruption,[394] and Her food in abundance and Her sons in Her house ... and She will radiate from the light of the Infinite in an excessive manner, without any lack, and in this state She was before the diminution, and forever She is under Her Husband[395] and his dominion. And by this the secret of the diminution will be amended.[396]

The three phases of the model are evident here: the starting point is the elevated state of *Malkhut* sitting beside Her Husband, then Her diminution, and finally Her restoration to the primordial position. By ascending, She sits *vis-à-vis* the Husband on His right, and Her limbs correspond to His, as part of some form of sexual union. According to other numerous passages by Cordovero, the moment of sexual union is also a moment of the divine Feminine reaching a size equal to that of the Male.[397] In the above passage, Cordovero does not accentuate the corporeal equality, but he does state explicitly that the eschatological situation does not obliterate the gender difference. This is, to be sure, not a new approach in Kabbalah, as no less than R. Moshe de Leon wrote at the end of the thirteenth century that "the Female stands in Her femininity forever."[398] Therefore, the first and the last stages in the above-mentioned model do not consist of a male androgyne, nor do they reconstruct one, as it has been repeatedly claimed.[399]

The apotheosis of the Female consists also in receiving two out the three biblical obligations of the husband: the conjugal debt, sexual intercourse, and food,

---

394 Compare, however, to the opposite view in Wolfson, which offers a generalized vision, to the effect that: "Redemption in the ultimate sense does not signify the perpetual pairing of male and female but the reconstruction of the androgyny in the Godhead, in which the gender dimorphism is superseded." See his "*Tiqqun ha-Shekhinah*," 291. For the problem of a monolithic vision of gender in Kabbalah in Wolfson's phallocentrism, see below in Concluding Remarks.

395 Compare to *Tiqqunei Zohar*, fol. 39a.

396 '*Or Yaqar*, to *Tiqqunim* (Jerusalem, 2009), 6: 209–210, Sack, *R. Moshe Cordovero, Ma'ayan 'Ein Ya'aqov*, 159–160:

לעתיד...שהיא תתעלה ותעמוד עם בעלה לימינו, זה כנגד זה ותתעלה למעלה פנים אל פנים ראש בראש שלוש ראשונות שבה שלוש ראשונות שבו זרועות בזרועות גופא בגופא שוקין בשוקין ולעולם נקבה זכר והיינו שתמיד היא מושפעת והוא משפיע אלא שהיא כאשה תמיד לימין בעלה ויהיו לה עתות עונתה בלי טרדה ויהיו לה מזונותיה בשופע ובניה בביתה...ותהיה מאירה מאור א"ס בשעור מופלג בלי חסרון ועל המציאות הזה היתה קודם המעוט ולעולם היא תחת בעלה ורשותו. ובזה יתוקן סוד המיעוט.

397 "*Male and Female*," ch. 14.

398 See the untitled treatise in Ms. Munich 47, fol. 366a: עולם תחתון היא נקבה העומדת בנקבות עולמית ועל כל פנים אינה חוזרת לעולם זכר.
The authorship of the text was established by Gershom Scholem, "Eine unbekannte mystische Schrift des Moses de Leon," 109–123.

399 Compare, e.g., Wolfson, *Language, Eros, Being*, 50, 55, 110, 156, 166, 267, 366–367, 374–375, 384, 386, 387–388, who considers the reconstitution of the Female within the Male as a basic myth in Kabbalah. See also Abrams, *The Female Body of God*, 3–4.

as the Kabbalist states in several other instances.[400] In other words, the eschaton does not eliminate the femininity but, on the contrary, this is the moment that it culminates. Moreover, Cordovero mentions some form of direct contact between the Female and the Infinite, as She is radiating from its light, a sign of equality. Later, on the same page, nevertheless, Cordovero says that the divine Feminine does receive from the Infinite.[401] On the other hand, the subordination of the Female to the Male is also explicitly mentioned, in a clear manner that contradicts what has been said earlier in the same passage: first, She is ascending and sitting at the right side of the Male, later, She is under the Male. In any case, according to this seminal passage, She was not masculinized or obliterated.

I want to emphasize the special importance of what I called above "the circular theosophy" in Cordovero's writings and in some other earlier and later Kabbalists.[402] This term designates the theosophical view that, unlike the vertical, emanational hierarchy evident in the widespread diagrams of the ten *sefirot* as a tree or as an anthropos, depicts the same ten *sefirot* by their names written on the circumference of a circle, where the first *sefirah*, *Keter*, is the starting point of the series of *sefirot* that ends with *Malkhut*, which is found in the immediate vicinity of *Keter*, moving in a clockwise direction or inversely.[403] An originally composite syntagm from the grammatical point of view, *Keter Malkhut* refers in pre-Kabbalistic sources to one single entity, a specific type of crown,[404] but under the pressure of the intricate theosophical structure, this locution has been divided between the two sefirotic entities. Both the uroboric and the vertical theosophy, however, preserve the original affinity between these two terms. In a way, the circular theosophy short circuits the hierarchical picture with regard to the lower location of the last *sefirah*, although not in the cases of other *sefirot*. This

---

400 For Kabbalistic sources and other discussions in Cordovero and his disciple see M. Idel, "On the Performing Body in Theosophical-Theurgical Kabbalah: Some Preliminary Remarks," 254–264.

401 *'Or Yaqar*, to *Tiqqunim*, 6: 210.

402 See above, nn. 215, 232.

403 For such a diagram, see *Pardes Rimmonim*, 6: 1. It is evident that Cordovero brings material already found in Kabbalah, although he himself does not accept this view. The same diagram is found also in the commentary on *Pardes Rimmonim*, in *'Asis Rimonnim* by R. Elisha Gallico, ad locum, who noticed the similarity of the sefirotic diagram to that of the zodiacal signs.

For two forms of emanation, the downward one from *Keter* to *Malkhut* and, inversely, the upward one, from *Malkhut* to *Keter*, see R. Abraham Azulai's quotation in *'Or ha-Ḥammah*, vol. 3, part 2, fol. 27d and see also n. 350 above as well as in ch. 9 below.

404 See Esther 2: 17, 6: 8, *'Avot*, IV: 13, *'Avot de-Rabbi Nathan*, ch. 41, R. Shlomo ibn Gabirol's famous poem *Keter Malkhut*. See also below, n. 428.

depiction is articulated in the context of the statement in *Sefer Yetzirah* as to the
sefirot qua entities whose beginnings are fixed to their end. For example, we read:

> There is no entity that there are no male and female in it[405] ... and when they[406] will connect
> to each other, their existence will be "their end is fixed to their beginning, and their begin-
> ning to their end," namely, the existence of *Keter* in *Malkhut* and of *Malkhut* in *Keter*.[407]
> And [the meaning of] "its end is fixed," is that *Malkhut* [is fixed] to its beginning that is the
> supernal Thought, and in order that the ways will be ten, their existence was connected
> before their being, and also "their beginning is fixed to their end" as *Keter* refers to the
> lower [level] just as it refers to the higher [level] and points to the existence of His power in
> all the creatures.[408]

This by no means exceptional view appears explicitly in Cordovero's *Commentary
on Sefer Yetzirah* ad locum[409] and in other passages of his works, and it is far
from merely a noble departure from earlier Kabbalistic views.[410] Whether the
circular diagram refer to the *sefirot* or only to the preexistent *sefirot*, referred by
the syntagm "before their being" as connected to each other in this way, is not so
clear, but theological circularity, or uroboric theosophy is nevertheless a theme

---

405 This is a slogan for the more comprehensive theory I call "dual ontology." See *Tiqqunei Zohar*,
fol. 89b, and also *'Or Yaqar*, 8: 230, 231 and9: 6. For more details, see my *"Male and Female."*

406 Namely, the consonants of the Tetragrammaton, which in the regular order refer to the
male and in the inverse manner HWHY refer to the female. See also in the *Commentary to Sefer
Yetzirah*, 70 and in his commentary to the prayerbook *Tefillah le-Moshe*, fol. 356b.

407 See especially the interesting passage in *'Or Yaqar*, on *Tiqqunim*, 3: 46 (Jerusalem, 1975) p.:

מדת המלכות שהיא נמצאת מא״ס

"The attribute of *Malkhut* that is found out of the Infinite." See also above, n. 379.

408 *'Or Yaqar*, to *Tiqqunim*, 4: 191 (Jerusalem, 2004):

דלית בריה דלית ביה דכר ונקבא, בענץ שסוד יהו״ה הם עשר ספירות, וסוד הוה״י הם עשר ספירות, וכאשר יתקשרו
אלו באלו ימצא מציאותם נעוץ סופן בתחלתן ותחלתם בסופן דהיינו מציאות הכתר במלכות ומלכות בכתר. ונעוץ סופו
שהוא מלכות בתחלתו שהוא המחשבה העליונה וכדי שימצאו הדרכים עשר היותם נקשרים במציאותם קודם היותם, וגם
תחלתן נעוץ בסופן כי הכתר רמז למטה כדרך שהוא רמז למעלה מורה המצא כוחו בכל הנמצאות.

Compare also to *'Or Yaqar*, on *Tiqqunim*, 3: 46, interpreting the views cited above from the introductions to *Tiqqunei Zohar*, and especially *'Or Yaqar*, 7: 183:

כתר במלכות מלכות בכתר והיינו אנ״י אי״ן,

See also the view found in the *Zohar* III, fol. 171, as to the close relationship between beginning
and end, a passage quoted at length in Cordovero's *Pardes Rimmonim*, 14: 3 and *'Or Yaqar*, 17: 15
(Jerusalem, 1989), (*Derishot be-'Inianei Mal'akhim*, part 5), and in his *'Elimah Rabbati*, fol. 145b.
Extremely interesting in this context is another passage in Cordovero's *Shi'ur Qomah*, fol. 93ab,
where he writes about the *sefirot* as found in a state of unity within a circle, referring also to the
prooftext from *Sefer Yetzirah*.

409 See p. 70 and also the many discussions in *Pardes Rimmonim*, e.g., 3: 1, 4: 5, 6: 1, 15: 1, 23: 22;
'Or Yaqar, 5: 6 (Jerusalem, 1987).

410 Sack, *From the Fountains of Sefer Elimah*, 119–120; compare to *'Or Yaqar*, 3: 38 and 14: 114.

that indubitably interested Cordovero. In any case, at least in one instance, this theme is connected explicitly to the pseudo-Aristotelian dictum.[411]

The identification of *Malkhut* with *Keter* poses some quandaries, as the former is conceived of as the source of judgement, whereas the latter stands for absolute mercy. In order to overcome this inconsistency, Cordovero claims that at the beginning, namely within the divine Thought, *Malkhut* was mercy, and only afterwards it became judgement, a feature that starts from the *sefirah* of *Binah*.[412] A somewhat similar solution is offered in order to solve the discrepancy between the masculine nature of the term *Keter* and the feminine one of *Malkhut* as represented by the term *'Ateret:* According to one of Cordovero's discussions, by the ascent of the latter, She becomes Male, in the vein of the phallocentric model, but on the same page, he nevertheless speaks about Her ascent to the Infinite and Her return full of the light of the Infinite.[413] In another instance, however, he suggests that the future situation of *Malkhut* will be one of equality to *Tiferet*, in the vein of some early Kabbalists who dealt with the myth of the diminution of the moon.[414] Those are examples of the conceptual fluidity of Kabbalistic thought, which, in principle, relativizes any definitive statement about a certain issue, part of multivocality that leaves little space for monolithic conceptualization of Kabbalah on the topic of gender, as is the case with other topics, too. The two theosophies are not necessarily consonant and do not resonate easily with one other; nevertheless, they share a similar attempt to privilege the Female, although in very different ways.

Let me draw attention to Cordovero's comparison between *Keter* as the ruler over the *sefirot* and the Diadem/*Malkhut* as the ruler over the lower worlds.[415] This is a functional comparison that does not speak about emergence or return but about a similar structure shared only by those two *sefirot*, seen as hegemonic in their respective realms. One of the disciples of Cordovero's writing, R. Elijah da Vidas, in his classic work of mystical-ethical instructions, *Reshit Ḥokhmah,*

---

411 *See Shi'ur Qomah*, par. 2, printed in *'Or Yaqar*, 21: 94 (Jerusalem, 1992):

אם כן נחזור החותם ונשלשל אותם שעלו במחשבה ויהיה שלשולם כחותם המתהפך, הראשונה אחרונה והאחרונה ראשונה בענין שתחלת המחשבה סוף המעשה, אם כן זאת האחרונה שהיא באמת ראשונה אין לה עקירה ממקומה אלא עומדת על ענין המחשבה מפני שסוף המחשבה הוא תחלת המעשה ודאי שכך הוא סוד החותם המתהפך שנעוץ קצהו בקצהו, ולכך זאת שהיא עולה במחשבה שם במציאות שנזכרה במחשבה עמדה על ראש המעשה, ואותה שהיתה תחלת המחשבה היא סוף המעשה.

412 See the text of *Sefer 'Eilimah* printed by Sack, ed., *R. Moshe Cordovero, Ma'ayan 'Ein Ya'aqov*, 3–4, 10.

413 See *R. Moshe Cordovero, Ma'ayan 'Ein Ya'aqov*, 135. For a discussion of material found in this part of Cordovero's book in the context of the myth of the fall of the Sophia, see Melila Hellner-Eshed, "On Love and Creativity" (Hebrew), 173–174.

414 *'Or Yaqar*, 17: 77. Compare to my "The Divine Female and the Mystique of the Moon."

415 *'Or Yaqar*, 9: 60.

connects the governance of *Malkhut* in the lower worlds to the pseudo-Aristotelian dictum, which means that divine thought intended from the very beginning to appoint *Malkhut* to govern the worlds: "'Thy kingdom is the kingdom of all the worlds, and your governance is generation after generation,'[416] and the aspect of the essence and root of all the worlds. And it is also said that 'Thy kingdom is the kingdom of all worlds,' and its matter should be understood as 'the end of action is the beginning of thought.'"[417]

Another disciple of the Safedian master, R. Abraham Galante, wrote in his commentary to the book of Lamentations that the ultimate intention of God's creation was to emanate the last attribute, as only by means of Her, the divine directives descend.[418] The other, more influential follower of Cordovero, R. Eleazar Azikri, the author of *Sefer Ḥaredim*, imagined *Malkhut* as related to *Keter* in a rather circular manner, in the vein of his master's thought:

> *'Attah* [you] refers to *Malkhut* namely, *Malkhut* is revealed,[419] and we intend that the light of the Emanator that is the essence of all will come to *Malkhut* called *'Attah* and also Elijah by saying 'Thou are'[420] ... He, blessed be He, united the *sefirot* with Him, since *'Attah* refers to *Malkhut* and *Hu'* [He] refers to *Keter*, as it is said in *Sefer Yetzirah*, 'He fixed their end in their beginning and their beginning in their end.'"[421]

---

416 Psalms 145: 3.

417 Gate I, ch. 1, ed. J. Ch. Waldman, (Jerusalem, 1984), I: 48:

(תהלים קמה:ג) מלכותך מלכות כל עולמים וממשלתך בכל דור ודור, ובחינת עיקרא ושרשא דכל עלמין גם כן נאמר באומרו: מלכותך מלכות כל עולמים, ויובן ענינו בסוד סוף המעשה תחלת המחשבה.

Da Vidas resorts to the dictum also in two other cases in his book, but those discussions do not concern us in this context.

418 *Qol Bokhim*, fol. 2a.

419 Compare, however, Wolfson's claim as to the hiddeness of the Female, in his *Language, Eros, Being*, 484, n. 164; his *Through a Speculum that Shines*, 339, 396; and his discussion of the "paradox" of the revealed and hidden divinity in his "Occultation of the Feminine," 148–149, endnote 1 and compare to my *"Male and Female,"* n. 211, and especially in Sack, *From the Fountains of Sefer Elimah*, 123: סוד היותה מפורסמת וגלויה לכל העובדים למטה "the secret of Her being famous and revealed to all the worshippers below," and see also below, n. 437. The worshipers are, probably the same as those mentioned above, namely the Kabbalists. In this context, it is worth emphasizing the concept of the "world of disclosure" or of "revelation" עלמא דאתגליא as a reference to the last *sefirah*. Cf. e.g., *Zohar*, I, fol. 18a, where Rachel, a symbol for the *Shekhinah*, was designated as the world of disclosure. See also Abraham Abulafia, e.g., *Sefer ha-'Ot*, 14, or *'Otzar 'Eden Ganuz*, 215.

420 Aziqri quotes the introduction to *Tiqqunei Zohar*, in Aramaic, where it is written *'Ant Hu*, which is misinterpreted as referring to Thou and He.

421 Eleazar Azikri, *Sefer Ḥaredim* Ch. 6, fol. 14ab:

שאתה רומז למלכות, רוצה לומר שהמלכות שהוא נגלה אנו מכוונים שיבוא האור מן המאציל שהוא עיקר הכל אל המלכות שנקרא אתה. וגם אליהו באומרו אנת הוא, ... שייחד ספירותיו יתברך עמו דאנת רמז למלכות והוא רמז לכתר על דרך שאמרו בספר יצירה נעץ סופן בתחלתן ותחלתן בסופן.

The passage refers to the intention in prayer that the references to God as "You" and "He" point respectively to *Malkhut* and *Keter*. These two *sefirot* are described as the beginning and the end, although they are related to each other.

Last but not least in the context of Cordovero: A somewhat later follower of his, R. Shabbatai Sheftel ha-Levi Horowitz, brought together some of the themes discussed above in a book written at the end of the sixteenth or early seventeenth century in Prague.[422] He paraphrased some of the formulations of the Safedian Kabbalist, writing:

> In the place where the holiness was [once], it remained in its existence, in a selected exist-ence, as it was before its expansion, despite its having expanded and revealed itself more, in accordance with the secret "The *Shekhinah* did not move away from its place"[423] ... as it is linked on high with[in] *Keter*, which is called head and scalp ... and *Keter Malkhut* ... and it is appropriate to refer to *Malkhut* as the limb of mouth, because it is found in the head as its end is fixed to its beginning.[424]

Although Horowitz does not refer explicitly to Alqabetz's poem, his passage illus-trates, nevertheless, what we attempted to show above, namely, that the term *Rosh* in the poem is related in a certain manner to *Malkhut,* as She is connected to the divine head. In the same context, Horowitz also writes: "Because the super-nal *Keter* is *Keter Malkhut*, namely *Malkhut* is united in *Keter* according to the secret of 'He tells from the beginning the end,'[425] the beginning is *Keter*, the end is *Malkhut*, because of Her prolongation and emanation from the supernal *Keter*,

---

422 On this Kabbalist, see Bracha Sack, *Shomer ha-Pardes, The Kabbalist Rabbi Sabbetai Sheftel Horowitz of Prague* (Hebrew). His views influenced in particular those of R. Naftali Hertz Bakharakh, which will be discussed in the next chapter.

423 See, e.g., *Yalqut Shimeoni* on Micha 4, no. 552.

424 R. Shabbatai Sheftel Horowitz ha-Levi, *Shefaʿ Tal,* fol. 29c:

במקום שהייתה הקדושה הגם שנתפשטה ונתגלתה יותר נשארה שם קדושתה במציאותה הראשון במציאות מובחר כמו שהייתה קודם התפשטותה בסוד לא זזה השכינה ממקומה.... ומפני שהיא נעוצה למעלה בכתר שהוא נקרא ראש וקרקפת... כתר מלכות ומטעם זה בעצמו ראוי למלכות לכנותה וליחסה באבר הפה שהוא בראש והוא בסוד נעוץ סופה בתחילתה.

This passage reflects the deep influence of Cordovero's discussion found in *Pardes Rimmonim*, 4: 5.

כתר עילאה איהו כתר מלכות, ועליה אתמר 'מגיד מראשית אחרית'. ואיהו קרקפתא דתפילי'.

The source is to be found in "another introduction" to *Tiqqunei Zohar,* fol. 11b. This text has been printed in the "prayers before the prayer" in Cordovero's *Tefillah le-Moshe*, fol. 23a. For *Malkhut* as mouth, see fol. 11a and *'Or Yaqar*, 22: 28, and my discussion in *"Male and Female,"* n. 222. Is this image of mouth related to Cordovero's description of disclosure of secrets that we mentioned above, beside n. 329?

425 Isaiah 46: 10. Compare also above, n. 227 and below, 574.

as *Malkhut* has also a hidden existence within *Keter* in accordance with the secret of Male and Female."[426]

The passage describes the hidden existence or presence of some aspect of *Malkhut* within *Keter*, following Cordovero, in terms of a sexual duality, which is part of what can be called "dual ontology,"[427] a much wider ontological world-view found in many Kabbalistic writings. Here, unlike the case mentioned earlier, the feminine dimension of the last *sefirah* when found on high is still evident, which means that it was not absorbed or masculinized.[428] It seems that the Plotinian view of the dual existence of the soul, in this and in the supernal world simultaneously, has been transposed into an understanding of the double existence of the Female in the supernal world.[429] In other discussions, Horowitz deals with the emanation of *Malkhut* from "pure thought," identical to the Infinite or to the first *sefirah*. In this context, he indicates that *Malkhut* was created first, designating Her as "the first emanation,"[430] a statement that denotes Her privileged status. This is the reason why, when found in Her primordial stage, She was called *Keter*. Apparently, as pure mercy, She loses Her identity there, despite what Horowitz wrote some lines beforehand about the theme of "first emanation."[431] In principle, the resort to the term *Malkhut* could be understood as referring to the

---

426 R. Shabbatai Sheftel ha-Levi Horowitz, *Shefa' Tal*, fol. 29c:

כי כתר עילאה איהו כתר מלכות ר"ל כי מלכות היא מיוחדת בכתר בסוד מגיד מראשית אחרית ראשית הוא הכתר
ואחרית הוא מלכות המשכותה ואצילותה מכתר עילאה כי יש למלכות ג"כ מציאות נעלם בכתר בסוד זכר ונקבה

This passage draws on Cordovero's *Pardes Rimonim* 4: 6:

כתר עלאה איהו כתר מלכות ועליה אתמר וכו'. פי' עתה בה לבאר בענין הכתר למה המלכות נקראת פה שהיא
למעלה בראש נעוצה בקרקפתא שהוא הכתר ולכן הראש נקרא כתר מלכות מפני ששניהן מיוחדים כתר מלכות
בסוד מגיד מראשית אחרית (ישעיה מו:י) ראשית הוא הכתר ואחרית המלכות והמשכתה ואצילותה מכתר עלאה.

427 See Mopsik, *Recherches autour de la lettre sur la sainteté*, 152–172, and my *"Male" and "Female."*

428 See also above, n. 403 and below, beside n. 680. See also the lengthy discussion in *Shefa' Tal*, fol. 46c-47a.

429 See the material collected in Tishby, *The Wisdom of the Zohar*, 3: 752. This theme occurs also in R. Nathan ben Sa'adyah Har'ar's *Sha'arei Tzedeq*, a contemporary of the gist of Zoharic literature; see 20. For the identification of the soul with *Shekhinah*, see Idel, "Ascensions, Gender, and Pillars," 61, 63–64, and Horowitz's *Shefa' Tal*, fol. 65b. The Neoplatonic cyclic view in the context of the soul is found in hundreds of discussions in Kabbalah. Compare, however, to Scholem's, *On the Mystical Shape of the Godhead*, 166, where he claims that some images found in the book of *Bahir* about the *Shekhinah* are reminiscent of the Gnostic views of the psyche.

430 *Shefa' Tal*, fol. 46a:

נמצא שבתחילת המחשבה הבלתי סוף ובלתי תכלית אין סוף ברוך הוא עלה במחשבה הטהורה הבלתי סוף ובלתי
תכלית להאציל מלכות להנהיג על ידה כל העולמות ונאצל מלכות...כי תיכף שעלה רצון המחשבה הטהורה לגלות
אלוהותו על ידי הנהגתו נאצלה מלכות...האצילות הראשון שנאצל ממנו היה ג"כ בלתי תכלית בתכלית הפשיטות
לקורבתו למאצילו...האצילות הראשון היתה מלכות.

431 *Shefa' Tal*.

concept of royalty and thus not specifically to the Female, but in a parallel discussion, this Kabbalist speaks about *Tiferet* and *Malkhut* in sexually differentiated terms.[432] Nevertheless, he declares that the essence of the thought was directed at emanating *Malkhut*, although he mentions in this context also *Tiferet*[433]; yet, on the next page, he says the same about *Tiferet*.[434] Gynocentric and androcentric approaches are mixed on the same pages, as we have seen above also in the context of Cordovero.[435]

Horowitz describes some form of circularity in another discussion:

> Although the *Shekhinah* is in exile, do not think that She is, God forbid, separated from *Keter*; this is not so, God forbid, as you cannot find *Keter* that *Malkhut* is not united with It, even less, you cannot find the unity of *Malkhut* without the union of *Keter* with Her, in every place that the First is found, also the Last is found, which means as the first adheres to the last, as it is impossible to attribute the number first to anything if not in relation to the last thing to it, as if there is no last, it is impossible to say first. We learn from it that the first thing is united with the last thing, that immediately when the first thing is known, also the last one is known, too, and the last one is found with it, and is not separated from it. So, too, is the issue of *Keter* and *Malkhut*, as they are forever not separated from each other, as they are always united with each other ... so we find that they are near each other in accordance to the secret of *Barukh ʾAttah*, even though they are distant [from each other] by ten ranks, as this is the secret of the unity.[436]

I see no better interpretation of this passage than assuming that the design of the ten *sefirot* in a circle, where the last *sefirah* touches the first, informs this

---

432 *Shefaʿ Tal*, fol. 22c. See also above at the end of ch. 3.

433 *Shefaʿ Tal*:

שהמחשבה הטהורה היתה שיתאצל תפארת ומלכות עכ"ז עיקר המחשבה היתה במלכות שתתגלה מפני שהנהגתה יותר מתגלה בעולם הזה.

See also below, n. 436. On the Female as essence, עיקר, in the later layer of Zoharic literature, see Roi, *Love of the Shekhinah*, 120–122.

434 *Shefaʿ Tal*, fol. 22d.

435 *Shefaʿ Tal*, fols. 22d–23a.

436 *Shefaʿ Tal*, fol. 64c, in his commentary to a certain R. Aharon Abraham ben Barukh's *ʾIggeret ha-Teʿamim*, ch. 1:

שהשכינה בגלות לא תחשוב שהיא נפרדת ח"ו מכתר לא כן ח"ו כי לא תמצא כתר בלא יחוד מלכות עמו וכן לא תמצא יחוד מלכות בלא יחוד כתר עמה בכ"ל מקו"ם שנמ"צא ראש"ון נמ"צא אחר"ון פירוש כמו שהראשון מדובק באחרון כי לא תוכל לייחס מספר ראשון לשום דבר אם לא בערך הדבר שהוא אחרון לו כי אם אין אחרון לא יתכן לומר ראשון נמצא שבמספר הראשון מתייחד עמו האחרון כי תכף שנודע מספר ראשון נודע ג"כ אחרון ואחרון נמצא עמו ולא נפרד ממנו כמו כן הוא העניין בכתר ומלכות כי לא נפרדים זה מזה לעולם כי לעולם הן מיוחדים זה בזה ... נמצא שהם סמוכי' זה לזה בסוד ברוך אתה, הגם שהם רחוקים י' מדריגות כי זה סוד הייחוד.

Compare also to the passage of Cordovero cited above beside n. 347 and n. 433.

discussion. Indeed, the very last page of his book contains such a drawing. His way of exemplifying the affinity of the first and the last in terms of numbers – I assume one and ten – implies that the Female, designated as *Shekhinah* or *Malkhut,* is privileged in comparison to any of the other *sefirot.* The interpretation of the blessing *Barukh 'Attah* is that the first term refers to the absent divine entity, while *'Attah* refers to the present one, which is referring to disclosure or revelation, as we have seen above in this chapter in the passage of his older contemporary, R. Eleazar Aziqri.[437] Closeness of the two *sefirot* certainly does not entail an absorption of one by the other or a shift in gender of one of them.

Cordovero himself depicts another instance of the distinguished existence of the Female on high: "That in [the case of] the *sefirot,* their end is fixed in their beginning, *Keter* in *Malkhut* and *Malkhut* in *Keter.*"[438] Although someone may interpret this passage as dealing only with the aspect of *Malkhut* that is found within *Keter* and vice-versa, as is the case of all the *sefirot* that contain aspects of each other *sefirah* according to Cordovero's theosophy, the uroboric imagery is nevertheless evident, as the existence of a feminine dimension in the highest *sefirah.*

R. Isaiah ha-Levi Horowitz, author of the widely read Cordoverian compilation *Shnei Luḥot ha-Berit* (Two tablets of the law), draws a connection between some of these images in this widespread mid-seventeenth century Kabbalistic text. Following to a great extent the path initiated by the Safedian master,[439] Horowitz adopted some of his theosophical views and applied his insights to more moralistic issues. The wide circulation of this book, especially in Eastern Europe, enabled him to disseminate the above topics that concerned him. With regard to the uroboric theosophy, he reiterated the views of circularity and wrote, e.g., that the entire realm of the emanation has its end in its beginning.[440] Once, he describes the two movements of two sets of the ten *sefirot:* "*Yod* in the plene spelling[441] is the ten *sefirot* from above to below, according to the straightforward

---

437 *Shefaʻ Tal*, fol. 64c: שמורה על הגילוי. See above, n. 419.

438 *Tefillah le-Moshe*, fol. 79a:

שבספירות נעוץ סופן בתחלתן כתר במלכות ומלכות בכתר.

See also in his *'Or Yaqar*, 15: 137, 206, and the Cordoverian passage quoted in R. Abraham Azulai's *'Or ha-Ḥammah*, vol. 3, part 1, fol. 69a, and Cordovero's widespread *'Or ha-Neʻerav*, 6: 5.

439 See the discussions of the two lights in similar contexts in Cordovero's *'Or Yaqar,* 3: 38, 4: 146 (Jerusalem, 1967).

440 *Shnei Luḥot ha-Berit*, vol. 1, fol. 190b:

ולפי שכל האצילות נעוץ סופו בתחלתו.

See also *Shnei Luḥot ha-Berit*, fol. 190a, where he speaks about the hidden emanation in identical terms.

441 *Yod* in its plene spelling *YWD* is equal in gematriah to 20, which means two sets of ten. Such a view is found already in the thirteenth century Kabbalah. See, e.g., M. Idel, "Sefirot above the

light, and the ten from below to above, according to the returning light, according to the secret 'the beginning is fixed in its end.'"[442]

Although not strictly a circular theology, here we have a short circuit between the two extremities of the theosophical structure that skips the intervening *sefirot*. Likewise, when dealing with the syntagm *Keter Malkhut*, Isaiah Horowitz writes, in a rather historiosophical manner, that the beginning contained the end, insofar as the storage and revelation of the primordial light unfolds in a context of a circular theology: "In the future, its end will be fixed in its beginning and its beginning fixed in its end, namely, and God will say 'let there be light,'[443] as at the beginning of creation, it [the light] was stored, and it will be revealed at the end, and the end is fixed in its beginning, the beginning of thought is the end of action."[444]

The uroboric position is thus regarded as the ideal, to be attained only in the future, not as an ontological given. Even though a gender dimension is not explicit here, the very resort to *Malkhut* in this context suffices in order to illustrate the phase one and three of the model we discuss here. There is a clear connection between the circular theosophy and an interpretation of the pseudo-Aristotelian dictum, both presented as an explanation of the phrase *Keter Malkhut,* understood in a theosophical manner as referring to a polarity of divine powers. These passages, like Cordovero's, neglect most of the *sefirot* when referring to the specific affinities between the first and last *sefirah*, *Keter* and *Malkhut.* Horowitz's work enjoyed a very wide audience, especially in the Ashkenazi communities, thus disseminating a view of the privileged status of the Female. In conclusion, one can trace the significant impact of Cordovero's views about the special status of the Female on a variety of influential Jewish works. His views and those of his followers are representative of a major school in theosophical Kabbalah.

Sefirot," 247–248.

442 *Shnei Luḥot ha-Berit*, 2, fol. 201a:

יוד' במילואה, וזהו סוד עשר ספירות מלמעלה למטה באור הישר, ועשר מלמטה למעלה באור החוזר, בסוד נעוץ תחילתו בסופו.

443 Genesis 1: 3.

444 *Shnei Luḥot ha-Berit*, 2, fol. 54a:

כתר מלכות: ולעתיד נעוץ סופו בתחלתו ותחלתו בסופו, דהיינו 'ויאמר אלהים יהי אור' שבתחלת הבריאה נגנז ויתגלה בסוף, והסוף נעוץ בהתחלת ראשית המחשבה סוף המעשה.

8 R. Isaac Luria Ashkenazi, His Kabbalist and Sabbatean Followers

"And She will ascend up to the Head"

וְתִיסַק עַד רֵישָׁא

R. Isaac Luria's "Hymn to Sabbath."

One of Cordovero's many disciples, R. Isaac Luria Ashkenazi [1534–1572] – better known by the acronym *ha-'Ari,* namely, the divine R. Isaac – became even more famous than Cordovero or any other of his disciples. Several months after Cordovero's death in 1570, Luria and his own disciples succeeded in articulating a basically different type of theosophy, which comprises a more comprehensive, variegated, and voluminous literature than the Cordoverian one. The extensive corpus of Lurianic Kabbalah – only a very small part of which was authored by Luria himself – is significantly less inclusive of earlier Kabbalistic views and much closer to the anthropomorphic theosophy of some parts of the *Zohar.* One the one hand, Luria and his disciples were more concerned with philosophy in general than with the pseudo-Aristotelian dictum, and in the theosophies elaborated in the Lurianic corpus of writings, feminine divine powers play an important role.[445] On the other hand, these writings were deeply concerned with the imagery of the three divine heads constituting the highest divine sphere and with the Female as emerging from the highest among these three, as hinted at in the theosophy of some parts of the Zoharic literature. As the scholarly view of the ontological marginality of the Female and the theory of an alleged reintegration of the Female into the Male are based mainly on Lurianic Kabbalah, a more detailed analysis of this Kabbalistic

---

445 The secondary literature on this Kabbalistic school is vast. Let me mention first the most pertinent studies for our topic. See, e.g., Ronit Meroz, "Redemption in the Lurianic Teaching" (Hebrew), 208–211, 230, 242, 246; Yoram Jacobson, "The Aspect of the 'Feminine' in the Lurianic Kabbalah," 239–255; Devorah ben David Gamlieli, *Psychoanalysis and Kabbalah: The Masculine and Feminine in Lurianic Kabbalah* (Hebrew); or Idel, "Ascensions, Gender and Pillars," 55–108. For a fine English monograph see Fine, *Physician of the Soul.* See also Yehuda Liebes, "Two Young Roes of a Doe. The Secret Sermon of Isaac Luria prior to his Death" (Hebrew); Meroz, "Redemption in the Lurianic Teaching," and Shaul Magid, *From Metaphysics to Midrash, Myth, History, and the Interpretation of Scripture in Lurianic Kabbalah.* For Wolfson's views on the topic, see the next footnote and in nn. 508, 483, and his "Engenderment," 212, 215, n. 38, and "Constructions of the Shekhinah," 60–61, n.153.

https://doi.org/10.1515/9783110599800-008

school is pertinent.[446] To be sure, this does not mean that this school of Kabbalah is homogenous, as the major ramification of R. Israel Saruk demonstrates.[447]

In an interesting passage, Luria, or perhaps his primary student R. Ḥayyim Vital, decodes the Hebrew consonants of the noun *'EleH* [those] in the verse of Isaiah 40: 26: "Who created those?" as referring to the three highest divine heads, namely, supreme configurations found in the highest divine realm, as follows: *'E*, the first head, *L*, the head that is not known, and *H*, the third head that is the occult brain, known as *'Attiqa' Qaddisha'*. *MiY* [Who] – which together with

---

446 See Wolfson, *Circle in the Square*, 116–121 and, following him, Shaul Magid, "Constructing Women from Men: The Metaphysics of Male Homosexuality Among Lurianic Kabbalists in Sixteenth-Century Safed," 4–28, especially 8, n. 11, where he emphasizes the alleged marginality of the role attributed by Luria to feminine elements! See also "Constructing Women from Men," 22–23, n. 66. This and his other studies show no evidence that he checked the Lurianic texts translated and interpreted by Wolfson; yet he relies uncritically on the findings related to the gender theory. Moreover, he shows no awareness of the existence of serious critics of the phallocentric gender theories such as, e.g., in Mopsik's studies, or Abrams's *The Female Body of God*; Daniel Abrams, "'A Light of Her Own': Minor Kabbalistic Traditions on the Ontology of the Divine Feminine," 7–29; Garbs, "Gender and Power in Kabbalah," or Shifra Asulin's studies. Compare also to a similar adherence to the unqualified phallocentric understanding of Kabbalah in Sarah Pessin, "Loss, Presence and Gabirol's Desire: Medieval Jewish Philosophy and the Possibility of a Feminist Ground," 33–34, 39. If she were not limited to exposure to the artificially imposed phallocentric "theory" but was more familiar with certain Kabbalistic texts, she would easily find the Female at the summit of the theosophical system, in a manner reminiscent of ibn Gabirol's understanding of the hypostatic hyle. See also the studies mentioned below in nn. 466, 906.

It is unnecessary to counteract the claim of an alleged marginalization of the Female, and I recommend that an uninformed reader read a part of the most widespread Lurianic text, sung widely in some Orthodox Jewish circles on Sabbath eve: the first song he composed for the three meals of Sabbath. The part pertinent to our discussion can be perused conveniently in an English translation in Scholem, *On the Kabbalah and its Symbolism*, 143–145. For a Hebrew translation of the Aramaic text and a detailed commentary, see Liebes, "The Songs for the Sabbath-Meals Written by the Holy Ari," 540–455. Another introduction to the importance of the *Shekhinah* relative to other topics is by reading the widespread seventeenth century book *Ḥesed le-'Avraham* by R. Abraham Azulai, a compendium of Cordoverian thought, where the *Shekhinah* plays a central role. In any case, the early Luria resorted many times to the polarity of masculinity versus femininity. See his *Commentary to Sifra' di-Tzeniu'ta'* (Hebrew), in ed. J. Avivi, in his *Kabbalat ha-Ari*, (Makhon Ben Zvi, Jerusalem, 2008), 2: 947, 948, 949, 951, 953, 954, 965, 1005–1006. Moreover, the so-called amendments of the configurations of Rachel and Leah, conceived of as two divine Females, as part of the Lurianic practice of the widespread *Tiqqun Ḥatzot*, militate in quite a different direction, and I would warmly recommend in this context reading Shaul Magid's earlier essay "Conjugal Union, Mourning and Talmud Torah in R. Isaac Luria's *Tikkun Hazot*," written before the ascent of the phallocentric theory. See also Idel, *Messianic Mystics*, 220, and Wolfson, "Gender and Heresy in the Study of Kabbalah," 260, n. 139.

447 See also my *Il male primordiale*, 266–299, or Liebes, *On Sabbateanism and its Kabbalah*, 310, n. 79.

'*Eleh* constitutes the word '*Elohim*, and also generated another *MiY*, as the plene writing of *M* is *M-M* and of *Y* is *Y-WD* [*WD* = 10].[448] Then the Kabbalist writes: "The end of the action is called '*Elohim*, and it is *Malkhut*, and the beginning of thought is '*Elohim*."[449] This identification of *Malkhut* with the first in Thought is reminiscent of what we have seen in Cordovero's text in the previous chapter, and She is also seen as the last divine power. Interestingly, Vital understands the role of *Tziytziyt*, as referring to Thought, while *Malkhut* is referred to by action, by dint of Her being the first in thought and last in action.[450]

The pre-axial aspect is found in Luria's own *Commentary to 'Idra' Zutta'*, an important theosophical treatise in the Zoharic literature; when dealing with configurations in the highest part of the sefirotic realm, the Head is conceived as the source of the Female.[451] We shall discuss only some of the lengthy series of Lurianic texts that put into relief the sublime status of the Female in comparison to other *sefirot*. All of them reveal the profound impact of the theory of divine configurations, countenances, or heads, especially of the three supernal heads, as found in the Zoharic composition '*Idra' Zutta'*.[452]

We shall next examine one of the few Kabbalistic documents authored by Luria himself, followed by a discussion of parallels in other Lurianic texts:

> And the Head that is higher than the two other [heads], which is called the "Supernal Head that is not known,"[453] is higher than the nine *sefirot*[454] mentioned earlier and together

---

448 Although it is not obvious in this context, *MiY* stands in many Kabbalistic texts for the third *sefirah*, *Binah*.

449 R. Hayyim Vital, *Sefer ha-Liqqutim*, Genesis ch. 1, 14.

450 R. Hayyim Vital, *Peri 'Etz Ḥayyim*, fol. 17c:

כי הציצית נקראין תשמישי מצוה, שמאירין אל הנוקבא, הנקראת מצה. ציצית, שהוא משמש לשכינה, בסוד תחלת המחשבה סוף מעשה.

451 See above, in the passage from *Ra'aya' Meheimna'*, printed in *Zohar* I, fol. 24a, referred also above in n. 261 regarding the ascent of the *Shekhinah* to the head of all the heads. Luria, was more inclined than Cordovero to discussions of the theosophy of the *Idra'*. The latter inclined toward the orientation of *Tiqqunei Zohar*, which deals with the plight of the Female. See also Roi, *Love of the Shekhinah*, 252, n. 59.

452 See *Zohar* III, fols. 288a, 289b, Matt, *The Zohar, Pritzker edition*, 9: 774, n. 23, 24, 786–787, n. 58. For the views about the divine configurations in Zoharic literature, see Sobol, *Transgression of the Torah and the Rectification of God*, 14–24, 143–174. See also Jonathan Benarrosh, "An Edition of Early Versions of *Idra Zuta* and an Unknown Hebrew Translation from Ms. Vatican 226, copied in 1311" (Hebrew), 157–247.

453 This head is identifiable with the Infinite in some Lurianic texts.

454 The nine lights or *sefirot* that emerge from the supernal light called *Botzina' de-Qardinuta'* as discussed in '*Idra' Zutta'* cf. *Zohar* III, fol. 295a. See the parallels mentioned in Matt's translation of this treatise in *The Zohar, Pritzker edition*, 9: 772, nn. 19, 20.

with It the ten absolute *sefirot* are completed. And behold the aspect of *Malkhut*[455] has not been mentioned and neither revealed in those nine original [*shorshiyyot*] *sefirot*. However, *Malkhut* is revealed afterwards from the secret of that "Supernal Head that is not known," which stands higher than the nine, above-mentioned original *sefirot*. And by this you should understand the [high] rank and the grandeur of *Malkhut*, as 'She is the diadem on the head of the Righteous,'[456] "She is the cornerstone"[457] who in the Time to Come will be greater than the sun.[458]

The primary claim here is that the Female, referred to as both *Malkhut* and *'Atarah* and in relation to the masculine, righteous, is found already in the highest of the three divine Heads, one that is virtually identical with the Infinite according to the theosophy stemming from the *Idra'* literature. The theory of three heads first appears in Kabbalah in *Idra' Zutta'*, although the contemporary thirteenth century Kabbalist, R. Abraham Abulafia expresses a similar view.[459] His book *Sefer ha-'Ot* was written in

---

455 The precise meaning of aspect here is questionable. Compare to R. Hayyim Vital's *Sefer ha-Heziyonot*, 186, where this aspect is related to *'Attiq Yomin* and to the encompassing light. See also Wolfson, "Engenderment," 212, n. 28.

456 BT., *Berakhot*, fol. 17a. This statement should be compared to the feeling of the presence of the *Shekhinah* on the head while in this world, cf. BT., *Qiddushin*, fol. 31a. Compare to Wolfson, "Engenderment," 212, where he claims that the image of the diadem on the head of the husband, cf. Proverbs 12:4, and on the head of the righteous, refer unqualifiedly to the restoration of the split male androgyne within the divine structure.

457 Psalms 118: 22.

458 R. Hayyim Vital, *Sha'ar Ma'amarei Rashby*, 236–237:

והראש העליונה על שתיהן שהיא הנקראת רישא עלאה דלא אתידע היא למעלה מן התשעה ספי' הנז' ועמה נשלמין לעשר ספירות גמורות והנה בחינת המלכות לא נזכרה ולא נתגלית באלו התשעה ספי' השרשיות אמנם אח"ך נגלית המלכות מסוד האי רישא עלאה דלא אתידע העומדת למעלה מן התשעה ספירו' שרשיות הנז'. ובזה תבין מעלת וגדולת המלכות כי היא עטרה בראש צדיק היתה לראש פינה אשר לעתיד תהיה גדולה מן השמש.

In my opinion, Vital's text cited here and another one he preserved that is mentioned below in this footnote convey a much better representation of Lurianic Kabbalah than the text adduced by Wolfson and interpreted phallocentrically; the latter, moreover, is more comprehensible in the context of the texts dealt with here. For the theme of the Female of *'Arikh 'Anppin*, see Vital's *Sha'ar ha-Kavvanot*, fol. 23a, in particular fol. 24a:

ואמנם לפי שזווג א"א נעלם מאד כי הרי אין בחינ' נקבה נזכר אצלו בפירוש אלא בהעלם גדול וע"כ נעלם זווג א"א במקום הזה ואין אנו מזכירין רק זווג דאו"א.

"Indeed, as the intercourse of *'Arikh 'Anppin* is a very hidden one, as the aspect of the Female is not mentioned explicitly, but in a very occult manner, and this is the reason why the intercourse of *'Arikh 'Anppin* in this place in hidden, and we do not mention or refer but to the lower intercourse of '*Abba*' and '*Imma*'." To be sure, mentioning hidden intercourse does not mean absent or being masculinized.

459 See n. 452 above. See Abulafia's assumption that there are three supernal heads stemming from the *sefirah* of *Keter* in his *Sefer ha-'Ot* in A. Jellinek, ed. "Abraham Abulafia, *Sefer ha-Ot*": *Jubelschrift zum 70. Geburtstag des Prof. H. Graetz*, 71. The theme of the three-headed God is found also in Hinduism in the form of the deity Trimurti.

Sicily between 1285–1288, after a long period of absence from the Iberian Peninsula, and he plausibly was aware of the existence of the theory of three heads in the highest divine sphere in Spain before 1273, the last year that he was in Castile or in Spain in general. The earlier nexus between a supreme divine head and the divine feminine, which we discussed in chapter 5, is addressed by Luria/Vital in the framework of a theosophy that is different from Cordovero's and thus qualifies the three-phases model in a significant manner. Interestingly, perhaps unconsciously, a feminine adjective and verb qualify the grammatically masculine term *Rosh* – head. The preeminence of the Female, *Malkhut,* is evident, both in the primordial past and in the eschatological future, when She is depicted as even transcending the light of the Sun, namely the Male, as Her Husband. Her description in the eschaton as higher than the sun is indicative of the *imaginaire* of Her grandeur. From this point of view, Luria's claim transcends even the positive attitude toward Her in Cordovero's Kabbalah.

This text became paradigmatic in this type of Kabbalistic literature: a significant series of other Lurianic Kabbalists similarly address Her superiority in comparison to the nine *sefirot*. For example, in similar terms, Luria's principal disciple, the famous Kabbalist R. Ḥayyim Vital Calabrese, cites Luria's oral teaching:

> Once I heard from my teacher, blessed be his memory, that those nine *sefirot* … and that what I have heard from my teacher, blessed be his memory, on this issue that: Behold, you should know that we have interpreted first that the nine original *sefirot*,[460] [together] with the head that is not known and they are the ten original [*sefirot*] and the source of the entire [realm of] emanation. However, the topic of the existence of the *sefirah* of *Malkhut* has not been revealed yet, but we shall interpret first that "the head that is not known" and by it you shall understand the rank of *Malkhut*, as She is the diadem on the head of the righteous and "She is the cornerstone,"[461] and in the future, Her light will be greater than the sun … and behold that *Malkhut* of *'Arikh 'Anppin* was not discernible as it has been commented upon in the introduction to the commentary on *'Idra' Zutta'* as in *'Arikh 'Anppin* there were only nine *sefirot* from *Keter* to *Yesod* as the head that is not known is an aspect of *'Attiq* and *'Arikh 'Anppin*" remained with nine *sefirot* alone but from the light of the expansion of *Netzaḥ, Hod,* and *Yesod* within *'Arikh 'Anppin* thence the aspect of *Malkhut* of *'Arikh 'Anppin* emerged. Thus, the ten *sefirot* have been completed in it and from it you should understand that always the aspect of *Malkhut* is higher than the Male that is higher than Her, and this is the reason why She is called[462] "the diadem of Her husband."[463]

---

460 According to another version, it is written *neqqudot*, the points. See n. 496 below.

461 Psalms 118: 22.

462 Proverbs 12: 4. Compare, however, the inverse interpretation offered by Wolfson, "Engenderment," 214, to a view of R. Efrayyim Penzieri, one of the students of R. Hayyim Vital, who uses the verse from Proverbs in a manner quite similar to that of his teacher.

463 *'Etz Ḥayyim*, Gate 13: ch. 2:

פ"א שמעתי ממורי ז"ל כי הט"ס הנ"ל... זה מה ששמעתי ממורי ז"ל בענין זה והוא דע כי הנה ביארנו תחלה כי הט"ס המקוריות (נ"א הנקודות) עם רדל"א והם י"ס מקוריות ושרשיות לכל האצילות אבל ענין מציאת ספי' המלכות

The occurrence of the diadem theme as related to the Female that is higher than the Male is quite obvious in the two passages quoted thus far. The first one depicts Her neither as totally absent from the highest Configurations or heads nor as "alone" within the structure of nine *sefirot*; rather, She is only together with *Yesod*, namely, as the feminine dimension of the masculine divine potency. Moreover, here, too, the Kabbalist distinguished between two phases of the Female: the primordial and the eschatological constitute the two phases in the three-phases model. In both passages, She is understood as related to the highest aspects of the divinity, higher than the nine *sefirot* that emerged before Her. Perhaps, we have here an implicit use of the pseudo-Aristotelian dictum under scrutiny, as Her appearance from the higher divine head is later. Whether the "Head that is not known" is to be viewed in the context of Thought is not clear.

The sun is indubitably a reference to the Male, and the future elevation and brilliance of *Malkhut* is conspicuous proof of Her sublime status, at least in the soteriological future, when She will transcend the Male, *Ze'yir Anppin*, although She transcended Him on the basis of the supreme status of Her source.[464] The final statement in Vital's *'Etz Hayy*im bolsters our thesis: the verse from Proverbs as to the relationship between wife and husband has been interpreted univocally as referring to Her supremacy, not Her absorption in an androgyne unit, and this supremacy is evident also in various ways in a series of earlier texts.[465]

As mentioned earlier, this view of the supremacy of the Moon/Feminine over the Sun appears already in some Kabbalistic texts from the mid-thirteenth century.[466] Last but not least: Luria was very fond of the anthropomorphic aspects of the higher entities in the divine realm, conceived of as countenances and heads, following as he was the theosophy found in the Zoharic *Sifra' di-Tzeni'uta'*, a book on which he wrote a commentary, and the two theosophical compositions called *Idrot*. There the concept of the *matqela'*, the necessary equilibrium between the masculine and feminine elements in the theosophical structure, is a principle

---

לא נתגלה עדיין עתה אמנם נבאר תחלת הכל האי רדל"א ובזה תבין מעלת מלכות כי היא עטרה בראש צדיק והיתה לראש פנה ויהיה לעתיד אורה גדולה מן השמש...והנה המלכות דא"א לא היתה ניכרת כמבואר אצלינו בהקדמת ביאור אדר"ז כי לא היה בא"א רק ט"ס מכתר עד יסוד כי רדל"א הוא בחי' עתיק ונשאר א"א בבחי' ט"ס לבד אבל מן האור של התפשטות נה"י דע"י המתלבשין בא"א משם נעשה בחי' המלכות דא"א ונשלמו בו י"ס ובזה תבין איך לעולם בחי' המלכות גדולה מהזכר העליון ממנה ולכן נקראת עטרת בעלה.

For the term מקוריות in the context of divine attributes, see also R. Nathan of Gaza's *Sefer ha-Beriy'ah*, ms. Berlin, 8° 3077, fols. 12b, 14a.

464 For the background of aggrandizing Her light, see discussions in my "The Divine Female and the Mystique of the Moon."

465 See below, n. 736.

466 See above, beside n. 144 and see also below, n. 472. Strangely, this interesting passage did not figure in the discussions related to Wolfson's phallocentric theory.

that informs the stable processes of emanation, which otherwise cannot persist.[467] Such an equilibrium is also found elsewhere: "The last point *Malkhut* ... and the peak of her growth is that she will include all her ten *sefirot* and she will be in a face-to-face position with *Ze`ir `Anppin*, totally equal, and the two kings[468] will use the same crown."[469] [This is just one of the many instances in which the equality between the feminine and the masculine divine powers is described as taking place during the daily theosophical process.

In another work, *Mevo' She'arim*, R. Hayyim Vital expresses a view similar to the one cited above, depicting the presence of the Female in the context of various supernal heads:

> And, behold, the aspect of *Malkhut* that is revealed alone[470] is not found in *'Arikh 'Anppin* alone, but only the aspect of *'Ateret* of *Yesod* within it, as all this is Male ... but the Female in a concrete manner is not found ... and so, too, in the [configuration of] *'Attiq Yomin*, the Female is not found by Herself, solely as the *'Ateret* of *Yesod* of the *'Attiq* is the Female, just as in *'Arikh 'Anppin*. However, afterwards, *Malkhut* **is revealed from the secret of the Head that is higher than all** [the heads] and it is not known, which is called *'Attiq Yomin* that is higher than all those nine *sefirot* of *'Arikh 'Anppin*, and this is the prooftext "the valorous wife is the diadem of Her Husband,"[471] which will be in the Time to Come **greater than the sun**, "and She will be the cornerstone."[472]

The allusion to the verse from Proverbs is especially interesting because it refers not to the head of the Husband, namely, *Tiferet* but to the highest divine Head, which, implicitly at least, is depicted as Her husband. *Malkhut* is juxtaposed here to the *'Ateret ha-Yesod*, the latter feminine power being dependent on the *Yesod*,

---

467 *Sifra' di-Tzeni'uta'*, printed in *Zohar*, vol. II, fol. 176b, translated in Matt, *The Zohar*, 5: 535. On the concept of *Matqela'*, see Liebes, *Sections in the Zohar Lexicon*, 329–330 and Wolfson, "Woman, The Feminine as Other in Theosophic Kabbalah," 183–184.

468 *BT. Hullin*, fol. 60b.

469 `*Etz Hayyim*, Gate 36, ch. 1: שהיא נקדה מלכות האחרונה שבה כנ"ל ותכלית גידול שלה הוא שיהיה בה
כל הי"ס שלה ותהיה עם ז"א פב"פ שוה לגמרי וישתמשו ב' מלכים בכתר א'.

470 Namely, as a separate *sefirah*, not as a feminine dimension of the *sefirah* of *Yesod*. This is the reason why one should not confound different states of feminine components of the divine world.

471 Proverbs 12: 4.

472 Vital, *Mevo' She'arim*, 95:
והנה בחינת מלכות נגלית לבדה לא נמצאת בא"א לבדה רק בחי' עטרת היסוד שבו כי כל זה הוא דכורא... אך נוקבא
ממש לא נמצאת וכן בעתיק יומין לא נמצא בחי' נוקבא בפני עצמה רק עטרת היסוד דעתיק היא נוקבא כמו בא"א.
אמנם אח"כ נתגלית... נמצאת המלכות מסד האי רישא עילאה מכולהו דלא אתיידע שהוא הנקרא עתיק יומן שהוא
למעלה מכל אלו הט"ס דא"א ח"ס אשת חיל עטרת בעלה אשר תהיה לעתיד לבא גדולה מן השמש היתה לראש פינה.
Emphasis added. Describing the moon's light as greater than that of the sun may reflect the view found already in the mid-thirteenth century. See n. 466 above.

while the former is conceived of as higher than the supernal Husband. Only this version relates the diadem to the supernal Head, not to the righteous, as in the passage of Luria, and in the one noted below from R. Naftali Bakharakh's book. Needless to say, according to those passages, the Female will not be obliterated in the future, but She or Her light will be enhanced even more than the Male's. An explicitly restorative view as to the ascent of the Female is evident elsewhere in R. Ḥayyim Vital's writing: "Behold, the angels do not know the place from which She has been hewn, when *Malkhut* ascends to the Infinite, as She is higher than they."[473] The "place" that is found with the Infinite will become a motif in R. Nathan of Gaza's theosophy, as we shall see below.

A very similar passage occurs also in a mid-seventeenth century classic of Lurianic Kabbalah, R. Naftali ben Jacob Elhanan Bakharakh's *Sefer ʿEmeq ha-Melekh*, which adopted a variety of themes from R. Israel Sarug's special version of Lurianism[474]:

> Nine *sefirot* of *Malkhut*, the original ones [*meqoriyyot*],[475] are found in "the supernal Head that it is not known," and the existence of *Malkhut* was not revealed yet. However, afterwards, *Malkhut* was revealed from the secret of that "Head that is not known" and because of it, you should understand the grandeur of *Malkhut* that is "the diadem on the head of the righteous," "and She became the cornerstone",[476] and so it will be also in the future, [She will be] greater than the sun.[477]

The evident repetition of some of the main components in the four last passages represents a skeleton of the three-phases model with a few variations. One of them is the repetition of "the head that is not known," which is not found in the two other versions of this passage. I consider this a mistake, which can be corrected by a comparison to the earlier passages adduced above, which precede Bakharakh chronologically. In the earlier texts, the Female's grandeur derives

---

473 *Shaʿar Maʾamarei Rashby*, 21: הנה המלאכים בעלות המלכות למקום שחוצבה עד אין סוף אין יודעים מקומה כי גבהה מהם

474 About him and his Kabbalistic thought, see Liebes, "On the Image, the Writings, and the Kabbalah of the author of 'Emeq ha-Melekh,'" 131–157; Eliezer Baumgarten, "Comments on Rav Naftali Bachrach's Usage of Pre-Lurianic Sources" (Hebrew), 1–23; Sharron Shatil, "The Doctrine of Secrets in *Emek ha-Melekh*," 358–395.

475 Compare to Nathan of Gaza's *Sefer ha-Beriyʾah*, ms. Berlin, 8° 3077, fol. 37a.

476 Psalms 118: 22.

477 R. Naftali Bakharakh, *ʿEmeq ha-Melekh*, Gate 16, ch. 67, fol. 162a:

כי תשעה ספירות מלכות מקוריות הם ברישא עילאה דלא אתידע עלייהו, והנה מציאות מלכות לא נתגלית עדיין, אמנם אחר כך נתגלית מלכות מסוד האי רישא עילאה דלא אתידע. ובזה תבין ענין מעלת מלכות, כי היא עטרה בראש צדיק, היתה לראש פינה, ותהיה גם כן לעתיד לבוא גדולה מן השמש.

from her emerging from a higher head than the nine *sefirot*. Based on the earlier passages, it should be understood here, too, that *Malkhut* emerges from a higher theosophical level in comparison to the phallic power = *Yesod*, Male = *Tiferet*, or even to the Father = *Hokhmah*, which belong to the realm of the nine *sefirot*. Her belated manifestation is not a matter of inferiority but, on the contrary, of superiority that is determined by the elevated ontological status of Her source, the "head that is not known." In any case, elsewhere this Kabbalist speaks about the *Malkhut* of "the Head that is not known."[478]

Bakharakh adopted a circular theosophy, while polemicizing with Cordovero's rejection of the same in *Pardes Rimmonim*, apparently unaware of other passages to the contrary discussed above. He promised to write an entire treatise on this topic, but, unfortunately, he did not do so or it was not found.[479] In the short discussion, Bakharakh quotes anonymous "ancient Kabbalists" who, according to him, said, "All the *sefirot* are in a circle."[480] In this context, he adduces a diagram of a circle where the ten *sefirot* are on the circumference, indicating that he revisited the thirteenth century uroboric theory. In this context, he also mentions R. Abraham Abulafia's "Book of the Circle," which allegedly adopted this view.[481] He claims, however, that this was indeed the status of the *sefirot* when they were within the first *sefirah*, before they were revealed in the anthropomorphic structure. He asserted that this topic was unknown to Cordovero, who debated it, but it was hinted at later by R. Isaac Luria. Bakharakh depicted his understanding of the Lurianic view in another diagram in his book that arranged the *sefirot* in a different kind of circular diagram, related to the type of *sefirot* that circumvent the primordial "world of *Tehiru*," namely, the space that *tzimtzum* generated, where the *reshimu*, namely, the

---

478 *'Emeq ha-Melekh*, Gate 7: 11, fol. 44d:

נתקנו תלת רישין, ובפרט רישא דלא איתידע עצמו, עם מלכות.

See also the interesting discussion *'Emeq ha-Melekh*, Gate 8: 8, fol. 46b.

479 *'Emeq ha-Melekh*, Gate 6, ch. 8, fol. 15d.

480 *'Emeq ha-Melekh*, fol. 15d-16ac:

שאמרו המקובלים הקדמונים ז"ל שהספירות הן כלם בעיגול

481 *'Emeq ha-Melekh*:

ובדרך זה דרך רבי אברהם מבולעפי"א [!] בספר הגלגל שלו

Most of his discussion has been copied in the anonymous Lurianic-Sarugian text, which is a late elaboration of an earlier Lurianic text, and was printed as *Ma'ayan ha-Hokhmah* (Koretz, 1784), fol. 1ab, found also in several manuscripts. See, e.g., Ms. New York, Columbia X 893 L 97393, fol. 1b. The printed text quotes Abulafia's book as *Sefer ha-Gilgulim*, which is evidently a mistake. On other instances where a "Book of the Circle" was mentioned in the name of Abulafia, see M. Idel, *The Writings and the Doctrines of Abraham Abulafia*, 1: 62–63, and see also Baumgarten, "Comments on Rav Naftali Bachrach's," 10. See also above, n. 403. For the various editions and printing of this treatise see Avivi, *Kabbalat ha-Ari*, 2: 564–568.

vestiges of the divine lights remained after the retreat of the divine.[482] In any case, this discussion and diagram show, graphically, that within the circle found in *Keter* the female was already present, near the first *sefirah*. The existence of the two diagrams in this classical Kabbalistic text, in print since 1648, thus constitutes the surge of the circular theosophy in the mid-seventeenth century.

Although it is difficult to speak about Lurianic Kabbalah as a unified field conceptually, it suffices to see here the stable elements that indicate the sublime root of the Female. The occurrence of the diadem theme as related to the Female that is higher than the Male is worth noting. The Female is depicted not as totally absent from other high Configurations or heads but as not "being alone" there, which means that She is found only together with *Yesod*.

In all those texts, the Female emerges from the highest layer of divinity, and the negation of the existence of feminine dimensions in the nine lower points does not signify the absence of the Female at a higher level. A similar discussion occurs in a text of R. Hayyim Vital: "And, indeed, provided the intercourse of 'Arikh 'Anppin is very hidden, as the aspect of the Female was not mentioned explicitly, but in a greatly esoteric manner, and the intercourse of 'Arikh 'Anppin is hidden in this place, [and] we know only the intercourse of 'Abba' and 'Imma.'"[483]

Although there is no negation of the ontological existence of the Female in the highest pleromatic entity, an epistemological problem exists: The supreme level of the divine head is not purely masculine; it contains also a Female, who is found in a state of intercourse with the Male, although this event remains transcendental to the Kabbalistic discourse, namely hidden to human cognition, unlike that of the relationship between Father and Mother.

The three-phases model is evident also in the works of R. Moshe Yonah (his Italian family name was Colombo), another important member of R. Isaac Luria's small Kabbalistic group, who wrote:

> Because the point of *Malkhut* is found now in the place of the head of 'Arikh 'Anppin as in this place Her root[484] is, and She was hewn from there.... Therefore, as here, the head of 'Arikh 'Anppin is Her place, we have the power to elevate Her by our good deeds and our

---

482 *'Emeq ha-Melekh*, Gate 5, ch. 4, fol. 14c.

483 For the theme of the Female of 'Arikh 'Anppin, see Vital's *Sha'ar ha-Kavvanot*, fol. 23a, in particular fol. 24a:

ואמנם לפי שזווג א"א נעלם מאד כי הרי אין בחינ' נקבה נזכר אצלו בפירוש אלא בהעלם גדול וע"כ נעלם זווג א"א במקום הזה ואין אנו מזכירין רק זווג דאו"א.

See also the Moroccan Kabbalist R. Shalom Buzaglo, *Hod Melekh*, fol. 203ab and above, n. 375. Compare, however, to the opposite view presented in Wolfson, *Language, Eros, Being*, 179–180, 182.

484 The term "root" that occurs in many cases in referring to the sublime source of the Female is part of the model we discuss here. See also below, the sentence cited from R. Nathan of Gaza's

prayers, which we pray with *Kavvanah,* [in order] to elevate *Malkhut* upward to the place of *'Arikh 'Anppin,* as you should know in accordance to the elevation of Sabbath [by the help of God?], as this is Her place, where She was at the beginning.[485]

Here the three phases are explicit, and the theurgical operation of the Kabbalists plays a central role. I attribute conceptual fluidity to the Kabbalists, and I doubt the existence of a unified Lurianic theology. In the specific case discussed above, however, the sublime status of the Female is quite evident and stable in this theosophy, at least in terms of the examples I cited from major exponents of this lore. In this context let me mention again the interpretation of Luria's hymn to Sabbath as mentioning the ascent of *Malkhut* to the head, as *'Attiqa',* as indicated in the previous chapter.

The supreme source of the divine feminine may help in understanding Her superiority versus the Male in the eschaton. According to Vital:

> You should know that all the lights surround all the above-mentioned particulars that are comprised in the Male and the Female, all are an aspect of the light of the *Binah* that surrounds the Sons ... and now the light that surrounds them is the light of *Binah.* But in the Time to Come, "God will create something new on earth"[486] as the Female of *Ze'yir 'Anppin* that is *Malkhut* "will surround the Male" in the manner that *Binah* surrounds it now, and the reason is that *Malkhut* will ascend higher than *Ze'yir 'Anppin,* according to the secret[487] "the Righteous sit and their Diadems on their heads."[488]

Sefer ha-Beriy'ah. For "place" in this context, see also his view referred to in n. 506 below. See also the references to "root" in his book, in some quotes below in this chapter.

485 *Kanfei Yonah,* Ms. Sasson 993, 35:

כי להיות הנקודה של מלכו' עתה במקום ראש אריך אנפין, שבמקום זה הוא שורשה וחציבותה...שנקודת כתר היתה כלולה מעשה. אם כן, מאחר שבכאן במקום ראש אריך אנפין הוא מקומה יש כח לנו במעשינו הטובים וגם בתפלותינו, אשר אנו מתפללים בכונה, להעלות את המלכות למעלה עד מקום אריך אנפין, כמו שתדע בסוד העלאת שבת ב"ה, להיות שזהו מקומה אשר היתה שמה בתחילה.

The manuscript is an autograph. The text was already printed by Ronit Meroz, *Redemption in the Lurianic Teachings,* 174, and see also in that work, 208–211 and Ada Rapoport-Albert, *Women and the Messianic Heresy of Sabbetai Zevi, 1666–1816,* 221–222. On R. Moshe Yonah and this manuscript, see Meir Benayahu, "Rabbi Moshe Yonah, A Disciple of Luria and the First of those Who Copied His Doctrine" (Hebrew), 4: 7–74; Avivi, *Kabbalat ha-'Ari,* 1: 194–203; and Uri Safrai, "The *Kavvanot* Homilies of R. Moses Jonah" (Hebrew), 197–251, especially 240–241, speaking about the ascent of *Malkhut* to *Keter* during some parts of the Sabbath service.

486 Jeremiah 31: 21.

487 *BT. Berakhot,* fol. 17a.

488 See Vital, *'Etz Hayyim,* Gate 44, ch. 6, fol. 100b, where the "greatness" is explained in terms of the Female surrounding the Male:

דע כי כל האורות המקיפים לכל הפרטים הנזכרים הנכללים בזכר ונוקבא כולם הם בחינת אור הבינה המקיף את הבנים...ועתה אור המקיפים אותם הוא אור הבינה, אבל לעתיד לבא ברא ה' חדשה בארץ כי הנוקבא דז"א היא

The term "particulars" parallels the "Sons" and refers to the lower seven *sefirot*, surrounded in the present by the light of *Binah*. In the eschatological future, however, the last *sefirah*, the Female will ascend and then replace *Binah*, as the power that is higher than the Male and surrounds Him. We can see here that two other prooftexts – Jeremiah 31: 21 and *BT. Berakhot*, fol. 17a – refer to the higher position of the Female after ascending to a place where She is superior to Him, as the *sefirah* of *Binah* is, just as other prooftexts such as Proverbs 12: 4 do. Those views reverberate in several later Lurianic treatises and served as the starting point for additional discussions.[489]

An interesting formulation of the privileged status of the Female in the context of the pseudo-Aristotelian dictum is found in the late sixteenth–early seventeenth century famous Italian Kabbalist R. Menahem 'Azaryah of Fano, who was first a disciple of Cordovero's Kabbalah and then turned to Lurianic forms of Kabbalah, while living mostly in Venice.[490] This major Kabbalist depicts the Female in the vein of *Tiqqunei Zohar* as discussed in ch. 5, as follows: "the first from down upward, in the plain sense, and so, too, She is the first from up downward, in accordance to the secret of the beginning of the thought is the end of the action, as it is written[491] 'Many daughters are valorous but you surpassed them

---

המלכות 'תסובב את גבר' הוא כדמיון מה שעתה מסבבת אותו הבינה, והטעם כי תתעלה המלכות למעלה מן הז"א
בסוד צדיקים יושבים ועטרותיהם בראשיהם.

See also below, in ch. 11, the passage of R. Elijah of Vilna.

489 See also *Sha'ar Ma'amarei Rashby*, fols. 49c, 50d, where *Malkhut* of the high Configuration of *'Attiq Yomin* is mentioned several times and *Sha'ar Ma'amarei Rashby*, fol. 5ab, 12, where the restorative ascent of *Malkhut* to the Infinite is explicitly related to Her primordial place, together with an interesting discussion of Her being equal to Her Husband, *Tiferet*. This is also the case in a discussion found in R. Nathan Shapira of Jerusalem, *Sefer Maḥaberet ha-Qodesh*, fol. 15a, which is paralleled by a rare version of Vital's *Sefer ha-Qavvanot* as found in a manuscript that is basically a compilation, Ms. Jerusalem, Benayahu, Kabbalah 35 fol. 2a. In the name of R. Moshe Najjara, the following statement is found: "during the [prayer of] Minḥah of the eve of Sabbath, *Malkhut* ascends to Her place that She was there before She complained.להר"ם נאגרא זלה"ה דע כי. The matter of "Her return to Her place" is found במנחה דע"ש מלכות עולה למקומה שהיתה קודם הקטרוג" also elsewhere in Shapira's book. See *Sefer Maḥaberet ha-Qodesh*, fols. 136c, 138a.

490 On this Kabbalist, see also Joseph Avivi, "R. Menahem Azariah of Fano's Kabbalistic Writings" (Hebrew), 347–376, and Reuven Bonfil, "Halakhah, Kabbalah, and Society: Some Insights into Rabbi Menahem Azariah da Fano's Inner World," *Jewish Thought in the Seventeenth Century*, eds. I. Twersky, B. Septimus, (Harvard University Press, Cambridge, MA., 1987), 39–61; Bonfil, "New Information Concerning Rabbi Menahem Azariah of Fano and his Age" (Hebrew), 98–135. This Kabbalist was strongly influenced by R. Moshe Yonah's version of Lurianism.

491 Proverbs 31: 29. For the use of this verse in a similar context, see the interesting passage adduced in Abraham Azulai's *'Or ha-Ḥammah*, vol. 3 part I, fol. 24b.

all' and She is second to <u>H</u>okhmah, as it is said that She precedes the Mother, as the Father founded the Daughter."[492]

Two divine females are portrayed as directly related to the Father, and as such, higher than the masculine *sefirot* of *Tiferet* and *Yesod*. Further on in the same section, the Italian Kabbalist describes the *sefirot* as having the end in their beginning and their beginning in their end, mentioning in this context the two extremities: the Infinite and *Malkhut*.[493] Earlier in the same section, he speaks about the much earlier Kabbalistic view that *Shekhinah* is found both below and on high.[494] Further in the same treatise he speaks about the ascent of *Malkhut* to the *sefirah* of *Binah*.[495] Elsewhere, R. Menahem 'Azaryah displays another type of privileging the Female. In his booklet *Yonat 'Elem* he wrote:

> Because from the days of *'Olam ha-Tohu*,[496] *Malkhut* was in the place of the supernal head, and despite the fact that afterwards all the ten *sefirot* expanded in their full stature from his head to his feet, the *Shekhinah* did not move from the first point,[497] and She is that head, literally, as the imprint of the entire structure, and *Malkhut* has been fixed in the place of the attribute of the back that is found there, but actually it is not true to attribute back to *Keter* … and there the three heads are comprised [with]in [the head called] *'Attiqa*,'[498] and there is no distinction [there] between front and back.[499]

---

492 R. Menahem 'Azaryah of Fano, *Ma'amar Me'ah Qeshitah*, par. 18, fol. 8b:

אמרנו שהיא ראשו' ממטה למעלה כפשוטו וכן היא ראשונה ממעלה למטה בסוד תחלת המחשבה סוף המעשה דכתיב בה רבות בנות עשו עשו חיל ואת עלית על כלנה והיא שניה לחכמה כדאמרן בהיותה קודמת לאם דאבא יסד ברתא

493 *Ma'amar Me'ah Qeshitah*.

494 *Ma'amar Me'ah Qeshitah*, fol. 8a.

495 *Ma'amar Me'ah Qeshitah*, fol. 11c.

496 This is the situation of the world of discreet points in the condition before the construction of the structured supernal Anthropos, *'Adam Qadmon*. Compare to the view of Bakharakh, above, beside n. 481.

497 This is a Kabbalistic version of the rabbinic theory that the *Shekhinah* did not move from the Temple or the Wailing Wall, despite the destruction. See, e.g., *Shemot Rabbah*, 2: 2 and in R. Israel Saruk's *Limmudei ha-'Atzilut* fol. 4a. For the resort to the imagery of points in similar contexts, see below in this chapter the discussions about R. Nathan of Gaza, and in ch. 9.

498 Following the view of the *'Idra*, in *Zohar* III, fol. 288b.

499 R. Menahem 'Azaryah of Fano, *Yonat 'Elem*, fol. 32a, ch. 39:

כי מאז בעולם התהו היתה מלכות בכח במקום הראש העליון ואע"פ שנתפשטו אח"כ כל י' ספירות כמלא קומתו מראשו ועד רגליו לא זזה שכינה מן הנקודה הראשונה והיא ההוא רישא ממש כי נשאר שם הרושם מכל הכלילות ומלכות הוקבעה במקו' מדת אחורים שבו אלא שלא יצדק בעצם ליחס אחורים בכתר... וכאן כלהו תלת רישין לאת כללו בעתיקא אין שום הפרש בין פנים לאחור.

I assume that we may discern some influences of the formulations of one of Luria's disciples, R. Israel Saruk. See, e.g., n. 497 above.

The Italian Kabbalist's insistence on not only considering the source of the Female in the highest Head but also on identifying that head with the Female had a certain career in Kabbalistic literature.[500] Although he qualifies it by saying that She is situated in the back part of *Keter*, he obliterates the distinction between back and front there. In principle, this distinction would also abrogate the difference between Female and Male there, but from the specific context of the translated passage, it is not a plausible reading. In any case, R. Menahem 'Azaryah of Fano here follows the classical Lurianic texts mentioned and analyzed above, by privileging the Female in his discourse, both by mentioning Her alone, and by insisting on Her supreme source. In my opinion, Lurianic Kabbalah adopted the theory that the last, which is the Female, is higher and found within the supernal Head, thus constituting another version, more implicit, of the Kabbalistic interpretations of the pseudo-Aristotelian dictum.

These quotes from R. Menahem 'Azaryah's writings and other Lurianic texts cited earlier in this chapter can facilitate an understanding of another passage from the writings of this Kabbalist that has been misrepresented in scholarship, as part of the effort to detect a phallocentric orientation in Lurianic Kabbalah. I shall adduce the full context of a short quote that reflects the line of thought analyzed above. The following passage is a discussion of the concept of "supernal head that is not known":

> *Keter* of the point[501] that is prolonging the heights of its size, **filling the entire space that was the place of the ten points, as we explained in ch. 27,**[502] which is the world of the

---

500 Compare, however, to Bakharakh's *'Emeq ha-Melekh*, 8: 8, fol. 46c, where the Kabbalist says that the name "Head that is not known" was given to *Malkhut*, and see also *'Emeq ha-Melekh*, 16: 10, as well as above, n. 478, and R. Jacob Koppel Lipshitz, *Sha'ar Gan 'Eden*, fols. 30b, 30d, 92b. Those authors reflect the apotheosis of the Female in theosophical thought. See also below, n. 503.

501 *Yonat 'Elem*, ch. 27, fol. 22ab. The point that contains ten other points is mentioned in some texts in early Kabbalah, at least from the time of R. Azriel of Gerona. See also Vital's *Sha'ar ha-Kelalim*, ch. 1, as introduction to *'Etz Hayyim*, and the Lurianic text translated in Wolfson, *Language, Eros, Being*, 181, cited from Vital, *Liqqutim Hadashim*, 22, where the Keter is described both as a point and as comprising ten points. Compare also to Vital, *Liqqutim Hadashim*, 18–19, where *Keter* is described not only as comprising ten other points, but also ten aspects, *behinot*. Compare also to R. Jacob Koppel's discussion in *Sha'arei Gan 'Eden*, fol. 30c, where he mentions "the secret of *Malkhut* from the point of *Keter*." סוד המלכות מנקודת הכתר. See also *Sha'arei Gan 'Eden*, fol. 18d: נקודת המלכות שהיתה גנוזה באין סוף "the point of *Malkhut* that was stored within the Infinite." See also *Sha'arei Gan 'Eden*, fols. 2b, 3a. See also above, n. 345.

502 *Yonat 'Elem*, ch. 27, fol. 22b. See also the text of this Kabbalist printed by Alexander Altmann, "Notes on the Development of Rabbi Menahem Azaryah of Fano's Kabbalistic Doctrine," 262, where נקודות המלכות namely "the [ten] points of *Malkhut*" are mentioned. Thus, points are

Male, and *Malkhut* is not discernible there, but according to the secret of the *'Atarah* that is comprised in *Yesod*. **And this Configuration[503] is compounded of the seven last[504] of this Malkhut, as we shall explain below in chapter 33[505] ... and this is why "the Head that is not known" is called Place[506] of the root.**[507]

In my opinion, Vital's texts and the others adduced above in this chapter convey a better representation of Lurianic Kabbalah than the truncated passage presented by Elliot R. Wolfson in order to herald his phallocentric point. In fact, in the context of the texts dealt with here, a full citation of the section he adduced leads to a more satisfactory understanding of the passage.[508]

---

related also to the Female. The points refer to a theosophical structure of divine powers that are arranged vertically, not in an anthropomorphic structure.

503 Namely, the configuration of *Keter*, or perhaps of *'Attiqa'* "the Ancient One." See also the view of another leading seventeenth century Lurianic Kabbalist, R. Jacob Hayyim Tzemah, *'Adam Yashar*, fol. 6b, and in particular fol. 22c, where this configuration is described as containing a unified structure of Male and Female. See also above at the end of n. 228 and n. 500.

504 This is an elliptic formulation, the "last" referring in my opinion, to the last seven points.

505 *Yonat 'Elem*, ch. 33, fol. 27b–28a.

506 For place as a designation for God in ancient Jewish and rabbinic texts, see Ephraim E. Urbach, *The Sages, Their Concepts and Beliefs*, 1: 66–89; and for later discussions, see Brian P. Copenhaven, "Jewish Theologies of Space in the Scientific Revolution: Henry More, Joseph Raphson, Isaac Newton and Their Predecessors," 489–548; M. Idel, "Universalization and Integration: Two Conceptions of Mystical Union in Jewish Mysticism," 33–50. Interestingly, place, *maqom*, is understood by R. Nathan of Gaza as female, הבקן. See his *Sefer ha-Beriy'ah*, 8° 3075, fols. 11b, 12b, 16a.

507 *Yonat 'Elem*, ch. 29, fols. 24a-24b:

כתר של נקודה בהתאריך רום קומתו מלא כל החלל שהיה מקום לי' נקודות כמו שבארנו בפ' כ"ז הוא עלמא דדכורא ואין מלכות נכרת בו אלא בסוד עטרה נכללת ביסוד, ופרצוף זה נתקן מז' אחרונות של מלכות זו על דרך שנפרש לקמן בפרק לג...לפיכך נקרא רישא דלאו רישא אלא מקום שורשו.

See Wolfson, *Circle in the Square*, 119–120, and *Language, Eros, Being*, 187. For the earlier Lurianic sources of this passage, see Wolfson, *Language, Eros, Being*, 512, n. 276; see also R. Menahem 'Azaryah of Fano, *Kanfei Yonah*, 14–15. Compare, however, Wolfson, *Language, Eros, Being*, 187, where he interprets another text of the same Kabbalist to fit in with his analysis of the translated passage mentioned above. He concludes there, rather fascinatingly, that "we can speak of the female enveloping the male, which converges symbolically with the image of the female being contained in the male, that is, encompassing is a form of integration, the feminine is the crowning part of the male." Indeed, he -- "we" – can speak in such a way, because of the bias of the rigid phallocentric theory, but it is questionable whether the Kabbalist did so. Whether the act of enveloping means, to believe such a type of analysis, in fact, integration into what is encompassed, namely an inversion of its plain meaning, is a matter to be proven not just stated as if self-evident in order to defend a problematic essentialist gender theory. See also below, n. 923 and compare the characterization of Aaron Hughes to Wolfson's approach, in the introduction to *Poetic Thinking*, 4–5: "Wolfson respects the integrity of the original texts as he undertakes the task to translate their messages."

508 See above, n. 458 and especially in *Language, Eros, Being*, 183.

The zone discussed here is what happens in the highest divine manifestation, hidden as it is. This is evident from the entire chapters from which we have quoted and from the two other chapters from the same book to which he refers. As to the existence of the Female within *Keter*, we learn also from a passage in R. Joseph ibn Tabul, one of Luria's close disciples.[509]

I emphasized in bold the sentences not translated by Elliot Wolfson's rendering of the passage, which forms the basis for his subsequent analysis, dealing with the absence or the occulation of the Female. Here, as in the case of the other Lurianic texts translated above, however, the Female is not occultated, as it appears in the English translation, but actually regarded as an entity higher than the nine *sefirot*, rendering the phallocentric interpretation rather dubious, to say the least. To describe Lurianic Kabbalah on the basis of this type of presentation of the text in an English translation is, indubitably a *tour de force* but a problematic scholarly enterprise. The occultation of the Female in these Lurianic texts derives from ignoring the context and from considering R. Menahem 'Azaryah of Fano's text only in its truncated form.

This type of presentation leads to dangerous distortions in which demonstrating the validity of the "theory" becomes more important than the specific meaning of the Kabbalistic texts to be interpreted by that theory. The selective texts are quoted basically to illustrate the theory,[510] which does not take in consideration the general background in the Lurianic system or even in the writings of Fano. In any case, Fano, like Cordovero and Luria, attributes a feminine spouse to the supreme countenance of *'Arikh 'Anppin,* both found within the higher Configuration of *'Attiqa' Qaddisha'.*[511] When quoted in its fuller version, the Lurianic text that supposedly exemplifies the phallocentric view actually means the very opposite: namely, it constitutes a reference to the superior origin of the Female, from a source that transcends all the nine *sefirot*, which include the Male. I see no other way to understand the insistence on Her supernal source than pointing to Her preeminence, in comparison to lower forms of existence of the Female, as part of the constitution of the lower *sefirah* or *sefirot*. The feminine elements in Luria's system are omnipresent in the gigantic theosophical structure he forged because of their multi-functionality.

---

509 See Joseph ibn Tabul, *Commentary to 'Idra' Rabba'*, 2: 143.

510 See my *"Male and Female,"* ch. 16.

511 See *Yonat 'Elem*, fol. 35b and *Yonat 'Elem*, fols. 29a, 36a: מלכות שבכתר "*Malkhut* within *Keter*". Compare, however, the views discussed by Wolfson, "Gender and Heresy in Kabbalah," 260–261, where the existence of the Feminine in the higher divine zone is envisioned in a more unified manner.

The seventeenth-century Kabbalist, R. Jacob Hayyim Tzemah, presents – from a slightly different angle – a locative interpretation of Alqabetz's verse similar to that proposed in the previous chapter. He interprets the term *R'osh* – head – as referring to Sabbath, as the consonants following each letter, *R*, is *Sh*, *'o* [– *'Aleph* -] is *B*, and *Sh* is *T*, constitute together the word *Shabbat*; he then: "and during the Sabbath, *Malkhut* that is called Sabbath, ascends to the place of the Head."[512] Capitalizing on this gloss, the anonymous author of the early eighteenth century classic of Jewish Kabbalistic customs, probably of Sabbatean extraction, entitled *Ḥemdat Yamim,* wrote:

> ... the end of the action is the beginning of thought, which is the secret of *Malkhut*, which was stored within the essence of God, blessed be He, since by Her means it was appropriate to build worlds, as in each and every rank of the nine supernal *sefirot*, there was no need to create worlds ... but [only She] is an attribute to Him, namely the Governance and the Dominion of the King ... and this is why He actualized all the worlds solely but from the point of *Malkhut*,[513] as She is the Governance and the Dominion of the King ... and this is the secret of what has been said, "the end of action is first in thought," namely, that despite the fact that *Malkhut* is the last of the ten *sefirot*, within the [divine] Thought She nevertheless is the first, in order to create the world first.[514]

The theory of the nine *sefirot* emanated first indubitably follows the Lurianic approach as described in several earlier quoted passage.; it represents an explicit elaboration of phase one in the three-phases model. Elsewhere, the anonymous Kabbalist describes another part of Alqabetz's poem as dealing with the ascent of the husband's Diadem "up to the head."[515] He also subscribed to the uroboric

---

512 See the gloss printed in R. Hayyim Vital, *Peri 'Etz Hayyim,* fol. 94c:

מראש מקדם נסוכה, כי באלפא ביתות אותיות המאוחרין אל אותיות ראש, הם שב"ת. ובשבת עולה המלכות הנקראת שבת, במקום הראש.

Compare to the theosophic discussion preserved in *Sefer ha-Hokhmah,* the mid-thirteenth century treatise attributed to R. Eleazar of Worms as discussed above, in ch. 5, and see Scholem, *Origins of the Kabbalah,* 98, about *Malkhut* as found as a diadem on the head of God, in a context where it is depicted in conspicuously feminine terms. See also Idel, *Kabbalah & Eros,* 40–41. This is a clear contamination of *Malkhut* by the valence of '*Atarah.* See below, ch. 12.

513 It refers to the center of *Malkhut.* Compare also to Cordovero, *'Or Yaqar,* to *Tiqqunim,* 5: 11, who speaks about the point as the center of *Malkhut.*

514 *Hemdat Yamim,* vol. 1, *Shabbat,* ch. 5, fol. 41c:

סוף מעשה במחשבה תחלה הוא סוד המלכות שהיתה גנוזה בעצמותו יתברך, כי בה ראוי לבנות העולמות. לפי שבכל מדריגה ומדריגה הט' ספירות העליונות אין צריך להיות [פועל] עולמות ... אבל לא יצא לתאר לו מלכות דהיינו שלטנותא והרמנותא דמלכא...ולכן הוציא לפועל כל העולמות מן נקודת המלכות, להיות שמלכות הוא שלטנותא והרמנותא דמלכא... וזה סוד אומרו "סוף מעשה במחשבה תחלה", כלומר כי אף כי מלכות היא אחרונה שבעשר ספירות, אבל במחשבה כדי לבראות העולמים היא תחלה.

515 *Hemdat Yamim,* fol. 42b.

theosophy, writing about the custom of beginning the study of the first chapter of Genesis immediately after concluding the study of the last chapter of the Pentateuch, part of the pericope entitled *Zot ha-Berakhah*:

> This pericope refers to the last attribute that is called *Berakhah*, in order to link Her to the attribute called "the valley of *Berakhah*."[516] And immediately [the pericope] *Bereshit* [is read] in accordance with the manner of "their end is fixed in their beginning" in accordance with the [verse] "The Lord founded the earth by means of *Hokhmah*"[517] "the Father founded the Daughter" and *Bereshit* has been translated[518] "By means of *Hokhmah*."[519]

Thus, when reaching the end of the Pentateuch, someone is asked to return to the beginning, which is the meaning of *Bereshit,* a move that is motivated theosophically, namely, as moving from the last *sefirah* to the first one, utilizing the theosophy of *Tiqqunei Zohar*, as seen above. The feminine elements are hinted at by the imagery that contains feminine nouns: the Daughter, *Hokhmah*, *Berakhah*.

The importance of the above discussions, however, extends beyond the content of a restricted number of explicit discussions to the possibility that their views of the Feminine spread to other cases, as is evident in the last quoted passage. It also holds true for R. Hayyim Vital's discussion of the cult of the Moon in the section called Gate of the Head of the Month, in his influential *Peri 'Etz Hayyim*,[520] which followed much earlier traditions that were discussed elsewhere.[521]

This is the standard understanding of Lurianic Kabbalah up to the late nineteenth century. When asked by an anonymous Kabbalist where it is possible to find in a Lurianic text the ascent of the *Malkhut* to the highest divine level, R. Joseph Hayyim ben Elijah, a leading Kabbalist in Bagdad, also known by the title of his major work as *Ben 'Ish Hay*, answered him by quoting the passages from *Sha'ar Ma'amarei Rashby* and *'Etz Hayyim* that were discussed above and other Lurianic texts, and then he writes:

> Behold this thing is explicit in the words of our teacher Isaac Luria, blessed be He. And the reason for Her grandeur is that She is revealed from the secret of "the Supernal Head that

---

516 2 Chronicles 20: 26.
517 Proverbs 3: 19.
518 In the translation known as the Jerusalem Aramaic translation: אמכחב
519 *Hemdat Yamim*, Hag ha-Sukkot, ch. 8, vol. 3, fol. 94b:
כי פרשת וזאת הברכה רמז למדה אחרונה הנקראת ברכה, לקשר אותה במדה הנקראת עמק ברכה, ותכף ומיד "בראשית" על דרך נעוץ סופן בתחלתן, בסוד ה' בחכמ"ה יסד אר"ץ, באבא יסד ברתא, וכדמתרגמין "בראשית" "בחכמתא".
520 *Peri 'Etz Hayyim*, fols.107ad, describing also the ascent of the Female to the *sefirah* of *Keter*.
521 See e.g., Idel, "The Divine Female and the Mystique of the Moon."

is not known," standing higher than the nine *sefirot* that are the roots, that *Tiferet* is one of them. And this issue is necessary in accordance to [the path of] nature as water that emerges from a high place and then descends to a lower one, it ascends [afterwards] to the high place, in accordance to the height from where it descended, and understand this well.[522]

This seems to be the only Kabbalistic effort to explain the three-phases model in a naturalistic manner, namely, by means of the theory of connected vessels, although in early Kabbalah this theory was already used in order to explicate the nature of the soul. Thus, in Lurianic texts adduced in this and the following two chapters, the model of descent-ascent is conceived of as reflecting an orthodox type of Lurianism.

The circular theosophy is also well represented in Lurianism. Commenting on the statement in *Sefer Yetzirah* to the effect that "Their end is fixed in their beginning," R. Ḥayyim Vital states briefly: "*Keter* and *Malkhut* are hewn from the same place,"[523] alleging some form of essential identity between them, although the distinction between them in their roots is also evident. Perhaps the diagram of a circle wherein the ten *sefirot* are depicted on the circumference influenced this statement, too. In any case, as seen above, Bakharakh attributed it, in some way, to Luria himself. Last but not least: Bakharakh envisioned the Sabbath as the time of the ascent of the Shekhinah. Citing Alqabetz's hymn, he interprets it as referring to Her ascent: "Come, Bride, Come Bride, immediately the *Shekhinah*, that is the Bride, the Queen, ascends on high, and all the worlds go with Her, and then She sings the Song of Songs, and so the souls in Paradise also go with Her

---

522 Joseph Ḥayyim ben Elijah, *Rav Pe'alim*, vol. 3, fol. 3bc:

הרי דבר זה מפורש בדברי רבינו האר״י ז״ל ומפורש הטעם של הגדלות שלה כיון שהיא נגלית מסוד האי רישא עלאה דלא אתידע, העומד למעלה מן התשעה ספירות שרשיות אשר התפארת הוא מהם, וענין זה הוא מוכרח על פי הטבע כי המים שיוצאין במקום גבוה, ואחר כך יורדין למקום נמוך הנה הם עולין מאליהם למקום גבוה לפי שיעור הגובה שממנו יצאו ובאו, והבן זה היטב.

See also, *Kabbalah & Eros*, 310, n. 26. For the theory of "original" *sefirot* – he uses the term מקוריות - within the Infinite; see also in R. Jacob Koppel Lipshitz of Mezdiretch, *Sha'arei Gan 'Eden*, fols. 29c, 30bc. Those are later reverberations of the late thirteenth century theory of ten luminosities, or inner *sefirot*, found within the Infinite or the first *sefirah*. See Idel, "The Image of Man above the *Sefirot*."

523 *Sefer 'Etz Ḥayyim*, Gate 25, derush 6:

נעוץ סופן בתחלתן כי כתר ומלכות ממקום א' חצובים

See also *Sefer 'Etz Ḥayyim*, Gate 39, derush 15:

כתר במלכות וחכמה ביסוד כו' עד מלכות בכתר וז״ס נעוץ סופן בתחלתן ותחלתן בסופן.

"*Keter* within *Malkhut* and *Hokhmah* within *Yesod*, etc., until *Malkhut* within *Keter*, and the prooftext is "their end is fixed in their beginning, and their beginning [fixed] in their end." This view is evident also in R. Nathan of Gaza's *Sefer ha-Beriy'ah*, whose views will be discussed further on in this chapter.

and sing with the angels to go with Her too."[524] The *Shekhinah*, evidently, plays an active, leading role in the ascent: during Sabbath, She is the Queen accompanied by an entourage The very pronouncing of the words in the prayers may be understood theurgically, as causing this ascent.

We shall mention briefly a topic that deserves a separate study – the correlations between the apotheosis of the Female in Safedian Kabbalah, as discussed in this and the preceding chapter, and evidence of the important spiritual role played by women in Safed in this period, as shown in some recent studies.[525] However, it should be pointed out that not all the branches of Lurianic Kabbalah agreed as to the themes discussed above. For example, these themes do not appear in the Kabbalistic writings of R. Israel Sarug, a student of Luria himself.

The Sabbatean literature written by Kabbalists of diverse orientations, such as Sabbatai Tzevi, Abraham Michael Cardozo, Nehemiah Ḥayyun or, more eminently, R. Nathan Benjamin Ashkenazi of Gaza, is particularly variegated. The latter, a famous Sabbatean prophet and an accomplished Lurianic Kabbalist, adopted the uroboric theosophy combined with the concept of the privileged status of the Female, and established a link between metaphysics, history, and a historical figure, Sabbatai Tzevi qua Messiah. [526] In his major Kabbalistic opus *Sefer ha-Beriy'ah* Nathan wrote:

> In the Time to Come, the secret of the Face of the Queen will be revealed, and She will become the All, according to the secret of the Face, like *Keter*, "a diadem [situated] above Her Husband" ... and a perfect building[527] will be built like *Tiferet* and *Malkhut*, and the Holy One, Blessed be He, is a diadem above them,[528] and then the right [side] stands over

---

524 *'Emeq ha-Melekh, Sefer Tiqqunei Shabbat*, ch. 1, repr.,

'באי כלה באי כלה' ותכף השכינה שהיא כלה מלכתא, עולה למעלה, וכל העולמות הולכים עמה, ואז היא משוררת 'שיר השירים' וכן הנשמות שהם בגן עדן הולכים עמה, ומשוררים עם המלאכים ההולכים גם הם עמה.

See also above, n. 260.

525 See Jeffrey H. Chajes, "In a Different Voice: The Non-Kabbalistic Women's Mysticism of Early Modern Jewish Culture" (Hebrew), 139–162; Chajes, "He Said She Said: Hearing the Voices of the Pneumatic Early Modern Women," *Nashim* 10 (2005): 99–125; Morris N. Faierstein, "*Maggidim*, Spirits and Women in Rabbi Hayyim Vital's Book of Vision," 186–196; Faierstein, "Women as Prophets and Visionaries in Medieval and Early Modern Judaism," 251–282.

526 On his thought, see Gershom Scholem, *Sabbatai Sevi, the Mystical Messiah*, passim; Chaim Wirszubski, *Between the Lines, Kabbalah, Christian Kabbalah and Sabbateanism* (Hebrew), 121–188; Liebes, *On Sabbateaism and its Kabbalah*, passim; Avraham Elqayam, *The Mystery of Faith in the Writings of Nathan of Gaza* (Hebrew) and my *"Male and Female,"* appendix K.

527 The context deals with the rebuilding of the Jerusalem Temple. Nathan follows the Midrashic attitude as to the ideal place of the *Shekhinah* in the Temple, as we have seen also in ibn Gabbai's discussions in ch. 6.

528 See a similar view discussed in a text that probably precedes Sabbateanism, in note 85 above.

the [lower] right and the left [side] stands over the left [side], just as the Father and Mother[529] stand over the Male and the Female.[530]

The "Parents" standing over the Son and Daughter refer to the positions of Father and Mother as the *sefirot Hokhmah* and *Binah* respectively, according to the sefirotic scheme of ten *sefirot*. The transformation of the Queen, whose precise sefirotic identity is not clear in this context, into a Crown – *Keter* – is a continuation of earlier traditions and this is also the case of Her becoming "the All,"[531] a transformation that probably refers to Her enhancement, which is not explicated in the context but certainly refers to a preeminent status. The description of the Diadem, *'Atarah*, as being higher than the lower divine couple demonstrates that this is not a phallic symbol, but an indication of Her superiority over the Male. In any case, the supernal Females mentioned in the passage will not be absorbed by either of the two Males, nor masculinized, but they will keep their position on the left side *vis-à-vis* the place of the Males in the sefirotic scheme. Is this diadem constituted by the revelation of the Face of the Female? Elsewhere in his major theosophical book, Nathan of Gaza speaks about "precisely the *Shekhinah* that is [identical to] the root of the Face, the root of right,"[532] thus allowing an identification of the Queen in the first

---

529 The Father and Mother stand for *Hokhmah* and *Binah*, which constitute together with the Son and the Daughter, the fourfold family. On this divine family, which has a long history in Kabbalah, see Idel, *Ben, Sonship and Jewish Mysticism*, 382–383, 436–437, and *"Male and Female."*

530 *Sefer ha-Beriy'ah*, ms. Berlin, Or. 8° 3077, fol. 15a: ולעתיד לבא שיתגלה סוד הפנים של המלכה ותהיה היא הכל בסוד פנים דגוונא דכתר, עטרת על בעלה...ויבנו בנין שלם כגוונא דת״ת ומלכות והב״ה עטרת עליהם ואז עומדים ימין על ימין ושמאל על שמאל כגוונא דקאים אר״א על זו״ן. See also *Sefer ha-Beriy'ah*, Or. 8° 3077, fol. 14ab on the connection between *'Atarah* and *Keter,* another case of circular theosophy. Interestingly, God is supposed to become a diadem over the head of the lower divine couple, while in the well-known pre-Kabbalistic and Ashkenazi traditions, the ascending prayers were regarded as constituting a diadem or a crown on the head of God. For an example in Cordovero, see *'Or Yaqar*, 11: 33, 34; 6: 123. Compare to Wolfson's analysis in "Engenderment," 242–243 of another passage from this book. Here and below, I use the unedited version of *Sefer ha-Beriy'ah* prepared by the late Prof. Chaim Wirszubski.

531 Compare to the text discussed in Abrams, *The Female Body of God*, 122, n. 231. For the various meanings of "All" in medieval thought, see Elliot R. Wolfson, "God, the Demiurge and the Intellect: On the Usage of the Word *Kol* in Abraham ibn Ezra," 77–111; and Howard Kreisel, "The Term *Kol* in Abraham Ibn Ezra: A Reappraisal," 29–66; and Jacques E. Schlanger, "Sur le Rôle du 'Tout' dans la Création selon Ibn Gabirol," 125–135; Adi Tzemach, *Studies in the Work of Shlomo ibn–Gabirol*, 'Yesh be-mo Yesh' (Hebrew), 9–22; and Wolfson, "The Tree that is All: Jewish-Christian Roots of the Kabbalistic Symbol in 'Sefer ha-Bahir,'" 31–76.

532 *Sefer ha-Beriy'ah*, ms. Berlin, Or. 8° 3077, fol. 10b: דווקא השכינה שהיא שרש פנים, שרש ימין In the same book, fol. 97ab, *Keter* and *Thought* are related to Head.

quote with the *Shekhinah*. Here, too, the positive approach to the *Shekhinah* is evident. Moreover, a certain form of circular theosophy is mentioned in *Sefer ha-Beriy'ah*, where he indicates that the *'Atarah* stems from the place of *Keter*, which is the reason for Her return there: this return is not a reconstitution, but a restoration of the diadem to the root, שרש, that is found together with the root of *Keter*.[533] This means that She is not derived from *Keter*, but from a very high root that is deemed to be parallel to the root of the highest *sefirah*. Needless to say, the term "root" is quintessential for understanding this passage. It appears repeatedly in Nathan's treatise and should be seen as a seminal term that refers to the three-phases model, under the impact of Luria's Kabbalah, where, as seen above, one finds the term ספירות שרשיות. Moreover, even the two types of primordial light, already present within the Infinite, are described as having roots.[534] In this context, the existence of "places" for the lights within the "primeval thought" and in the Infinite should also be mentioned.[535] We may, therefore, speak about the architecture of supernal powers populating the Infinite and existing in a certain type of tension.

I assume that Lurianic Kabbalah and R. Nathan adopted the theory of the hidden *sefirot*, or the ten luminosities, stemming from much earlier forms of Kabbalah, although not adopted by Cordovero, and they have been treated as the source of the ten lower *sefirot*.[536] The return to the source or to the root thus is not necessarily a gender discourse or a matter of fluidity but of regaining the place a *sefirah* had in the primeval theogonic stage. This is true, in my opinion, even when dealing with the verse from Proverbs 12: 4 that mentions wife and husband: it should be understood in many cases as referring to a certain place, namely, a special theosophical zone rather than a reference to gender. In any case, without quoting these passages from *Sefer ha-Beriy'ah*, it is hazardous to speculate about the implicit meanings of *Keter* as Male and then the restitution of the Female into the alleged Male androgyne, a theme that is introduced in the analysis of texts as part of what I call the oblique fallacy.

---

533 See *Sefer ha-Beriy'ah*, Or. 8° 3077, fol. 14a:

מציאות הארץ תלוי בכתר ששרשה בעת הצמצום היה כפי שרש מקום הכתר ...ומזה הטעם חוזרת בסוד העטרה

See also *Sefer ha-Beriy'ah*, Or. 8° 3077, fols. 16ab, 59a. 75b, 96b.Compare, however, to the assumption of Wolfson, "Engenderment," 243, who "surmises" that the return of the Female to "the masculine Keter" is actually an act of restitution.

534 See *Sefer ha-Beriy'ah*, fol. 96a: שרשים של שני מיני אורות ב' In some other cases, the source – מקור – is used instead of root. See, e.g., fols. 4a, 13a, 16a.

535 See *Sefer ha-Beriy'ah*, Or. 8° 3075, fol. 2a

536 See above, n. 236.

This passage should be compared to Nathan's statement in his famous *Treatise on the Dragons*, where he discusses the ascent and the occultation of the Messiah:

> Just as the Holy One, blessed be He, ascends to this level[537] so, too, the messianic king will ascend to a high level in body and soul, for his body will be purified like the pavement of sapphire, and this is the secret of "under His feet there was the likeness of a pavement."[538] The word *ve-taḥat* [under] is numerically equivalent to his name and to his cognomen.[539] And he is [tantamount to] *raglav* [his feet], because he is the secret of the heels. *Raglav* is *regel Yah*, which is the secret of the corona of the phallus of the Father, for *Yesod*, too, is called foot..[540] "The likeness of a pavement of sapphire" refers to the diadem, in the secret of the "diadem of the husband,",[541] for She ascends to the supernal world above which there is nothing.[542]

The subject matter of the passage is Sabbatai Tzevi qua Messiah. Nevertheless, per the last sentence, it is the diadem alone that ascends, and Her ascent to the highest zone of the divine world is well attested in the Lurianic sources adduced above. The assumption here is that the diadem will reach a level that is higher than that of the Male, represented by the phrase "The Holy One, blessed be He," which should be seen as identical to the Husband, or perhaps to *Ze'yir 'Anppin*, as we have seen in the passage from *Sefer ha-Beriy'ah*. It is important to emphasize that both the King Messiah and the diadem transcend the theosophical level of the Male as husband,[543] and, perhaps, reach higher than the highest *sefirah*, hinted at by the phrase "above which there is nothing."[544] According to several Sabbatean traditions, there is a connection between Tzevi and the "power of the

---

537 Of the Sabbath. This is a hypostatic reading of the sacred time, found already at the beginning of Kabbalah.

538 Exodus 24: 10.

539 *Ve-Tahat* = 814 = *ShBTY TzVy*. See Elliot R. Wolfson, "The Engenderment of Messianic Politics: Symbolic Significance of Sabbatai Sevi's Coronation," 235, n. 109. See also Elqayam, "The Burden of Silence," 208, n. 106.

540 *Sefer ha-Beriy'ah*, 8° 3077, fols. 86b–87a.

541 Proverbs 12: 4.

542 See G. Scholem, ed., *be-'Iqvot Mashiyah*, 15–16, as translated by Wolfson, "The Engenderment of Messianic Politics," 235, cited here with some minor changes.

543 On this point, my interpretation differs dramatically from that of Wolfson. See "The Engenderment of Messianic Politics," 235, n. 107 and his entire claim in this article. See, especially, the passage he quotes from *Sefer ha-Beriy'ah*, where the verse from Proverbs 12: 4 is adduced as a prooftext and analyzed phallocentrically, 242–243. See also my *Saturn's Jews*, 75, 159–160, nn. 127, 128.

544 Wolfson did not address this theme in his study.

supernal crown,"[545] which may reinforce the reading that the Messiah, related to the configuration of the Father, will transcend it.

These traditions hint at a relationship between a historical figure, the Sabbatean Messiah, Sabbatai Tzevi, and the diadem, and, indeed, in some cases, Tzevi has been identified as the *Shekhinah*.[546] In this case, therefore, we may speak about an apotheosis *in corpore* and *in spiritu*. Especially relevant for our discussion is the ascent of Tzevi qua *Shekhinah* to *'Attiqa' Qaddisha'*, in accordance with a passage of R. Jonathan Eibeshuetz,[547] in a manner reminiscent of the Lurianic discussions of the origin of the Female. In an early testimony concerning Tzevi, Eibeshuetz attributed a certain change in the Jewish ritual to the *Shekhinah*.[548] Is the vision of Tzevi as both supernal crown and as *Shekhinah* related to some form of circular theology?

The ascent of the Diadem is a matter of returning not only to the highest levels of the sefirotic world but also to a lower one. In his book, Nathan mentions the ascent of the diadem to the *sefirah* of *Da'at*, Knowledge, a divine power that is considered to be the external aspect of *Keter*, namely higher than _Hesed_ and *Gevurah*; he describes this event by means of the verse from Proverbs 12: 4, in terms of a return to Her first place, a view reminiscent of the three-phases model.[549] Elsewhere, the diadem is mentioned in the context of the divine dwelling on the bodies of the purified righteous, in a context of the concept of the divine chariot, and the way I understand it is that the diadem is higher than the bodies.[550] To be sure, in this book, too, the vision of the Female/diadem as the corona of the phallus is found – another case of inconsistency or plurivocality.[551] In another composition of R. Nathan, we read about a more egalitarian approach: "In the Time to Come ... the power of the moon will intensify, with two kings sharing a single crown, which is alluded to in the verse "the diadem of her husband," and the light of the moon will be like the light of the sun – not like the light it has in

---

545 See my *Saturn's Jews*, 159, n. 125.

546 See, e.g., the text printed in Wirszubski, *Between the Lines*, 232, and discussions in Wolfson, "Engenderment," 232–233; Elqayam, "'The Burden of Silence,'" 206–209, 248.

547 Cf. Liebes, *On Sabbateaism and its Kabbalah,* 129, 366, n. 181.

548 See Scholem, *Studies and Texts Concerning the History of Sabbateanism*, 224–225. The cult of the divine *Shekhinah* is evident also in Abraham Michael Cardozo; see Wolfson, "Constructions of the *Shekhinah*," especially 16–17, 25–26, 30.

549 *Sefer ha-Beriy'ah*, Or. 8° 3077, fol. 59b. In this context, the ascent to *Keter* is also mentioned.

550 *Sefer ha-Beriy'ah*, Or. 8° 3075, fol. 6b.

551 *Sefer ha-Beriy'ah*, Or. 8° 3077, fol. 85b.

the present, but after the sevenfold intensification of its light ... then the light of the moon will be like that of the sun."[552]

These ascents of the diadem should be compared also to some accounts about the ascent of Sabbatai Tzevi in the sefirotic realm. In an explicit passage, the ascent of Tzevi to the *sefirah* of *Binah*, a *sefirah* related in many texts to the planet Saturn, is quite conspicuous.[553] The so-called Yemenite Sabbatean apocalypse, which is a fragment from a lost treatise stemming from a rather early period of the Sabbatean movement, describes the Messiah as ascending from "one degree to another, [all] the degrees of the seven *sefirot* from *Gedullah* to *Malkhut* ... [and] after two years he ascends to the degree that his mother is there."[554] Gershom Scholem has correctly interpreted this text as pointing to Tzevi's soteriological ascent to the third *sefirah*, *Binah*, which is commonly symbolized in theosophical Kabbalah by the symbol of the Great Mother.[555] He even hypothesized, on the basis of this passage, the existence of a mystical event in the spiritual life of Tzevi in 1650. Moreover, as pointed out recently, in Sabbateanism there is a cult of the Virgin, identified as Queen Esther. conceived as an archetypical messianic figure.[556]

In Nathan of Gaza's famous epistle, he mentions that the believers' belief in Sabbatai Tzevi as Messiah will ensure the reception of "'the inheritance of the Lord,'[557] which is the mystery of the Jubilee Year that will become manifest at this time and the 'rest,' which is the mystery of the manifestation of *'Attiqa' Qaddisha'*, within the configuration of *Ze'ir 'Anppin*, in the year 1670."[558] This

---

552 Nathan of Gaza, "The Treatise of the Menorah" (Hebrew) in Scholem, ed., *be-'Iqvot Mashiyah*, 114–115. I followed basically the translation of Rapoport-Albert, *Women and the Messianic Heresy of Sabbetai Zevi*, 222. See other discussions of Sabbateanism adduced in *Women and the Messianic Heresy*, 222–223. For changes in Nathan's thought, see Elqayam, *The Mystery of Faith*, and Liebes, *On Sabbateaism and its Kabbalah*, 304–305, n. 29. Compare, however, the claims of Wolfson, *Language, Eros, Being*, 511, n. 267, regarding the approach of Nathan as phallocentric.

553 See my *Messianic Mystics*, 187–197; *Saturn's Jews*, 54–69; and Elqayam, "'The Burden of Silence,'" 215, n. 124.

554 Gershom Scholem, *Researches in Sabbateanism* (Hebrew), 214–215. For more on the possible non-Yemenite background of this treatise, see Yehudah Nini, "Sabbatean Messianism in Yemen" (Hebrew), 5–17 and Joseph Tubi, *'Iunim be-Megillat Teiman* (Hebrew), 82–150. For a Freudian interpretation of this passage, which emphasizes the importance of mentioning "his mother," see Avner Falk, "The Messiah and the *Qelippoth*: On the Mental Illness of Sabbatai Sevi," 25–26. For a Jungian interpretation, see Siegmund Hurwitz, "Sabbatai Zwi, Zur Psychologie der haeretischen Kabbala," 2: 239–263. See also Idel, *Ben*, 457–458.

555 See above, n. 26.

556 See the important study of Elqayam, "'The Burden of Silence,'" 173–250.

557 See I. Tishby's remark in R. Jacob Sasportas, *Tzitzat Novel Tzvi* (Hebrew), 7, n. 8.

558 See Sasportas, *Tzitzat Novel Tzvi*, 7–8; Scholem, *Sabbatai Sevi*, 270, and his footnotes there.

passage explicates two different topics: let me start with the most obvious one: in 1670 a lofty revelation will take place, when the highest divine hypostasis, the countenance of 'Attiqa' Qaddisha', will illuminate the lower configuration within the intra-divine world.[559] Those who merit it will then gain "rest," menuẖah. Though "rest" is explicitly related to redemption, I assume that it is also related to the concept of Sabbath.[560] The term "secret" hints at this redemptive significance. An earlier phase of the salvific drama is already emerging, however, "in this time," which is referred to by the "secret of the Jubilee." I assume that this secret designates a lower – but already present in 1665 – form of deliverance.

What is the theosophical significance, however, of this present mystery of Jubilee? The Jubilee, as most Kabbalists agree and as indicated in the above discussions, is a symbol of the third sefirah. This symbolism points to the present presiding power, namely the sefirah of Binah. Although Scholem overlooked this distinction between the two phases in his analysis, he, nevertheless, correctly pointed out the salvific meaning of Binah in this context. He did not pay due attention to its possible implications, thus conveying the impression that one global redemptive event is mentioned here.[561] Moreover, in one of the later sentences of the same epistle that describes the future events during the next seven years, Nathan wrote explicitly that the miracles mentioned in the book of the Zohar will not take place until "the year of the next Shemittah.[562] And in the seventh [year], ben David will come[563] and in the seventh year is Sabbath, which is the King Sabbatai, and at that time, the above-mentioned rabbi [namely Sabbatai Tzevi] will come from the river of Sambatiyon together with his spouse, the daughter of Moses, our master."[564]

In the light of the above, I shall address an important issue in Nathan of Gaza's original theosophical thought that is related, in my opinion, to the possible

---

559 This is a view found both in the Zoharic theosophy and in Lurianic Kabbalah, which is connected sometimes with the glory of redemption. See Zohar, III, fol. 136b, and Liebes, Studies in the Zohar, 44–46, 60–62.

560 See also below in the next chapter.

561 Sabbatai Sevi, 275–276.

562 Namely within the span of maximum six years. In Kabbalistic texts, the term shemittah does not always refer to the cosmic cycles.

563 Isaiah Tishby, in his edition of Tzitzat Novel Tzvi, 11, n. 9 mentions the parallel to BT, Megillah, fol. 17b.

564 Sasportas, Tzitzat Novel Tzvi,. 11; Scholem, Sabbatai Sevi, 273–274. My interpretation of King Sabbatai as referring to Saturn is related to the citation adduced above from p. 7, where the Jubilee and the revelation of the 'Attiqa' Qaddisha' are mentioned and to the reading offered by Sasportas himself, adduced on 9, n. 44. See also Tzitzat Novel Tzvi, 13: "this Rabbi, whose name points to him, Sabbatai."

repercussion of the earlier discussions. As Yehuda Liebes proposed, the two concepts "light that is thoughtless" – 'or she-'eyin bo mahashavah – and "the light that possesses thought," 'or she-yesh bo mahashavah or "the light of the thought" – 'or ha-mahashavah – both found primordially within the Infinite, and struggling as part of the theogonical and cosmological process, should be identified with Sabbatai Tzevi and Nathan, respectively.[565]

This type of specific complexity within the zone of the Infinite may be cast also in gender terms: the "thoughtful light" as masculine, and the "thoughtless light" as feminine, as the former is depicted several times as inseminating the latter.[566] In my opinion, it is possible to reinforce Liebes's suggestion by emphasizing the main characteristic of the "thoughtless light": its opposition to the process of creation or, in the term used by Nathan, as related to destruction, Horban, a term that recurs several times in this book.[567] A main feature of the planet Saturn, in Hebrew Sabbatai, is its being associated with destruction, the Hebrew term Horban as it is found in a series of Hebrew texts, most of them Kabbalistic, written long before the emergence of Sabbateanism.[568] The destructive nature of Chronos in Greek mythology, and of Saturn in the Latin one, reached Judaism through a variety of sources and inspired the vision of Nathan's original theosophy. In my opinion, this conceptual and terminological convergence related to the theme of destruction strongly supports my contention that Tzevi's self-understanding and that of some of his followers, and

---

565 See Yehuda Liebes, *From Shabbetai Tsevi to the Gaon of Vilna, A Collection of Studies* (Hebrew), 29–38, especially 35–36.

566 *Sefer ha-Beriyah*, ms. Berlin, 8° 3077, fol. 76a; Or. 8° 3075, fols. 2a, 4a, b. The supposition in *Sefer ha-Beriyah*, fol. 5a is that the two thoughts should connect to each other מתקשרים, without assuming an absorption of one by another. The non-absorptive nature of the union of Male and Female in the eschatological future is evident in *Sefer ha-Beriyah*, 8° 3077, fol. 26a, where the union of the Male is depicted as being in the day and that of the Female in the night.

567 *Sefer ha-Beriyah*, ms. Berlin, Or. 8° 3077, fol. 96a, b; Or. 8° 3075, fols. 5a, 25b.

568 See the occurrences of this term in a passage from R. Joseph ben Shalom Ashkenazi, *Commentary on Sefer Yetzirah*, fols. 51c-52a, and copied almost verbatim in *Sefer ha-Peliy'ah*, 1, fol. 57b. The latter was a book studied by Tzevi, which had a decisively influence in my opinion, on his self-perception and that of others. See also the anonymous fourteenth century treatise *Sefer Toledot 'Adam*, Ms. Oxford-Bodeliana 836, fol. 180b and the same passages found in the writings of the late fifteenth century R. Yohanan Alemanno, the sixteenth century R. Joseph ibn Tzayyah, R. Abraham Yagel, and R. Shlomo ha-Levi Alqabetz, or the seventeenth century R. Abraham Azulai, translated and discussed in Idel, *Saturn's Jews*, 24–29, 62–63, 70–71, 163. It should be noted that the attempt to counteract the creative processes by the sefirots' striving to return to the supernal source is found in late thirteenth century Kabbalah. See Idel, *Kabbalah, New Perspectives*, 163–164, 184–186, or Mopsik, *Les grands textes de la cabale*, 100–103.

particularly Nathan's theosophy emerged in relation to astrology, especially the theory of *shemittot*, the cyclical cosmic times.[569] It goes without saying that Nathan's portrayal of the Messiah of Izmir, or those of other Sabbatean authors, do not represent the more theistic approach of Tzevi himself.[570]

A somewhat later major thinker, Abraham Michael Cardoso,[571] the most theological of Sabbatean authors, displayed a special interest in the divine Feminine, dedicating an entire sermon to the *Shekhinah*. Wolfson, who published this text for the first time and other discussions of the *Shekhinah*,[572] analyzes the text in accordance with his phallocentric theory. This is problematic as the various discussions do not mention the absorption of the *Shekhinah* by the Male, at least not explicitly. The sermon does, however, refer very clearly to some issues mentioned above regarding the special status of the divine Feminine. For example, the opening statement reflects a circular theosophy that includes a privileged status of the Female:

> "It is better the end of a thing than its beginning."[573] This verse has been stated in an unqualified manner, so it must be understood [as referring] to all the worlds and all the ranks, and despite the fact that commentators said that the intention is that the final cause is eminent, as the intention of the actor is to accomplish his action and for the end that is the final intention, he starts from the beginning and operates by several [intermediary] means to attain his intention. Nevertheless, there is an inner secret and in order to understand it, the verse "He tells from the beginning the end"[574] should be cited. For example, when the "Master of the will"[575] wanted, and it ascended in thought to create the world, He caused the emanation of all the emanated [entities] from *Keter* to *Yesod* and, nevertheless, He could not create the world but in the moment that the last countenance of the countenance of the [world of] emanation [emerged]. And [only] after the last *sefirah* out of the ten *sefirot* emerged and it has been amended as in the existence of the countenance called Female [*nuqba'*] of Ze'yir 'Anppin, it was possible that the world

---

569 Compare to Liebes, *From Shabbetai Tsevi to the Gaon of Vilna*, 14, n. 4.

570 Liebes, *On Sabbateanism and its Kabbalah*, 20–34, and Cristina Ciucu, "The Metaphysical Foundations of the Sabbatean Messianism as reflected in Nathan of Gaza's *Sefer ha-Beriah*," 149–179.

571 On this Sabbatean theology, see Nissim Yosha, *Captivated by Messianic Agonies, Theology, Philosophy and Messianism in the thought of Abraham Miguel Cardoso* (Hebrew), especially 153–155; Liebes, *On Sabbateaism and its Kabbalah*, 35–48, and a selection of passages translated into English, in David Halperin, *Miguel Cardoso, Selected Writings*, especially 273–308.

572 See his "Constructions of the *Shekhinah*."

573 Ecclesiastes 8: 9. This verse has been interpreted in a similar manner later on in a passage of R. Moshe Hayim Luzzatto, from *'Adir ba-Marom ha-Shalem*, 94–95.

574 Isaiah 46: 10. For the occurrence of this verse as part of the circular theosophy, see above, nn. 227 and 425.

575 This is a reference to God in Jewish philosophy and in the writings of R. Menahem Azaryah of Fano. See M. Idel, "Conceptualizations of Tzimtzum in Baroque Italian Kabbalah," 33.

of creatures will emerge.... And how should we explain that the end of the thing is better than the beginning ... *Keter* is called beginning ... up to the moment that *Malkhut* has been revealed that is called lower *Shekhinah* ... the end and the good.[576]

The conspicuous opening passage of the sermon, with its description of the feminine power as good[577] and as the final cause is a continuation of many texts discussed earlier in this study, and it constitutes the basic pattern for many of Cardoso's following discussions. The circular theosophy found in the above passage appears more explicitly elsewhere, when he describes the emergence of *Malkhut* directly from *Keter*,[578] and he also mentions Her emergence from the "supernal head that is not known" in the vein of the Lurianic texts adduced above in this chapter.[579] In any case, he claims that "*Malkhut* is higher than any blessing and praise in the existence of Her root and Her growth and Her emanation than *Ze'yir 'Anppin*."[580] The root of the *Shekhinah* is perceived as found in the First Cause,[581] and She is depicted as "I am superior, up to the Infinite."[582] In my opinion, the above passage reflects also the theosophical interpretation of the pseudo-Aristotelian dictum, which should be taken into consideration when attempting to make sense of this passage. Elsewhere, the Female is described as ascending to *'Attiqa' Qaddisha'* and becoming a cornerstone,[583] which means that She will maintain Her independent status even after Her ascent to Her source. Cardoso also mentions the non-eschatological ascent of the *Shekhinah* to the highest level and then Her return full of all good things,[584] in the manner many earlier Kabbalists claimed. Moreover, the logic that sees the best in the last is applied also to the

---

576 Wolfson, "Constructions of the *Shekhinah*," 93–94. Compare also a parallel passage translated into English by Wolfson, "Constructions of the *Shekhinah*," 75.

577 See also "Constructions of the *Shekhinah*," 95.

578 "Constructions of the *Shekhinah*,": מלכות שברר טוב בעבור שורשה מן ראשית שהוא הכתר. See also "Constructions of the *Shekhinah*," 116--117, and another text of Carodoso's translated by Wolfson, "Constructions of the *Shekhinah*, 75.

579 "Constructions of the *Shekhinah*,": מלכות ...שהוא כלי מתגלה מכח ההיא רישא עילאה דלא אתיידע

580 "Constructions of the *Shekhinah*," 116 מלכות מרומם על כל ברכה ותהלה במציאות שורשו וצמיחתו והשתלשלותו יותר מז"א.

581 "Constructions of the *Shekhinah*,"117. See also the text translated by Wolfson, "Constructions of the *Shekhinah*," 74.

582 "Constructions of the *Shekhinah*,":ס"א עד עליונה אני .

583 "Constructions of the *Shekhinah*,". 136 אחר היות אל השכינה כ"ז תעלה עד ע"ק בסוד עתיק יומין See also "Constructions of the *Shekhinah*,", 122.

584 Constructions of the *Shekhinah*, 131.

creation of the woman at the very end of the creational process,[585] in a manner similar to that seen at the end of chapter 6, in discussions about the eminence of women.

In his study on the *Shekhinah*, Wolfson dealt with a variety of other texts by Cardoso, which, indeed, support his androcentric reading. Surprisingly, Wolfson's lengthy analysis ignores the content of the above cited Hebrew text, without explaining the reason for his omission, presumably because it does not fit into the androcentric approach. In my opinion, we have in this case, too, an example of conceptual fluidity, and one must not be so selective in elaborating his views. If one takes this text into consideration, it is difficult to consider that Wolfson accurately characterized Cardoso when he wrote: "In the final analysis, Cardoso embraced the androcentric anthropology of the kabbalistic tradition."[586] Much more nuanced approaches that do not skip the dissenting voices are necessary before reaching a "final" analysis and conclusions. Grand theological claims, especially when formulated in the singular, often preclude an understanding of specific texts, an incongruity that is sometimes amusing, as we shall see in the next chapter.

Interestingly, a mid-eighteenth-century Sabbatean treatise known as "And I come this day to the Fountain," by the famous Rabbi Jonathan Eibeschuetz,[587] states at the very end of the book:

> A time will come when the higher *Shekhinah* will be above "the God of Israel,"[588] in accordance with the secret of [the verse] "as a valorous wife is the diadem of Her Husband,"[589] this being the significance of [the verse] "then Moshe will sing."[590] As matters stand now, the *Shekhinah* serenades whenever She wants sex.... But a time will come when "the God of Israel" will serenade.... This is the inner meaning of the verse[591] "The light of the moon shall become like the light of the sun," conveying that the *Shekhinah* will be in a lofty place like "the God of Israel," who is symbolized by the sun, while the sun's light will take the place of

---

585 "Constructions of the *Shekhinah*," 94, 95.
586 "Constructions of the *Shekhinah*," 80. See also 78. Nota bene the singular, an issue to be discussed below in the Concluding Remarks.
587 On his Sabbatean thought, see Liebes, *On Sabbateaism and its Kabbalah*, 103–197, and Moshe A. Perlmuter, *Rabbi Jonathan Eibeschuetz and His Attitude towards Sabbatianism* (Hebrew).
588 Namely, the *sefirah* of *Tiferet* in Sabbatean parlance. See Liebes, *On Sabbateanism and its Kabbalah*, 158–168, 170–174, 177–180.
589 Proverbs 12: 4. See also above, n. 204.
590 Exodus 15: 1.
591 Isaiah 30: 26.

the moon ... but the rank of the *Shekhinah* will be sublime so that the "God of Israel" will in comparison to Her be as the *Shekhinah* is now in comparison to Him.[592]

The complete reversal of the present gender hierarchy is more prominent than ever before, especially as, rather than turning into the other, the luminaries change places and, I assume, also their functions, without a gender shift. Nevertheless, the sun-moon relationship does not essentially differ from what we have seen in the previous Lurianic and Sabbatean passages that said that in the future, the moon will shine stronger than the sun, although the late Sabbatean author expresses it more dramatically. Unlike in the Lurianic sources, however, the *Shekhinah* is identified here with the "true Messiah," who is Sabbatai Tzevi, and they ascend to have intercourse with the head, or the countenance of *'Attiqa'*.[593] Although these two discussions differ, and both deal with the eschatological situation, I see the Female as occupying a privileged status in comparison to the "God of Israel." In any case, the identification of the Messiah with the Female is another indication of the privileged status of the latter.

In other words, the Sabbatean passages adduced in this chapter can reasonably be inscribed in the theoretical Lurianic line concerning gender, as depicted earlier. They are far from deviant speculations. In my opinion, the texts presented here do not corroborate the comprehensive phallocentric "theory" that dominates the entire Kabbalistic discourse nor do they support the exclusively phallocentric-oriented reading of main thinkers in Sabbateanism, who introduce terms such as the integration of the feminine and the reconstitution of the androgynous phallus, or overcoming dimorphism.[594]

Another important question concerns whether the Sabbatean discussions are related to the prominent role played by some Jewish women as prophetesses in Sabbateanism, a messianic movement that depended so much on R.

---

592 For the Hebrew original see R. Jonathan Eibeschuetz, *And I come this day to the Fountain*, 160:

ולעתיד יהיה שכינה עילאה למעלה מן בסוד 'אשת חיל עטרת בעלה' הז"ס 'ואז ישיר משה' שעכשו כשהשכינה רוצה לזווג משוררת בסוד 'אני חבצלת השרון' אבל לעתיד תשורר א"י...הז"ס 'והיה אור הלבנה כאור החמה' היינו כשהשכינה תהיה למעלה כא"י שהוא בסוד חמה ואור החמה יהיה במקום לבנה...רק שישגב מעלתה של השכינה עד שיהיה א"י נגדה בערך כמו שהייתה השכינה עכשו נגדו.

Cf. the English translation by David Halperin, reprinted in Pawel Maciejko, ed., *Sabbatean Heresy*, 121, modified here in some cases. See also Jonatan Benarroch's study ""Piercing What Has Been Sealed' – The Blasphemer (Lev. 24: 10–16) and Toledot Yeshu: From the Homilies of the Zohar to R. Jonathan Eybeschutz's 'Va'avo haYom 'el ha'Ayin'" (Hebrew), printed in *And I come this day unto the Fountain*, 243–277.

593 See *And I come this day to the Fountain*, 158–159.

594 Compare Wolfson, "The Engenderment."

Nathan's literary activity?[595] Or, more generally: does the dissemination of Jewish mysticism in the early modern period, which includes its popularization by adopting a much simpler type of discourse, coincide with the somehow greater role played by women in the available testimonies about spiritual life in Judaism in the past?

I shall turn next to a series of discussions, most of which continued some elements of the Lurianic themes discussed in this chapter, although sometimes they were combined with earlier, mainly Cordoverian themes.

---

595 See Rapoport-Albert, *Women and the Messianic Heresy*; Ciucu, "Messie au fèminin," 70–78. See also Scholem, *Sabbatai Sevi*, 405.

9 R. Moshe Ḥayyim Luzzatto: 1707–1746

"When *Malkhut* comes down, She is in the secret of *Keter* itself, and from there everything exited, and this is the secret of *Keter Malkhut*."

וכשבאה מלכות למטה, הנה היא סוד הכתר עצמו, שמשם יצאו השאר. וסוד העניין הזה הוא כתר מלכות

'Adir ba-Marom ha-Shalem, 119.

"Behold, the link of *Keter* is with *Malkhut* and it is a very great secret."

והנה קשר הכתר הוא עם המלכות, והוא סוד גדול מאד.

'Adir ba-Marom ha-Shalem, 119.

"The perfection of All is the end, and the perfection of the Male is the Female."

שלימות הכל הוא הסוף, ושלימות הזכר היא הנקבה .

'Adir ba-Marom ha-Shalem, 96.

The eighteenth-century paragon of Kabbalah, R. Moshe Ḥayyim Luzzatto,[596] was basically the most original follower of Lurianic Kabbalah in its various forms. His originality stems partially from a greater philosophical understanding of the mythical theosophy of Lurianism, under the influence, to some extent, of Kabbalists who had been active in Italy for some time.[597] Many scholars have addressed Luzzatto's views in general, and even his vision of gender. A recent paper dedicated to his approach portrayed his theosophy as if unqualifiedly subscribing to a phallocentric gender theory.[598] In order to reach such a conclusion, much of the

---

596 Jonathan Garb, *Kabbalist in the Eye of the Storm* (Hebrew); Garb, "Authentic Kabbalistic Writings of R. Moses Hayyim Luzzatto" (Hebrew), 165–222, where he summarizes some of his earlier studies on the topic; Isaiah Tishby, *Studies in Kabbalah and Its Branches*, vol. 2 (Hebrew); Tishby, *Netivei 'Emunah u-Minut* (Hebrew), 169–202; Tishby, *Messianic Mysticism: Moses Hayim Luzzatto and the Padua School*; Joelle Hansel, *Moise Hayyim Luzzatto (1707–1746), Kabbale et philosophie*; Elisheva Carlebach, "Redemption and Persecution in the Eyes of Moses Hayim Luzzatto and His Circle," 1–29; Carlebach, *The Pursuit of Heresy: Rabbi Moses Hagiz and the Sabbatian Controversies*, 195–255; Liebes, *On Sabbateanism and Its Kabbalah*, 59–60, 66, 314–15, n. 112, 316, n. 119, 398, n. 18; Yirmeyahu Bindman, *Rabbi Moshe Chaim Luzzatto: His Life and Works*.
597 Idel, "Conceptualizations of Tzimtzum in Baroque Italian Kabbalah," 28–54.
598 Elliot R. Wolfson, "'*Tiqqun Ha-Shekhinah*': Redemption and the Overcoming of Gender Dimorphism in the Messianic Kabbalah of Moses Hayyim Luzzatto," *History of Religions* 36 (1997): 289–332; Wolfson, *Language, Eros, Being*, esp. 75–77, 375; Wolfson, "Gender and Heresy in Kabbalah," 261–262. This is Wolfson's third study dedicated to a specific Kabbalist's view of gender; the other two, dealing with the coronation of Sabbatai Tzevi and the views of Cardoso,

https://doi.org/10.1515/9783110599800-009

pertinent material that Luzzatto wrote and which appeared in print has been over-looked, and some of the passages that were adduced for that purpose have been misunderstood.[599] Rather than repeating my earlier analyses of some of Luzzatto's other passages as to the privileged status of the *Shekhinah* that portray Her as having direct affinities to the highest divine sphere, I shall restrict my discussion here to a few passages that have not yet been analyzed in this context.

Following the lead of Cordovero, Luzzatto, more than other Kabbalists, was concerned with the amendments of the *Shekhinah*.[600] He also deals explicitly with the pseudo-Aristotelian dictum and with the divine Female as part of what I termed above circular theosophy:

> But in the time to come "the mountain of the Lord's house shall be established on the top of the mountains."[601] This is the supernal *Keter*. Then indeed "the light of the moon will be as the light of the sun."[602] At that time, "I shall lift my eyes to the hills, from whence [*me-'Ayin*] comes my help"[603] – this is the *Shekhinah*. '*Ayin* – it is '*Attiqa' Qaddisha'*.[604] What is *Yavo'* [will come]? This is the sublime secret, as it is written "together with me from *Lebanon*, bride, together with me from *Lebanon* you shall come."[605] Come and see: the *Shekhinah* is

---

were discussed in the preceding chapter. For a somewhat more complex picture of this topic, see Abrams, *The Female Body of God*, 52, 53, 120–121. See more recently Wolfson's "Retroactive Not Yet: Linear Circularity and Kabbalistic Temporality," 37–48. In this essay, he deals also with Luzzatto's book *'Adir ba-Marom*, although he skips some of the sections concerning time that do not fit his theory and sometimes even invert the meaning of the texts he cites. See, *'Adir ba-Marom*, 31, n. 50. On 44, n. 101, he translates a text from Luzzatto's *'Adir ba-Marom ha-Shalem*, 94 and interprets it without explaining why, strangely, it deals with "gender transvaluation." As I have indicated in "On Gender Theories in R. Moshe Ḥayyim Luzzatto," and also below, the translated text and others that I have adduced in my discussions talk explicitly about the escha-tological future as the time of the governance of the Female.

599 See Idel, *Kabbalah & Eros*, 293, n. 143 and Idel, "On Gender Theories in R. Moshe Ḥayyim Luzzatto." For the general role of the *Shekhinah* in Luzzatto's thought, see Garb, *Kabbalist in the Eye of the Storm*, 209–216.

600 See, e.g., Garb, *Kabbalist in the Eye of the Storm*, 209–216; Luzzatto, *'Adir ba-Marom ha-Shalem*, 26, 231, and in one of the letters printed in *'Otzrot ha-Ramḥal*, 351–352 and in one of his letters to one of his teachers in *'Iggerot Ramḥal*, 268–269.

601 Isaiah 2: 2.

602 Isaiah 30: 26.

603 Psalms 121: 1.

604 For the pun '*Ayin* – '*Aniy*, in the context of a circular theosophy, see Luzzatto's *'Adir ba-Marom ha-Shalem*, 53 and compare to *'Adir ba-Marom ha-Shalem*, 53, 228, 231.

605 Song of Songs 4: 8. For *Lebanon* as a symbol for *Keter*, see, e.g., Cordovero, *Pardes Rimmonim*, 3: 7; 7: 2; 23: 12; 23: 14; 23: 22; *'Or ha-Ne'erav*, part 7; *'Or Yaqar*, 7 (Jerusalem, 1975), 7: 8, 10, 28; *Sefer ha-Gerushin*, R. Abraham Azulai, *'Or ha-Ḥammah*, vol. 1, fol. 33d, 55b, 74c, 147cd, 148b, vol. 2, fol. 2c, vol. 3, part 1, fol. 43a, part 2, fol. 55b; and Idel, *Kabbalah: New Perspectives*, 124, 181–182, 335, n. 103. In other texts, some of them Cordoverian and in Lurianic Kabbalah, *Lebanon* stands in

the linkage of all the ranks, as in it is the beginning of thought [and] the end of action,[606] and everything is the linkage from the beginning [or from the head] of all to the end of all. The *Shekhinah* is the linkage of all and this is the reason why it is written: "whence comes my help" – this is *'Ayin*, the supernal *Keter*, as from there the *Shekhinah* is dwelling, in order to link the linkages. And the secret of this issue is "the valorous wife is the diadem of her husband."[607] This is the stone that is elevated endlessly … [the *Shekhinah*] is the [woman] partner to the king,[608] indeed, as it is appropriate, and this is the meaning of "from the *Lebanon* come with me, bride!" Despite the fact that She ascends to the Infinite, Her [sexual] linkage is with Her partner, "from the *Lebanon* come with me."[609] This is the reason why [it is said] "My help is from the Lord." This is if She is with the Lord … Come and see: when the *Shekhinah* ascends to that supernal *Keter*,[610] it is written,[611] "the mountain of the Lord's house shall be established on the top of the mountains."[612]

In my opinion, Luzzatto operated here, *inter alia*, with what I call the three-phases gender theory.[613] Two phases of this theory are quite explicit: the first one

---

many cases for the *sefirah* of *Ḥokhmah*. See, e.g., R. Abraham Azulai, *'Or ha-Ḥammah*, 1, fol. 29c, 58c, 74c, vol. 3, part 1, fol. 43b, part 2, fols. 94c, 126c. In other cases, it may stand for three higher *sefirot*. See, *'Or ha-Hammah*, vol. 1 fol. 54d. In some cases, it stands for *Malkhut*; see Azulai, *'Or ha-Ḥammah*, vol. 1, fol. 147d. For the descent of *Malkhut* from Lebanon see *'Or ha-Ḥammah*, vol. 1, fol. 6c and for Her ascent to Lebanon see, *'Or ha-Ḥammah*, vol. 1 fol 7b. For the ascent of *Malkhut* to *Keter* see also Cordovero's *Tefillah le-Moshe*, fol. 354b and above in n. 375.

606 See also the much later treatise *Quntres Kelalei Hathalat ha-Ḥokhmah*, fol. 13c.

607 Proverbs 12: 4. For the use of this verse to describe the excellence of the Female, not Her subordination, see, e.g., Cordovero's *Tefillah le-Moshe*, fol. 353a. See also above, n. 589 and below, n. 629.

608 The king, like the Lord, is referring to the divine Male, corresponding to the *sefirah* of *Tiferet*.

609 Compare also to the passage from Cordovero's *'Or Yaqar*, vol. 12, translated and discussed above.

610 See also Luzzatto's *'Adir ba-Marom ha-Shalem*, 119, where the Female is described as arousing *Keter*. This ascent has a mark of both Zoharic and Cordoverian modes of thought. See also *'Adir ba-Marom ha-Shalem*, 95, where Luzzatto speaks about the Female as higher than the Male, in the context of Proverbs 12: 4. See n. 607 above.

611 Isaiah 2: 2.

612 *Tiqqunim Ḥadashim*, no. 44, 104–105:

אבל לזמנא דאתי 'נכון יהיה הר בית ה' בראש ההרים' (ישעיה ב:ב) דא כתר עלאה. כדין 'והיה אור הלבנה כאור החמה' (שם ל:כו) ודאי. בההוא זמנא 'אשא עיני אל ההרים מאין יבוא עזרי' (תהלים קכא:א) דא שכינתא. אין דא ע"ק. מאי 'יבא'? אלא הכא הכא רזא עלאה כד"א 'אתי מלבנון כלה אתי מלבנון תבואי' (שיר השירים ד:ח). ת"ח שכינתא ודאי קשרא דכל דרגין איהי, דבה תחלת המחשבה סוף המעשה. וכלא אתקשר הכי מרישא דכלא עד סופא דכלא. ושכינתא הכי איהי קישורא דכלא. בג"כ מאן יבוא עזרי, דא אין כתר עלאה דמתמן שראת שכינתא לקשרא קשרין. ורזא דמלה אשת חיל עטרת בעלה (משלי יב:ד). ודא אבן דסליקין לה עד אין תכלית ... כדין אזדמנת למהוי בת זוג למלכא ודאי, והכי אתחזי. ורזא דא 'אתי מלבנון כלה', אע"ג דאהי עד א"ס סלקת, יחודא דילה דילה בבת זוגה, 'אתי מלבנון תבואי'. בג"כ 'עזרי מעם ה'' דא אי' דקיימת עם ה'...ת"ח: בזמנא דתסלק שכינתא עד ההוא כתר עלאה, דכתיב בה 'נכון יהיה הר בית ה' בראש ההרים'.

Compare to Cordovero, *'Or Yaqar*, 7: 7–8.

613 For more on this issue, see my "On Gender Theories in R. Moshe Ḥayyim Luzzatto."

argues that the *Shekhinah* stems from the highest level within the divine realm, represented here by the terms *Keter 'Illa'ah, 'Ayin, 'Attiqa' Qaddisha', Lebanon*,[614] and most probably also Thought, and presents Her as returning to that sublime place in the eschaton, either to *Keter* or to the Infinite. The resort to the verse from Proverbs here should be understood, as on many other occasions in Kabbalistic literature, as referring to the Female's superiority to the Male/Husband, who is the partner mentioned here.[615] The additional phase, the middle one, is implicit in the concept of the divine Female's descent and then Her ascent, as an interregnum, in which some form of androcentric approach is plausible. This passage constitutes a certain parallel to Luzzatto's discussion in his other book *Da'at Tevunot*, in a passage that includes a reference to the pseudo-Aristotelian dictum:

> ...as from the moment She was emanated from Her source, it is incumbent that the maximum perfection that will be attained at the very end will be within her nature, but it has been said to her from above "go and diminish yourself" up to the moment she will return to her original place by her elevation in accordance to her deeds. However, it is not the case that Her creation has been diminished from the very beginning and Her ascent will be greater afterwards, because "there is nothing new under the sun."[616] However, the order is inverse, as She is in her great power since She was emanated, and then it will diminish, until She will return to her strength. In any case, "the end of the action is found in the first thought," and this is the reason why the perfection of the human has been established first, and afterwards [comes] its diminution, in order to return to the degrees upon which he descended, to elevate to his perfection that has been embedded in his nature from the very beginning.[617]

---

614 Compare also to the use of this symbol in *Tiqqunim Ḥadashim*, no. 67, 129.

615 For Luzzatto, see, e.g., *'Adir ba-Marom ha-Shalem*, 96.

'אשת חיל עטרת בעלה 'שזכרתי, שלפי הסדר הזה הנוקבא סודה למעלה מן הזכר בסוד 'צדיקים יושבין ועטרותיהם בראשיהם' שהוא בזמן הגיעם אל המנוחה...ועל כן הוצרך הגלות, בסוד הזכר, להחזירה למקומה וכשתחזור אז תהיה היא בתחלה בסוד שם שלם, ובסוד: אשת חיל עטרת בעלה.

From the context it is evident that it is the superiority of the Female that is the correct understanding of the biblical verse.

616 Ecclesiastes 1: 9.

617 Luzzatto, *Da'at Tevunot*, 77–78:

המצב השלם שראוי להיות לאדם בזמן השלמות האחרון אשר יהיה לו. והדבר מבואר מעצמו, שהמדרגה התכליתית, אשר היא תהיה סוף כל עילוי האדם, היא הנקבעת ראשונה, כי מאז התאצל הנשמה ממקורה צריך שיהיה בחקה השלמות היותר גדול שתוכל להגיע אליו בסוף הכל, אלא שיאמרו לה מלמעלה, לכי ומעטי את עצמך, עד אשר תשוב אל מקומה הראשון בהתעלותה על פי מעשיה. אך לא שבריאתה ממועטת בתחלתה, ויהיה עילויה מרובה אחריה, כי אין כל חדש תחת השמש, אבל הסדר הוא הפך מזה, כי בכחה הגדול מאז התאצל, אחר - ימעטו לה, עד אשר תשוב לאיתנה. ועל כל פנים - סוף המעשה תחלת המחשבה. על כן שלמות האדם הוא הנקבע ראשונה, ואחריו - מיעוטו, לשוב במעלות אשר ירד בן, להתעלות אל שלמותו כאשר הוחק לו מתחלה.

I provide as literary a translation as possible, and the shift from male to female gender is found in the Hebrew original. Compare also to *'Adir ba-Marom ha-Shalem*, 5:

"לכן בתחלה נמצאת גדולה ואחר כך קטנה".

As mentioned above, this is just one of the expressions of the three-phases model in the later forms of Lurianic Kabbalah.

Based on Lurianic discussions of the root of the Female in the highest head, and perhaps also on R. Nathan of Gaza's views, as seen in the previous chapter, Luzzatto writes – when alluding again to Proverbs 12: 4 that "'the head that is not known' is [situated] upon them,[618] and It is the root of the recipient, that is the *Shekhinah*."[619] The assumption seems to be that a feminine power is found in that head, which is also the root of the lower divine Feminine. According to another version, the end of the quote is "the secret is 'the valorous wife is the diadem of the Husband.'"[620] Luzzatto repeatedly mentions the return of the *Shekhinah* to Her primeval status[621] and at least once in the context of the pseudo-Aristotelian dictum.[622] In some cases, he mentions the ascent of the *Shekhinah* or the *Nuqba'* on high, even to the Infinite,[623] and he resorts to the image of the stone that is thrown on high, although the concept of retrieval is not indicated.[624]

Most importantly, Luzzatto regards the celebration of the Sabbath as the repose that corresponds to the divine Feminine, unlike the weekdays that are the days of action and of exile, related to the Male powers.[625] During the Sabbath, *Malkhut* is

---

See also my "On Gender Theories in R. Moshe Ḥayyim Luzzatto," and Luzzatto's *'Adir ba-Marom ha-Shalem*, 94. See also in one of Luzzatto's letters printed in *'Otzrot ha-Ramḥal*, 343 and the interesting discussion in *Sha'arei ha-Ramḥal*, 109–110, to be read in the context of the discussion on 112. For a different use of the dictum, see *Sha'arei ha-Ramḥal*, 299.

618 Namely, over the other two heads.

619 *Qelaḥ Piteḥei Ḥokhmah*, no. 104, fol. 61b:

ורדל"א שעל גביהם היא שורש למקבל, שהיא השכינה.

For a similar view, see also Luzzatto's other important discussion in *'Adir ba-Marom ha-Shalem*, 121–122.

620 In the commentary on this statement, it is said that this is

סוד זה הוא אשת חיל עטרת בעלה.

"This secret is that a valorous wife is the diadem of Her Husband." See fol. 66b.

621 *Tiqqunim Ḥadashim*, no. 39, 94–95.

622 *Tiqqunim Ḥadashim*, 94. See also above, beside n. 612.

623 *'Adir ba-Marom ha-Shalem*, 53, 54, 229.

624 *'Adir ba-Marom ha-Shalem*, 53.

625 *'Adir ba-Marom ha-Shalem*, 94, 96, 135–136, 183, 191 and my "On Gender Theories in R. Moshe Ḥayyim Luzzatto." Compare, however, to Wolfson's claim in his "*Tiqqun ha-Shekhinah*," 319, n. 131: "In Luzzatto's writings, following zoharic and Lurianic sources, Sabbath also represents the reintegration of the feminine to the masculine in a manner that overcomes gender dimorphism.... The Sabbath, therefore, symbolically represents the ascent of the *Shekhinah* and the consequent rule of the masculine potency over the feminine." The claims in the last part of the passage do not correspond to Luzzatto's thought but are part of the inertial reading of texts in the light of the phallocentric theory.

related to *Keter*, as hinted by the locution *Keter Malkhut*,[626] and in this context, he speaks about the equality of the two divine powers.[627] Here, again Sabbath and its relation to the Female combined with the ritual at a privileged moment in time – a paramount convergence in theosophical Kabbalah and Hasidism, as we shall see below. In yet another text, Luzzatto describes *Malkhut* as referring to the prime matter – *hiyuly* – but also as related to the phallic sign.[628] The complexity of the attitude to the divine Feminine is evident in another passage:

> The matter of "a valorous woman is a diadem for Her husband"[629] for the Feminine is a single, separated point, and the nine *sefirot* come to Her by the secret of a supplement. This means that *Malkhut*, which is verily the root of the lower beings,[630] is the sole one that gives a place to darkness in the act of governance and actual evil; for deficiency is caused not by the Emanator to the world but by the recipient. Indeed, from one perspective this is surely Her lowliness, but from another perspective this is Her excellence and eminence,[631] for this is not done except to reveal the supernal unity ... and the excellence of the Lord, blessed be He, is not disclosed except through Her as has been explained above.[632] And there is no praise for the Lord, blessed be He, revealed except through Her. Therefore, this is the reason why the Lord, blessed Be He, has made Her in such a manner, deficient and dark by nature, to allow a place to actual evil. This is the reason why She needs so many amendments, which are not necessary to the Emanator, who is not deficient at all from His perspective. But when She is perfected and received Her amendments, even more so, She transformed

---

626 '*Adir ba-Marom ha-Shalem*, 135–136. Compare, however, '*Adir ba-Marom*, 133, where the Female is described as stemming from *Yesod*. Luzzatto combines in his writings androcentric views together with privileged approaches to the Female.

627 '*Adir ba-Marom*, 136:

כי אנו אומרים שנוקבא היא בסוד כתר, והוא סוד, כתר מלכות, וזהו גם כן, אני ראשון ואני אחרון. אך ההקדמה הכוללת היא, כי כל ראש וסוף שוים בבחינה אחת. אלא שלפעמים תתחיל ההנהגה מכתר בסוד בחינה אחת, ולפי זה תהיה נוקבא כתר. ולפעמים מחכמה, ותהיה הנוקבא חכמה.

The question of equality between the polar sexual entities in Luzzatto requires a closer examination. Compare, however, Wolfson's phallocentric analysis of R. Moshe Ḥayyim Luzzatto's Kabbalistic understanding of the locution *Keter Malkhut* in *Language, Eros, Being*, 76, 375. See also below, n. 692.

628 See his fragmentary *Commentary on Sefer Yetzirah*, printed in *Sha'arei Ramḥal*, 217.

629 Proverbs 12: 4. See above, n. 607.

630 See, especially, *Sefer ha-Kelalim*, no. 25, 275, where Luzzatto claims that the essence of the lower beings is Yisra'el, and the Female is depicted as the "root of Yisra'el." See also *Sefer ha-Kelalim*, no. 15, 260. See also elsewhere, *Sefer ha-Kelalim*, no. 18, 262, where the question of the root of evil is mentioned. See also in his '*Adir ba-Marom ha-Shalem*, 357, for another strong linkage between the *Shekhinah* and the Jewish people and also 448, 471.

631 Here my translation differs from Wolfson's. Compare *Sefer ha-Kelalim*, no. 28, 277: שבח ומעלה Here excellence is related to the free will of the lower entities. See the entire discussion in *Sefer ha-Kelalim*.

632 This is a leitmotif in Luzzatto. See, e.g., his *Da'at Tevunot*, no. 160, 179, and '*Adir ba-Marom ha-Shalem*, 394. See also below, beside n. 655.

evil into good, as explained above. Then Her excellence ascends up to 'Adam Qadmon,[633] as the excellence of the Lord, Blessed be He, is revealed through Her, as we have explained, and then She is called "the diadem of Her husband."[634]

Two types of perfection are presented here: one of the emanator, which is relatively static, and the other of the more active recipient, namely, the Female. Her perfection comes after imperfection, due to Her being amended, despite Her imperfect nature. This imperfection is, according to this passage, congenital, although it serves as the reason for amendments and thus for perfection.[635] She is the location of two different states, as lowliness and eminence are mentioned together in the same paragraph, and there is no gain in understanding Luzzatto by referring solely to only one of those states. Though related to reception and changes, She is nevertheless privileged by being the only way of revealing the divine unity. In my understanding, Luzzatto mitigates the negative aspects of *Malkhut* that he mentions by assuming that they are related to the lower beings as recipients, part of a longer tradition in the Middle Ages.[636] To a certain extent, this is a nominal understanding of evil, at least from the point of view of the nature of the Female, especially if we read it in the context of the above translated passage from *Da'at Tevunot*.[637] Such an interpretation will also impact our

---

633 On the nature of this Lurianic concept in Luzzatto, see *Sefer ha-Kelalim*, kelal 8, 251–252. Compare also to the view in *'Adir ba-Marom ha-Shalem*, 471, where the transformation of evil to good is related to the ascent of the *Shekhinah* and the verse in Proverbs.

634 Luzzatto, *Sefer ha-Kelalim*, kelal 26, 275:

ענין אשת חיל עטרת בעלה ושנוקבא היא נקודה אחת לבד וט' ספירות באים לה בסוד תוספת הנה המלכות שהיא שורש התחתונים ממש היא לנדה הנגתנת מקום לחושך בהנהגה ולרע ממש כי אין החסרון מפאת המשפיע לעולם אלא מפאת המקבל ואמנם זה הוא שפלות לה ודאי מצד אחד אך מצד אחר הוא שבח ועילוי כי אין זה עשוי אלא לגלות יחוד העליון כמבואר למעלה ואין שבחו של האדון ב"ה מתגלה אלא בה ונמצא שמפני כך עשאה האדון ב"ה חסרה בטבעה וחשוכה לתת מקום לרע ממש, ולכן היא צריכה תיקונים רבים מה שאין צריך במשפיע שאינו חסר מצד עצמו. אך כשהיא נשלמת וקיבלה תיקוניה תיקונה שיצאה מן הרע ואדרבא החזירה הרע לטוב כמבואר למעלה אז שבחה עולה עד אדם קדמון כי שבחו של האדון ב"ה מתגלה בה וכמו שביארנו ואז נקראת 'עטרת בעלה'.

A part of which was translated in Wolfson, *Language, Eros, Being*, 375, 591, n. 11, adduced here with some changes.

635 See my *Il male primordiale*, pp. 330–334.

636 This is a philosophical approach that accounts for alleged changes in the supernal world by assuming a different reception of the same act by lower and diverse entities. It appears also in another work of Luzzatto's *Qine'at H' Tzeva'ot*, 106. This view entered Kabbalah already in the thirteenth century. See, e.g., Abraham Abulafia, *Shomer Mitzwah*, 27, Abulafia, *'Imrei Shefer*, 71, and Cordovero's *Pardes Rimmonim*, 4: 4.

637 The two books do not display the same theory of the Feminine: one emphasizes Her perfection, while the present quote emphasizes Her deficiency. For a nominalistic understanding of the myth of the diminution of the moon, see Cordovero in his *Sefer 'Elimah*, 54–55, where the Female is described not just as growing but, as in the case of the moon, Her body is gradually

understanding of Luzzatto's use of the verse from Proverbs 12: 4 as referring to the superiority of the Feminine, in the vein of the passage translated above from *Tiqqunim Hadashim*. This is also the case in a seminal passage from *'Adir ba-Marom,* where Luzzatto writes:

> But when this cycle will be completed, then the Female ascends to be a diadem to the King. And the secret of this is that then "the Female will encircle the Male,"[638] namely, that *Ze'yir 'Anppin* will be operating by the power of the Female, what She prepared during the time of the exile, because thus She is the diadem on His head, what She prepared is what He will do, neither less nor more. Therefore, in accordance to Her aspect, power is drawn to Him, and He operates solely as the *Shekhinah* did [...]; the governance is Her governance, in accordance to the secret of causing the return of evil to good. But at the end, *Ze'yir 'Anppin* will behave by means of this diadem of His, which is indeed "the valorous wife is a diadem on His head.[639]

The prominent role of the Female as preparing the power for the governance in the eschaton, and Her empowering the Male, who precisely implements Her directives, represents a fascinating example of Her privileged status in comparison to the Male, despite the existence of opposite views in the very same book.[640] In some cases in this book, Luzzatto resorts to the locution *'Atrot ha-hanhagah,* the diadems of the governance, a depiction that underscores the importance of the diadem.[641] In any case, according to another text of Luzzatto's, even the governance of the Male depends ultimately on a feminine source, described as an "occult root" that is higher than the Male – the supernal configuration of *'Imma',* corresponding to the *sefirah* of *Binah,* which emanates upon the Small

---

illumined by the sun, and thus its full size becomes visible after it is covered and thus invisible, thereby allowing a more egalitarian approach to the question of the dimensions of the two bodies. See also Cordovero's *'Or Yaqar* 5: 222. For a nominalist vision of the *sefirot*, see Luzzatto's *Sefer ha-Kelalim,* kelal 1, 247.

638 Jeremiah 31: 21.

639 *'Adir ba-Marom ha-Shalem*, 362:

אבל כשנשלם זה הסיבוב, אז עולה נוק' להיות לעטרה למלך. וסוד הדבר, כי אז, נקבה תסובב גבר (ירמיה לא, כא), והיינו שהז"א יהיה הפועל בכח הנוק' מה שהכינה היא כל זמן הגלות, כי כך היא עטרה בראשו, מה שמוכן בה הוא מה שיעשה, לא פחות ולא יותר. ונמצא, שלפי בחינתה נמשך לו כח תמיד, והוא פועל רק כפי מה שעשתה השכינה... ההנהגה היא הנהגתה, בסוד החזרת הרע לטוב. אך בסוף, ז"א ינהג בעטרתו זאת, והוא ממש 'אשת חיל עטרת בעלה'.

640 *Adir ba-Marom,* 5:

כי באמת הנוקבא איננה עשויה אלא לקבל מן הזכר ולהשפיע לתחתונים. ונמצא ששלימות מציאותה היא הקבלה מן הזכר וההשפעה.

641 *'Adir ba-Marom,* 90–91.

Configuration, – the Male – and then upon the *Nuqva'*.[642] Elsewhere, he equates the governance of *Ze'yir 'Anppin*, described as that of mercy, on the one hand, and that of the Female, representing the governance of the *Nuqba'* and related to judgement, on the other hand.[643] Interestingly, in one case, the attribution of judgment to the *Nuqba'* is sweetened by the supernal Mother, the *Binah*.[644] Let me emphasize, however, that *'Atarah* occurs in Luzzatto also in some clearly phallo-centric treatments, as part of what we call conceptual fluidity.[645]

Although Luzzatto subscribes to the vertical theosophical system in most of his discussions, he was also concerned with what I term circular theosophy. In his major theological work, *'Adir ba-Marom*, he wrote about the secret of the twenty-two letters in their different configurations, constructing divine names and appellations; they were also, however, in a chaotic state, without order. Then he wrote: "Afterwards, they were constituted in the secret of a circle, whose end is fixed in its beginning, so that they all remain in the secret of one *Yod* alone, in the secret[646] of the formless diameter fixed in the ring."[647]

Luzzatto organizes the letters into a sequence in accordance with the two hundred thirty one combinations of two letters, as proposed in *Sefer Yetzirah*, then into divine names, that are fewer, and then into one letter, *Yod*; he then mentions the image of the diameter and the ring. In short, this is a pyramidal structure. Thus, the circle and the ring point to circularity, while the shape of *Yod* stands for the diameter, which is formless because *Ḥokhmah*, the second *sefirah*, represented by the letter *Yod*, is conceived of as formless, versus the third *sefirah*, *Binah*, which is a circle. Another interesting treatment of circularity is found elsewhere in the same book.[648]

---

642 See the fragment from an epistle of Luzzatto sent to the "sages of Livorno," written in 1730, printed in Meir Benayahu, *Kitvei ha-Kabalah shel ha-Ramhal*, 269.

643 *Sefer ha-Kelalim*, 278, no. 29.

644 *'Adir ba-Marom*, 72–73.

645 See, e.g., *'Adir ba-Marom*, 5, 9, 98, 134, 208, 282, 284, 360–361.

646 Cf. *Zohar*, I, fol. 15a, Matt, *The Zohar, Pritzker edition*, 1: 108, translates "a cluster of vapor … thrust in a ring" but *qutra'* should be understood, in my opinion, as a diameter, following the use of the Barcelonese author in the first part of the twelfth century R. Abraham bar Ḥyya', *qoter*. See also the similar interpretation of the Zoharic text in *Sha'arei Ramhal*, 420.

647 *'Adir Ba-Marom*, 336:

סוד הכ"ב אותיות היו מצטרפות בצירופים רבים בכח שני שמות אלו דאלהי"ם, ונעשים רל"א שערים פנים ואחור. ובכח הצירופים האלו היו מאירים כל הכינוים כנ"ל. אך עדיין היה הכל בסוד תהו ובהו, והכינוים מתערבים ומאירים זה בזה בלי שום סדר, אלא הכל בערבוביא. ואחר כך חזרו ונכללו כל אלו השמות בסוד עיגול אחד ונעוץ סופו בתחלתו, עד שנשאר הכל בסוד י' אחד לבד, בסוד קוטרא בגולמא נעיץ בעיזקא והה' שזכרנו נשארה בסוד ד"ו העולה י'.

648 *'Adir Ba-Marom*, 440–441:

והוא סוד כתר מלכות, והוא הד' של אחד, ונחשב לעטרת בעלה. ואז נאמר 'עיקר שכינה בתחתונים'...ומתעטרת ברישא ואז מתחבר חיבור יאהדונה"י, בסוד זיווג של רישא וסופא. ואז נשלם אחד ממש.

Circular theosophy is evident also in another text from Luzzatto's above-mentioned *Qelaḥ Piteḥei Ḥokhmah,* where he claims:

> In the *sefirot* there are the straightforward light and two kinds of returning light: [a] one is after the ranks[649] descended from *Keter* to *Malkhut,* [then] *Malkhut* returns and becomes *Keter,* and in this manner until *Keter* becomes *Malkhut.* And this shows the perfection of the Infinite, blessed be He, that from It everything emerges and It is the end of All, namely that "I am the first and I am the last."[650] And It reveals itself at the beginning, just as it does at the end. And each of the ranks that are near to It is aggrandized by Its name, and what was *Malkhut* becomes *Keter.* [b] And the second one is that no light perfects Its issue but only when it exists and returns to its source, namely when it descends downwards forcefully, and afterwards it immediately returns, leaving below the rank that it leaves, and it ascends. And then the rank remains in its state of being built, and so on for all of them."[651]

[A] is an excellent example of the dynamic nature of the sefirotic system, which speaks about transformation, presumably, of the entire spectrum of the divine powers, but the Kabbalist specifies only *Keter* and *Malkhut* as the beginning and the end. The symmetry between the transformations at the beginning and at the end is evident: the two extremes are not antipodal entities but are transformed into each other. Whether this theogonic description implies some gender overtones is not clear, despite the use of the term *Malkhut,* as She may be just the last as the opposite of the first. No matter the authorial intention regarding gender issues, the circularity of the system is evident, as we can discern also from a variety of other discussions in this book, where the recurrent use of the verb *SBB,* to encircle, occurs.[652] In short, perfection is explicitly related to the image of the circle and to circularity.[653] In [B], however, the theory of the two lights, already discussed in the previous chapter, again serves this idea of circularity, especially as the immediacy of the movement of the lights is mentioned. The topic

---

649 Namely, the *sefirot.*

650 Isaiah 44: 6. This verse serves in a similar context in Luzzatto's *'Adir ba-Marom ha-Shalem,* 53, 64, 67, 96, 136.

651 No. 16, fol. 14ab:

יש בספירות אור ישר ואור חוזר משני מינים. א', שאחר שירדו המדרגות מכתר עד מלכות, חוזר מלכות ונעשה כתר, וכן בדרך זה, עד שכתר נעשה מלכות. וזה מראה שלמות הא"ס ב"ה, שממנו יוצא הכל, והוא סוף הכל, והיינו, "אני ראשון ואני אחרון", והוא מתגלה כך בראשונה כמו באחרונה. והמדרגות - כל הקרוב קרוב אליו מתגדל בשמו, ומה שהיה מלכות נעשה כתר. והמין הב', שום אור אינו משלים ענינו אלא כשיוצא ועוד חוזר למקורו. והיינו כי יורד עד למטה בכח, ואחר כך מידי עלותו מניח למטה מדרגה מה שמניח, והוא מתעלה. ואז המדרגה נשארת בבנינה, וכן כולם.

652 See *'Adir ba-Marom,* no. 9, fols. 10b–11a, no. 12, fol. 12a, no. 13, fol. 12b, no. 14, fol. 13a, or *'Adir ba-Marom ha-Shalem,* 119, and *Sha'arei Ramḥal,* 420.

653 *'Adir ba-Marom,* no. 9, fols. 10b–11a, no. 12, fol. 12a, no. 13, fol. 12b, no. 14, fol. 13a, or *'Adir ba-Marom ha-Shalem,* no. 13, fol. 12b.

differs from [A], when the *sefirot* are transformed into each other; [B] deals with the creation of a certain rank, namely a *sefirah*, by the moving light, without mentioning its transformation into another *sefirah*. In a way, the two lights are one but moving in different directions. In an important passage in *'Adir ba-Marom*, Luzzatto writes:

> And what is said about the Female of the [World of] Emanation that "they enjoy the radiance of the *Shekhinah*"[654] so we may call all the *sefirot* the radiance [of the light of] the powers of the Infinite, blessed be He. And in all the places radiance is *Malkhut* of that rank … and the *sefirot* in general are the radiance, and the parts of the aspects of the radiance are numerous, and they are the *sefirot*. And when the Infinite, blessed be He, reveals in order to govern, all the *sefirot* and their matters will return to be counted but as "*Malkhut* of the Infinite," when the Infinite governs. And this is what is intended by the "secret of the *Shekhinah*".… And She will govern because of the unity that will be revealed in Her,[655] until all the ranks will ascend so that they will be counted within Her as solely *Malkhut* of the Infinite … and you should understand that when the *Shekhinah* is in Her place, She is only Her small aspect, namely, *Malkhut* after [namely lower than] *Ze'yir 'Anppin*, as when the nine supernal *sefirot* allude to the hidden supernal powers … [the place] from where the radiance emerges, then *Malkhut* will descend beneath them alludes to the light that emerges from them. However, indeed, everything is *Malkhut* alone. And when the union will be revealed within Her, She is enhanced and elevates Herself to Her source, so that She causes the return of all the worlds to their aspect – to be counted solely as *Malkhut* of the Infinite, blessed be He, and then it is the time of the great and perfect *Tiqqun*.[656]

The feminine aspect of the terms *Shekhinah* and *Malkhut* is evident from the use of the term *Nuqva'*, the Female, at the beginning of the passage. Her centrality is also obvious as She is the main instrument of the divine revelation during the non-redeemed period, as well as in the eschaton.[657] It should be mentioned that the process of elevation is connected in many cases in this book to that of augmenting

---

654 *BT, Berakhot*, fol. 17a.

655 See also above, n. 632.

656 *'Adir ba-Marom*, part 2, 160:

כענין שנאמר למטה בנוק'[בא] דאצילות "ונהנים מזיו השכינה" כן נוכל לקרוא לכל הספירות "זיו" כחותיו של א"ס ב"ה, ובכל מקום "זיו" הוא המלכות של המדרגה ההוא שהזיו שלה. והצדיקים אינם נהנים אלא מזיו של השכינה... אך נדבר על ספירות בכלל כי הם הזיו, אלא שחלקי בחי' הזיו רבים, והם הם פרטי הספירות. ובהיות הא"ס ב"ה מתגלה לשלוט, יחזרו כל הספירות ועניניהם להיות נחשבים רק למלכות א"ס בהיות א"ס שולטת. וזה מה שתכוון בסוד השכינה ...והיא תשלוט הרבה מפני היחוד המתגלה בה, עד שיתעלה כל המדרגות להחשב בה רק מלכות של א"ס ב"ה ...ותראה כי השכינה במקומה הוא רק בחינתה הקטנה, שר"ל מלכות אחר ז"א, כי בהיות הט"ס העליונות רומזים הנסתר בכחות העליונות שאמרתי, שמהם יוצא הזיו, אז מלכות תרד תחתיהם לרמז האור היוצא מהם, אך באמת הכל הוא רק מלכות. ובהתגלות בה היחוד - היא מתגדלת ומתרוממת למקורה, עד שמחזירה כל העולמות לבחי' זאת - להחשב רק מלכות של א"ס ב"ה, ואז הוא זמן התיקון הגדול והשלם.

657 See *Sefer ha-Kelalim*, no. 36, 287.

the size or the power,[658] a motif found in several instances also in Cordovero in the context of the Female. In the former era, She represents the Infinite on the various levels of reality, each containing its own *Shekhinah*, whereas in the final epoch, that of *Tiqqun*, all the beings will be elevated by Her to Her supernal hypostasis within the Infinite, or according to another discussion, to *'Adam Qadmon*.[659] According to yet another discussion, the theme of sexual intercourse within the "Head that is not known" reverberates on all the lower planes, an interesting exposition of the comprehensive nature of a widespread concept in Kabbalah that I designate as dual ontology.[660] It is plausible to conceive *Malkhut* of the Infinite as a primordial entity and the return of all beings to Her as an eschatological event. According to this passage, She is not dissolved within the Infinite, nor masculinized, rather, it is the starting and the final point of a broader cosmogonic process, which assumes that everything has been created within Her and will return to Her.[661] This passage speaks clearly about the process of *Tiqqun*, reparation or amendment, but without any reference to an obliteration of *Malkhut*. In this latter phase, the various levels of existence of *Malkhut* within the worlds, like *Malkhut* of the world of emanation which is described, as the result of Her descent, as smaller and lower than *Ze'yir 'Anppin*, will be aggrandized and return too to the realm of *Malkhut* of the Infinite. This "small aspect" of *Malkhut* presupposes a concept of a greater *Malkhut*, which I assume is *Malkhut* of the Infinite or another higher status within the world of emanation.[662] It is important to note

---

658 See, e.g., *'Adir ba-Marom ha-Shalem*, 22.

659 See *Sefer ha-Kelalim*, *kelal* 26, 275, and *'Adir ba-Marom*, 105.

660 *'Adir ba-Marom*, *kelal* 35, 284–85.

661 See also the Lurianic text discussed in Yoram Jacobson, "The Problem of Evil and Its Sanctification in Kabbalistic Thought," 254–255, and Luzzatto's *'Adir ba-Marom*, 394:

"שכל העולמות נבראו במלכות, אלא שאף על פי כן מתחלקים, שזה נקרא זכר וזה נקרא נקבה"

"All the words have been created within/by *Malkhut*, but nevertheless they are divided, that this is called male and this is called female."

662 See *'Adir ba-Marom ha-Shalem*, 4. Even after Her final ascent, when She is described as not descending again, part of a clear restorative situation, She does not seem, according to this text, to disappear. This passage seems to be influenced by Cordovero's discussion in *Tefillah le-Moshe*, fol. 230a:

"והי' אור הלבנה כאור החמה דהיינו אל השמי' יקשר המלכות בת"ת ושוב לא תרד".

The term *Malkhut* of the Infinite is found in Lurianic Kabbalah and it plays an important role in the writings of Luzzatto's older contemporary R. Ya'aqov Koppel of Mezritch; see Shaul Magid, "The Metaphysics of *Malkhut*: *Malkhut* as *Eyn Sof* in the Writings of Ya'aqov Koppel of Mezritch," 245–267. The Lurianic term *Malkhut* of the Infinite seems to echo a concept found in Cordovero, as to the preexistence of *Malkhut* to the ten *sefirot* and the Womb of the Infinite. See my article "The Womb and the Infinite in R. Moshe Cordovero's Kabbalistic Thought," 41–64.

that Luzzatto mentions, explicitly, the return of the Female to Her source, which is part of the gender theory I proposed above as constituting the third phase.

Elsewhere this Kabbalist speaks about the special affinity of *Keter* and *Malkhut* that allows the latter to arouse the former.[663] In this case, the sexual connotation of the act related to *Malkhut* is evident, as is the feminine dimension of *Malkhut*. Others in Luzzatto's circle assumed that the secret of the connection between *Keter* and *Malkhut*, as epitomized by the locution *Keter Malkhut*, is still unknown, which helps explain the length of the exile. In the future, however, the secret will be revealed.[664] In this context, Luzzatto's view as to the redemptive role played by women in the past and the future, which includes transgressive acts, should be mentioned.[665]

In short, Luzzatto, the most prolific and original post-Lurianic Kabbalist, followed, *mutatis mutandis*, the path opened by Luria insofar as the nature and activity of the Female is concerned, and he did so in more explicit terms than we have seen in the preceding chapter. At the same time, probably under the influence of Cordovero, he also adopts the circular theosophy and the centrality of the amendment of the *Shekhinah*. In my opinion, the continuity between Luzzatto's views and those of earlier Kabbalists in terms of the topics studied here is quite obvious, despite his more abstract modes of discourse.[666]

---

663 *'Adir ba-Marom ha-Shalem*, 119:

וסוד הענין הזה הוא כתר מלכות. והנה בכח הקשר הזה מלכות מעוררת את הכתר.

See also his *Sefer Kelalim Rishonim*, kelal 35, printed in *Sefer ha-Kelalim*, 284–285.

664 See the commentary on Psalms, from Luzzatto's milieu: *'Otzrot ha-Ramhal*, 155:

וטעם אריכות הגלות הוא, לפי שאינו מתגלה החיבור של מלכות בכתר, בסוד כתר מלכות, אבל לעתיד לבא יתגלה זה התיקון.

See also at the beginning of the next chapter, beside n. 668.

665 See Kaniel, *Holiness and Transgression*, 101–103.

666 The impact of the cult of the Virgin Mary on Luzzatto's views discussed above is still debatable. See Garb, *Kabbalist in the Eye of the Storm*, 215–216. Indubitably Luzzatto, like Cardoso before him, was aware of the Christian cult of the Virgin Mary, and it might have had an impact on the vision of the *Shekhinah*. See also above, n. 90.

10 The Privileged Female in Some Later Kabbalists in Ashkenaz

Early in the history of the themes discussed above, Middle Eastern elements – in the case of the book of *Bahir*, the Spanish ones that deal with the relationship between thought and action – and the mainly Ashkenazi anthropomorphic ones were combined in various ways. Those combinations do not articulate a unified picture, a fully coherent worldview, although the importance of the connected concepts of beginning and end is prominent. Most of the Kabbalistic sources cited thus far stem from Spanish Kabbalists or those who wrote under their direct impact. This applies also to the views of R. Isaac Luria or of R. Isaiah Horowitz, both Ashkenazi figures by extraction, despite the fact that the voluminous Ashkenazi literature written in Germany and France – Halakhic, exegetical or speculative – from the tenth to the end of the thirteenth century did not mention the pseudo-Aristotelian dictum. The two Kabbalists, who spent some time in the Ottoman Empire, were in direct contact with Spanish Kabbalists.

Kabbalists who were active later in Ashkenazi territories in East Europe, however, show signs of having adopted identical or similar views to those discussed here. For example, R. Samson Ostropoler, the mid-seventeenth century Kabbalist active in Poland,[667] wrote in *Dan Yadin*, a commentary to the book *Karnayyim*, written by a certain obscure figure R. Aharon of Kardina, as follows: "In the secret of *Keter* and *Malkhut* etc.,[668] you should know that the interpretation is that when *'Ateret* is higher than *Paḥad*, in accordance to *Keter Malkhut*, when *Malkhut* ascends on high [becoming] an emblem on *Keter* [*nezer la-Keter*], and then She is called *'Ateret Tiferet*, as She is higher than *Tiferet*. Then all the *sefirot* imbibe peace and the blessing of God."[669]

In the Hebrew Bible, the term *Nezer* signifies an emblem on the high priest's turban.[670] Implicitly, therefore, the head as *Keter* is also hinted at in the context of *Malkhut* and *'Ateret*, which is described as ascending, understood as a very positive action. When *Malkhut* ascends on high, Her elevated

---

667 See Yehuda Liebes, "Mysticism and Reality: Towards a Portrait of the Martyr and Kabbalist R. Samson Ostropoler," 221–255.
668 This text is the subject of the following analysis. On the secret of *Keter* and *Malkhut*, see also above, at the end of ch. 9, in R. Moshe Hayyim Luzzatto's discussion translated there.
669 Samson Ostropoler, "Dan Yadin," 63:

בסוד כתר ומלכות וכו', פירוש ידוע תדע שכאשר עטרת למעלה מפחד בסוד כתר מלכות שמלכות עולה למעלה נזר
לכתר ואז היא נקראת עטרת תפארת שהיא למעלה לתפארת אז כל הספירות יונקים שלום וברכה וברכת ה'
670 Exodus 29: 6.

https://doi.org/10.1515/9783110599800-010

status is clear; we may ask, however, whether the reference to sucking/imbibing reflects a gender role of *Malkhut*.

A passage by the late eighteenth-century Hasidic Kabbalistic author R. Isaac Aizik ha-Kohen shows the impact of Lurianic views, where he writes: "All the aspect [sic] of the moon [*ha-Yareaḥ*], which is a lower rank, is grounded first in its place in the Thought, and it is the shape of the moon [*ha-Levanah*] that was shown by the Holy One, blessed be He, to Moses, and He told him, 'So, Watch and Sanctify!'[671] which means that the lower moon [*ha-Yareaḥ*] should be seen in the form of what you see above."[672]

I am not familiar with earlier texts that portray the moon as found within the divine thought. In my opinion, the moon stands for the Female, as in many other pre-Kabbalistic and Kabbalistic interpretations.[673] Whereas the primordial shape within the divine thought is referred to in Hebrew by the feminine term for moon, *Levanah*, Her lower manifestation is alluded to by the masculine term, *Yareaḥ*. Whether there is an implication of gender in this distinction is not so clear. In another discussion, R. Isaac Aizik ha-Kohen applies first in Thought as referring to Sabbath, Repose, and the Female. In a manner recalling some earlier analyzed views in Lurianic Kabbalah and in Luzzatto's other writings, they are seen as superior in comparison to the weekdays, which are related to the Male.[674]

The constellation of ideas discussed above is well represented in the massive encyclopedic work of R. Jacob Tzevi Yalish, a Hasidic author who was also an accomplished Kabbalist, writing in the first half of the nineteenth century in Poland:

> *Keter* is made from *Malkhut*, in accordance with the secret of the Returning Light, which ascends from *Malkhut* to *Keter* in the secret of "its end fixed in its beginning," and so it descends in the secret of straightforward light [from] *Keter* to *Malkhut*, and their beginning is in their end, and this is the secret of *Keter Malkhut*, that *Malkhut* is contained in *Keter* and *Keter* is contained in *Malkhut*, in accordance with the secret of the straightforward light and of the returning light.[675]

---

671 See *BT, Rosh ha-Shanah*, fol. 20a.

672 Isaac Aizik ha-Kohen, *Berit Kehunat 'Olam*, 425:

כי כל בחינת יר"ח שהוא בדרגא תתאה נשרש במקומה במחשבה תחילה, והוא סוד צורת הלבנה שהראה הקדוש ברוך הוא למשה ואמר לו כזה ראה וקדש, רצונו שהירח התחתונה תראה כתבניתה אשר אתה מראה למעלה.

673 See my "The Divine Female and the Mystique of the Moon."

674 *Berit Kehunat 'Olam*, 50–51. Compare to Idel, "On Gender Theories in R. Moshe Hayyim Luzzatto."

675 Jacob Tzevi Yalish, *Qehilat Ya'aqov*, fol. 45b:

כתר כלול ממלכות בסוד אור חוזר שעולה מלכות אל הכתר, בסוד נעוץ סופו בתחילתו, וכן יורד בסוד אור ישר כתר עד המלכות ותחילתן בסופן, זה סוד כתר מלכות, שמלכות כלולה בכתר וכתר כלול במלכות, בסוד אור ישר ואור חוזר.

In this instance, the ongoing circular movement of the two lights, mentioned already in Safedian Kabbalah, for example by Cordovero, Luria, and Luzzatto,[676] is described here more forcefully as linking between the two poles of *Keter* and *Malkhut*. Although the author invokes secrecy several times, the content is revealed immediately afterwards. The uroboric dimension is not indicated explicitly, but this seems to be the meaning of the passage. The sexual polarity is introduced elsewhere in the encyclopedia, when Yalish wrote: "The essence of the name of *Keter* is the feminine aspect that it receives from itself … that *Malkhut* is called *Keter Torah*, *Keter Kehunah*, *Keter Malkhut*,[677] when She ascends on high, in accordance with the secret[678] of 'the valorous wife is the diadem of Her husband'".[679]

The circular meaning of the term "crown" probably entailed the assumption that this *sefirah* has a feminine significance. This is a rather daring discussion – by ascending, the lower feminine power reaches *Keter*, thus encircling the higher Male.[680] In any case, the ascent does not attenuate the feminine dimension of the Female, as this high *sefirah* was depicted as feminine. Elsewhere,[681] Yalish describes the pseudo-Aristotelian dictum by adding the equally Aristotelian theory of final cause in the case of the relationship between cause and causatum, the latter being considered the telos. He thus interprets the rabbinic myth of the diminution of the Moon, which refers to the Female.[682] Again, the teleological mode of thought is adopted within an obviously theosophical context. Let me emphasize that here, as in many other cases, ascent does not mean a sexual transformation.

From the late eighteenth century, Kabbalah developed in Lithuania primarily in the direction of Lurianic thought, sometimes influenced by Luzzatto's views. The first and most important figure in this school is the famous R. Elijah ben Shlomo, known as the Vilna Gaon. In his *Commentary to Sifra' di-Tzeni'uta'*, he wrote: "Everything is one; their end is fixed in their beginning, as it is written in *Sefer Yetzirah*. This is the reason why *Malkhut* is 'Aniy [I] and *Keter* is 'Ayin [Nought] compounded of the same consonants."[683] Further on in this book, he

---

676 See, e.g, *Pardes Rimonnim*, 15: 1; Cordovero, *'Or Yaqar*, 3: 38, 4: 146, and the two previous chapters.

677 Avot, 4: 13.

678 Proverbs 12: 4.

679 *Qehilat Ya'aqov*, fol. 45c:

ועיקר שם הכתר הוא צד הנקבות שמקבל מעצמו...פירוש דמלכות נקרא כתר תורה כתר כהונה כתר מלכות, כאשר היא עולה למעלה בסוד אשת חיל עטרת בעלה.

680 See above, nn. 375, 428.

681 *Qehilat Ya'aqov*, fol. 13b.

682 See my "Divine Female."

683 Elijah ben Shlomo, *Commentary to Sifra' di-Tzeni'uta'*, ch. 2, fol. 38a:

שהכל א' נעוץ סופן בתחלתן כמ"ש בס"י שלכן מלכות אני וכתר אין באותיות שוות.

states: "*Malkhut* Herself became *Keter* to them as every *Keter* in the lower world is *Malkhut* of the supernal world, in accordance with the secret of *Keter Malkhut* as it is written in *Sefer Yetzirah*: their end is fixed in their beginning."[684]

Evidently, some form of special affinity between the beginning and the end has been established as part of the uroboric theosophy, although here a more cosmic picture is intended. The feminine nature of *Malkhut* is not, however, emphasized in this context or in a brief but interesting discussion by R. Isaac Ḥaver, who claims that "the secret of *'Ayin* and *'Aniy* [is that] their end is fixed in their beginning and this is the return of the wheel to its root."[685] On the basis of many discussions in very similar contexts, the term *'Aniy* stands for the last *sefirah* and most plausibly for the last feminine power.

Elsewhere in the same commentary, R. Elijah discusses the meaning of the Diadem, in a manner that is very relevant for our discussions:

> ... in the seventh millennium, all will return to their mother, "and the earth will be obliterated." ... This is the secret of Sabbath, but Sabbath does not return to Her root to *Binah* but *Binah* illuminates Her by means of the six extremities, which are the six weekdays of deeds, and She is equal to him, and this is the reason that this is the time of intercourse. And then[686] "the righteous sit and their diadems are on their heads,"[687] "the diadem of her husband,"[688] and then "there is no food or beverage or procreation, etc.,"[689] as it is on the day of Atonement, the rank of *Binah*, as it is written in the *Tiqqunim*, as then it is in accordance with the secret of "the sign" that is a diadem on the head, "and one that uses the sign, will die,"[690] as there is no intercourse when *Malkhut* is [found] on the head of the husband, and there are no new souls ... and *Binah* alone remains as everything is hidden within Her.[691]

The *'Aniy* – *'Ayin* is a Cordoverian pun. See, e.g., Cordovero, *'Or Yaqar*, (Jerusalem, 1985), 13: 120, 7: 133; Asulin, "The Double Construct of the Image of the *Shekhinah*," 94, n. 94, and the material cited above in n. 439, and Idel, *Hasidism: Between Ecstasy and Magic*, 109–110. It is also found, however, in Lurianic texts such as Vital's *'Etz Ḥayyim.*

684 *Commentary to Sifra' di-Tzeni'uta'*, ch. 4, fol. 39c:

ומלכות עצמה נעשית כתר להם שכל כתר שבעולם התחתון הוא מלכות של עולם עליון בסוד כתר מלכות כמ"ש בס"י נעוץ סופן בתחלתן.

685 Isaac Ḥaver, *Sefer Pithei She'arim*, Netiv ABY'A, Petah 1, II, fol. 147a:

והוא סוד אי"ן ואנ"י נעוץ סופם בתחלתם והוא חזרת הגלגל אל שרשו

686 I assume that here R. Elijah refers to the seventh millennium.

687 *BT. Berakhot*, fol. 17a.

688 Proverbs 12: 4.

689 *BT. Berakhot*, fol. 17a.

690 *Avot*, 1: 13.

691 *Commentary to Sifra' di-Tzeni'uta'*, ch. 1, fol. 17c:

אלף השביעי יחזרו כלם לאמם ואתבטלת ארעא שתשוב לאמה...וזהו סוד השבת אלא ששבת אינה חוזרת לשרשה אל בינה אלא בינה מאיר לה שלא ע"י ו"ק ששת ימי המעשה והיא שוה לגביה לכן זמן הזיווג בו. אבל העה"ב דוגמת יה"כ ששבה אל אמה ואז צדיקים יושבים ועטרותיהן בראשיהן (בבלי, ברכות, דף יז ע"א) עטרת בעלה ואז אין בו

I propose distinguishing between two periods informing this passage – one in the seventh millennium, the other in the sixth. In the latter, *Malkhut* is a female who is depicted as illumined by *Binah,* the mother, and reaching a state or a size equal to the Male, with whom She has intercourse.[692] In the seventh millennium, however, *Malkhut* is described as ascending on the one hand onto the head of the Male and on the other, onto the Mother. The verse from Proverbs is understood here in a totally asexual manner, as referring to the superiority of the Feminine power, as is evident from the context. Interestingly, the Male is barely mentioned, as the divine Feminine is depicted as depending on the *Binah,* and She returns to Her root there.[693] The Female is, therefore, either equal to the Male or superior to Him, and there is no indication of Her absorption or masculinization because of this ascent. Her return to the root may reflect a ramification of the three-phases theory.

It is worth pointing out that in describing the ascent of *Malkhut* to *Binah,* not to a higher source, R. Elijah diverges from the theory of Lurianic texts discussed in ch. 8, as R. Shlomo Eliashiv pointed out in his *Commentary on Sifra' de-Tzni'uta'.*[694] No matter how low the source of the Female is considered here in the sefirotic hierarchy in comparison to the Lurianic views, She is nevertheless distinctly privileged. It is noteworthy that a direct disciple of R. Elijah, R. Menahem Mendel of Shklov, mentioned the theory of the nine points that are completed by a higher, tenth point that encompasses the lower nine, without emphasizing however, the feminine aspects of this point, a term that in Hebrew is grammatically feminine.[695] It is not clear whether the Female is mentioned in this context; it depends on whether one explicates the shorter form 'נק as *neqeivah* or as *nequddah.* I prefer to decode it as Female, as it refers to the occultation of the feminine divine there. Elsewhere, he speaks about the source of *Malkhut* in "the Head that is not known" in an explicit manner; from the context, a feminine entity is plausible, as Tamar and the emergence of her sons Peretz and Zerah from there is mentioned.[696]

לא אכילה ולא שתיה ולא פ"ו כו' כמו ביה"כ דרגא דבינה כמ"ש בתיקונים שאז היא בסוד תגא עטרה בראש וכל המשתמש בתגא חלף שאין שימוש כשמלכות בראש בעלה ואין נשמות חדשות לכן אין בו אכילה כו'. ה"ס וארעא אתבטלת, ונשאר בינה בלבד שכלם בקרבה נעלמים.
See also Liebes, *From Shabbetai Tsevi to the Gaon of Vilna,* 275–276.

692 This view is found in a plethora of earlier Kabbalistic texts. See above, nn. 383, 627.

693 *Commentary to Sifra' di-Tzeni'uta',* ch. 1, fol. 17b, and see above, n. 484.

694 *Commentary to Sifra' di-Tzeni'uta',* fol. 70b, no. 39. See also immediately below, our discussion of his views, in line with R. Elijah of Vilna.

695 Menahem Mendel of Shklov, *'Mayyim 'Adirim,* 4–5, discussed also in Liebes, *From Shabbetai Tsevi to the Gaon of Vilna,* 158–160.

696 Menahem Mendel of Shklov, *Sefer Raza' de-Meheimanuta'.* 1: 63.

Another member of the Lithuanian school of Kabbalists, R. Isaac Eisik Haver Wildman, active in the mid-nineteenth century, the author of *Pithei She'arim*, refers to the theme of the "diadem of Her Husband," writing:

> And just as in the [process of] emanation of Male and Female, they were together within the womb of *'Imma'*, impregnated in the secret of *du-partzufin* within the letter *H*[697] that is in *'Imma'*, as there the Female is onto the Male, "the diadem of Her Husband" … and from the side of *'Imma'*, it is governance of the World-to-Come, in the seventh millennium, the rank of the Female will be higher than that of the Male, which is the secret of the amendment of [the name of] *Ben* and will ascend to *SaG*, the diadem onto the name *MaH*.[698]

The structure of the *du-partzufin* within the womb of the Mother assumes the superiority of the Female over the Male according to both Cordovero and R. Hayyim Vital.[699] The metamorphosis of the *du-partuzfin* in the lower sefirotic world assumes an inversion of the hierarchy, which will be restored in the eschatological time.

Overall, some Lurianic Kabbalists employ the concept of *Malkhut* of the *'Ein Sof*, namely, *Malkhut* of the Infinite, and its reverberations in the other, lower kinds of *Malkhut* that correspond to and stem from the highest one.[700] In one instance, this theme is articulated by referring to the pseudo-Aristotelian dictum. R. Shlomo Eliashiv, a major late nineteenth century and early twentieth century Lithuanian Kabbalist, active in the last part of his life in Jerusalem, wrote:

---

697 Namely, the first H in the Tetragrammaton, which corresponds to the third *sefirah* or the countenance of *'Imma'*.

698 Isaac Eisik Haver Wildman, *Pithei She'arim*, 2, fol. 162b:

וכמו שבאצילות זו"ן היה תחילה ברחם אימא בעיבור בסוד ד"ו פרצופים...כי שם הנוקבא ע"ג דכורא עטרת בעלה כמ"ש בכמה מקומות, שמצד אימא הוא הנהגת עוה"ב, באלף השביעי תהיה מדרגת הנוקבא למעלה מדכורא שהוא סוד תיקונים של ב"ן שיעלה לס"ג עטרת על גבי שם מ"ה.

See also his *Berit Yitzhaq*, fols. 4c, 38b. Haver was influenced by Luzzatto's Kabbalah and the passage from Vital's book *Mevo' She'arim* on the divine names; this is discussed in a different manner than my gender theory by Wolfson, "Gender and Heresy," 259–260. This passage seems to be influenced by Vital's *'Etz Hayyim*, Gate 39, sermon 5. One can discern a rather androcentric approach to what happens in the present from other parts of Eisik Haver Wildman's *Pithei She'arim*. See e. g., 2, fol. 80ab.

699 See Idel, *Male and Female*, n. 69.

700 See the early eighteenth-century Polish Kabbalist, R. Jacob Koppel Lipshitz, *Sha'arei Gan 'Eden*, fols. 21d–22a; and the discussion of the topic in Moshe Perlmuter, *Rabbi Jonathan Eibeschuetz and His Attitude to Sabbateanism*, 96, 109–110; Idel, *Kabbalah & Eros*, 208–209, 310, n. 26, and compare to Magid, "The Metaphysics of *Malkhut: Malkhut* as *Eyn Sof* in the Writings of Ya'aqov Koppel of Mezritch," 245–267.

Malkhut of the [world of] emanation touches the light of *'Ein Sof*, indeed, that is found within *Malkhut* of *'Ein Sof*, as the end of the action is [found] in the Thought first, and *Malkhut* is there, and the entire revelation of *Malkhut* of *'Ein Sof*, is only for the sake of Her, so that She will be revealed, and this is the reason that the entire emanation has been emanated for the sake of *Malkhut*, so that She will reign over all the actions [*ma'asim*] ... and this is the reason that at the time of *Tiqqun*, when His Kingdom[701] [*Malkhuto*] will be revealed in the entire world, and "He alone will reign in awe,"[702] then the light of *Malkhut* will expand, and She will unite from low to high and from high to low, and She will ascend higher than all,[703] up to *Malkhut* of *'Ein Sof*, blessed be His name."[704]

Eliashiv may have been influenced by the Kabbalistic thought of R. Moshe Hayyim Luzzatto, whose views were addressed in the previous chapter. We may distinguish between the theogonic moment of the generation of *Malkhut* after She was in the divine Thought and it descended, and the final phase, the return to the source, namely, two phases of the three-phases theory we mentioned above. Implicitly, the middle phase dealing with the exile of the Shekhinah is also implied here. If we consider whether the term *Malkhut* refers only to the divine dominion over the extra-divine world or whether it also contains some feminine aspects, the latter seems to be the case when the Kabbalist mentions the union from beneath

---

701 Another translation would be royalty, namely the attribute of the Infinite as a king.

702 This is a quote from the liturgical poem *'Adon 'Olam*, recited during the morning prayer.

703 On the syntagm "higher than all," see also above, the passage from Cordovero's *'Or Yaqar*, to *Tiqqunim*, 5: 2, referred to in n. 244 above. Eliashiv uses this syntagm several times in this book in the context of the Female or *Malkhut*.

704 Shlomo Eliashiv, *Leḥem, Shevo ve-'Aḥlema'*, part 2, 3, ch. 1, Haqdamot U-She'arim, fol. 46d:

המלכות דאצילות היא מגיעה באור א"ס ממש שהוא בהמלכות דא"ס כי סוף מעשה הוא במחשבה תחילה ושם מלכות אחד הוא וכל הגילוי דהמלכות דא"ס הוא רק בשבילה כדי שתתגלה היא ולכך נאצל כל האצילות כולו בשביל המלכות כדי למלוך על כל המעשים... ולכן בעת התיקון כשיתודע מלכותו יתברך בכל העולם כולו והוא לבדו ימלוך נורא אז תתפשט אור המלכות ותתייחד מתתא לעילא ומעילא לתתא ותתעלה היא למעלה מהכל שהוא עד המלכות דא"ס ית"ש.

and also in his other volume from this book, *Leḥem, Shevo ve-'Aḥlema'*, Sefer De'ah, vol. 2, fol. 158b, where *Malkhut* and *Keter* are depicted as two aspects of one entity, the former revealed, and the latter hidden:

הרי יש בה העלם וגילוי פנימית וחיצונית. שבפנימיותה היא למעלה מהכל ושורש הכל והכל הוא ממנה. כי היא השורש והראשית לכל י' ספי' שבכל עולם. אלא שכ"ז הוא נעלם בה

"And behold, within Her there is hiddenness and revelation, an inner dimension and an external one, and by the dint of Her inner dimension, She is higher than all, and is the root of all and everything emerged out of Her, as She is the root and the beginning of all the ten *sefirot* found in every world, but all this is hidden within Her." See also *Leshem*, fol. 158c, where the assumption that *Malkhut* is generated only by aspects of the higher nine *sefirot* is presented as an external view, while in a concealed manner, She is the source of these *sefirot*. In this context, he mentions that the essence of *Malkhut* is identical to the essence of *Keter*, another indication of Her privileged status. This view is reminiscent of earlier discussions in R. Jacob Koppel Lipshitz's *Sha'arei Gan 'Eden*, fols. 21d–22a.

on high and vice-versa. Those two forms of union are found in Cordovero's discussions of the sexual union of the divine female.[705] Moreover, the Kabbalistic traditions analyzed in this study that identify the entities described by the pseudo-Aristotelian dictum militate in this direction. The ascent to the Infinite that is described as taking place after union parallels discussions of the ascent of a couple to the higher levels in the divine world, as seen in ch. 7. Elsewhere in the same book, Eliashiv summarizes his view as follows:

> *Malkhut* consists[706] of two aspects: as Her essence and innermost [aspect] is higher than all, as She is the root of all ... She is from the *Malkhut* of the Infinite, as everything is from Her, and anything else is nought. However, She is changing from one revelation to another, and from one rank to another, and descends to the end of each of all supernal ranks, to become the root of the lower rank. This is the meaning of "I am the first and I am the last,"[707] *Keter Malkhut*, as on high She is *Keter*, that is *'Ayin* [Nought], hidden from cognition, and beneath it is *Malkhut*, called *'Aniy* [I].[708]

This is a nice summary of some of the topics dealing with the privileged approach to the Female. It adds an essential link between the two *sefirot*, the last representing a transformation of the first. Despite those hints at the feminine background of *Malkhut*, which is invariably referred to in Hebrew by verbs in the feminine form while it is in the zone of *Keter*, in earlier discussions in this book, Eliashiv firmly denies the feminine role of this power, claiming that She assumes a feminine nature only when She descends to Her lowest place.[709] According to this discussion, *Malkhut*, although not a feminine power, serves as a source for the lower divine powers, as a recipient that turns into a source.

It is difficult to state definitively whether Eliashiv differentiated sharply between the category of femininity as understood by the term *nuqba'* and the term *Malkhut*, conceding feminine overtones only to the former. Eliashiv's statements constitute very firm affirmations, which are extraordinarily rare in Kabbalistic literature, and they would strongly support the phallocentric model. Despite the

---

705 See, e.g., Cordovero's *'Or Yaqar*, (Jerusalem, 1970), 5: 102–103, *'Or Yaqar*, 11: 13; *'Or Yaqar*, on *Tiqqunim*, 5: 28, 30. See also R. Abraham Azulai's *Ḥesed le-'Avraham*, fols. 16d–17a and the Cordoverian passage quoted by him in *'Or ha-Ḥammah*, vol. 2, fol. 3d, vol. 3, part 1, fol. 85c.
706 Literally "stands on."
707 Isaiah 44: 6.
708 Eliashiv, *Leḥem, Shevo ve-'Aḥlema'*, Sefer De'ah, vol. 2, fol. 158b: כי עומד המלכות בשני בחי'. כי עצמותה ופנימיותה היא למעלה מהכל כי הרי היא שורש כולם וכמו שאמרנו שהיא מהמלכות דא"ס שהכל הוא ממנה ואפס זולתו. אמנם היא מתחלפת מגילוי לגילוי וממדרגה למדרגה ויורדת בסוף כל מדרגה עליונה להיות שורש להמדרגה התחתונה. והרי היא בסוד אני ראשון ואני אחרון. כתר מלכות. כי למעלה היא הכתר שהוא נקרא אי"ן, נעלם מהשגה. ולמטה היא מלכות שנקרא אנ"י .
709 Eliashiv, *Leshem*, Sefer De'ah, vol. 2, fol. 158bc.

categorical formulations to this effect, however, elsewhere in the same book, the Lithuanian Kabbalist wrote:

> Within the *Nuqba'* there are seven ranks,[710] and the seventh one will be equal to Him and they will both employ the same crown,[711] and this never happened [in the past] until the Time to Come[712] ... as always [in the past] the Male's rank was higher than the *Nuqba'*[713] and this is a function of the lack of amendation, but in the Time to Come, all this will be amended and even more so, She will be in the aspect of[714] "the diadem of Her Husband."[715]

This passage employs the term *Nuqba'*, which is the paramount term for the Female as a sexual entity, not *Malkhut*. Mentioning the husband afterwards definitively indicates a sexual understanding of this power, not just in its lower position, as he claimed elsewhere, but also when ascending higher than Him in the eschaton. At least in this case, the ascent on high is to be understood, therefore, not as a divestment of the feminine element; She maintains it while being superior to the Male. We may thus discern conceptual fluidity in Eliashiv's approach to the Female. Another discussion pertinent to the topic of the privileged Female shows that *Malkhut*, nevertheless, has some feminine connotations:

> The essence of the existence of humanity and of the world is indeed only the first nine *sefirot*, but the *sefirah* of *Malkhut* is only the generality, root and cause and telos. And this is, as we said, that all the ten *sefirot* are solely [for the sake of] the revelation of *Malkhut*, as the light of the Infinite is revealed by their means. But the individual *Malkhut*[716] is the very splendor of Her essence, which has been revealed at the end in order to bring them all

---

710 Perhaps the seven palaces, in accordance with the Zoharic cosmology. See also Cordovero, *'Or Yaqar*, 4: 25 and 4: 65 about the various degrees found within the *Shekhinah*, and also 5: 154; 11: 53, 63, 75, 77, 133; 13: 158, 186. The last text referred to here speaks about aspects of the *Shekhinah* that are found not only within the divine world but also in the three other cosmic worlds. See also *'Or Yaqar* on *Tiqqunim*, 5: 258. These texts are good examples of the need to resort to the term "realm" in the context of the nature of the *sefirot*, namely, to regard them as a zone where different processes take place.

711 As part of the rabbinic legend of the diminution of the moon. On this issue, see Idel, "The Divine Female and the Mystique of the Moon."

712 Eliashiv, *Leshem*, Sefer De'ah, vol. 2, fol. 154d.

713 This is a principle discussed in the context of this quote.

714 Proverbs 12: 4.

715 See Eliashiv, *Leshem*, Sefer De'ah, vol. 2, fol. 154c:

וכן ישנם להנוק' ז' מדרגות והמדרגה הז' הוא להיות שוה בשוה אליו ושישתמשו שניהם בכתר אחד וזה לא היה מעולם עד לעתיד לבוא... והרי לנו כי מעולם הוא שהזכר הוא גבוה למעלה מהנוק'. וזה נמשך מחסרון התיקון כי הרי לעתיד יתוקן כ"ז ולא עוד אלא שתהיה היא בבחי' עטרת בעלה.

716 Eliashiv distinguishes in several cases between *Malkhut* found in a certain *sefirah* as its feminine aspect and the general *Malkhut* that is identified as the last *sefirah*. See, e.g., *Leshem*,

to their telos, as at the beginning, *Malkhut* of the Infinite has been revealed and She has expanded in the essence of existence of humankind and the world, in order to take out and innovate that entire world by means of that light of the first nine *sefirot*. Afterwards, Her intention concerning them has been revealed, which is to encompass them all within Her and to reign over them, and this is the *sefirah* of *Malkhut* that is from the essence of the splendor of the very *Malkhut* of the Infinite, and this is the secret of what has been said "the valorous wife is the diadem of Her husband,"[717] and it has also been said, "you surpassed the others"[718] as She ascends to "the place She has been hewn from"[719] ... as She ascends up to *Malkhut* of the Infinite, by [means of] the light that is found in Her essence. And behold, the revelation of the light within them is the intention of the *sefirah* of *Malkhut*, and this is their telos and She is their cause at the beginning, and their telos, as for Her sake they emerged, and the cause itself is the telos and the root ... as because of Her revelation, they have been perfected.[720]

We have another example here of circular theosophy, as the *sefirah* of *Malkhut* of the Infinite is both the cause and the telos, which means that the supernal light that emanated from *Malkhut* of the Infinite to the lower *Malkhut* returns to Her as the telos, which means as privileged. The circuit of light, reminiscent of the circuit of the two lights we have seen in several instances above in the writings of both Cordovero and Luria, is also evident here. The citation of the two verses from Proverbs points to the feminine overtones of *Malkhut* in this context. In any case, R. Shlomo Eliashiv speaks several times quite explicitly about the *nuqba'* as found in the higher realms, like *Keter*, in a way that is reminiscent of the approach of R. Elijah of Vilna, but nevertheless closer to Lurianic Kabbalah.[721]

From the point of view of the theme of this study, the privileged status of *Malkhut* is evident: the other nine *sefirot* are not mentioned by name nor

---

fol. 7abc, and it is found already in classical Lurianic texts. See, e.g., R. Jacob Ḥayyim Tzemaḥ, *'Adam Yashar*, fols. 5a, 17a.

717 Proverbs 12: 4.

718 Proverbs 31: 29

719 See *Tiqqunei Zohar*, no. 21, fol. 61b, quoted above, beside n. 255.

720 Eliashiv, *Leshem*, Heleq ha-Be'urim, part 2, fol. 30bc:

כי עיקר המציאות דהאדם והעולם הוא באמת רק הט' ספי' הראשונים אבל ספי' המלכות הנה היא רק כללותו ושורשו וסיבתו ותכליתו, והוא כי הרי אמרנו שכל הי' ספי' הם רק גילויי המלכות דאור אין סוף שתתגלה על ידם, אך ספי' המלכות הפרטי הוא זוהר עצמותה עצמה שנתגלה לבסוף להביא כולם לתכליתם, כי מתחילה נתגלית המלכות דא"ס ונתפשטה בעצמותה המציאות דהאדם והעולם להוציא ולהמציא את כל אותו העולם כולו שהיא ע"י האור דהט' ספי' הראשונים, ואח"כ נתגלה בכוונתה בהם שהוא לכלול כולם בה ולמלוך עליהם והוא ספי' המלכות שהיא מעצמות זוהר המלכות דא"ס גופה והוא בסוד שנאמר חיל עטרת אשת בעלה וכן נאמר עליה ואת עלית על כולנה שהיא עולה לאתר דאתגזרת ... שהיא עולה עד המלכות דא"ס והוא באור עצמותה שבה, והרי הוי ספי' המלכות גילוי אור הכוונה בהם שהוא תכליתם. וכן היא שורשם שבתחילה וסיבתם, שבשבילה יצאו כולם, והסיבה הוא התכלית והוא השורש... כי בגילויה נשלמו כולם

721 See, e.g., *Leshem*, vol. 2, fols. 63c, 65a, 72c, 74d, 95c.

considered to be instrumental for the realization of the intention of creation of both humankind and the world. In other words, we may discern here the first and last phases of the three-phases model. The middle phase is represented in another discussion found in the same book, which explains that the descent of *Malkhut* to the lower world takes place in order to redeem the people of Israel by elevating them to the eschaton.[722] We see here a fascinating example of a technique of privileging the Female that differs from the classical Lurianic sources cited above; R. Shlomo Eliashiv seems to avoid the latter's description of Her as emanated from the highest divine Head in favor of a more Sarugian theory of *Malkhut* of the Infinite. I would say that this Kabbalist even polemicizes with the Lurianism as described in chapter 8 above, which posits the emergence of *Malkhut* from the highest divine head. In any case, the differing views found in the writings of the same Kabbalist testify to the intricacy of the sex theory in his thought.

The substantial agreement on the privileged concept of Malkhut as stemming from the very high divine realm – despite some interesting divergences in details – between the two major Kabbalists active at the end of the nineteenth century, R. Joseph Hayyim ben Elijah in Bagdad and the somewhat later R. Shlomo Eliashiv, in Lithuania and in Jerusalem, is very revealing as to the widely accepted status of the Female as privileged in Lurianic Kabbalah. Nevertheless, the question that was sent to R. Joseph Hayyim shows that it was not a universally accepted view.

---

722 Eliashiv, *Leshem*, Sefer De'ah, vol. 2, fol. 158a.

11 Some Hasidic Examples of the Three-Phases Gender Theory

Following the Safedian cult of the *Shekhinah*, many Hasidic masters also elaborated on this topic, regarding the fate of the Female as a major religious issue. From the start, the founder of Hasidism, R. Israel ben Eliezer, the Besht, insisted that worship be directed toward the *Shekhinah* for Her own sake.[723] Her redemption, related to Her elevation to the higher theosophical realm, is tantamount to the redemption of the people of Israel.[724] Her exile is often connected to the exile of the soul.[725] Hasidic authors, from the very inception of this phase of Jewish mysticism, adopted the play on words of *'Aniy – 'Ayin*, found in Cordovero and Luria, in order to express the ascent or the connection of *Malkhut* to *Keter*; sometimes they joined it with the statement from *Sefer Yetzirah* as to the beginning and the end being fixed in each other.[726] In some cases, the Besht speaks about the unification of the deed with the thought, sometime in terms of the *'Aniy – 'Ayin*,[727] and in another case, in terms of *Malkhut*'s elevation to the rank of *Mahashavah*, presumably *Hokhmah* or *Keter*, by means of some form of total devotion, even when performing the most ordinary type of activity.[728] In my opinion, unifying deed and thought echoes the pseudo-Aristotelian dictum. In one of the Besht's teachings, the *Shekhinah* will become a Bride in the eschatological future.[729]

Although Hasidic thought in general was less oriented to the technical side of theosophical structures, it nevertheless gave prominence to terminology related to the Female. One sees this with regard to Her dynamic aspect of ascending or being elevated to *Binah* or *Keter*. Less concerned with speculations about the

---

723 See e.g., R. Jacov Joseph of Polonnoye, *Toledot Ya'aqov Yosef*, fol. 23c; Jacov Joseph of Polonnoye, *Tzafnat Pa'aneah*, fols. 1b, 13d, 35d, 39b, 43b, R. Moshe Hayyim 'Efraim of Sudylkov, *Degel Mahaneh 'Efraim*, 106.

724 See *Tzafnat Pa'aneah* fols. 5a,d, 22c, 69a.

725 See *Tzafnat Pa'aneah* fol. 19bc. See also M. Idel, "Multiple Forms of Redemption in Kabbalah and Hasidism," 57–65.

726 See especially *Tzafnat Pa'aneah*, fol. 67ab.

727 See e.g., *Toledot Ya'aqov Yosef*, fol. 117b.

728 *Toledot Ya'aqov Yosef*, fol. 144b:

עניין המלוכה נמשך מן בחי' מלכות שהוא השכינה, וכ"כ בתיקונים כ"א דף ס' ח"ל, ובגין דשכינתא היא מלכות...והנה שמעתי ממורי ממורי זלה"ה פירוש הפסוק כל אשר תמצא ידך לעשות בכחך עשה (קהלת ט: י), כי חנוך מט"ט היה מייחד על כל תפירה קבה"ו וכו' ודפח"ח. א"כ מיד במחשבה זו שאמר אשימה על"י מלך, אז מעלה מלכות עד המחשבה. Compare also to *Tzafnat Pa'aneah*, fols. 4d, 22c and R. Moshe Hayyim 'Efraim of Sudylkov, *Degel Mahaneh' Efraim*, 91.

729 *Tzafnat Pa'aneah*, fol. 5b.

https://doi.org/10.1515/9783110599800-011

supernal origin of the *Shekhinah* than the Kabbalists were, they devoted greater attention to the cult of the *Shekhinah*, Her amendment, and Her elevation. Nevertheless, in earlier Hasidism, one can find the theory of the emergence of the *Shekhinah* out of <u>H</u>okhmah and the necessity to unify speech, that is *Malkhut*, with Thought, *Mahashavah*, which is <u>H</u>okhmah.[730]

Hasidic masters were acquainted with the three-phases model, especially in the Lurianic form analyzed in chapter 8 with regard to the exalted status of the Female, whose light in the future would exceed that of the Sun. Similar views to those analyzed above regarding the status of the Feminine in the context of the pseudo-Aristotelian dictum are found in additional Kabbalistic writings and those of eighteenth and nineteenth-century Hasidism.[731] In line with earlier sources, Hasidic ones depicted the *Shekhinah* as a stone hewn at a higher level that had to be thrown, namely, restored to its root.[732] Hasidic masters adopted the pseudo-Aristotelian dictum in other contexts, too.[733] Those additional texts, which combine earlier traditions on the topics discussed above, deserve separate analyses in order to offer a balanced picture of the role played by the different conceptualizations of the feminine in Kabbalistic literature. Indeed, a plethora of other interpretations of the dictum have been omitted here as they do not deal with the status of the Feminine.

In the first two generations of Hasidic thought, however, I could not find elaborations on the topic with the sort of statements mentioned above,[734] but the situation changes in the third generation of Hasidic masters. In this context, I would like to discuss the theme of God's encrownment with *Knesset Yisra'el* in

---

730 *Tzafnat Pa'aneah*, fol. 3b. For more on this issue, see below, n. 755 in this chapter. For *Malkhut* as having been taken from *Hokhmah*, see the introduction to *Tiqqunei Zohar*, fol. 11b.

731 See, e.g., R. Hayyim of Czernovitz, *Be'er Mayyim Hayyim*, vol. 1, fols. 7e, 25a, 112b, 161b or R. Shne'ur Zalman of Liadi, *Torah 'Or*, fol. 43c, Shne'ur Zalman, *Sefer ha-Tanya'*, 'Iggeret ha-Qodesh, ch. 20, R. Moshe of Kobrin, epistle 51 printed in R. Abraham Weinberg of Slonim, *Yesod ha-'Avodah*, 2: 102.

732 See R. Moshe Hayyim 'Efraim of Sudylkov, *Degel Mahaneh Efraim*, 220, R. Hayyim of Czernovitz, *Be'er Mayyim Hayyim*, vol. 1, fol. 20d, 159d, 2, fol. 10d,f, R. Abraham Yehoshu'a Heschel of Apta, *'Ohev Israel*, fols. 7d, 12bc, 29b, 50d, and below, in the passage translated from R. Nahman of Bratzlav.

733 See, especially, R. Dov Baer of Mezhirech, *Maggid Devarav le-Ya'akov*, 78, 135, 140, 196; and R. Abraham Yehoshu'a Heschel, *'Ohev Yisrael*, fols. 12bc, 29b and 64cd, the last two to be quoted and translated below.

734 To what extent the descent of the Hasidic *Tzaddiq*, for the sake of ascent, ירידה לצורך עליה is connected to the Neoplatonic and theosophical schemes discussed here is a matter of further investigation. This katabatic model, which is central in Hasidism, deserves a separate study. See Idel, *Hasidism: between Ecstasy and Magic*, 103–107.

the eschatological future and in the present.[735] R. Abraham Yehoshuʻa Heschel of Apta, a well-known Hasidic author active at the beginning of the nineteenth century in Podolia (now Ukraine), wrote as follows:

> In the future, the action of the sun and all the other signs of the Zodiac and stars will be delivered to us, as nowadays each star performs its actions that is imprinted in it. But in the future, everything will be delivered into the hand of *Knesset Yisraʼel* in the aspects of "a valorous wife is the diadem of her husband,"[736] namely, God, blessed be He, as if will encrown Himself by *Knesset Yisraʼel*,[737] and *Knesset Yisraʼel* will be in the aspect of *Keter*, higher than all the worlds, and [then] all the worlds, supernal and lower, will be governed by us. And this will be the consequence of the [people of] Israel's enthroning God, blessed be He, on themselves and will accept the yoke of the kingdom of heaven on themselves, out of great love.... As the primordial and simple will [of God] was that he should be described by the attribute of King, this being the reason why in His thought it ascended to emanate the world so that His Kingdom in the world should be noticed, *Malkhut* ascended in the [divine] thought at the beginning, and this is what has been composed in the [liturgical] poem "*Malkhut*, is preexistent, before everything that existed,"[738] and this is the cornerstone from which the entire world was founded as it is said in the Gemara,[739] and the *Shekhinah* is called Stone.[740] ... And behold that when someone is enthroning the Holy One, blessed be He, on each and every limb [of his], by performing the will of the Creator, blessed be He, that desires to have the attribute of King, then this person elevates the holy *Melukhah*,[741] up to the Supernal Thought, as She was in the primordial times, when all the worlds ascended in

---

735 For gender and Hasidism, see, e.g., Nehemia Polen, "Miriam's Dance: Radical Egalitarianism in Hasidic Thought," 1–12, and Ada Rapoport-Albert, "On Women in Hasidism: S. A. Horodecky and the Maid of Ludmir Tradition," 495–525; Elliot R. Wolfson, *Open Secret;* 200–223; Wojciech Tworek, "Time and Gender in the Teachings of Shneʼur Zalman of Liadi" (Hebrew), 57–74; and Schwartzman, "From Mystical Vision to Gender Equality Aspirations," 149–155.
736 Proverbs 12: 4. Nota Bene: here, as in many other cases, although not always, this verse is used as a prooftext for the superiority of the Female, not for Her inferiority. See above, beside nn. 462, 471, 607, 678, 714, 717. There is no consensus on regarding the biblical prooftexts as illustrating one single gender theory, as is implied in the practice related to demonstrating the existence of the phallocentric model. See also Menussi, "'Arise from Dust,'" 116–120.
737 Perhaps the impact of Jeremiah 31: 21. See above, n. 283 and below, n. 790.
738 This is the opening line of a liturgical poem. Here *Malkhut* does not stand for a hypostatic entity in a theosophical system but for the reign of God in the world. Nevertheless, in the verse that follows the opening sentence cited here, it is written that *Malkhut* is the beginning and the end and the middle. Afterwards the term *Kallah*, bride, is mentioned.
739 *BT., Yoma'*, fol. 54b.
740 See above, the pertinent passages on the last *sefirah* as stone cited in ch. 5. See also above, n. 732.
741 Literally, it means royalty. This is another term for *Malkhut*. Compare also *'Ohev Yisraʼel*, fols. 23b, d, 33d, 64d, 87b. This view is repeated elsewhere in the same book, fol. 46cd, in the context of the interpretation of the diminution of the moon.

thought of God, blessed be He,[742] and this is the issue of linking the lower _Hokhmah_ to the supernal _Hokhmah_ as this is [the meaning] of the words of _Tiqqunim_[743] of the Holy _Zohar_ ... namely, to Her source and origin, the holy Thought.[744]

The occurrence of the feminine nouns: _Shekhinah, Knesset Yisra'el_, stone, together with the verse about the valorous wife, does not leave a doubt as to the feminine nature of the entity called _Malkhut_ or _Melukhah_. The mystic touches on the link of _Malkhut_ to _Hokhmah_ or of the Daughter to the Father. The ambiguity of the nation in the lower realm, and its representation as the divine Feminine in the supernal realm as _Knesset Yisra'el_ is evident: "and [the concept of the people of] Israel ascended in the divine Thought to be created first, and then _Knesset Yisra'el_ is in an aspect of _Yod_, and it was hidden and stored within the supernal hidden Thought."[745] In any case, the Female is conceived of as stemming from the hypostatic divine thought; this derivation explains Her return by elevation, a scenario related explicitly to the theme of Her primeval supernal root or Her preexistence. As part of their theurgical approach, Kabbalists or Hasidim regard the elevation as the result of the performance of the divine imperatives. The three-phases gender model is also represented here and in other texts in early Hasidism that I have addressed elsewhere.[746] Although the Kabbalist enthrones the Kingdom, _Malkhut_, on each of his limbs by means of the performance of the commandments, a theme found already in R. Joseph Gikatilla's theosophical

---

742 Namely, when God contemplated, in _illud tempus_, the idea to create those worlds.

743 The citation from _Tiqqunei Zohar_, fol. 61b, which was translated and discussed in chapter 5, is introduced for the second time in the wider context of the quoted passage.

744 _'Ohev Yisra'el_, fol. 29b:

לעתיד לבא יהא נמסר לנו פעולת השמש ושאר המזלות והכוכבים. כי לעת עתה הנה כל כוכב הוא פועל פעולתו שהוטבע בו. אבל לעתיד יהא הכל מסור ביד הכנסת ישראל בבחינת (משלי יב:ד) 'אשת חיל עטרת בעלה' היינו שיכתיר את עצמו כביכול השם יתברך בהכנסת ישראל ויהיה הכנסת ישראל אז בבחינת כתר שהוא יותר גבה מכל העולמות ויהיו כל העולמות עליונים ותחתונים מתנהגים על ידינו. וזה יומשך ממה שישראל ימליכו את הש"י על עצמם ויקבלו עול מלכות שמים באהבה רבה.... ולהיות רצון הקדום הפשוט היה להתתאר בתואר מלך לכך עלה במחשבה לפניו ית' להאציל העולמות כדי שיתגלה ויוכר מלכותו בעולם. ונמצא שמלכות עלה במחשבה תחלה וזהו שיסד הפייט, מלכות עד לא קדם קדומה. וזהו אבן שתיה שממנה הושתת העולם כולו כנזכר בגמרא (בבלי, יומא, דף נד ע"ב) היינו השכינה נקרא אבן והנה כשהאדם ממליך את הש"י על כל אבר ואבר ובזה עושה רצון הבורא ית' שהיה לו תואר מלך. אז האיש הלזה מעלה מלוכה הק' עד מחשבה עליונה כמו שהיתה מימי קדם כשעלו כל העולמות במחשבה לפניו ית'. וזהו ענין קישור חכמה תתאה בחכמה עילאה וזהו ג"כ פי' דברי התיקונים זה"ק דידינן לזרקא אבנא היינו אבן שתיה בחי' מלכותא קדישא לאתר דאיתגזרת מיניה. היינו לשורשה ולמקורה. הוא מחשבה הקדושה.

745 See _'Ohev Yisra'el_, fol. 64cd:

שישראל עלו במחשבה תחלה להבראות והי' אז הכנסת ישראל בבחי' יו"ד והיה טמיר וגניז במחשבה עילאה סתימאה.

Compare also _'Ohev Yisra'el_, fols. 65c, 88b.

746 See also my "Some Observations on Gender Theories in Hasidism,' 81*–101*. See also Idel, "Revelation and the 'Crisis of Tradition,'" 282–283.

Kabbalah, those enthronements cause, perhaps dialectically, the ascent of the *Shekhinah* on high. This process should be understood as part of Kabbalistic theurgy. It is important to differentiate between the final triumph of the Jewish nation and of the Female in the future, on the one hand, and the possibility of effecting Her elevation through the performance of commandments at privileged moments in the present such as the Sabbath, on the other hand.[747] An interesting feature of this passage is the forceful language of power, which culminates with the capacity to dominate the natural world, at least in the eschaton. In another passage, this Hasidic author deals with the ascent of the Female to a position higher than that of the Forefathers, namely the *sefirot* of *Ḥesed, Gevurah* and *Tiferet,* up to the Primordial Will.[748]

Elsewhere in the same book, R. Abraham Yehoshuʻa Heschel discusses the equality related to the circular movement in a dance, as the ascent and the descent cause the beginning and the end to touch each other, and he also refers to the first and last letters in the Hebrew alphabet that may touch each other.[749]

A contemporary of R. Heschel, the more famous R. Nahman of Bratzlav, epitomized the three-phases model by commenting on the earlier Kabbalistic discussions on the *zarqa'*, saying, for example:

> Each time that someone comes to a learned person and tells him what preoccupies him, and that learned person is an aspect of Moses, that is the aspect of *'Ayin*,[750] as it is written, "Wisdom is found out of *'Ayin*,"[751] by this [confession] you are contained within the Infinite, as this is the aspect of *"zarqa'* that is thrown to the place that it was taken from there"[752] that you will cause the return of *Malkhut* to the Infinite.[753,754]

---

747 *'Ohev Yisrael*, fol. 46d.

748 *'Ohev Yisrael*, fol. 23bc.

749 *'Ohev Yisrael*, fol. 12ab. See also Polen, "Miriam's Dance."

750 The full spelling of the letters of *Moshe*, when the first letters are removed, *M-m Sh-yin H-'*, equals the word *me-'Ayin*, in the biblical verse. This nexus between *Moshe* and *me-'Ayin* is found in several Ashkenazi Hasidic texts and in Kabbalah.

751 Job 28: 12, as interpreted by theosophical Kabbalists.

752 *Tiqqunei Zohar*, no. 21, fol. 61b, no. 64, fol. 95b.

753 See also *Sefer Liqqutei Moharan*, 1, paragraph 4, fol. 3c.

754 *Sefer Liqqutei Moharan*, 1, paragraph 4, fol. 4b:

זה בכל פעם שבא אצל תלמיד חכם ומספר לפניו כל לבו, והתלמיד חכם הוא בחינת משה, שהוא בחינת אין, כמו שכתוב: "והחכמה מאין תמצא". ועל ידי זה אתה נכלל באין סוף. וזה בחינת 'זרקא דאזדריקת לאתר דאתנטילת מתמן', שתחזיר את המלכות לאין סוף.

For the translation of the fuller context of the passage, see the discussion of Zvi Mark, whose analysis deals mainly with the mystical absorption of the person in the Infinite. Cf. *Mysticism and Madness, The Religious Thought of Rabbi Nahman of Bratslav*, 28–29. Compare also to *Sefer Liqqutei Moharan*, 1, par. 35, fol. 49a.

The Hebrew term translated as learned person is *Talmid H̲akham*, a wise scholar, which is related to the *sefirah* of *H̲okhmah*, understood by R. Nahman, as by many other Kabbalists, as emerging out of the supernal *'Ayin*, the *sefirah* of *Keter*. The speeches are identical with the so-called "world of Speech" and *Malkhut* or *Shekhinah* in early Hasidism,[755] in which the elevation of speech is conceived as an ideal.[756] Going to the wise person in order to speak with him thus amounts to an ascent of *Malkhut* to the two higher *sefirot* and then even higher, to the Infinite. Although R. Nahman interprets *Malkhut* specifically as dealing also with speech, the image of *Malkhut* as stemming from and returning to the Infinite is very reminiscent of the earlier traditions. The verb *tah̲ziyr* – translated as "to cause the return" – therefore, points to the retrieval of an early stage of *Malkhut*, when She was found within the Infinite. The constellation of themes – Moses, *Me-'Ayin*, *H̲okhmah*/Wise person may refer also to R. Nahman himself.[757] Many other sources related to R. Nahman also quote the passages from *Tiqqunei Zohar*, testifying to the concern with the linguistically interpreted special version of above the model, which was probably influenced by the founder of Hasidism and the great-grandfather of R. Nahman. Two main Hasidic figures thus adapted the three-phases model in different ways, although they share the centrality of employing language. Nevertheless, the two differ on certain major issues: the Apter Rebbe speaks mainly about the eschaton whereas R. Nahman concentrates mainly on the present. The former focuses on the national body; the latter

---

755 Regarding an attribution of the phrase "world of speech" to the Besht, see in the compilation of traditions of the Great Maggid [i.e., Dov Baer of Mezhirech], *'Or ha-'Emmet*, fol. 1b, and Rivka Schatz Uffenheimer, *Hasidism as Mysticism: Quietistic Elements in Eighteenth-Century Hasidic Thought*, 191 and note 8; and R. Dov Baer of Mezhirech, *Maggid Devarav le-Ya'akov*, 52. I cannot delve here into the analysis of the widespread Beshtian instruction to unify speech and thought or "the world of speech" with "the world of thought," teachings that represent a different set of questions related to the coordination of human acts and to attaining a unified mode of activity. See also R. Jacob Joseph of Polonnoye, *Tzafnat Pa'aneah*, fol. 3b, R. Shne'ur Zalman of Liadi, *Sefer ha-Tania*, *'Iggeret ha-Qodesh*, ch. 20, and R. Aharon Kohen of Apta, *'Or ha-Ganuz la-Tzaddiqim*, fols. 5d, 8a, 28d, 29b. This identification of speech with the last *sefirah* reflects earlier views, where She was related to the mouth and to the oral nature of the "oral Torah." See, e.g., above, nn. 329, 424; R. Moshe Hayyim Efrayyim of Sudylkov, *Degel Mahaneh 'Efrayyim*, 222, or R. Reuven ha-Levi Horowitz, *Dudaim Ba-sode*, fols. 86a, 103a, 115a. For an interesting parallel of the dichotomy of world of speech and thought, see R. Jacob Ifargan, *Sefer Minhat Yehudah*, 2: 554.

756 See Idel, "Modes of Cleaving to the Letters in the Teachings of Israel Baal Shem Tov: A Sample Analysis," 299–317 and "East European Hasidism: The Emergence of a Spiritual Movement," 35–61.

757 See Arthur Green, *Tormented Master, A Life of Rabbi Nahman of Bratzlav*, 119–121, 205; Zvi Mark, *The Revealed and Hidden Writings of Rabbi Nachman of Bratslav, the World of Revelation and Rectification*, 52–53.

emphasizes the individual, whom he describes as capable of reaching some form of mystical union with the Infinite, reflected by the verb *KLL*, translated as "contain/include."[758] The efficacy of speech, not necessarily the ritual performance, turns confession into a perlocution.

Another Hasidic author, a younger contemporary of the three figures mentioned above, is R. Qalonimus Qalman Epstein of Cracow. In a widely-read treatise, he reiterates the eschatological apotheosis of the divine Feminine to Her source, in the vein of passages in Lurianic Kabbalah:

> The coming of the Messiah will happen when the [*sefirah* of[*Malkhut* ascends to [the configuration of] '*Attiqa' Qaddisha*',[759] and the *Tzaddiqim* will draw then the influx from the Supernal Constellation [*Mazzal 'Elyon*], from the "thirteen amendations of the Supernal Beard"[760] to *Malkhut*, and therefrom to *Knesset Yisra'el*. Behold that in every Sabbath[761] there is a semblance of this [process] that the *Tzaddiqim* are drawing down the influx from '*Attiqa' Qaddisha*', from the Supernal Constellation ... to *Knesset Yisra'el*.... On each and every Sabbath, it is done in this way so that the *Tzaddiqim* cause the ascent of *Malkhut* to '*Attiqa' Qaddisha*' and draw down the influx from there onto *Knesset Yisra'el*.[762]

The author combines the '*Idra*' theosophy as understood by Luria with the astro-magical concept of drawing down power from the highest point. He does

---

758 On the verb *KLL* for referring to integration in divinity, see M. Idel, "Universalization and Integration: Two Conceptions of Mystical Union in Jewish Mysticism" in *Mystical Union and Monotheistic Faith, An Ecumenical Dialogue*, 27–58, 157–161, 195–203.

759 According to this author, in his *Ma'or va-Shemesh*, 1: 186, in this Configuration there is no aspect of Male and Female. Some pages later (189), however, he speaks about the "masculine waters" that emerge from there, yet another case of incoherence.

760 This is another symbol for the first *sefirah*, both in the book of the *Zohar* and in R. Joseph Gikatilla. He seems to have been substantially influenced on this point by Cordovero, whom he quotes on this issue by name. See *Ma'or va-Shemesh*, 1: 83. This Hasidic master resorts numerous times in his book to these two terms for designating the source of the influx to be drawn down.

761 Compare to the passage quoted in the name of the Besht by his student R. Menahem Nahum of Chernobyl, as discussed in Idel, *Messianic Mystics*, 222–225, where there is a nexus between a messianic attainment, human activity, and Sabbath.

762 *Ma'or va-Shemesh*, 1: 103.

והנה בביאת משיח...יהיה זה שתעלה המלכות הקדושה למעלה עד עתיקא קדישא והצדיקים ימשיכו אז השפע ממזל
עילאה מי"ג תיקוני דיקנא עילאי למלכות ומשם לכנסת ישראל. והנה בכל שבת ושבת יש דוגמא זו שהצדיקים מושכים
שפע מעתיקא קדישא ממזלא עילאה...לכנסת ישראל.. בכל שבת ושבת נעשה דוגמא זה שהצדיקים מעלים ומייחדים
את המלכות בסוד עתיקא קדישא וממשיכים משם השפע לכנסת ישראל.

For more on this passage, see M. Idel, "Sabbath: On Concepts of Time in Jewish Mysticism," 86–87. On the Sabbath and the drawing down of spirituality and vitality, see also R. Abraham Yehoshu'a Heschel, '*Ohev Yisra'el*, 107–108.

so by a common denominator: *Mazzal* – technically the zodiac sign with a patent astral connotation, but in its occurrence in theosophical Kabbalah as Supernal Constellation, it refers to *Keter*. This represents a transformation of an astro-magical mode of thought by projecting the magic from the celestial world onto the higher, divine one and also of the theosophical Kabbalah because it concedes access to the Supernal Configuration not only to *Malkhut* but also to the righteous envisioned as a magician.[763] Indeed, whereas in the astro-magical model and in the mystical-magical one, only the human male magician ascends and brings down power, here both the divine Female and the righteous do so, although on different levels. Elsewhere in his book, R. Qalonimus Qalman writes: "He hints at *Malkhut* of the World [the Queen] ascending to *'Arikh 'Anppin* to receive from there the influx from the Infinite."[764] Causing the return of *Malkhut* recalls R. Nahman's passage discussed in this chapter.

Familiarity with these Hasidic discussions can facilitate a better understanding of the Lubavitch Hasidism's views concerning the Female. For example, R. Shne'ur Zalman of Liadi adopted the circular theosophy on the one hand, while negating the regular concatenation of causa and causatum, in the form of the concentric circles, in the context of the phrase *Keter Malkhut,* on the other hand.[765] Moreover, we learn from his *Commentary on the Pentateuch*, which articulated a view that is fully consonant with the gender theory related to dual ontology as mentioned in some cases above:[766]

> The union of the Holy One, blessed be He with His *Shekhinah*, is found up to the Height of the Degress,[767] namely, within the [world of] Emanation they are the union of Male and Female, and higher [is] the degree that is called the Line that descends from the light of the

---

763 For the magical-astral dimensions of the concept of *Tzaddiq*, see Idel, *Hasidism: Between Ecstasy and Magic*, 189–203.

764 *Ma'or va-Shemesh*, 2: 663:

רומז שבראש השנה המלכות שמים עולה אל האריך אנפין לקבל משם שפע מאין סוף.

On the affinity between *Malkhut* and the configuration of *'Arikh 'Anppin*, see also *'Or Yaqar*, (Jerusalem, 1989), 16: 56, and *'Or Yaqar*, on *Tiqqunim*, (Jerusalem, 2004), 4: 91–92, and much more in Lurianic Kabbalah, e.g., in *"Male and Female,"* n. 500. See Meroz, *Redemption in the Lurianic Teaching*, 174, as well as some texts adduced in my *"Male and Female,"* appendix K.

765 *Sefer ha-Tania'*, 'Iggeret ha-Qodesh, ch. 20, where he refers twice to the theory of *Sefer Yetzirah*, in the context of the *sefirot* that emerge and return to their origin.

766 My view on duality differs from what Rachel Elior designates as "the dual meaning of the existence," in her *The Paradoxical Ascent to God, The Kabbalistic Theosophy of Habad Hasidism*, 25–33. The two forms of duality do not contradict each other, as they constitute totally different aspects of Habad thought.

767 *Rum ha-ma'alot*, a phrase that means, in Lurianic Kabbalah, the world of Emanation.

Infinite,[768] blessed be He, *Shekhinah*,[769] that is descending from *Malkhut* of the Infinite, and the essence of the Emanator blessed be He, is called, the Holy One, blessed be He. And this is the reason why in the writings of Isaac Luria, blessed be his memory, it is written [that the Holy One Blessed be He] and His name[770] is the aspect of *Malkhut*.[771]

Three couples are mentioned here in an explicit manner. The first, found in what I call the core formula of theosophical-theurgical Kabbalah, is of *Tiferet* and *Malkhut*.[772] It is paradigmatic for two others, one found in the world of Emanation, the other one even higher, which consists, I assume, of the Line and the *Shekhinah*. A fourth couple, which is only implicit, probably exists – that of the Infinite and *Malkhut* that belongs to It, referred to as "*Malkhut* of the Infinite." Interestingly, at the beginning of the paragraph from which we adduced the quotation, the Hasidic master speaks also about the unification of Father and Mother by the recitation of *Qeriyat Shemaʿ*.[773]

Indeed, this author contends that prayers of Jews at the end of the prayer service of Yom Kippur can cause the elevation of the *sefirah* of *Malkhut*, probably the feminine power found in the world of emanation, to *Malkhut* of the Infinite, which is conceived as the aspect of the inner dimension of the configuration of

---

768 As to the power of procreation of the light of the Infinite, see Shneʾur Zalman of Liadi, *Liqqutei Torah*, on Song of Songs, fol. 40a. The line of the Infinite is reminiscent of the phrase "thread of the Infinite" found in Vital's *ʿEtz Hayyim*, Gate 1 ch. 2, or Vital, *Mevoʾ Sheʿarim*, 4. For the sexual overtones of the relationship between the line and the *tehiru*, namely the circular place that remains after the evacuation of the infinite light, or the withdrawal, see R. Jacob Koppel, as discussed by Tishby, *Paths of Faith and Heresy*, 219. On its possible source in early forms of Kabbalah, see Idel, "Visualization of Colors," 23–24. See also above, the discussion of R. Qalonimus Qalman Epstein.

769 The Hebrew here is not so smooth. Compare, however, to *Sefer Liqqutei Moharan*, Balaq, fol. 68c, where the light is described as enclosed in the aspect of *Malkhut*.

770 *Pirqei de-R. Eliezer*, ch. 3. See also *Liqqutei Torah*, Hosafot, fol. 52a, where it is obvious that the name is *Malkhut* of the Infinite.

771 *Liqqutei Torah*, Piqqudei, fol. 7cd:

יחוד קוב"ה ושכינתיה ימצא עד רום המעלות דהיינו באצילות הם יחוד זו"ן ולמעלה מעלה נק' קו הנמשך מאא"ס ב"ה שכינה שהוא נמשך ממלכ' דא"ס, ועצמות המאציל ית' נק' קוב"ה ולכן בכהאריז"ל כ' דשמו הוא בחי' מל'[כות] דא"ס נק' ג"כ שמו.

See also the view of his disciple, R. Aharon of Staroselye, in an important discussion of the aspect of *Malkhut* as higher than the emanation in his *Shaʿarei ha-ʿAvodah*, Shaʿar ha-tefillah, fols. 37a–38a, translated and discussed in Rachel Elior, *The Theory of Divinity of Hasidut Habad, Second Generation* (Hebrew), 225–227. Here the primordial status of *Malkhut* is presented quite clearly as the reason for Her ascent back to Her source, an example of a three-phases theory.

772 *Kabbalah & Eros*, 1–3.

773 *Liqqutei Torah*, Piqqudei, fol. 7c.

'Attiq.[774] A restorative ascent of the lower *Malkhut* thus brings Her back to Her supernal source within the realm of the Infinite, called also by the name *Malkhut*.[775] In one instance, the founder of Lubavitch Hasidism speaks about the ascent of *Malkhut* higher than Her Husband, *Ze'yir 'Anppin*.[776] R. Aharon Kohen of Apta, another influential late eighteenth-century author, writing under the impact of Lubavitch Hasidism, describes the *Shekhinah* as the head because of her status, which adheres to the supernal root in the divine chariot, namely, the sefirotic realm, and is also described as the "head of all the heads."[777]

One of R. Shne'ur Zalman's more senior contemporaries and an acquaintance, R. Elimelekh of Lisansk, speaks about a future distinction: "the low, despised attribute of *Malkhut* is in bitter exile now, but with the advent of the Messiah, when the crown of *Malkhut* will ascend, he will understand the grandeur of *Malkhut*, how Her rank is sublime in an unreachable manner."[778] The Hasidic author seems to have conflated *Malkhut* with *Shekhinah,* although in other instances, he distinguishes between the two. In any case, this influential Hasidic leader formulated the fitting participation in the plight of the *Shekhinah* in exile, reminiscent of the cult of the Safedian Kabbalists, especially as it concerns the task of the Hasidic righteous.[779] The elevation of the *Shekhinah* sometimes up to the level of the *sefirah* of *Hokhmah* is a leitmotif from the time of

---

774 Shne'ur Zalman of Liadi, *Siddur Tefillot mi-kol ha-Shanah* (Brooklyn, 1981), fol. 250cd: כי הנה עלי' המ"ל ביו"ל ביו"כ הוא עד מ"ל דא"ס שהוא בחי' פנימיות דעתיק...א"כ ביכולת' לעלות עד שרש כל בחי' המ"ל. See also his *Siddur Tefillot mi-kol ha-Shanah*, fols. 74ab, 249c, 250ab. See also above, n. 215 and especially n. 715. Whether or not the ascent to the root of all the aspects of *Malkhut* is higher than *Malkhut* of the Infinite is not so clear.

775 For the distinct feminine nature of the series of *sefirot* in the different cosmic worlds called *Malkhut*, see *Tefillot mi-kol ha-Shanah*, fol. 46d. For the view of *Malkhut* as the realm of revelation, following the *Zohar*, see his *Sefer ha-Tania'*, 'Iggeret ha-Qodesh, ch. 20, and *Torah 'Or,* fol. 44d.

776 *Torah 'Or,* fol. 44d; see also the interesting discussion of the transformation of the Female from recipient to emanator in the eschatological time, in *Torah 'Or, ,* fol. 45ab, discussed in Menussi, "Arise from Dust," 118–119. This is just one more case of intricacy in theosophical thought, which cannot be reduced to just one stable concept of gender.

777 Aharon Kohen of Apta, *'Or ha-Ganuz la-Tzaddiqim*, fol. 26c.

778 Elimelekh of Lisansk, *No'am 'Elimelekh*, 159: שיבחין לראות איך מדת מלכות מושפלת עתה בגלות המר ויבחין בביאת משיחנו במהרה שיתנשא אז כתר מלכות ויבין גדולת מלכות איך מעלתה גדולה לאין חקר

779 *No'am 'Elimelekh*, in the unpaginated instructions at the beginning of the book, as well as 23, 30, 37, 40.

early Hasidism, as is the case also in this popular book.[780] This book reiterates the vision of the *Shekhinah* as the mother of Israel.[781]

At the end of the nineteenth century, a renowned Hasidic figure and prolific author, R. Tzadoq ha-Kohen Rabinovitch-Rubinstein of Lublin, reiterated themes found in earlier Kabbalistic literature and in Hasidism.[782] For example, he explains the meaning of the biblical locution '*Ateret Tiferet*, as a reference to "*Keter 'Elyon* that is *Keter Malkhut*, and *Knesset Yisrael* is called '*Ateret*, which encrowns and becomes a diadem for the Holy One, blessed be He … and *Keter 'Elyon* is onto the head, [and] it is the *Maḥashavah*, the brain … 'and a valorous woman who will find Her?'[783] this is *Knesset Yisra'el*."[784]

This passage follows a short reference to the ritual recitation of chapter 31 of Proverbs to one's wife about the virtues of the ideal woman on Sabbath eve. The recitation that is ordinarily directed at the wife has been transposed to the supernal Female. It contains both the idea of the ascent of the diadem to the supernal head, found in non-Kabbalistic sources, and a hint at circular theosophy related to the phrase *Keter Malkhut* in a non-phallocentric manner as it is related to *Keter 'Elyon* and to mental operations, and, last but not least, a clear connection to the Female as representative of the Jewish nation. The strong association of supernal *Keter* to Thought and to feminine entities once more contradicts the phallocentric concept of this zone conceived as if free of distinct feminine dimensions in Kabbalistic theosophy.

R. Tzadoq ha-Kohen also reiterates the speculations found in *Tiqqunei Zohar* about the head as tantamount to *Keter 'Elyon* and the daughter, tantamount to *Malkhut* – both hinted at in the word *Bereshit*. Alluding to the later theory that each of them comprise ten *sefirot*, he also mentions the phrase *Keter Malkhut* and the pun '*Aniy-'Ayin*.[785] Elsewhere, he ascribes a form of circular theosophy in his interpretation of the line "The beginning of wisdom is the awe of the Lord,"[786] in the context of a commentary on Luria's verse in the hymn that was discussed in

---

780 See e.g., *No'am 'Elimelekh*, 41, 42.

781 *No'am 'Elimelekh*, 26, 32, 193.

782 On his thought, see Alan Brill, *Thinking God: The Intellectual Mysticism and Spiritual Psychology of Rabbi Zadok of Lublin,* and Amirah Liver, *The Oral Torah in the Writings of R. Tzadoq ha-Kohen of Lublin* (Hebrew).

783 Proverbs 31: 10.

784 Tzadoq ha-Kohen Rabinovitch-Rubinstein of Lublin, *Peri Tzaddiq*, vol. 3, fol. 64b:

עטרת תפארת...והיינו כתר עליון איהו כתר מלכות ונקרא כ"י עטרת שמכתיר ונעשה עטרה להקדוש ברוך...כתר עליון שהוא על הראש שבה מוחא...אשת חיל מי ימצא.

Compare also to R. Shne'ur Zalman of Liadi, *Torah 'Or*, fol. 8b.

785 *Peri Tzaddiq*, vol. 5, fols. 51d-52b.

786 Psalms 111: 10.

chapter 7:[787] "*Keter Malkhut* that is called '*Ateret*, after the name[788] of the supernal *Keter*, in order to unify the beginning with the end, and in one name they are constituted and the 'beginning of wisdom' is called the head of All, and this was done by our forefather Abraham, blessed be his memory, who was the first to gain the aspect of '*Attiqa*'."[789]

In addition to discussing the privileged status of the female and circular theosophy, R. Tzadoq's writings also present the three-phases gender model, for example in the following:

> In the future, "the Lord performs new [wonders] and the Female will encircle the Male"[790] and She will ascend in accordance to the secret of the "valorous wife is the diadem of her husband,"[791] as it is known, namely, She will return to be the first *H*, by means of the perfection of the oral Torah in the understanding [*Binah*] of their heart, they will merit to unite to supernal *Binah*, namely, the *Binah* that was emanated by the Holy One, blessed be He, in order to create the world.[792]

The theory underlying this passage is that the Female represents the letter *H*, which is the last *H* of the Tetragrammaton, which now refers to the last *sefirah*. In the future, however, She will ascend to the third *sefirah*, *Binah*, or understanding, an ascent described as a return, related to the term *Teshuvah*, one of the cognomens of the third *sefirah*, which is indicated by the first *H* of the Tetragrammaton. In my opinion, the return to a higher theosophical level means, in this context, the encircling of the Male by the ascending divine feminine power. *Binah* is perceived as referring to the "supernal Mother" and as being naturally higher than the two masculine attributes.[793] The two verses cited in the last passage recur

---

787 See *Peri Tzaddiq*, vol. 2, fol. 104a.

788 Perhaps these a small error and instead of בשמא we should amend to כשמא, which would then be translated as "like the name."

789 *Peri Tzaddiq*, vol. 2, fol. 104bc:

ראשית חכמה יראת ה' שהיא כתר מלכות דאתקרי עטרת דכתרא עלאה רישא ליחדא רישא בסופא ובחד שמא אתכלילת ונקרא ראשית חכמה רישא דכלא וזהו על ידי אברהם אבינו ע"ה שזכה ראשון לבחינת עתיקא.

A similar discussion is found also *Peri Tzaddiq*, fol. 104a, where R. Tzadoq refers to the passage from *Zohar Hadash* discussed in ch. 5. Compare also to the view of R. Jacob Ifargan, *Minhat Yehudah*, 1: 369, where he quotes his uncle R. Yehudah ben Jacob's book '*Etz Hayyim*, to the effect that *Keter* is called "the great Diadem" העטרה הגדולה .

790 Jeremiah 31: 21: בָּרָא יְהֹוָה חֲדָשָׁה בָּאָרֶץ נְקֵבָה תְּסוֹבֵב גָּבֶר See also above, n. 737.

791 Proverbs 12: 4.

792 Tzadoq ha-Kohen Rabinovitch-Rubinstein, *Sefer Taqqanat ha-Shavim*, no. 6, fol. 35a:

לעתיד ה' עושה חדשות, דנקבה תסובב גבר ותתעלה בסוד אשת חיל עטרת בעלה כנודע, היינו שתשוב להיות ה' ראשונה על ידי שלימות התורה שבעל פה בבינה שבלבם יזכו לידבק במדת הבינה שלמעלה היינו הבינה שהאציל ה' יתברך להשפיע בעולם.

793 *Sefer Taqqanat ha-Shavim*, ibidem.

together elsewhere in R. Tzadoq's writings,[794] along with the mythical theme found in rabbinic texts about the "dance [or circle] that the Holy one blessed be He" will make for the righteous in the eschatological future.[795] The image of a circle, which appears in these three classical Jewish texts, may be related to circular theosophy, found indeed *in o*ther instances in this author's writings, as seen above. Interestingly, following the more general Hasidic trend, especially in the Pshiskha-Kotzk Hasidic school, the metaphysical speculation is channeled toward attaining an inner experience, represented in this passage by the phrase "*Binah* of their Heart."[796]

Those are just some few examples of this Hasidic master's reiteration of earlier material, combined in new ways. In principle, I do not see significant innovation in the way these Hasidic masters portrayed the divine Feminine; in any case, continuity is more evident than differences.

Several Hasidic texts, however, under the impact of R. Isaac of Acre's story consider contemplation of women's beauty as part of a technique to reach the contemplation of the *Shekhinah*.[797] This reflects another indubitable Platonic influence on Jewish mysticism. In another instance, although only implicitly, the supernal Feminine manifests Herself in a woman.[798] I have not yet found similar views regarding the beauty of man. This is just another instance of the privileged status of the f/Female. Last but not least, there are reports of a vision of the *Shekhinah* by R. Levi Isaac of Berditchev, a leading figure in early Hasidism, and by the somewhat later prolific thinker R. Isaac Eizik Yehiel Safrin of Komarno.[799]

---

[794] *Peri Tzaddiq*, vol. 2, fol. 45b.

[795] *BT., Ta'anit*, fol. 31a.

[796] See also below, n. 966.

[797] See M. Idel, "Female Beauty: A Chapter in the History of Jewish Mysticism" (Hebrew), 317–334; Idel, *Kabbalah & Eros*, 177. To those sources also the important discussion of the Great Maggid, *Maggid Devarav le-Ya'akov*, 332–333, should be added. See also Tworek, "Time and Gender in the Teachings of Shneur Zalman of Liadi," 62–63. For a very similar Platonic attitude see Cornelius Agrippa of Nettesheim, as discussed in Newman, *From Virile Woman to WomanChrist*, 231–232.

[798] See Idel, *Kabbalah: New Perspectives*, 315–316, n. 77, and Erich Neumann, "Mystical Man," 411.

[799] See Idel, *Kabbalah: New Perspectives* 83–84.

12 Some Wider Terminological Considerations

As indicated above, many important Kabbalists adhered to a complex and dynamic concept of the Feminine. Assessing Her different functions and mobility within the divine realm, they did not identify the Feminine with a single divine power, *sefirah,* or place in the theosophical hierarchy. In other words, according to many of the major theosophical systems, She is considerably less fixed in a certain place than any other of the *sefirot.* To refer to this fluid identity, Kabbalists employed a variety of feminine terms, which coincide only in part insofar as their functions are involved. The most common ones are *Shekhinah, Malkhut, Nuqba', Bat or Barta', 'Atarah/'Ateret, Bat Melekh, Malkhah, Matronita', Knesset Yisra'el,* Eve, Rachel, or in another manner, Leah. They are by no means simple symbolic synonyms. Inevitably, those different terms stem from different types of narratives, which in many cases have been conflated. For example, the Wife in Proverbs 12: 4 was identified by Kabbalists with *Knesset Yisra'el* and the *'Atarah,* or *Malkhut* with ' Matronita', and so on, all this in accordance with the specific contexts of discussions that are very exegetical. This type of free association is one of the reasons for my description of theosophical Kabbalah as kaleidoscopic. Each of the above terms can assume the meanings of the others because of the Kabbalists' strong associative tendencies. In other words, the relationship to the last *sefirah* creates a semantic field in which certain terms can be used interchangeably. In some cases, the meaning of a term in Kabbalah differs, or even is opposite to that of its Rabbinic narrative, as, for example, viewing the ascent of the *Shekhinah* on high as a positive development. To take another example, *Knesset Yisra'el* may be a spouse or also a Bride, i. e., *kallah,* and *Malkhut,* originally the divine royalty governing over the lower world, is also envisioned as ascending on high. These appellations cluster around the location of the last *sefirah,* which plays a role that can be designated as synthesizing or totalizing, as has been noticed by Georges Vajda, although with a somewhat different semantic nuance.[800]

As the contexts of the different discussions indicate, *Shekhinah* stands mainly for the dwelling of the divine in this world, but it can refer to the feminine component of the sexual couple, as in the widespread syntagm, *qudesha' berikh hu' w-shekhinteih,* the Holy One, Blessed be He, and His *Shekhinah.*[801] In theosophical

---

800 See *Le commentaire d'Ezra of Gérone,* 177.

801 This is the core formula in theosophical Kabbalah from the early fourteenth century. See Idel, *Kabbalah & Eros,* 1–3. See also Daniel Abrams, for scholars' exaggerated emphasis on the term *Shekhinah* in *Kabbalistic Manuscripts and Textual Theory: Methodologies of Textual Scholarship in the Study of Jewish Mysticism,* 119.

https://doi.org/10.1515/9783110599800-012

Kabbalah, *Malkhut* indicates primarily the dominion of the divine in this world, related in many cases to the symbol of King David, or divine royalty in general, but, as in many cases discussed above, this term connotes this power as a feminine hypostasis.[802] Although royalty and kingdom reflect the relationship of the divine world to the lower world, in many cases, as seen above, *Malkhut* ascends on high, even to the Infinite, namely, She operates along a different vector than governing, although the two directions may be combined. In light of the emphasis on dominion or royalty in many cases, this term does not automatically refer to a feminine power. *Nuqba'* or *Neqevah*, however, are the paramount terms for the feminine counterpart of the Male – in addition to the feminine dimension inherent in the Male; they occur mainly in later forms of Kabbalah, where the acronyms *ZU"N* or *ZKU"N* refer to *Zakhar u-Neqevah*.

Moreover, *'Atarah*, which has been discussed at length, stands for the diadem, an entity created by prayer in order to serve as the diadem of the husband, positioned higher than He is, on the Head, whether of the *sefirah* of *Tiferet* or even of a higher entity, but in other cases, it stands for the corona of the phallus, in subordinate or acquisitive contexts.[803] A more adequate reading will have to pay attention to this polyvalence. *Knesset Yisra'el* refers in these contexts to a feminine power, but prominently in the context of the representative of the people of Israel, as the wife of God, following earlier discussions in rabbinic Judaism. Those appellations come from different sources and have different denotations; they are hardly synonymous although some Kabbalists presented it that way. These appellations had, nevertheless, been attached in the vertical scheme of the ten *sefirot* to the last one, either in Her relationship to higher entities, as seen above, or to lower ones.

In some cases, Kabbalists' ambiguous use of terminology leaves room for misinterpretations. For example, the term *'Atarah* has at least two basic meanings in Kabbalistic terminology: on the one hand, the feminine aspect of the *sefirah* of *Yesod*, which is an essential aspect of its being a constituent part of the phallus after circumcision, and thus fixed in a certain place, and, on the other hand, a term drawing on rabbinic prayer ritual, thus a different, dynamic, and independent Female entity, *Malkhut, Kallah* or *Shekhinah*, sometimes designated as

---

802 En passant, this aspect of *Malkhut* as referring explicitly to the kingdom of David, *Malkhut Beit David*, which is found in hundreds of Kabbalistic texts as referring to the last *sefirah*, corroborates the thesis here as to the importance of the representation of the Jewish nation.

803 Regarding the assumption that there is one basic meaning of *'Atarah* in Kabbalah, a term that is a major topic of some of our discussions, see Wolfson, *Language, Eros, Being*, 452–453, n. 192. See, however, the survey of the various meanings of this term in Cordovero's writings in Idel, *"Male and Female,"* ch. 10.

'Atarah, which is a sefirah by Herself, drawing on ancient concepts of coronation of the king.[804] Although both Kabbalistic interpretations conceive the referents to be found in the divine realm, they are situated in different places in the pleroma. They also function in very different ways: the former is built into Yesod, thus fixed on the phallic organ, and entails a shift in meaning in order to refer to a feminine dimension of the phallus; the latter is perceived as extremely mobile, moving from one ontological level to another in the pleromatic ones, up to Keter or to the Infinite. Unlike Shekhinah, which is described as both ascending to the higher sefirotic worlds and as descending to the lower ones, the diadem is envisioned solely as ascending. Here we have been concerned solely with the latter, as part of the three-phases model. Conceptually speaking, an analysis based on fusing the two different meanings ultimately obliterates this significant distinction and creates confusion; in addition, it ignores the texts about Malkhut as an independent entity that stems from the highest divine realm. In any case, it seems that in theosophical Kabbalah, the diadem assumed an eschatological significance by Her ascent, perhaps grounded in the association with the ancient dictum of "returning the diadem to her former place."[805]

On the other hand, the term Malkhut, as referring to the divine governing of the lower worlds, or to the divine royalty, loses much of this meaning when applied to the concept of Malkhut of the Infinite, which is very remote from the lower world. It adopts connotations of points of transition from one cosmic world to another, referring basically to the view that the lowest entity of a higher world is the highest of the lower world, and thus She corresponds to the latter's Keter.

Those primary terms are sometimes differentiated in order to refer to Her various positions vis à vis the Male. For example, we read in a passage from Tiqqunei Zohar, as adduced by Cordovero in his commentary on this Zoharic book: "When She ascends onto His head, it is said of Her: 'a valorous wife is the diadem of Her Husband,' and when She descends beneath Him, She is called His spouse, with whom He unites."[806] Here we already have the dynamic nature of the

---

804 See Green, Keter, passim, and, e,g., in ch. 8 above, the passages from Luria, Vital, and Bakharakh, where the 'Ateret of the Yesod differs from the Malkhut that emerges from a much higher source. Compare also to Cordovero, 'Or Yaqar, 9: 60, where again this distinction is evident. In some of Wolfson's early analyses, he did not differentiate between the two meanings. See Idel, R. Menahem Recanati, the Kabbalist, 1: 222–223 and Idel, "Ascensions, Gender, and Pillars," 70–71.

805 Cf. e.g., Yalqut Shimeoni, Deuteronomy, ch. 19, no. 856.

806 Tiqqun 11, as quoted in 'Or Yaqar on Tiqqunim, 4: 92:

כד סליקת על רישיה איתמר בה 'אשת חיל עטרת בעלה' וכד נחיתת תחותיה אתקריאת בת זוגיה ייחודיה.

Female, depicted in Her two different positions *vis-à-vis* the Male: one superior to Him, related to Her preeminence, using as prooftext the verse from Proverbs 12: 4, and one inferior, depicting Her subordination. This is a nice illustration of feminine multi-functionality. Interestingly, neither the lower nor higher positions are depicted as "natural" but as the result of a move from one place to another, which, as we learn from the verbs used by the Kabbalists, She initiated in both cases. When commenting on this passage, R. Moshe Cordovero wrote:

> *"When She ascends onto His head"* – She is a woman ['ishah] and a female [neqeivah], but She is a valorous one, and She ascends onto His head, but on high, when She ascends, She is [called] *shir*, and on Her descent, She is [called] *shirah*,[807] as interpreted. When She is on high, "She is the valorous wife," but when She descends downward, *"When She descends beneath Him, She is called His spouse and His union,"* the issue being that *Shirah* has two aspects, which are not in their entirety His spouse, but [only] His Union. But *Shir* is masculine, that She was drawn on [the letter] *He*, that is feminine, but here the two aspects are feminine. One is the aspect of the ascent, "the valorous wife is the diadem of Her Husband," and the second aspect is below. And when She descends and the two existences will be united together, the two aspects will be feminine, one is the secret of His spouse, and the word *Bat Zugeih* comprises all Her limbs and Her amendments, as a spouse to His spouse. But the specific place that is the secret of the house of the womb,[808] the point of Zion,[809] is called His union, namely, the specific aspect in Her being where the union exists. And the matter is that when *Malkhut* elevates to [the position of] Her being "the valorous wife, the diadem of Her husband," She ascends by the specific aspect that is the median point toward the point of the Holy of Holies, the entrance of the *Yesod*, and all the other limbs remain in their place as they are.[810]

For the different relations of the *Shekhinah* with other *sefirot* and the different symbols that reflect those affinities, see also the work of the contemporary Kabbalist R. Menaḥem Recanati, – whose thought has other theosophical affinities to the views of *Tiqqunei Zohar* – in a passage analyzed in Idel, *R. Menaḥem Recanati*, 1: 225–226. See also above, n. 8 and in ch. 5. The Zoharic text is in Aramaic, and Cordovero translates it into Hebrew. I put the Aramaic sentences in italics.
807 *Shir* and *Shirah* mean song, the first grammatically is masculine, the second feminine.
808 In Hebrew, *Beit ha-Rehem.*
809 This is the meeting point of the phallus and the womb. See the study of Leah Morris, "*Neqqudat Zion, Sod Beit ha-Rehem*" (Hebrew), 112–147.
810 *'Or Yaqar* to *Tiqqunim*, 4: 92:
סליקת על רישיה איתמר בה **אשת חיל** אשה היא ונקבה היא, אלא שהיא עושה חיל ועולה על ראשו, אמנם למעלה בעלייתה היתה שיר וברדתה שירה כדפי', וכאן בהיותה למעלה היא אשת חיל וברדתה למטה כד נחיתת תחותיה איתקריאת בת זוגיח יחידיה העניין כי שיר"ה יש בה שתי בחינות, ואינה כלם בת זוגיה, אלא יחודיה, אלא שיר זכר שנמשכה על ה' שהיא נקבה, אמנם כאן הם שתי בחינות נקביות,הא' בחינת עלויה אשת חיל עטרת בעלה, הב' בחינתה למטה, וכאשר תרד ויתקשרו שתי המציאיות יחד יהיו שתי בחינות לנקבה, הא' הוא סוד בת זוגיה, והנה מלת ב"ת זו"ג מחייב כל איבריה ותקוניה כעין בת זוג לבת זוג, אמנם המקום הפרטי שהוא סוד בית הרחם נקודת ציון יקרא יחודיה, דהיינו הבחינה הפרטית בכל המציאות שבה היחוד, והענין כי המלכות כשמתעלית להיותה אשת חיל עטרת בעלה מתעלית בבחינה מיוחדת שהיא הנקודה האמצעית אל סוד נקודת קדש הקדשים שבה כניסת היסוד ושאר האיברים במקומן עומדים.

Before continuing with the translation of this longer passage, I shall first analyze the content of the translated section.. It includes a variety of terms: wife, woman, Female, diadem, spouse, and *Malkhut*, all of them feminine nouns. They differ from each other but nevertheless overlap. The term "spouse" refers to the entire body of the Female, whereas the union involves only the Female sexual organ. What seems evident in the phallocentric tone of the passage is the allusion to the diadem together with *Yesod* in a purely sexual setting, and the famous prooftext from Proverbs 12:4 is invoked in this context. This would mean that the Female's "superiority" is subsumed to Her becoming the corona around the penis of the husband, and thus this event alone would constitute Her ascent.

The seemingly evident meaning in accordance with the phallocentric way of reading of this fragment, does not, however, answer the crucial question of Her ascent: does this ascent mean solely Her being assimilated to the masculine sexual organ, Her masculinization, and thus Her obliteration? In order better to understand this quandary, let me translate the immediate continuation of the above passage:

> The secret of this aspect[811] will ascend in order to receive, up to the Infinite, in accordance to the secret of the linkage and the adherence of the Infinite to that aspect, as it has been interpreted in the pericope *Piqqudei*, paragraph 14, as to the matter of the adherence of the Infinite to the intercourse even during the weekdays,[812] as She is the matter of the secret of the median point that descends downward and becomes that median point as the secret of all the amendment[s] of Her other limbs, and this is the reason of Her being Her [!] Spouse and Her union. And this aspect is permitted to intercourse as humans are enjoying its existence since She is for the sake of governing the lower beings. However, the aspect that ascends in accordance to the secret of *Shir* that is masculine that ascends higher and higher.[813]

The ascent of the sexual organ of the Female and the adherence of the Infinite to it is explained here as the result of its earlier descent from a very high realm

---

811 Namely, the aspect of the Female that is the median point, mentioned at the end of the passage translated earlier.

812 This is just one example that the restrictions of sexual relationship to the Sabbath night were not actually respected and should not be used as an illustration of Jewish "asceticism." See Idel, *Kabbalah & Eros*, 223–233.

813 *'Or Yaqar* to *Tiqqunim*, 4: 92:

וסוד הבחינה הזאת תתעלה לקבל עד א״ס, בסוד קשר ודבקות א״ס בבחינה ההיא על הדרך שפירש בפ' פקודי סימ' י״ד ענין דבקות אין סוף בזווג אפי' בימי החול בענין סוד הנקודה זו האמצעית היורדת למטה ונעשית נקודה אמצעית לסוד כל שאר תקון איבריה, ולזה היא בת זוגה ויחודה, והנה הבחינה הזאת מותרת בתשמיש מפני שנהנים ממציאותה בני אדם שהיא צורך ההנהגה אל התחתונים, אמנם הבחינה שהיא עולה סוד שיר זכר העולה למעלה למעלה.

in comparison to the lower *sefirot*. This is a very common theme in Cordovero.[814] Such a reading implies another version of the three-phases gender theory. The ascent of the sexual female organ on high, as part of the act of intercourse, may be related to the preexistence of a womb there, together with the Infinite, as we may learn from certain other Cordoverian texts.[815] According to this passage, the masculine aspect of the Female ascends on high – referred to here by *shir* – in order to receive, and as recipient, it has a function that is characteristic of the Female. Moreover, earlier in the same context, this Safedian Kabbalist wrote: "Behold, Her elevation to [the rank] of 'a valorous wife the diadem of Her Husband,' She does not ascend but to the head of Her Husband. However, the quintessence is to ascend to *Hokhmah*, as it has been interpreted, 'A stone that has been hewn.'"[816]

The description of the divine Female ascending to the higher rank does not fit the phallocentric theory, especially as another ascent is mentioned immediately. The Female as a stone is a classical symbol, as we have seen in several cases, including in ch. 5 above; more examples can easily be adduced, and Cordovero follows *Tiqqunei Zohar*.[817] Cordovero assumes that *Malkhut*, stemming originally from *Hokhmah*, should ideally return or be caused to return there. This brief quote reinforces the reading of the entire passage as related to the three-phases model. A phallocentric reading focused mainly on transcendence of the Male/Female polarity would thus be misleading. An analysis based on separating an individual passage from a broader context and from a more complex theory can be highly problematic. Instead of assuming the prevalence of a basic uniformity throughout various versions, one should first detect and analyze a "theory" in each of the systems or works of Kabbalists to whom it is attributed. This exercise

---

814 For the ascent of the "point of Zion" to the Infinite, see, e.g., also in Cordovero's *Shiʿur Qomah*, fols. 89b, 96a.
815 See Idel, "The Womb and the Infinite." Whether there may exist an affinity between the superior status of matter in Shlomo ibn Gabirol's system, as higher than the Form, and that of Arabic texts translated as pseudo-Empedocles, and the womb as a supernal entity that generates, is an issue requiring additional studies. In any case, the parallel to Plato's receptacle as a generative entity is remarkable. See Pessin, "Loss, Presence and Gabirol's Desire."
816 *'Or Yaqar* on *Tiqqunim*, 4: 91:
והנה העלוי להיותה אשת חיל עטרת בעלה אינה עולה אלא עד על ראש בעלה, אמנם העיקר להתעלות עד החכמה כדפי' אבן דאיתגזרת.
See also *'Or Yaqar* on *Tiqqunim*, 4: 94, 154, and Idel, "*Male and Female*," n. 26.
817 See above, nn. 165, 255, 256, 472, 477, 612, 744, the quotes from the *Book of Bahir*, and some other Kabbalistic sources. For additional cases when stone stands for the last *sefirah*, see e.g., Cordovero, *Tiqqunei Zohar Hadash*, 1: 43, 283 – where he deals also with the *zarqa'* and the ascent to *Keter* – or 284, 286. For the secret of the *zarqa'* in Cordovero, see Sack, *R. Moshe Cordovero, Maʿayan ʿEin Yaʿaqov*, 104–125, especially 118, 119–120, and the text on 122. See also above, ch. 11, the discussion of R. Nahman of Bratzlav that draws on the passages from *Tiqqunei Zohar*.

is crucial, as I did not recommend extracting the three-phases gender model by means of extrapolating from a text found in a certain Kabbalist to another's writing, which I would call the oblique fallacy. For example, if a certain Kabbalist in many cases identifies the third *sefirah*, *Binah* as the Great Mother, and in some other cases depicts Her in masculine terms, this description should not obliterate the feminine aspects of this divine power in many other instances. Each Kabbalist should first be analyzed separately, as much as possible; one need not impose a uniform theory everywhere, even in the writings of a particular author. Both Cordovero's writings and the Lurianic corpus are fine examples of inconsistency or conceptual fluidity. The above passage clearly illustrates the danger of reducing a complex system to a simplistic theory by detaching an item from its immediate context.

In addition to the primary terms for the Female, we have also noted secondary ones, such as stone, precious stone – in Hebrew of feminine gender – or *zarqa'*, which refer to more specific moments in the Female's career. The earlier theosophical terminology is complicated by R. Moshe Cordovero's introduction of the concept of *behinah*, or aspect, found in each of the *sefirot*. This theory fragments the *sefirot* into a variety of smaller components, which enable each *sefirah* to connect to the other *sefirot* or to participate in a variety of different activities, perhaps even simultaneously.[818]

In the context of the Female's privileged status, it should be emphasized that in describing the activities of the last *sefirah*, *Malkhut*, most Kabbalists associate far more "symbols" – namely biblical and other terms stemming from classical Jewish literatures with Her than with any other *sefirah*. This is a form of paronomasia, which reflects Her manifold and different roles. Among the vast literature of commentaries on the ten *sefirot*, the greater number of discussions dedicated to the *sefirah* of *Malkhut* than to other *sefirot*, including the two paramount masculine powers, is striking.[819] Most of those symbols do not reflect anything acquisitive with regard to the attitude to the Female. This paronomasia may stem from the various hypostatic terms related to the divine feminine in older texts, such as *Hokhmah, Shekhinah, Knesset Yisra'el, Matronita', Stone, Zarqa'* etc., which were arranged in the context of the last *sefirah*; although they maintained some of their initial dynamic valences, they were brought together by the dynamic nature of the

---

818 See ben Shlomo, *The Mystical Theology of Moses Cordovero*, 181–182, 253–256.
819 On this literary genre see Gershom Scholem, "Mafteah le-Perushim 'al 'Eser Sefirot" (Hebrew), 498–515; Michal Oron, "The Literature of Commentaries to the Ten *Sefirot*" (Hebrew), 212–229; Idel, *Kabbalah: New Perspectives*, 210–214; or Idel, *The Angelic World*, 49–53. Compare, for example, the volume dedicated to the last *sefirah* in the anonymous *Sefer ha-Shem, Attributed to R. Moses de León* (Hebrew), 157–196, in comparison to all the other *sefirot* altogether, 49–156.

Neoplatonic processes of descent and ascent. Arranging the various cognomens around a certain divine power, in our case the last *sefirah*, also generated some forms of contamination of meanings, namely the transition of a meaning found in one term, such as the feminine, to other terms, such as *Malkhut*, which originally had nothing to do with femininity.[820] On the other hand, some of the appellations are clearly masculine, such as David, or Solomon, for example, which does not assume any transformation of the ancient king into a feminine power.

We may deduct something about the semiotic nature of the terms used by many of the Kabbalists from an analysis of the above passages. Their main concerns were to make sense of the classical texts, whether Biblical or Zoharic literature, in relation to their way of life and the performance of the commandments; for this purpose, they used the theosophical structures as primary exegetical codes. The words designated by scholars as symbols, a term that is absent in the nomenclature of Kabbalistic literature, were not utilized to explore the remote, inaccessible, or ineffable realm of the divine; inversely, an acquaintance with the conceptual and theosophical structures enabled them to interpret the classical texts and the valences of words that scholars call symbols. Unlike the Romantic understanding of symbolism as a mode of intuiting supernal mysteries, as formulated in the field of Kabbalah by Gershom Scholem, and his followers,[821] we may reasonably ascribe to most of the theosophical Kabbalists a significantly different approach to semiosis: to illumine texts by means of the most important sets of theological structures that they inherited or, in some cases, enriched by their theosophical speculations.[822] The contemplative aspects of the texts addressed above are marginal, in light of the Kabbalists' belief that they possess the ultimate clues for understanding both texts and any major event by applying the sophisticated interpretative apparatus that they controlled and in some cases even shaped. We may suggest four stages in the emergence of the theosophical symbolism of the Female: first, the ancient hypostatic figures of the Female, Sophia, *Hokhmah*, or *Knesset Yisra'el*; then the identification of those terms with the last sefirotic power; third, applying words and themes from canonical writings to

---

820 For similar semiotic processes in occult thought, see Brian Vickers, "Analogy versus Identity: The Rejection of Occult Symbolism, 1580–1680," 95–163; Vickers, "On the Function of Analogy in the Occult," 265–292.

821 See my discussion of the concept of symbolism according to Gershom Scholem, in *Old Worlds, New Mirrors, On Jewish Mysticism and Twentieth-Century Thought*, 83–108. The sixteenth-century Christian Kabbalist Johannes Reuchlin is the most important source for this terminology. See below, n. 957.

822 See my *Absorbing Perfections*, 234, 272–313, 331–332, and "Symbols and Symbolopoiesis in Kabbalah," 197–247. For our purpose, the polyvalence of the crucial terms *Malkhut, du-partzufin*, and *'Atarah* in Hebrew in general and in Kabbalah in particular is pertinent.

describe this feminine power; and, finally, the contamination of those appellations by valences found in other appellations.[823] The semantic contaminations differ from Kabbalist to Kabbalist, and they are one of the reasons for what I call the kaleidoscopic nature of theosophical Kabbalah. The broadening of the appellations attributed to the last *sefirah* is evident with the development of Kabbalah and is part of the strong interest in the divine Female.

The Kabbalists used their exegetical ingenuity, much more than their personal experiences with the alleged sublime divine realm, in creating the symbols, capitalizing on a polyvalent type of semiosis, according to which a single word may have different theosophical valences and one can use many different words to attribute divine power.[824] This underlies the predominantly exegetical nature of Kabbalistic literature, which is evident in the case of the voluminous commentaries on the Bible and the *Zohar*. The meanings of those books changed, particularly when new forms of theosophy emerged and were applied in those commentaries. For example, in many Kabbalistic books, including many of Cordovero's works, the Female ascended to the Infinite or to *Keter*, but in the Lurianic corpus, She retrieves Her existence within the 'Head that is not known,' whereas in other Lurianic texts, mainly stemming from R. Israel Sarug's school, it is *Malkhut* of the Infinite that She reaches.[825] Cordovero's theory of sefirotic self-inclusion – namely, the view that each *sefirah* contains also the other nine – endows a feminine dimension to each of the ten *sefirot*, in addition to the feminine character of the last *sefirah,* and substantially affected the discourse on the Female.[826] Nevertheless, those noteworthy theosophical changes did not significantly affect the phases of the three-phases model of gender. Though She is depicted as related to *Keter*, or to the head that is unknown, the important issue is that She is understood to stem from the highest divine manifestation, where She is present as a distinct entity, sometimes understood in a sexual relationship but in any case, as superior to the *sefirah* of *Tiferet* or *Yesod*. In other words, semantic multivalence, coupled with a gradual fragmentation of the divine potencies and thus their multiplication,[827] and, subsequently, the generating of more and more new affinities and processes between those "aspects," and between them and the rituals, rendered later Kabbalah and some parts of Hasidic thought much more kaleidoscopic.[828]

---

823 See my *Absorbing Perfections*, 301–302.
824 See *Absorbing Perfections*, 296–298.
825 On this term, see Liebes, *On Sabbateaism and its Kabbalah*, 308–309, n. 71.
826 See in more detail my "*Male and Female*."
827 See my *Old Worlds, New Mirrors*, 3–6.
828 See my *Kabbalah: New Perspectives*, 247–248.

Undoubtedly, legalistic strictures and social inhibitions curbed potential extremist consequences of the theosophical speculations; in most cases, these factors impeded the emergence of unrestrained conclusions arrived at as a result of systemic development. Speculations as to the special relationship between the Father and the Daughter were not inhibited, as we have seen in the above texts. In the case of Frankism, however, these speculations were transformed into action, as we see in reports about an incestuous sexual relationship between the eighteenth-century figure Jacob Frank and his daughter Eva/Rachel, identified as the *Shekhinah*, and his recommendation to regard her as a messianic figure.[829] Skeptical about the ubiquitous relevance of any form of psychoanalytical apparatus, I refrain from resorting to the concept of an Electra complex in order to explain theosophical structures, especially as they were forged by males. Perhaps one can explain those males' preoccupation with feminine images by assuming some form of complementariness, just as in Christian mysticism, monks were attracted to worship of the Virgin.[830] On the other hand, I assume that many of the innumerable references to the *Shekhinah* in theosophical Kabbalah are not necessarily informed by Her being perceived as a Daughter because, in many cases, the maternal imagery is quite evident, as is that of "the Daughter of the King found in exile," a classical national image.[831] This latter theme – when the Female is often presented as a princess – may include some forms of privileged attitude.[832] More than merely a Being, the divine Female is a Becoming, alternating between different states and actions.

Nonetheless, let me emphasize that in many other cases, the term *Shekhinah* or *Malkhut*, especially *nuqba'*, is, indeed, portrayed as having been subordinated to the two lower masculine divine powers; as part of the phallocentric model, She is regarded as the Back, *'Aḥorayyim*, in comparison to the Male, who represents the Face, *Panim*, and in many cases, She has some sort of affinities to demonic powers. We shall be careful, however, not to transfer automatically the connotations of one of the terms to others, as this would generate a homogenous

---

829 See Ada Rapoport-Albert, "On the Position of Women in Sabbatianism, 1: 168–169, 268–269, 279–294; Ciucu, "Messie au fèminin," 80–84; and Idel, *Kabbalah & Eros*, 177.

830 See the important observations to this effect in Bynum, *Jesus as Mother, Studies in the Spirituality of the High Middle Ages*, 18, 162. See also Idel, "The Spouse and the Concubine," 145 and Roi, *Love of the Shekhinah*, 413–414.

831 Norman J. Cohen, "*Shekhinta ba-Galuta*: A Midrashic Response to Destruction and Persecution," 147–159.

832 For the reverberations of the motif of *Bat ha-Melekh*, the Daughter of the King, in Kabbalah and Hasidism, see Biti Roi, "Lost and Found: the Evolution of Kabbalistic Interpretation from *Tiqquney ha- Zohar* to Rav Nachman of Breslav" (Hebrew), 654–694. See also the short statement of R. Jacob Ifargan, quoted at the end of this chapter.

semantic field: for example, the sexual connotations of the Female are not always significant, just as a woman is feminine but not necessarily a sexual partner. This fine distinction is pertinent for theories that regard gender as significant in its entirety, in all cases in which one of the above appellatives is mentioned.

In addition to surveying the various acts of the Female and Her different positions, I want to emphasize the importance of the verbs related to this entity. Governing, ascending, descending, nourishing, encrowning, and encompassing indicate activities that the Female initiates, in addition to the passive verbs referring to shifts She undergoes, such as hewn from the supernal source or thrown in order to return to it. Both the active events and the passive shifts define the Female, as much as Her shifting positions or Her subordination does, especially in a constellation of very dynamic systems. In any case, depicting the Female solely as passive, in the vein of Freud's sharp and phantasmagoric distinction between active males and passive females, is invalid for many Kabbalistic theosophical discussions. In this context, it should be mentioned that the Male powers in Kabbalistic theosophy, such as *Ze'yir 'Anppin*, are occasionally described as the recipients, which afterwards impart the effluence to lower realms of existence, becoming donors, in a manner that is reminiscent of the Female.[833]

In this context, I shall address an essential issue for the above discussions. Does the three-phases model that attributes to the Female such a sublime source explain Her special power and the emerging or intensifying impact of feminine theurgy[834] and of the Female's theurgy?[835] Does Her stemming from the source of power, or "the source of blessing," empower Her activity in the supernal realm and that of women in their relationship to the theosophical structure? In other words, are those types of theurgy a ramification of the three-phases model or of the privileged status of the Female? The answer to this question has implications for understanding the import of the theosophical Kabbalists' attitude toward the Female/woman, beyond the specific instances in texts where this model has been explicated, a phenomenon that I call radiation. In other words, if a Kabbalist

---

833 See, e.g., R. Shne'ur Zalman of Liadi, *Torah 'Or*, fol. 44d.

834 See, e.g., *Zohar*, I, fol. 49a; R. Menahem Recanati, *Commentary to the Torah*, fols. 61c, 89d; Idel, "The Spouse and the Concubine," 145–148; *Kabbalah & Eros*, 247–250, and Garb, "Gender and Power in Kabbalah," 90–91. See also the so-called *Holy Epistle*, attributed to Nahmanides, in *Kitvei ha-Ramban*, 2: 335–336 (Hebrew), written in the last third of the thirteenth century. Regarding the need for the woman's intention during sexual rapport, see also in R. Isaac of Acre, *'Otzar Hayyim*, Ms. Moscow-Ginsburg 775, fol. 159b, or in the anonymous treatise, described by Y. Zvi Langermann as perhaps written in Castile in the same period as the *Holy Letter*, in his article "MS. New York, JTSA Mic. 2497," 277. See also Abrams, *The Female's Body of God*, 110–111.

835 See *'Or Yaqar*, 6: 75 and 17: 79. See also *'Or Yaqar*, 22 108. See also Jonathan Garb, *Manifestations of Power in Jewish Mysticism* (Hebrew), 203–204.

adheres conceptually to the three-phases model, does he have to adduce it fully or refer solely to one of its phases in a certain context.[836] For example, R. Menahem Recanati, who was acquainted with the model as it is formulated in the *Book of Bahir*, quotes it *verbatim*, and he also deals, although in different places in his commentary, with feminine theurgy;[837] this is also the case with R. Isaac of Acre.[838] Accordingly, I propose interpreting other statements in their writings as implying part of the more comprehensive model.

With the much wider dissemination of Kabbalah, especially at the end of the fifteenth century and even more so in the sixteenth century, and especially its detailed elaborations in Safedian types of Kabbalah, those topics became more articulated and widely disseminated.[839] There was indeed a shift in the quantity of discussions, but much less in the quality.[840] In my opinion, later forms of Kabbalah occasionally display multiple sorts of continuities, which also implies discontinuities. Moreover, as I proposed elsewhere, some aspects of Kabbalah in Safed coalesced also in the context of different forms of reactions to the emergence of Christian Kabbalah in Italy.[841]

In certain Kabbalistic literature that was not influenced by Safedian types of Kabbalah, such as that written in southern Morocco at the end of the sixteenth and early seventeenth century, I cannot discern a significant shift in comparison to the Spanish Kabbalah, which was the major source of influence. For example, in a work by R. Jacob Ifargan, an early seventeenth century Kabbalist, he cites his uncle, R. Yehudah ben Jacob, a Kabbalist himself, to the effect that "the essence of his existence[842] is to worship the Bride, the Lady, and to bear the yoke of Her subjugation on his neck."[843] Ifargan's own book is replete with discussions about

---

836 See my "The Divine Female and the Mystique of the Moon," 158.

837 See above, nn. 165 and 834.

838 See above, end of ch. 4, and nn. 135 and 834.

839 For the impact of the *Zohar* and Recanati's *Commentary to the Torah* on Guillaume Postel, see Weiss, *A Kabbalistic Christian Messiah*. Recanati's book was translated by Flavius Mithridates for Giovanni Pico della Mirandola in the 1580s and again by Postel himself.

840 For another explanation of the prominent role of the Female and power in the sixteenth century, see Garb, "Gender and Power in Kabbalah."

841 See above, n. 323.

842 Basically, of the creation of man, as we can learn from the context.

843 *Sefer Minhat Yehudah*, 1: 165:

עיקר הוויתו הוא לעבוד הכלה, הגבירה, ולשאת עול שעבודה על צוארו.

This short statement is reminiscent also of the medieval Provencal *amour courtois* or *fin'amour*. See also Idel, *Kabbalah & Eros*, 45–46. For the wider phenomenon see Jean-Claude Vadet, *L'esprit Courtois et Orient, dans les cinq premiers siècles de l'Hegire*, and Moshé Lazar, *Amour Courtois et fin'amours dans la littérature du XIIe siècle*.

du-partzufin and the role of the *'Atarah*, in the vein of Nahmanides's followers; he also mentions Her drive to ascend to the *sefirot* of *Keter* and *Hokhmah*,[844] or Her ascents from *sefirah* to *sefirah*.[845] In some cases in this book, however, he depicts the last *sefirah* as not having an essence of Her own but as merely reflecting one of the other nine *sefirot*[846] – examples of conceptual fluidity. Although Ifargan, who was acquainted with many Kabbalistic books in print, wrote his work a generation after the decline of Safed as a Kabbalistic center, it does not clearly show the impact of the above-mentioned Safedian discussions.

Probably, Cordovero's endorsement of a cult of the divine Princess derived from common sources that also inspired the Moroccan Kabbalist. Kabbalah thus developed, in different centers – the Yemenite Kabbalah is another example – in different rhythms, at the very same time.

---

844 *Sefer Minhat Yehudah*, 2: 221.
845 *Sefer Minhat Yehudah*, 2: 518–519.
846 *Sefer Minhat Yehudah*, 2: 402–403. See also *Sefer Minhat Yehudah*, 405, 493.

13 Concluding Remarks

"Lying is done with words and also with silence."
Adrienne Rich, *On Lies, Secrets and Silence.*

"Especially at the present time,
when all places are accessible either by land or by water,
we should not accept poets and mythologists as witnesses of things that are unknown,
since for the most part they furnish us with unreliable testimony about disputed things,
according to Heraclitus.
Polybius, *Histories*, iv. 40.

One of the two biblical references to *Keter Malkhut*, which could serve as subtitle of this work, occurs in the context of Esther's receiving a crown in the book of Esther 2:17, namely, in the context of a woman's coronation as a queen. It is worth enumerating its various meanings: it stands for the location of the first divine manifestation and last, feminine *sefirah* as part of the circular theosophy. In other cases, it stands for the ascent of the last *sefirah* to the highest one, in the vein of Neoplatonism, and as part of the three-phases model. Last, but not least, it stands for the theosophical interpretations of the pseudo-Aristotelian dictum, thought and action as referring to the two divine powers. The three different interpretations combine in various ways that present a unique vision of the Female in comparison to other *sefirot*.

Semantically, those views stem from dissociating *Keter* and *Malkhut* – which in biblical and rabbinic literature refer to just one entity – and treating them as if they refer to two different divine entities, whose relationship Kabbalists formulate in various ways. An additional interpretation of this locution, associated with Cordovero's school, assumes the existence of each of these two *sefirot* in one another.

With regard to the last interpretation, several major Kabbalists, among them the *Zohar*, Nahmanidean Kabbalists, R. Isaac of Acre, Meir ibn Gabbai, Cordovero, Luria, Cardoso, or Luzzatto, and some of their followers made explicit use of the pseudo-Aristotelian dictum, many of them in the context of a divine feminine power. Some Kabbalists adapted and adopted this dictum, a way of thought unrelated to either divinity or feminine powers, to enrich their discussions on the nature of both theosophy and on gender topics. It should be mentioned that thought, as a prime action, and the head as the highest limb, have sometimes been amalgamated to refer to the supernal root of the Female as action or as Daughter. Various passages discussed above contain assorted mixtures of unrelated themes stemming from different sources: ancient biblical discussions of Wisdom, together with thoughts on the valorous woman in the book of Proverbs,

https://doi.org/10.1515/9783110599800-013

some views in *Sefer Yetzirah*, a Greek myth about Athena's special birth, and the theosophical vertical and circular approaches, or the schemes of the ten *sefirot*.

The intricate fabric of these texts, which are sometimes informed by the three-phases gender theory, may also reflect the adoption of a form of the Neoplatonic theory of cosmic processes of procession – *prohodos* – and reversion – *epistrophe* – and of descent and ascent of the soul and of other entities in general to the source.[847] Although the Neoplatonic way of thinking has nothing to do with the *Shekhinah* or the Feminine, Kabbalists adopted the Feminine and adapted the rabbinic vision of the ten ascents and descents of the *Shekhinah*, namely, Her mobile nature. Rabbinic thought envisioned the privileged locus of the *Shekhinah* below, in the Temple, whereas the ascents are provoked by human sins, and the good deeds of men drew Her back down. This represents the inverse situation as reflected in Neoplatonism, where the original place is located in the supernal world, and the descent is the effect of a fall that ought to be repaired by a return on high. This is a fine example of the deep impact of a philosophical view on a major Kabbalistic issue. Unlike the philosophical approach that deals with cosmic processes that are often only marginally connected to human deeds, however, the ascent of the Female is closely related to the performance of the commandments.

Nevertheless, the privileged status of the Female remains very conspicuous, despite the amalgams of various themes and diverging traditions, especially given the circular or uroboric theosophy. Rabbinic literature, which was not so concerned with problems of origins and endings, did not produce comprehensive metaphysical models, as was the case, in some instances, in Jewish philosophy and in Kabbalah in general and, especially, in theosophical Kabbalah. In the

---

847 Those views appear already in Plotinus and were adopted by Proclus, especially in his *Elements of Theology*, sentence 31: "All that proceeds from any principle reverts to respect of its being upon that from which it proceeds." A version of Proclus's book was known in the Middle Ages as *Liber de Causis*. For a detailed analysis of this scheme, called by a modern scholar the "spiritual circuit," see A. C. Lloyd, *The Anatomy of Neoplatonism*, passim and Jean Pépin, "Theories of Procession in Plotinus and the Gnostics," 297–335. This Neoplatonic theory was well known in Judaism from the thirteenth century, in part due to the various translations of the Arabic treatise, *Al-Bataliusi's Sefer ha-'Aggulot ha-Ra'yoniot*. See the fine introduction of Kaufmann to this work and n. 403 above, as well as M. Idel, "The Sources of the Circle Images in *Dialoghi d'Amore*," 162–166. For these two processes in Neoplatonism and early Kabbalah, see Steven Katz, "Utterance and Ineffability," 292–293 and Idel, *Ascensions on High*, 170–171, 186 and compare to its occurrence in Christian spirituality, as pointed out by Newman, *God and the Goddesses*, 291, where she quotes St. Bonaventura to the effect that "this is the whole of our metaphysics – emanation, exemplarity, and consummation: that is to be illumined by spiritual rays and led back to the ultimate source." See also Bernard McGinn, *The Flowering of Mysticism Men and Women in the New Mysticism 1200–1350*, 88–89 and now Michael Ebstein, "The Circular Vision of Existence."

latter type of Kabbalah, the Female plays an important role in those moments of divine activity.

Despite the keen interest in the primordial source, in the status, and in the dynamics of the Female, Kabbalistic literature does not provide sustained descriptions of Her appearance; even less, it attempts to offer some form of drawing. Although parts of the Hebrew Bible, the Song of Songs, and various parts of the Book of Proverbs offer significant descriptions of the feminine entities, the various Kabbalists did not produce a rich poetical erotic literature that elaborates a fuller picture of their thought on the Female or on human feminine figures. They used biblical verses or selected phrases from them, often detached from their immediate literary context, as prooftexts and in fewer cases as springboards, fashioning them into composite, skeletal narratives. This poverty in producing sustained discourses and poetic literature – Alqabetz's poem mentioned above is one of the few exceptions – ties in with their emphasis on the centrality of deeds, actions, and the performance of precepts, rather than on anatomical descriptions of the Female that are so characteristic of Greek art and poetry. To a certain extent, a preference for avoiding individual pictures – the biblical interdiction on producing visual images aside – is related to the centrality of the national myth, namely the collective, which we have mentioned several times. In short, theosophical Kabbalists judged individuals in a wider context, usually in terms of their performance, which means, in many cases, their belonging to the community, and not by their external, individual appearance. It is worth mentioning, however, that a few visual revelations of the *Shekhinah* are known since the second half of the sixteenth century.[848]

In contrast, a few pieces, although very important ones from the theosophical point of view, found in the Zoharic literature, *Sifra di-Tzeni'uta'* and the *Idrot*, contain detailed descriptions of the masculine divine heads and beards. Nothing similar exists in the case of the Female, with the exception of a long discussion in *Tiqqunei Zohar* and in one of Cordovero's books.[849]

Let me analyze the hermeneutical steps evident in a variety of Kabbalistic writings concerning topics discussed above: first, the content of the pseudo-Aristotelian dictum was projected from a human to the divine structure and mode of activity. The totally independent emergence of a complex structure of divinity that we termed Kabbalistic theosophy enabled this projection. Perceiving a

---

[848] See Idel, *Kabbalah: New Perspectives*, 80–84. Many of R. Joseph Karo's revelations over several decades are attributed to Feminine powers, *Shekhinah*, Mother, *Malkhut*, etc., although they are not visual experiences. See above, n. 358, and below, n. 874.

[849] See Roi, *Love of the Shekhinah*, 327–360, and Sack, ed., *R. Moshe Cordovero, Ma'ayan 'Ein Ya'aqov*, 39–66.

threat of centrifugal themes endangering the notion of divine unity within the complex structure of the divine realm, Kabbalists introduced a solution involving centripetal modes, in this case, interpreting the identity between the first and the last divine hypostases as referring to thought and action respectively. This means that the two main concepts of the dictum were reified to function in narratives related to the divine powers as distinct entities. Unlike R. Yehudah ha-Levi's application of the dictum to God's intention when creating the world, thus generating two poles, a divine one – thought – and an extra-divine one – the created world,[850] the Kabbalists confined their conceptualizations basically to the intra-divine realm.

This reification, in fact, a process of deification, is related to another major development: the introduction of sexual polarity in the divine realm that envisions in the terms mentioned in the dictum a potential for sexual polarization. This means that the action, transferred to the last *sefirah*, has been discussed in gender terms. The introduction of sexual polarized exegesis in interpreting and applying the pseudo-Aristotelian dictum is but one of many examples of this radical exegetical move.[851] In fact, the grammatical gender of the Hebrew terms for thought and action, *maḥashavah* and *ma'aseh*, are feminine and masculine respectively, namely, inverse to their referents in the sefirotic realm, *Keter* and *Malkhut*; this obvious inconsistency, however, did not deter the Kabbalists from a sexual reading of this couple.

The strength of the identification of the last *sefirah* as a feminine power transcends the inconsistency evident in the theosophical interpretations of the details of the pseudo-Aristotelian dictum. Instead of constructing an interpretation based on literal meaning in specific texts, Kabbalists attached greater importance to specific themes in their theosophical structures, often using interpreted texts as prooftexts for a predetermined theory. This is the major difference between many Kabbalists' treatment of rabbinic myths related to the phases of the moon and its light in comparison to the sun, on the one hand, and their interpretation of the pseudo-Aristotelian dictum, on the other. In the former case, the myths were rethought in a way that was more adequate to their rabbinic sense and then appropriated to the Kabbalists' own myths.[852] This example of freedom of interpretation is part of a more general phenomenon: the Kabbalists were radical or forceful readers and exegetes, who often employed extravagant exegetical techniques in order to project their myths onto the interpreted texts, as

---

850 See *Kuzari*, 3: 61–74. Compare also to R. Isaac Abrabanel, *Yeshu'ot Meshiḥo*, fol. 47a.
851 See, e.g., my "Leviathan and Its Consort: From Talmudic to Kabbalistic Myth," 145–187.
852 See Idel, "The Divine Female and the Mystique of the Moon."

evident already in the *Book of Bahir*.[853] In other words, the pre-axial attitude was projected onto the axial one.

One should compare the richness and the audacity of those Kabbalistic interpretations to the rather homogenous approach to the pseudo-Aristotelian dictum in Jewish philosophical writings. As Samuel Stern pointed out, medieval Jewish philosophy has a long history of appropriations of the dictum, some which indubitably served as intermediaries between the Greek and Arabic sources and the Kabbalists. This is evidently the case in some classics of Jewish thought such as R. Bahya ibn Paqudah's *Hovot ha-Levavot*, R. Yehudah ha-Levi's *Sefer Kuzari*, or, later on, in the fifteenth century, R. Joseph Albo's *Sefer ha-'Iqqarim*, R. Isaac Arama's *'Aqedat Yitzhaq*, or R. Isaac Abravanel, each of whom used different variants of this dictum.[854] Composed under the influence of various strands of Greek or Hellenistic philosophical literature, these Kabbalistic writings often reveal a congruency with the major conceptual impulses found in those literatures, which is particularly true of their various theologies.[855] This is also the case with regard to Christian medieval authors such as St. Thomas d'Aquinas or Meister Eckhart.[856]

On the other hand, the absence of a Kabbalistic interpretation of this dictum in some Kabbalistic writings, such as the many books of R. Abraham Abulafia, of R. Isaac ibn Latif, R. David ben Abraham ha-Lavan, or of R. Yohanan Alemanno, is connected to their attributing an insignificant role to the divine feminine power; this holds true in many forms of Jewish philosophy. They subscribed to the theology of divine perfection, basically a static one, which in some cases was adopted in part also by theosophical Kabbalists, such as the author of *Ma'arekhet ha-'Elohut* or some discussions in R. Hayyim Vital.[857] Whereas the earlier Jewish philosophers understood the pseudo-Aristotelian dictum in a way that was more faithful to its original sense, the above-mentioned Kabbalists brought in a variety of creative misunderstandings, especially by introducing the sexual polarities.

The specific nature of R. Azriel's text as discussed in ch. 2 is illuminating: he was not particularly concerned with the role of the Female in his theosophy and, at the same time, he was deeply influenced by various forms of Neoplatonism,

---

853 See my *Absorbing Perfections*, 250–271.
854 "The First in Thought is the Last in Action," Liebes, *Sections in Zohar Lexicon*, 260.
855 For the indifference to gender issues in Jewish philosophy see Julia Schwartzmann, "Gender Concepts of Medieval Jewish Thinkers and the Book of Proverbs," 183–202.
856 See however, our discussion of Cornelius Agrippa's gender-oriented discussion under Kabbalistic influence, in ch. 6 above.
857 For problems related to divine perfection and perfectibility in Kabbalah, see my *Il male primordiale nella Qabbalah,* passim.

as Scholem duly pointed out.[858] For this reason, his approach to the dictum focused on questions related to divine unity, and he did interpret it in gender terms, which had already appeared in the book of *Bahir*, as we saw in ch. 5. The tensions between the Neoplatonic, vertical, hierarchical, and emanative picture of the divine world, on the one hand, and the uroboric, circular theosophy, found embryonically in the formulation in *Sefer Yetzirah* 1:7, on the other hand, form the background for some of the discussions of the pseudo-Aristotelian dictum surveyed above. Kabbalists understood – or basically misunderstood – this dictum as itself having some uroboric overtones, and they combined this with the view of *Sefer Yetzirah* about the circular *sefirot*. Once again this is a creative misunderstanding.

We may conclude that the existence of strong theosophical structures, which included Feminine powers, one of which has sometimes been considered as "higher than all," or as emanated directly from the first divine power, *Keter*, impinged on some theosophical Kabbalists' eccentric interpretations of the pseudo-Aristotelian dictum.[859] The theosophical codes were sufficiently strong, at least from a certain moment, and they could impose their valences that were alien to the interpreted texts, whether or not they were Jewish.[860]

Although the *Book of Bahir* already showed evidence of the role of the Feminine power in Kabbalistic theosophy, as shown above,[861] the ascent of the Nahmanidean Kabbalah and of the Zoharic theosophies determined the main directions of later Kabbalists, especially the Safedian interpretations, as described in the previous chapters. One sees this, in particular, in the thought of Cordovero. who was well-acquainted with the two forms of Kabbalah mentioned above. These Kabbalists did not ascribe a status of transcendence for the Female, as part of putting Her on a pedestal; rather, they conferred upon Her a privileged position expressed sometimes by the syntagm "higher than all," which combines in some cases a supernal origin with a theology of divine immanence by means of the Female presence in the lower world. After all, depictions of Her in Her lower metamorphoses do not always portray Her as subordinate; in some cases, moreover, they describe Her as governing this world, or even mingling with

---

858 See, e.g., his *Origins of the Kabbalah*, 314, 322, 428–429, 439–441, 446–447, n. 195, Gabrielle Sed-Rajna, "L'influence de Jean Scot sur la doctrine du kabbaliste Azriel de Gerone," 453–463.
859 See my studies mentioned above in n. 42 and Weiss, *Cutting the Shoots*. In my earlier studies, as in this one, I am concerned with an entity in the theosophical realm, the divine Female, not with the status of women in Kabbalah.
860 See Idel, *Absorbing Perfections*, 301.
861 See the survey of the different scholarly views on this topic in Abrams, "The Condensation of the Symbol 'Shekhinah,'" 7–82 and Idel, *Ben, Sonship and Jewish Mysticism*, 385–399.

it in what can be called an exile of the *Shekhinah* – all these as part of the second phase in the three-phases gender theory.[862] We cannot, therefore, speak about an essentialist theory of even one single stage of the Feminine.[863] Kabbalists did not necessarily conceive the Female as having an inferior status, even in the case of the sexual encounter, however, as we see from a long series of discussions in R. Moshe Cordovero's writings that emphasize the issue of the equality and reciprocity between the bodies of the two supernal powers.[864]

In other words, Kabbalists, all of them males, attributed a much broader gamut of situations and roles to the Female than they did to the divine masculine powers. In many texts, they conceived Her as a supremely dynamic divine power, a trend evident already in the Ashkenazi passages discussed above, the early fourteenth century *Tiqqunei Zohar*,[865] and even more so in the thought of Cordovero, who was well acquainted with the theories of the latter book.[866] To be sure, this development does not mean that we should dismiss other views about the Female, many of them negative, some of which are related to Her contacts with the demonic powers, Her linkage to the *sefirah* of *Gevurah*, the power of strict judgment, or to Her subordinate status to the Male, but they should not be presented by means of categorical generalizations, as the only one model in the field, or even as a dominant one.

The discussions above and those on similar topics mentioned in the footnotes do not claim that one single or even one main theory of gender exists in Kabbalistic literature;[867] nor do they deny the existence of many androcentric views in the writings of some of the Kabbalists analyzed earlier or in other Kabbalists. As in many other cases, an individual Kabbalist, not to speak about Kabbalistic literature in general, subscribed to more than one single theory, as part of what I called "conceptual fluidity."[868] Kabbalists display ambivalent attitudes toward the Female and feminine, spread over a wide spectrum, from the privileged, as described above, to the demonic.[869] In my opinion, serious scholarship in the field should strive to form a picture that incorporates the conceptual

---

862 See Idel, "The Divine Female and the Mystique of the Moon."

863 For a non-essentialist vision of the Female in Cordovero, see Abrams, *The Female Body of God*, 122–123 and Asulin, "The Double Construct of the Image of the *Shekhinah*."

864 See my "*Male and Female*," ch. 14.

865 See Roi, *Love of the Shekhina* and ch. 5 above.

866 "*Male and Female*."

867 See below, n. 893.

868 See n. 13 above. As is well-known, major Kabbalists such as R. Moshe de Leon, R. Joseph Gikatilla, and the various parts of the Zoharic literature reflect significantly different views in their various writings.

869 See Mopsik, *Recherches autour de la lettre sur la sainteté*, 199–201.

structures of the varied theories, their independent histories, and the occasional interrelationships among them, without affirming the exclusivity or dominance of one single, overarching theory in Kabbalah, and even less so in Judaism. One must address the various ramifications of each model in greater detail before dealing seriously with the issue of hegemonic models. In this work, I attempted to draw scholarly attention to a somewhat neglected current in Kabbalistic thought that finds expression in certain passages by major Kabbalists,[870] in order to contribute to the understanding of the richness of Kabbalistic worldviews in matters of gender.[871]

My main purpose in the present study was to highlight the ideas of major Kabbalists, as expressed in specific passages dealing with the sublime roots of the Female – perceived as higher than what we find in other sources and in scholarship – or Her return by ascent to such a primordial status. At the same time, we must be aware of the development of a theme that is absent in some early Kabbalistic schools and in the ecstatic ones and should chart the later growth of this paramount development. Some discussions refer to the return of the Female to the higher source in religiously privileged moments – during the Sabbath, Holidays, or in the eschaton,[872] specific discussions that I view as part of the three-phases gender theory. The references to the privileged moments in time, plausibly imply that in ordinary times, *Malkhut* exists in a diminished condition, what I call the second phase of the three-phases model, although at the same time, She is thought of as reigning over this world as a Queen. This paramount role of the divine Feminine, recurring in thousands of theosophical texts using clear feminine imagery, such as Queen or as the daughter of the King, has been neglected in the phallocentric picture of gender in Kabbalah, which reduces the gamut of Kabbalistic *imaginaire* solely to the sexual role attributed to Her.

In the context of the above discussions, I adopted a hermeneutical approach without, however, reducing the apotheosis of the divine Feminine solely to exegetical explanations, namely, contending that the special status of the Female is solely the result of late medieval thought, emerging out of casuistic discussions. In my opinion, earlier traditions contributed to this apotheosis in some important Kabbalistic schools.[873]

---

870 Exceptions are discussed in Abrams, *The Female Body of God*, 112, n. 210, and Roi, *The Love of Shekhinah*.

871 For the variety of views of the feminine divine power in late thirteenth-century Kabbalah, see also Roi, *The Love of the Shekhinah*, 251.

872 See, e.g., the text cited in R. Abraham Azulai's *'Or ha-Ḥammah*, vol. 3, part 2, fol. 67d.

873 As mentioned above, this is not the case, for example, of Provencal Kabbalah and its Catalan extension, as it is absent in ecstatic Kabbalah or the writings of R. Isaac ibn Latif.

In a series of studies, I pointed to Kabbalistic texts claiming the existence of the Female's privileged status for a variety of reasons. Some other sources are pre-Kabbalistic, which means that feminine exegesis was used to insert some concepts already found in Jewish traditions, discussions that I shall not reiterate here.[874] Together with the material analyzed here, they constitute a significant voice in Kabbalah, which is far from marginal or exceptional. Nevertheless, I am not concerned here with the question whether this status is a matter of continuation, retrieval, or restoration of the alleged situation of an ancient matriarchate or of a "matriarchate consciousness," to use Erich Neumann's term.[875] This is, indeed, an interesting speculation, but the findings of the present discussions do not depend on such broad and often nebulous assumptions; in fact, one can explain their acceptance, sometimes verbatim, by other Kabbalists on the basis of certain earlier sources and systemic or structural developments.

As pointed out earlier, the transpersonal aspects related to the Female as representing the entire Jewish nation can be understood in terms that are not connected to a specific type of individual psychology in modern terms but as a continuation of pre-axial elements concentrating on the representation and the historical vicissitudes of a certain human group. The apotheosis of the Female is not part of a feminist approach but of the strengthening of Jewish national identity and self-aggrandizing of the nation.[876] This identification of the Female and the nation contributed to the dynamic image of the Female, unlike the passivity attributed to femininity by some thinkers such as Freud and, following him, in E.R. Wolfson's interpretation of Kabbalah. Theosophical texts relate dynamism to mobility and to reaching the highest and the lowest levels of divinity and of existence in general. By creating a direct affinity between the first and the last divine powers, as in the circular theosophies, motion is introduced as an essential part of the system.

In fact, there are good reasons to explain the recurrence of this privileged status of the Female by viewing some of the discussions about Her as profoundly related to the widespread theme of the people of Israel as a chosen nation. Biblical and rabbinic discussions sometimes portrayed the Jewish nation as

---

874 See, e.g., Idel, *Kabbalah & Eros*, 45–49, 137–147; Idel, "R. Joseph Karo and His Revelations: On the Apotheosis of the Feminine in Safedian Kabbalah"; and Idel, "The Triple Family: Sources for the Feminine Perception of Deity in Early Kabbalah."

875 *The Great Mother*, 78–79 or Chava Weissler, *Voices of the Matriarchs: Listening to the Prayers of Early Modern Jewish Women*. See also Idel, *Kabbalah & Eros*, 97.

876 To be sure, the other main type of Kabbalah, the ecstatic one, is much less concerned with this issue; it places more emphasis on inner developments, and it is much more universalist, indubitably because of the impact of Maimonides' thought and of Neoplatonism.

the wife of God, as *Knesset Yisra'el*; the elevation of the Female in theosophical Kabbalah has, therefore, overtones that in many cases privilege the Female as representative of a national entity in the divine sphere, as a Mother of the tribe.[877] A type of relationship thus emerged that did not necessarily place the Female as dependent on or subordinate to the Male, as Kabbalists ranked the gender issue as secondary to the ethnocentric one; they attached greater importance to the vicissitudes of national history and the manner of its development. Most analyses involving gender studies in Kabbalah diminish the centrality of this affinity of the Female and the Jewish nation, although, in my opinion, it is a significant element in Kabbalistic literature, which prefers methods that focus on the individual identity and experiences. The above chapters explicitly delineate the affinities of Israel as a nation in history and its ahistorical representative on high, *Knesset Yisra'el,* and their privileged status is also clear from the use of the phrase "precious stone." We see this clear imagery starting with the passages in *Sefer ha-Bahir* that we have adduced up to the passage from R. Abraham Yoshu'a Heschel of Apta's book. As seen from this ethnocentric perspective, the Female possessed Her ancient dignity, as did the ancient Israelites, and She is expected to regain it in the eschatological future, a vision that was reinforced by the Neoplatonic approach mentioned earlier. Moreover, Her role as the tenth *sefirah* that does not ascend should not be understood as dealing necessarily with a lower function. Numerous instances relate the *Shekhinah* to the act of procreation of souls, envisaged as born out of Her intercourse with the Male. As such, Biblical and rabbinic Judaism thus regard Her as an indispensable factor in a highly significant process; most Kabbalist sources similarly attach great importance to reproduction.[878] Last but certainly not least: She is part of the mythology of the sacred recurrent time, the Sabbath day, as we have seen frequently, especially in chapters 7, 8, and 9.

To be sure, all the authors discussed above were Jewish males writing for the consumption of other Jewish males, producing ethnocentric worldviews, with

---

[877] See, e.g., the late fourteenth century Byzantine treatise, the vast compilation *Sefer ha-Peliy'ah*, 1, fols. 56b, 85d, II, fols. 15d, 42d. See also the material discussed in my "The Triple Family," "The Divine Female and the Mystique of the Moon," and especially *Kabbalah & Eros*, 138–140, and my "On the Identity of the Authors," 100, n. 190, 105, and n. 217, 110, n. 243, 136, 145–147, 153, 183, 194–195 and n. 441, 212–213, n. 253, and n. 346. It should be emphasized that there are many Jewish sources where the people of Israel are represented on high by the head of Jacob, described sometimes in erotic relations to God. See Wolfson, *Along the Path*, 1–62 and the pertinent footnotes. For the cult of specifically the head of Jesus as found in some icons in Middle Ages in Western Christianity, see the study and the material assembled by Pietro Lazzarini, *Il Volto Santo di Lucca*, and Idel, "On the Identity of the Authors," 166, n. 375.

[878] See the texts discussed in, e.g., Idel, "*Male and Female*," nn. 93, 94, and 158.

prominent narcissistic biases. Moreover, the Female was often portrayed as privileged by an even higher power, which was not necessarily a King or a power
that functions as a male. Within the theosophical systems, however, the two predominantly masculine hypostases, the *sefirot* of *Tiferet* and *Yesod*, are perceived
as having been transcended by Her ascent, in many cases because She was conceived as stemming from an even higher divine entity, described sometimes as
the Father or one that is even higher. In other words, the phallocentric theory
as formulated thus far, in terms of the Female's subservient role to the Male,
ignores basic features of the various theosophical structures that are evident in
the Female's supernal origins, Her return there, and the rich dynamics that are
characteristic of the Female alone.[879] Scholars have dramatically impoverished
the Kabbalists' picture of the Female.

Finally, I find it very surprising that many texts discussed here – that are
pertinent to this topic and very explicit – have remained at the margin of gender
theories in Kabbalah, despite the special interest in this topic over the last two
decades. Only by neglecting or suppressing the content of so many pertinent
Kabbalistic texts,[880] and earlier scholarly discussions on topics addressed here,[881]
could a homogeneous, uniform, and rigid picture of a phallocentric gender theory
be offered to naïve readers who might believe simple generalizations taken from
feminist clichés. In a highly representative passage for his conceptual approach
to gender in Kabbalah, Elliot R. Wolfson confesses as follows:

---

879 Compare below, n. 881, as to Wolfson's claim of an alleged absence of even a fissure in his
phallocentric edifice. Indeed there are no fissures because the edifice itself is a very shaky construct. Examples include describing the views of R. Menahem 'Azaryah of Fano, without referring
at all to the material discussed in ch. 6 above or those of Abraham Michael Cardoso without
referring to the sermon he himself edited, as discussed in ch. 8.

880 See, e.g., my "The Divine Female and the Mystique of the Moon," or *Kabbalah & Eros*, and
"Male and Female."

881 See, e.g., the serious scholars' failure to engage the Kabbalistic material cited, translated,
and discussed already in 1988, in my *Kabbalah: New Perspectives*, 196–197, and especially in my
R. *Menahem Recanati*, 1: 217–220, 223, 228–229, published in 1998, in the studies referred to in n.
893 below, and *Kabbalah & Eros*, passim, in the homogeneously phallocentric picture of gender
in Kabbalah that rules in this literature without exception and recurs in Elliot Wolfson's studies.
See, e.g., his *Language, Eros, Being*, 446, n. 114, where he claims, as late as 2005, in a very polemi-
cal tone, that he believes that regarding "critical structures of thought" in Kabbalah, "uniformity
of approach is more telling than diversity," all this in addition to the ubiquitous phallocentrism.
See also *Language, Eros, Being*, 62–63: "uniformity … is astonishing," 78–79, and especially on
94–95, where he speaks about "inflexible structure" and "structural inflexibility." For more on
this issue, see below, n. 893. Are those inflexible statements appropriate tools for understanding
the performative and dynamic theology of the Kabbalists and even more the theurgical aspects?

[m]y *insistence on phallocentrism* of medieval kabbalah should be seen as a feminist reading. However, I must say with regret that the *portrayal of gender in kabbalistic sources themselves does not supply evidence for multivocality or even a fissure in the edifice that would support this slant...* On the contrary, *they exemplify a remarkable degree of homogeneity;* surprisingly, changes in time and place have had virtually no effect on the phallocentric disposition.[882]

In this passage, the author emphasizes his exclusive claims for a certain gender theory. The negative and subordinate nature of the Female has appeared in scholarship previously,[883] but the present "insistence" on exclusivity, on the one hand, and the adopting of a feminist approach, on the other hand, are, indeed, new. Wolfson's univocal edifice, which, he claims, does not have even one fissure, an inert, unchangeable model persisting over centuries, presents an interesting case in scholarship in the field, which has slowly moved toward a more complex and multivocal approach, but in this case is returning to monochromatism. Ironically, Wolfson's book has as its epigraph a statement of no other than Heraclitus. This explicitly monolithic approach to gender is not an exceptional statement, which is indeed quite telling from the scholarly point of view.[884] Elsewhere in the same book, he writes, in a somewhat more "open" manner: "Ontically, woman is derived from man and thus she must be subservient – a sexist orientation pervasive in the thinking of medieval kabbalists; I have yet to find one traditional kabbalistic source that proves to be an exception."[885]

---

882 *Language, Eros, Being,* 87, emphases added. See also in this work 389, 471, n. 436, and his claims in "Occultation of the Feminine," 153, n. 4. These statements were written long after publication of some mild critiques. See below, n. 913. In the same year that Wolfson's cited statement was published, some studies that strongly qualify or even reject this monolithic approach appeared. See Abrams, *The Female Body of God;* Garb, "Gender and Power in Kabbalah," and my *Kabbalah & Eros,* and "Androgyny and Equality in the Theosophico-Theurgical Kabbalah." Compare also to Rachel Elior's far-reaching general claim as to the absence of the feminine voice in her "'Present but Absent,' 'Still Life,' and a 'Pretty Maiden who has no Eyes': On the Presence and Absence of Women in the Hebrew Language, in the Jewish Religion, and in Israeli Life," *Studies in Spirituality* 20 (2010): 381–455.
883 See Gershom Scholem, *Major Trends in Jewish Mysticism,* 37, and the studies referred in n. 24 above.
884 See also his *Language, Eros, Being,* 471, n. 436: the "monolithic character of the androgyne in kabbalistic doctrine."! *Nota bene* the singular mode of the statement. In fact, the term androgyne is, symbolically speaking, quite polyvalent. Compare, for example, to my *Kabbalah & Eros,* 53–103; Idel, "Androgynes: Reflections on the Study of Religions," 17–48 and Idel, "Archetypes and Androgynes at Eranos," 193–221. As to the singular mode of describing Kabbalah, see Wolfson, *Language, Eros, Being,* 389 and compare to my *Kabbalah in Italy,* 312; see also above, n. 803.
885 Wolfson, *Language, Eros, Being,* 62. See also his "Woman: The Feminine as Other in Theosophic Kabbalah," 176–177. Compare, however, above, n. 356, where such a view is found in a text printed in a Ph. D. he supervised.

In light of the texts noted above, most of which he did not discuss, it is hard to believe such generalizations about an alleged essentialist nature of the edifice. Even less credible is the implicit claim as to the impossibility that the Female can originate from a much higher level in the divine pleroma than the Male/Husband, as if phallocentrism is invariably representative of Kabbalah as a whole, in fact also of Judaism as such – and in one case in his writings, even of the entire Western culture.[886] The search for general messages and universal keys implies a monolithic content that is quintessential, a gaze that immobilizes the most important topic Wolfson investigated. This monolithic drive is also evident when he declares the morphological "semblance" of the theurgical and the ecstatic categories in Kabbalah, as both are rooted in the allegedly shared assumption about the divine nature of the souls of the Jews.[887] I presume that Abraham Abulafia would certainly be shocked by such an assumption, as he centered his ecstatic Kabbalah on the development of the intellect, which is common to all intelligent persons, regardless of religious affiliation, a very universalistic approach.[888]

The drive to level stark differences is, therefore, not merely a matter of a specific erroneous reading, in fact, a sustained misreading, of some Kabbalistic texts, but part of a much wider phenomena that I would call essentialism. Wolfson reached this conclusion after producing a long series of studies for more than a decade.[889] This scholar fiercely defends against any opposing voices his scholarly legacy of phallocentrism, indubitably his most important thesis, which he argues that other scholars ignored but only he revealed.

Were such clichés, repeated *ad nauseam,* correct, they would amount to the view that the many passages discussed above are either not Kabbalistic or not precisely quoted or properly understood, or perhaps – what might be best for the "theory" – they are just my invention. In fact, by excluding most of these passages, Wolfson has created a distorted picture of the field on this topic, which has been widely disseminated in print for two decades; in addition, he misrepresented material that he quoted from Lurianic Kabbalah, and, in his analysis, skipped over a passage of Cardoso that he himself published and made available, as we saw in ch. 8 above.

---

886 See his *Language, Eros, Being*, 596, n. 57.

887 *Language, Eros, Being*, 209–210.

888 This type of monolithic assumption will be treated in detail elsewhere. Compare, for the time being, to M. Idel, "*Nishmat Eloha*: The Divinity of the Soul in Nahmanides and His School" (Hebrew), 338–380 and Idel, "'Higher than Time' – Some Observations on Concepts of Time in Kabbalah and Hasidism," 185–197.

889 See above, n. 28.

Naïve readers – a category that includes some scholars in the field who do not have access to the variety of Kabbalistic literature and to the broad spectrum of content in the Hebrew originals, or simply are not interested in consulting them, even when they may have the linguistic capacities, – tend to be no more than believers. If such readers depend exclusively on the scholarly analyses in English on Kabbalistic phallocentrism, they may know little about the existence of several major "exceptions," about the various conceptual cross-currents, about the polyvalence of what scholars call symbols in theosophical Kabbalah, or of the existence of alternative models of gender theory in such a vast literature, written over several centuries in different continents. In short, it is surprising that in recent discussions of gender in Kabbalah and Hasidism, scholars have neglected, or perhaps even suppressed, the texts analyzed above that belonged to major figures in Jewish mysticism.

Moreover, this sustained "overlooking" is not the most striking phenomenon. In fact, in the 1930s, Scholem published one of the earliest and most outstanding passages that runs counter to Wolfson's exclusivist theory, a lengthy passage found in R. Isaac of Acre's elaboration on R. Jacob ben Jacob ha-Kohen; this passage was reprinted and discussed, inter alia, in Daniel Abrams's 1993 Ph. D. thesis, which was supervised by no other than Wolfson himself.[890] In my opinion, the phallocentric theory excludes many pertinent texts concerning gender in Kabbalistic theosophy that should have been part of the gender-oriented discourse; a perfect illustration is Wolfson's treatment of Cardoso's view, which ignores the important text he himself edited, as noted in ch. 8. Such an overemphasis creates a grievous imbalance, distorting an understanding of many issues related to gender in both Kabbalah and Hasidism.

The recurrent resort to just one gender model on this complex topic, evident in the generalizations about the alleged phallocentric nature of Judaism and Kabbalah as a whole, cannot do justice to a rich gamut of situations in theosophical conceptions. Explicit statements of major Kabbalists that present a totally different approach have been ignored, and one major Kabbalist's view, that of Cordovero, has been treated, surprisingly, as a "departure." In this work and in some earlier studies elsewhere,[891] I am not proposing another exclusive single model, which is supposed to inform the Kabbalah as a whole, nor do I assume that the model should be found in all the theosophical forms of Kabbalah. I tried to avoid a comprehensive claim, which is part of a larger scholarly phenomenon

---

890 See above, at the end of ch. 4.
891 See, especially, "The Divine Female and the Mystique of the Moon."

that I called "the totalizing quandary," which is evident in some of Gershom Scholem's descriptions of Kabbalah.[892]

I have attempted to facilitate comprehension of some specific texts, based on a broader approach to the supernal origin of the Female, considered in many cases the telos of the entire emanational process. This does not exclude the existence of other gender theories in Kabbalah, including the androcentric/phallocentric/acquisitive one, as formulated by Elliot R. Wolfson. One should, however, carefully evaluate their relative importance, while remaining cognizant of the existence of a variety of models, of their relative weight, their ramifications, source, and specific history in this literature. Whereas I adopt an inclusive approach, allowing for the existence of several models of the relationship between Male and Female, as I pointed out already in my book *Kabbalah & Eros,* Wolfson formulates his theory in a stark, exclusive manner, making hyperbolic statements. One may dispute my selection of texts and their interpretations, from several points of view, as the gates of casuistry are not closed, as some rabbis would say. In my opinion, however, what cannot be disputed is the fact that for the most part, the stream of scholarly discussions about recent gender theories, whether phallocentric or not, do not cite or even allude to the vast majority of the texts translated and analyzed above. More importantly, even when a scholar published for the first time an important text such as Cardoso's sermon on the *Shekhinah,* he or she did not take it into consideration in the analysis of the topic, as seen in ch. 8.

Indeed, when seen as a whole, and this applies to many vital topics – including issues of gender – Kabbalistic literature is both variegated, complex, and in a continuous conceptual flux, although still operating with several stable models.[893]

---

892 See Idel, *Representing God,* 142–148.

893 On the coexistence of different models in Kabbalah and Hasidism, see, e.g., my works: Idel, *Hasidism, Between Ecstasy and Magic,* 45–145; *Messianic Mystics,* 17–18, 272–273, *Kabbalah & Eros,* especially 213–233; and *Enchanted Chains,* passim, as well as, e.g., Garb, *Manifestations of Power in Jewish Mysticism,* 54, 79–82, 88, 167–168, 169; and Ron Wachs, *The Secret of Unity, Unifications in the Kabbalistic and Hasidic Thought of R. Ḥayyim ben Solomon Tyrer of Czernowitz* (Hebrew).

On the existence of different models of the supernal Female found in various stages of Judaism, see Idel, *Kabbalah & Eros,* passim, especially 131–133, 213–223, and some earlier discussions of this topic in my "The Bride of God" (Hebrew), 44–46; Idel, *R. Menachem Recanati the Kabbalist,* 1: 223; Idel, "The Spouse and the Concubine, the Woman in Jewish Mysticism" (Hebrew), 141–157; Idel, "Eros in der Kabbalah: Zwischen Gegenwaertiger Physischer Realitaet und Idealen Metaphysischen Konstrukten," 59–102, and "Ascensions, Gender and Pillars," 55–108; Jonathan Garb, "Gender and Power in Kabbalah," 79–107; and Ciucu, "Messie au fèminin," 67–68. See also above, n. 881. For a critical reflection on my theory of models, see Elliot R. Wolfson, "Structure, Innovation, and Disremptive Temporality: The Use of Models to Study Continuity and Discontinuity in Kabbalistic Tradition," 159–184.

Although significantly traditional, with classical books and sacred figures, this literature adopted themes from a variety of sources and adapted itself through the generations. The gender metamorphoses of the pseudo-Aristotelian dictum discussed here represent just one modest example, and this may also be the case with the Zeus/Athena myth.[894] It should be mentioned nevertheless that, at least in one case in East European Hasidism, the pseudo-Aristotelian dictum was interpreted in national terms, when applied to the patriarch Jacob, a male, as the telos of creation. This means that Jacob's role in "history" is conceived of as the "end of action," just as Adam was the "beginning," which emerged in the divine thought. However, Adam's original sin had to be rectified later by the patriarch, most probably as a representative of the collective of the Israelites, who become the telos of creation.[895]

This vast literary corpus awaits the careful application of scholarly approaches – philological, historical, psychological, phenomenological, sociological, or others – which are not so heavily invested in specific modern agendas or in repetitions of overarching generalizations that are imposed on Kabbalistic literature as a whole. Scholars who try to subsume medieval traditions to fashionable but unsuitable modern theories merely obscure texts by inventing harmonizing interpretations.[896] I propose more flexible approaches: a toolbox of methods, in fact, which is applied when someone is aware of their respective weaknesses, will facilitate a proper understanding of modes of thought on sex and gender that differ so dramatically from the modern ones.[897] As part of a polychromatic approach to this literature, scholarship should pay greater attention to the expressions of ambivalence toward the Female. Moreover, modesty and less aggressive language may also serve as indispensable qualities for sensitive reading of the texts and then interpreting them. By listening only to one melody, scholars are prone to be deaf to other important voices.

My perusal of the texts in the field convinces me that the Kabbalistic writings have little to do with those modern agendas and cultural fashions that are trying to build monolithic edifices. In my opinion, some of the quoted passages adduced

---

894 For other Greek myths adopted by Kabbalists, see, e. g., R. Isaac of Acre's and another Kabbalist's appropriation and Kabbalistic interpretation of a version of the myth of Prometheus, M. Idel, "Prometheus in a Hebrew Garb" (Hebrew), 119–123. See also Idel, "From Italy to Ashkenaz and Back: On the Circulation of Jewish Mystical Traditions," *Kabbalah* 14 (2006): 64–65, n. 66; Idel, *Ben: Sonship and Jewish Mysticism*, 647 and Liebes's study mentioned above, n. 263.

895 See the late eighteenth century R. Moshe Hayyim Efrayyim of Sudylkov, *Degel Maḥaneh 'Efraim*, 34–35. This is another case of imposing a tribal, pre-axial national topic on an axial one.

896 See e.g., n. 375 above.

897 See my survey of different methodologies in *Ascensions on High in Jewish Mysticism*, 1–13.

in order to prove such theories resist such a reading, not to speak about numerous other discussions that were conveniently ignored or, in some instances, even acutely misinterpreted, as in the case of Cordovero's, Luria's, or Cardoso's Kabbalistic thought.[898] When cultivated in a dogmatic manner, the new twentieth-century methodological mirrors are, intellectually speaking, too narrow in their scope, and tend to lead, at times, to ideological inflexibilities or axiomatic attitudes that ignore the associative, fluid type of thought characteristic of Kabbalistic writings, especially in the fundamental corpus of Zoharic literature, which had a great impact. Moreover, the multifunctional aspects of the feminine are obliterated.

Modern scholars' convictions that they possess the clues to a universal truth regarding Kabbalists' attitude to the Female inclined them to choose in a highly selective manner,[899] – I would say even in a strongly biased way – what material to consider as pertinent representative sources and what to ignore. These "selective affinities" ignore significant aspects of a certain literature and reduce major voices to silence, thus diminishing what I see as both the breadth and the substantial variety of the old conceptual worlds under scrutiny. In other words, gross exaggerations diminish the credibility of the scholarly analyses.

Gender scholarship's presentation of the phallocentric model in Kabbalah has focused mainly on what I see as one of the stages of the complex career of the divine Female, the lowest one, understood, however, as if invariably determined by Her subordinated position. Even while She was commonly perceived in this lower position in the theosophical hierarchy, however, She was nevertheless governing the lower world, and She solely represents the entire range of the constellation of themes in theosophical Kabbalah, from the first to the tenth divine power.[900] The androcentric model that emphasizes the acquisitive approach did not take in consideration the recurrent *imaginaire* concerning Her origin and Her return to the highest levels of the divine world; it thus reduces and simplifies the complexity of the Female's metamorphoses and Her diverse functions in many forms of theosophical Kabbalah. In contrast to the more passive Males, the feminine hypostatic power that we discuss here often plays the most dynamic and, I would say, also the most dramatic roles in many of the theosophical systems.[901] For example, the

---

898 See, e.g., the discussions in chs. 6, 7, and 8 above.

899 See, for example, the theories regarding the meaning of religion of Carl G. Jung, Mircea Eliade, and, to a certain extent, also Henry Corbin.

900 For an interesting intersection of many of the functions of the Female in the higher and lower worlds, see Luzzatto's 'Adir ba-Marom ha-Shalem, 53.

901 Compare, however, to Scholem, *On the Mystical Shape of the Godhead*, 196 and the view of Heinrich Zimmer he cited there.

higher Female is described as a Mother giving birth to offspring, namely to the seven lower *sefirot* in the case of the third *sefirah, Binah,* and to human souls in the case of the last one, *Malkhut,*[902] and perhaps in the case of the hypostatic supernal womb in Cordovero's theosophy, found high in the sefirotic realm, or perhaps higher than it, as mentioned above, as the mother of the supernal divine realm.

In fact, in addition to what I termed the conceptual fluidity of the Kabbalists, we should also take in serious consideration the ontological fluidity of the position of the divine feminine power, not just Her alleged "absorption" by the Male as an axiom, but also Her sublating Him, or even nourishing Him subsequently, as we have seen above.[903] In one instance, we find the assumption that the limbs of the Male are absorbed into those of the Female.[904] To be clear: in the way I use the syntagm, ontological fluidity means mobility on the vertical axis of the ten *sefirot*, not a change in sex.[905] This fluidity/mobility has more than one form in theosophical Kabbalah, however, as in some cases the Female ascends, presumably in Her entirety, on high, whereas in some cases in Cordovero's opus, it is only one of Her aspects that does so.

Nor does the phallocentric theory, gravitating almost exclusively around the moment of sexual encounter between the Male and the Female as divine hypostases, seriously take into account the positive role of maternal,[906] procreative, and sometimes affective and consoling aspects, indubitably important roles ascribed to the divine feminine power by Kabbalists. These other dimensions of the Kabbalistic *imaginaire* of the Female, in addition to the sexual one, are very significant for understanding both the range of Kabbalists' conceptions and the wide impact Kabbalah has had since the end of the sixteenth century, which extends beyond the concept of the subordinate role of the *Shekhinah* to the divine Male.[907] The stunning success of Alqabetz's poem mentioned earlier,[908] which

---

902 See, e.g, *Tiqqunei Zohar*, no. 6, fols. 22a–22b, and Cordovero's *'Or Yaqar*, 15: 7.

903 Those two forms of fluidity differ from the textual fluidity that was proposed by Daniel Abrams, *Kabbalistic Manuscripts and Textual Theory*. See also above, n. 13. A fourth type of fluidity, of gender, differs from the other three.

904 See R. Jacob Ifargan, *Minhat Yehudah*, 1: 321.

905 On fluidity of Kabbalistic systems, see, e.g., Idel, *Hasidism: Between Ecstasy and Magic*, 50–51.

906 See Wolfson's opposite view in *Language, Eros, Being*, 81–82; he relies on the view of Caroline Walker Bynum that motherhood was not considered important in the Middle Ages. Thus, the divergences between Judaism and Christianity – and Bynum addresses only the latter – are ignored in favor of another simplistic generalization.

907 See, e.g., Schneider, *Kabbalistic Writings on the Nature of Masculine & Feminine.*

908 See Kimelman, *The Mystical Meaning*, passim, and Scholem, *On the Kabbalah and its Symbolism*, 141–142 and Moshe Hallamish, *Kabbalistic Customs of Shabbat* (Hebrew), 203–205.

soon after its composition became an integral part of the Sabbath Eve ritual in many Jewish communities, is just one example of the impact of a piece that gravitates around some form of cult of the divine Feminine, referred to in the poem both as Sabbath and as Bride.

This was not merely a theoretical formulation but a myth found in different forms in the two main types of theosophies that are pertinent for our discussion here, the vertical and the circular. It soon became part of the way many Jews imagined the encounter with what they considered to be holiness in time, as personified by the Female. The experiential aspects of the poem and of the Sabbath day as a mode of life considered to be delightful as understood by Kabbalists, have little if anything to do with acquisitive dimensions of the feminine divine power by the males who chanted it.

The present study examines only some aspects of a vaster topic concerning the complex status of the Female within the theosophical structure: the many instances She has been privileged in comparison to the other divine powers in the complex conceptual structures or the sefirotic systems that include many other divine hypostases. Having drawn upon the writings of a variety of major Kabbalists, I consider the three-phases gender-model to be one of the major models for understanding gender in theosophical Kabbalah. This vision of the plurality of divine hypostases, conceived of as quintessential components of Kabbalistic theosophies, puts into sharper relief the special, dynamic status of the Female in the system as privileged. Moreover, a comparison in these literatures of the attitude to the divine Daughter, as illustrated by the above passages, to that of the divine Son clearly reveals both the privileged attitude toward the supreme root of the Female and the dynamic nature that is characteristic of the Daughter or the Female.[909] The Son was, to the best of my knowledge, never described as a "precious stone"; neither was He depicted as descending from or ascending to the highest divine head, except for a few cases, – and then almost always together with the Female – despite the great importance of a human masculine offspring in the traditional forms of Judaism. Nor is the teleological attitude emphasized so much in the case of the divine Son, as we have seen above concerning the Daughter in numerous examples. The Female as manifested in the *sefirah* of *Malkhut* is, at least statistically speaking, more prominent in the theosophical Kabbalistic books in comparison to the other main feminine hypostasis, the *sefirah* of *Binah*, or the supernal Mother. Nevertheless, the common denominator of discussions about the divine Female and the divine Son is their

---

909 For the many discussions of the theme of Son as a hypostasis within the sefirotic realm in Jewish mysticism, see Idel, *Ben, Sonship and Jewish Mysticism*.

special relationship to the people of Israel, indubitably the result of their striving to belong to a supernal entity, as the Israelites have been regarded in many pre-Kabbalistic and Kabbalistic texts as the sons of God. The specific nature of the gender of the supernal entity seems less important than the sense of belonging that derives from establishing an affinity between the nation and its components and a divine entity.

We should, therefore, acknowledge the conceptually complex aspects of the privileged status of the Female as described above in all its main components in order to avoid simplifications that could transform Kabbalah into a systematic theology or some form of coherent philosophy. The recent dominant approach in Kabbalah scholarship that regards Kabbalah as a conceptually unified corpus, or a theologically coherent system, informed by a consistent theosophy, displaying an invariably androcentric ontology, expressed in univocal symbols, or a single hegemonic gender theory, is part of a much broader phenomenon evident in the field that I call the theologization of this complex and conceptually fluid literature. This process was evident already in the work of Gershom Scholem and many of his followers.[910]

Through either ignorance of the existence of certain classic Kabbalah texts or systematic unwillingness to discuss them, a neat myth about a phallocentric edifice, conceived of as ubiquitous in Kabbalah or in Judaism as a whole has been skillfully forged and then fiercely defended. Contemporary neo-Hasidic/Kabbalist authors, Sarah Schneider and Nil Menussi, both inspired by the thought of the contemporary Kabbalist R. Yitzhaq Ginzburg, present another one-sided view of the existence of a single gender theory in Kabbalah and Hasidism, although it is diametrically opposite to Elliot R. Wolfson's edifice of the allegedly hegemonic

---

910 See M. Idel, "On the Theologization of Kabbalah in Modern Scholarship", 123–174, *Enchanted Chains*, 19–26, and my earlier discussions in *Kabbalah: New Perspectives*, 27–29; Idel , *Hasidism: Between Ecstasy and Magic*, 50–51; and Idel, "Kabbalah-Research: From Monochromatism to Polychromatism," 27–32. See also Wolfson's return to monochromatic conceptualization in the case of the gender theory in Kabbalah, as cited above in nn. 881, 882. Although he protests against my characterization of his views as monochromatic (see his *Language, Eros, Being*, 93–94), he nevertheless adheres to these views in the very contexts where he protests. This is a case of scholarly conceptual fluidity, which is multivocal and monolithic at the same time. See also the characterization of Wolfson's approach in Garb, "Gender and Power in Kabbalah," 84–85, 100–101.

For another extensive instance of theologization, this time unrelated to Luria's theory of gender, see Joseph Avivi's two different depictions of Luria's Kabbalah in his two different books on the same topic. Treating it as a systematic and most coherent mode of thought, he ignores the many discrepancies, contradictions and tensions found in Lurianic texts. Compare to my very different approach to Lurianism as a heterogenous corpus, in *Il male primordiale*, 272–274.

phallocentrism. Their rather idyllic views on gender as found in Kabbalah and mainly in Hasidism, which have been presented in very detailed studies, totally ignore the existence of androcentric aspects and texts in Jewish mysticism, including Wolfson's studies, on the one hand, and also the existence of the three-phases model, on the other hand.[911] The two extreme exclusive approaches to gender are essentialist and thus highly problematic from both the philological and conceptual points of view. Wolfson constructed his edifice by systematically blocking out instances of explicit discussions of the privileged divine Female – including one he published for the first time – passages that are both numerous and conspicuous and more explicit than the material adduced for the phallocentric model. During the decades when this model has been upheld almost exclusively, there has been no significant attempt to respond to the existence of opposite views in scholarship or in Kabbalistic texts, although some of the latter are classics in the field. Nor am I aware of his seriously acknowledging the pertinence of any of the scholarly critiques of some of his mistaken interpretations;[912] he dismissively terms scholars who criticized his unsubstantiated phallocentric thesis as mere "detractors."[913] Thus far he has not admitted the possibility that his phallocentric theory misrepresents any specific Kabbalistic material or admitted the existence of "exceptions" labeled as a noble departure that "detract" from alleged general axioms. This study aims at showing that alleged exceptions, which were only rarely recognized, are much closer to the center than to the margin.

Surprisingly, some of the scholars writing on Kabbalah had cooperated, at least passively, with such a monolithic approach, for example as lecturers, editors, or reviewers for academic presses or journals, contributing to the emergence of what may become a blind alley in scholarship in this field. Moreover, most of the

---

911 "Arise from Dust," 87–135. My position is much closer to the content of the critique of this essay by Tamar Ross, "A Response Article," (Hebrew), 189–203.

912 See Idel, "Androgyny and Equality in the Theosophico-Theurgical Kabbalah," or Idel, *Kabbalah & Eros*.

913 See the list of scholars designated as "detractors" as enumerated in this context by Elliot R. Wolfson, *A Dream Interpreted within a Dream: Oneiropoiesis and the Prism of Imagination*, 439–441, n. 65. See also above, n. 446. Calling such names, to which we can add elsewhere the term "obsessive," is not a very strong argument in an academic debate. It reflects less the validity of the phallocentric theory but much more a weakness in both the "theory" and the scholarship of the author of the theory. On the other hand, it exerts an authoritarian pressure, prone to deter younger scholars from criticizing him. For some of the critiques of his approach, quite mild in my opinion, see also Arthur Green, "Kabbalistic Re-Vision: A Review Article of Elliot Wolfson's *Through a Speculum that Shines*," 265–274; Mark Verman, "Kabbalah Refracted," 123–130,.; Mopsik, *Sex of the Soul*, 27; Liebes, *From Shabbetai Tsevi to the Gaon of Vilna*, 274 and n. 821, Abrams, *The Female Body of God*; Garb, "Gender and Power in Kabbalah;" or Ciucu, "Messie au fèminin," 67.

recent studies written in Hebrew and mentioned above do not sufficiently deal with the details of the interpretations of specific texts about gender adduced by Wolfson in order to articulate his phallocentrism. This is a problematic academic silence. For example, this unsubstantiated phallocentrism renders it impossible to account for the emergence of so many discussions of the Female, even less for the contribution to feminist attitudes among Christian thinkers who showed an interest in Kabbalah during the Renaissance and even later.[914]

Perhaps, when carefully checking the specific contexts of some of the most "phallocentric" passages in their original language,[915] some younger, more open-minded scholars in the field will recognize the existence of a more complex, and, in my opinion, also more interesting picture, or mosaic, of a vital topic in theosophical Kabbalah.[916] What could have been a fresh approach to Kabbalah, in this case, some fresh questions adopted from feminist theories, has turned into an axiom, actually an academic ahistorical dogma, allowing no exceptions, and speaking openly, and amusingly I must say, about detractors, heresies and obsessions, in publications that are deemed academic. This mathematical model assumes that if a certain theory is correct in certain specific cases, one may extrapolate to apply it to many other as yet unexamined cases, especially if one believes that there are no exceptions to the supposed rule. More recently, namely, a decade ago, a fissure can be discerned in the monolithic approach. Wolfson declares, after referring to some of my critiques of his approach[917] that he nevertheless assumes what he calls an "immutability of system," which has multiple subsystems,[918] and he attributes to the Kabbalists a so-called "monological pluralism," without, however, exemplifying or elaborating how this works in specific Kabbalistic texts.[919] In my opinion, systems appear in time and they also

---

914 See above, in ch. 6, the discussion about Cornelius Agrippa's view and here in Concluding Remarks.

915 See, e.g., my earlier discussion of an alleged phallocentric Kabbalistic passage, copied by R. Isaac of Acre from ibn Gaon's book *Keter Shem Tov*, based on an erroneous version of the text that Wolfson used to anchor his analysis of its alleged phallocentrism. I analyzed it in my *R. Menahem Recanati, the Kabbalist*, 1: 217–219, 225 in a very different manner based on its source and parallel texts. See also my "Ascensions, Gender, and Pillars," 70–71. Wolfson was apparently not acquainted with this critique, as he never mentions it.

916 See, e.g., Ciucu, "Messie au fèminin."

917 See my *Kabbalah & Eros*, 100–101, 130–131, addressed by Wolfson in "Structure, Innovation," 177–178.

918 Wolfson, "Structure, Innovation,"179. Compare my earlier view of the existence of a variety of systems and orders in Kabbalah, which, however, escaped his attention, Idel, "Some Forms of Order in Kabbalah," xxxi–lviii.

919 Wolfson, "Structure, Innovation," 176.

change over time, and we have attempted above to show that there is more than one theosophical system that should be taken in consideration when dealing with gender in Kabbalah. Instead of repeatedly conjuring the Kabbalistic texts by means of sophisticated terms such as "gender transvaluation,"[920] "gender dimorphism," or "male androgyne," as if they are hovering monolithically over the entire Kabbalistic literature by some form of scholastic magical words, it would be preferable to give attention to the actual claims made in the texts.

Theoretically, any proposal is welcome provided it is backed by textual analysis. Those fascinating rhetorical terms aside, his recent studies, as far as I am acquainted with them so far, do not yet represent the diversity of ideas noted above, different as they are from phallocentrism or any qualification of monolithic vision. They still ignore or suppress systematically other main voices on gender in the literatures they claim to analyze. Nor is it clear how the new terminology is connected to the theory of gender as no specific example has been adduced. Declarations made in this essay, many of them new in his axiology, and the appealing new terms culled from Franz Rosenzweig or Jacques Derrida, a practice in which Wolfson indubitably excels, are, at the end of the day, no more than shell games if they are not applied to addressing the entire spectrum of different views. What matters in my opinion is not merely the existence of some sophisticated declarations by a scholar, but also some form of dealing with and admitting the existence of what he would call disruptive voices, which are, nevertheless, found in many major Kabbalists, in some cases in a very explicit manner. Hopefully, in the near future, Wolfson will apply his many intellectual gifts to implementing those declarations issued a decade ago, in a more pluralistic manner. Meanwhile, I wait with trepidation to see this new approach with regard to his gender theory.

The inherent intellectual despotism of the monolithic "theory" about gender, which obliterates the various voices in the texts, reducing them to a single melody, is a sad academic story, detracting from the richness, ambiguity, and ambivalence of the topics under investigation.[921] The diversity of voices, polyphony – although not a symphony – is a more accurate portrayal of the diverse conceptual reality of the texts as I see them. Scholars may legitimately debate the specific weight of each of those voices in the general economy of Kabbalistic literature, but this question will be better addressed after accepting the concept of a different type of arena, where there are no solo performers, but a chorus with differing understandings of phenomena related to sex and gender that interact and sometime confront each other. Let me remind the reader that more detailed studies provide

---

920 See above, in n. 598.
921 See also, above, n. 446.

additional examples related to many of the topics dealt with here, and the choice of the texts offered in this study does not exhaust the available Kabbalistic treatments.[922]

In other words, the monolithic phallocentric theory acts as an ahistorical common denominator, for which the various Kabbalistic texts are merely linguistic containers in which this theory dwells, with some variations. As a result of this essentialist approach, certain themes that are not actually present are propelled into many texts, by dint of the belief in a universally accepted comprehensive theory.

Adopting a rigid phallocentric conceptualization of the woman exacts a high price: it results in ignoring many pertinent texts by major Kabbalists that run counter to the scholarly imposed monolithic theology; in addition, some of the texts that are cited resist the biased reading imposed on them. This leads not only to distortion but also sometimes to an inversion of meaning as it was explicated in the full version of the Hebrew texts: one sees this in Wolfson's denial of the feminine components in the first *sefirah*.[923] In a more methodological vein, I assume that a less homogenous scholarly approach to both Kabbalistic theosophies and to gender, which will be grounded in a broader conceptual spectrum of pertinent primary material, without excluding what does not fit in with feminist "theory" (actually, solely the specific theory of Luce Irigaray), will do greater justice to the complexity of the variegated material and the Kabbalists' conceptual fluidity.

Normally, scholarship progresses by accreting new understandings of both synchronic and diachronic complexities, not by subscribing to static beliefs. Part of these complexities is gaining an understanding of the existence of wider structures that include the feminine hypostases such as, for example, the three-phases model discussed above and not focusing solely on one of its stages as if representative of the allegedly "secret" logic of the entire structure. I do not contend, however, that all the negative aspects of the *imaginaire* of the Female that nourished the phallocentric hypothesis should be understood as the second phase of this three-phases model; sometimes they are part of independent types of negativities attributed to feminine hypostases within the theosophical systems or even to concrete women.

---

922 See *"Male and Female,"* and above, nn. 381, 599, 746.

923 See, e.g., above, ch. 8, the discussion of Wolfson's presentation of R. Menahem 'Azaryah of Fano's passage as phallocentric. On the issue of inversion of the explicit meaning of the texts, as they were analyzed in some of Wolfson's studies, although related to other topics, see, e.g., the many references adduced in my *"Male and Female,"* n. 120 and above, in nn. 375, 507 and Roi, *Love of the Shekhinah*, 53, n.28, 112 and n. 86, 369 n. 52, 384. Compare even Wolfson's discussion in "Constructions of the *Shekhinah*," 55.

Nevertheless, I assume that the conceptual reverberations of the three-phases model are wider than the specific instances in Kabbalistic literature in which the full model is explicated. In short, the phallocentric theory created too rigid a bed for the Kabbalists' kaleidoscopic *imaginaire* of the Female, and it soon turned into a narrow, procrustian one. In fact, one may ask why Kabbalists, whose approaches to the Female are so negative, devote so much space to discussing issues related to Her? Polyvalence, ambiguity, and ambivalence are more suitable tools for attaining findings in the field.

I did not address the important issue of whether the privileged status of the Female in the various theosophical systems had repercussions on the status of the historical women in Judaism, or at least in the Kabbalistic camp, because the sources with which I am familiar did not yield sufficient material. Nevertheless, in non-Kabbalistic circles, women in Judaism sometimes had a preeminent status in their family, as has been pointed out in the monograph of Avraham Grossman.[924] I would like not to confirm one type of causality: that the sociological "situation" influenced theosophy, or vice-versa, as I do not assume only one or any form of affinity between the two realms.[925] One can, however, discern such a nexus between the privileged status of the Female in the divine world and women in this world in some cases in modern Hasidism, especially in the Lubavitch school, [926] although the ascent of the role of the Female is evident already in both Safedian Kabbalah and in Sabbateanism and Frankism, as pointed out above. The affinities between the Kabbalistic discussions and the Hasidic theological ones are very evident, as seen for example in ch. 11 above; it is very difficult, however to determine whether the theosophical approach directly affected matters at the sociological level in the Middle Ages and early modern period, despite the recent studies of Avraham Grossman, Simhah Goldin, or Elisheva Baumgarten, which offer an excellent start in the historical direction.

In other words, I am not contending here or elsewhere that there was a feminist attitude in the modern sense of this term in Kabbalistic thought despite the elevated status of the Female in some form of theosophical *imaginaire,* claims of several types of equality between Female and Male, or reciprocity in their relationship.[927] My major claims above were based less on a uniform social reality

---

924 Avraham Grossman, *Pious and Rebellious, Jewish Women in Europe in the Middle Ages* (Hebrew).

925 Compare to Wolfson, "Woman, The Feminine as Other in Theosophic Kabbalah," 169.

926 See my "Some Observations on Gender Theories in Hasidism."

927 For more on my approach to these issues, see *"Male and Female,"* ch. 15 and appendix N, as well as "Ascensions, Gender, and Pillars," and see recently also Ciucu, "Messie au fèminin," 69, 76–77, 86.

in Judaism and more on considerations related to earlier traditions, exegetical efforts, and systemic developments. The three-phases model is found earlier than the emergence of Kabbalah in Europe: in the Middle East – the *Book of Bahir* – in Catalunia and Castile in the thirteenth century, Safed in the sixteenth century; the subsequent various Ashkenazi backgrounds – Hasidic and Kabbalistic in the eighteenth and nineteenth centuries – differ from each other, even though earlier Kabbalistic traditions shaped the views of later Kabbalists. Indeed, we discussed views formulated first in Islamicate provinces, then in Catholic lands, in the Ottoman Empire and in the Russian and Polish-Lithuanian empires, where there were mixtures of Russian Orthodox and Catholic forms of religion. The social realities of Kabbalists were as complex as their theologies. For this reason, the various treatments of the Female are more the result of the changing relationship between earlier traditions, pre-Kabbalistic and Kabbalistic, the various features of the theosophical structures, and the *imaginaire* of individual Kabbalists, than a response to immediate contexts.

The Kabbalistic *imaginaire* component consists also of linguistic associations, such as gematriahs or semantic associations – e.g., ʽ*Atarah, Keter*, namely diadem, crown – of symmetries and correspondences, in many cases not based on conceptual affinities. They were not interested in fixed theories with philosophical interpretations proclaiming some forms of universal truth. For example, there is no single "place of the feminine" in theosophical Kabbalah, as the divine Feminine may stem from the first, second, third, fifth, or from the sixth *sefirah*, and She may return to each of them, depending on the various Kabbalists or the different texts they interpret. Only the more popular forms of representing Kabbalah by means of the static drawing of the vertical ten *sefirot* established such a locus also in the imagination of Kabbalah scholars.

Moreover, it is noteworthy that the positive views about the divine Feminine surveyed above were not disruptive voices, and their authors were not dissenting figures who created tensions between Kabbalists and the legalistic authorities in Judaism in any significant manner, unlike what seems to have been the case in Christian Renaissance Kabbalah.[928] R. Joseph Karo, the most important legalistic figure of the last half of the millennium, regularly was visited for several decades by revelations stemming from feminine divine powers. He recorded most of those revelations in his diary of nocturnal revelations printed as *Maggid Meisharim*, in the feminine gender: ʼ*Imma' meyaseret,* admonishing mother, *Matronita',* *Shekhinah, Mishnah*, etc.[929]

---

928 See Newman, *From Virile Woman to WomanChrist*.
929 "R. Joseph Karo and His Revelations: On the Apotheosis of the Feminine in Safedian Kabbalah."

The matters related to the divine Feminine were not portrayed as especially esoteric, inaccessible secret topics. Although Kabbalah as such was often considered esoteric, as indeed it was in a few circles, especially in the thirteenth century, in many other cases, the Kabbalistic discourse does not center around the secrecy of topics, but more around ways of representation and the theurgical effects of the commandments, which is true of most of the texts dealt with above.[930] In my opinion, it is hard to speak about a rebellion of ancient broken images, as Scholem does, implying some form of antinomianism,[931] but about efforts to reinforce the rabbinic texts and a way of life by resorting to a map of the divine zone that can make sense of them.

Last but certainly not least in this context: better comprehension of the positive evaluation of the divine Feminine in many important texts in theosophical Kabbalah can facilitate an understanding of the later and even more recent elevation of the status of the divine Feminine in theological thought. For example, the preeminence of women in sixteenth century Christian Kabbalah was predicated on a Kabbalistic assumption, which Barbara Newman called "esoteric theology," as seen in ch. 6 above, in the case of Heinrich Cornelius Agrippa of Nettesheim. *Mutatis mutandis* it may be true also of the famous cardinal Egidio da Viterbo's lengthy discussions of the *Shekhinah* and the cult of Sister Juana by their younger contemporary, Guillaume Postel, as the mother of the world.[932] In all those cases, Kabbalah exerted an obvious impact in forging some aspects of the *imaginaire* of the preeminence of a feminine figure, human or/and divine.

This feminist orientation is also evident, to give some more recent examples, in the occult systems of Madame Helena P. Blavatsky and MacGregor Matters. The former, as well as her successor Annie Besant, in the Theosophist Society, were influenced, inter alia, by the [quasi-]Kabbalistic thought of Éliphas Lévi (Alphonse Louis Constant).[933] Likewise, Carl Gustav Jung and his disciple Erich Neumann showed significant interest in Kabbalah and Hasidism in the course of articulating and developing new directions in psychoanalysis.[934] This time

---

930 This is the case even when the term *sod*, secret, appears, as in my case, it refers to the theosophical or symbolical meaning that is immediately revealed, not to some form of hidden, undisclosed topic or something that is mysterious. For forms of secrecy in Kabbalah, see above, n. 250, and M. Idel, *Abraham Abulafia's Esotericism*: Secrets and Doubts.

931 *The Mystical Shape of the Godhead*, 125. Compare Idel, *Kabbalah: New Perspectives*, 156, and "Leviathan and Its Consort."

932 See, especially, Weiss, *A Kabbalistic Christian Messiah*, 194–195 and nn. 22–23.

933 See Jean-Pierre Laurent, "Un messianism à feminine," 50–51.

934 See Idel, *Kabbalah & Eros*, 146. For the elaboration of the feminine entities in another disciple of Jung's, see Karl Kerenyi, *Athene, Virgin and Mother in Greek Religion* and *Eleusis: archetypal image of mother and daughter*.

the information concerning Kabbalah is grounded in much more reliable channels of transmission than the above-mentioned two theosophists, which include Gershom Scholem, although also the psychoanalysts adopted Kabbalah in quite creative a manner. An issue that is especially worth more detailed attention is Jung's addition of the figure of the Virgin Mary to the supremely masculine divine trinity, generating by such an addition a divine quaternity that involves a case of elevation of a feminine entity to a divine status.[935]

Kabbalistic discussions of the privileged divine Feminine may well have found their way to some of the more recent feminist and New Age theories, which, indeed, drew upon a variety of religious sources[936] but also from the writings of Jung and Neumann.[937] Moreover, the flourishing scholarship on Kabbalah in recent decades supplied some themes to recent Jewish revival movements, and the *Shekhinah* became, again, at least in certain restricted circles, a Goddess.[938] In recent years, a few Orthodox rabbis have voiced such views, although in a more modest and hesitant manner, postponing the apotheosis of women to the Messianic future, as seen in some cases in Kabbalistic, Sabbatean, and Hasidic texts cited above.[939]

Needless to say, Kabbalists or Hasidic leaders were not feminists in any modern sense of the term, and their major concerns were not directed at the

---

935 See Newman, *God and the Goddesses,* 254–273. See, especially, Jung's 1952 letter to James Kirsch, translated in *Jung-Kirsch Letters: The Correspondence of C.G. Jung and James Kirsch,* 141–142. Jung compares the Kabbalistic view of conjunction of the Male and Female to the Christian *assumptio baetae virginis,* a comparison which is rather artificial, due to his superficial knowledge of Kabbalah that was mediated, as he recognizes in this context, mainly by means of Christian Kabbalists' Latin translations, which were sometimes theologically biased. Jung fell prey to a theory close to *prisca theologia,* which harmonizes the various sorts of preeminence of the Female. Compare also to his dream reported in Jung's *Memories, Dreams, Reflections,* 294.

936 See, e.g., Jonathan Cahana, "Dismantling Gender: Between Ancient Gnostic Ritual and Modern Queer BDSM," 60–75.

937 On Jung's writings as a possible mediator to some theories found in modern feminism, see Idel, *Kabbalah & Eros,* 146, and Diana Basham, *The Trial of Woman, Feminism and the Occult Sciences in the Victorian Literature and Society.* See also n. 26 above.

To be sure: those Kabbalistic considerations are indubitably not the sole type of elevation of women, as we can see from Ashley Montagu's book *The Natural Superiority of Women, A noted anthropologist destroys the myth of male supremacy,* which is built on totally different considerations, his Jewish background notwithstanding.

938 See, e.g., Luke Devine, "How *Shekhinah* became the God(dess) of Jewish Feminism," 81–91, for a survey of the scholarship that is related to the apotheosis of the *Shekhinah* in modern Jewish feminism. See also Wolfson, *Language, Eros, Being,* 85–86. For the proposal of Ewert H. Cousins to see what he calls the second axial age currently emerging, as characterized by the return of the feminine element to the forefront, see *Christ of the 21th Century,* 155–157, 160–162 and his "Male-Female Aspects of the Trinity in Christian Mysticism," 37–50.

939 Schwartzman, "From Mystical Vision to Gender Equality Aspirations," 152–155.

empowerment of women, including their own wives, and thus it was not a social phenomenon. Nevertheless, they forged the concept of "feminine theurgy," although it was systematically neglected in scholarship.[940] Is there a connection between "feminine theurgy" – which according to Kabbalists' visions of some of her acts, especially the sexual ones, empowers women – connected to the various versions of the privileged status of the Female in the divine realm and Her relation to the lower worlds as the Ruler? Some forms of affinity between the two feminine realms are conspicuous in theosophical Kabbalah,[941] especially in the Lurianic one, where the soul of a woman that ascends on high during sleep is thought to play an erogenic role, what I called erogenic theurgy, in the sexual encounters taking place in the divine realm.[942] Certainly, this was not part of a social reality but of the specific oneiric *imaginaire* of the various Kabbalists, which was anchored in their religious life.

Finally, let me frame the above discussions in a broader context. Ancient Greece was the source of a basic shift from the body to the intellect that influenced the higher culture in the West. This shift was emphasized already in the nineteenth century by the speculative and controversial essay of Johann Jakob Bachofen[943] and reformulated more recently by Grace Jantzen as follows: "from an interest in female bodies to an interest in men's mind,"[944] namely, from the

---

940 See my *Kabbalah & Eros*, 247–250. On the importance of the performance of commandments in most of the phases of Jewish mysticism, see my *Kabbalah: New Perspectives*, passim, and *Hasidism: Between Ecstasy and Magic*. To what extent the idea of the Female's performance and the women found in Kabbalah somehow figure in Judith Butler's feminist theory is a matter that may require additional attention. Whereas the theosophical Kabbalists considered that sexual identity defines the choice of the specific acts to be performed, some modern feminists conceive the performances as generating the sexual and gender identities. As in my other studies I am less concerned with the body per se than the importance of its actions, what I call 'the performing body.' See also above, n. 400 and below, n. 944.

941 See Abrams, *The Female Body of God*, 161–162, 167–178.

942 See Scholem, *On the Mystical Shape of the Godhead*, 187–188; Abrams, *The Female Body of God*, 110–111; Garb, "Gender and Power in Kabbalah," 89–90, and Idel, "Ascensions, Gender, and Pillars," 74–76, 79–84. See also my *"Male and Female,"* ch. 12.

943 See *Myth, Religion, and Mother Right, Selected Writings of J. J. Bachofen*, 88–91.

944 Grace M. Jantzen, *Power, Gender and Christian Mysticism*, 61, where she identifies Plato as the author where the shift crystallized. See also Jantzen's work, 26–42. For the pronounced importance of the body as an instrument of action, in my opinion since the thirteenth century Kabbalah, see Idel, "On the Performing Body in Theosophical-Theurgical Kabbalah," 251–271 and "From Structure to Performance: On the Divine Body and Human Action in the Kabbalah" (Hebrew), 3–6.

For the claim about the impact of the Renaissance Christian culture's new attitude to the body on Safedian types of Kabbalah, see the monograph of Roni Weinstein, *Kabbalah and Jewish Modernity* (Hebrew), passim, translated recently into English. See also Weiss, *A Kabbalistic*

pre-philosophical mystery religions in Greece, gravitating around goddesses, to Greek philosophy, concerned with the mental activity of men. Although I am not convinced as to the total rupture between the two modalities from a historical point of view, this observation as a phenomenological statement is fascinating. There is no need to remind the reader of the influential Aristotelian statement about the active nature of the male and the passive one of the female or the views on male as form and female as matter.[945] Another way of seeing it is to resort to Karl Jaspers's nomenclature about the pre-axial and axial religious or philosophical modes or Karl Popper's views of two different types of societies. The coexistence between the two religious modalities is part of the complexity of Kabbalistic theosophical thought, as well as of Hasidism, whereas the ecstatic Kabbalah and some other cases in Hasidism represent an appropriation of the mental penchant in Greek thought. The tensions between the two forms of Kabbalah can be understood against the background of the two different synthetic lines, the pre-axial and the axial.[946] Whereas the ecstatic Kabbalah had an articulate type of speculative literature, from where it derived its concepts – the Neo-aristotelian one and sometimes Neoplatonism, as part of what I call an intercorporal strategy – the theosophical-theurgical Kabbalah was much more intracorporal, namely, nurtured primarily from earlier theosophical treatises, which were looser conceptually and more open to innovation.[947]

This shift toward the ideal of a mental religion in some Greek circles indeed affected, in many ways, parts of elite culture in Christianity, Islam, and significant figures in Judaism such as Maimonides and his many followers. The eighteenth and nineteenth centuries Enlightenment movement in Western and Central

---

Christian Messiah, 195, n. 23. Compare also to Garb, "Gender and Power in Kabbalah," 91–92, who hypothesizes a shift, or a discontinuity in the sixteenth century Kabbalists's connection of the Female and power, in comparison to the medieval texts; see also his *Modern Kabbalah*, 34–35. For the role of the body in Judaism see also e.g., Mopsik, "The Body of Engenderment in the Hebrew Bible, the Rabbinic Tradition and the Kabbalah." Without a preliminary examination of the place of the body in the medieval period, it is difficult to appreciate shifts that took place later.

945 See Plato, *Timaios* 50c, and Aristotle, *De generatione animalium* 1: 20, par. 729a, which reverberated in many discussions in the Middle Ages. See, e.g., Maimonides, *The Guide for the Perplexed*, 1:17, about the matter/form duality as male and female and Joseph Stern, *The Matter and Form of Maimonides's Guide*, 114–117. Maimonides was followed by many medieval thinkers, e.g., Abraham Abulafia, *Sefer Mafteah ha-Sefirot*, 24, 55, Abulafia, *Sitrei Torah*, 169, and see also Scholem, *On the Mystical Shape of the Godhead*, 183, Wolfson, *Language, Eros, Being*, 189, 347, Wolfson, "Constructions," 55, and Newman, *Sister of Wisdom*, 128.

946 See my *Studies in Ecstatic Kabbalah*, 18–19.

947 See my *Absorbing Perfections, Kabbalah and Interpretation*.

Europe – its philosophies and their reverberations in some Central European Jewish circles – attest to such a shift. Inter alia, the emergence of the Kabbalah in the Middle Ages is, in various ways, a reaction to, although also a certain appropriation of the speculative, universalist tendencies.[948] The question is not whether Kabbalists were acquainted with or influenced certain philosophies but whether they adopted and adapted those philosophical themes, which scholars consider "universal," to strengthen their particularistic tendencies.[949] This trend is a continuation of some Central European Jews' Enlightenment type striving to become "universal" by decoding the monotheistic message or the "rational ethics" of Judaism – to use a phrase Gershom Scholem attributes to his father,[950] – a blatant tendency among many modern Jews, who reduced this complex and performative type of religion to a set of speculations as, for example, the assumption and the recommendation to adhere to the nomadic, exilic situation and belief in monotheistic abstractions as preached, for example, by George Steiner.[951] When applied to a culture that was considerably more specific in its terminology and forms of action and much less individualistic than imagined by some modern figures, too strong an axial orientation is prone to marginalize major aspects of the Kabbalistic literature.

Possibly, the new emphasis on the feminine from early Kabbalah – as in other cases – is not an innovation *ex nihilo* in Judaism but a reaction to the negativity of the feminine in philosophy, especially insofar as the divine is concerned, by adopting and adapting earlier Jewish traditions, some of which I mentioned in

---

948 See, e.g., Alexander Altmann, "Maimonides' Attitude toward Jewish Mysticism," 200–219; Charles Mopsik, "Maimonide et la cabale. Deux types de rencontre du judaisme avec la philosophie," 48–54; Shlomo Blickstein, *Between Philosophy and Mysticism: A Study of the Philosophical-Qabbalistic Writings of Joseph Giqatila (1248–c. 1322)*, , Elliot R. Wolfson, "Beneath the Wings of the Great Eagle: Maimonides and thirteenth century Kabbalah," 209–237; Wolfson, "The Impact of Maimonides' *Via Negativa* on Late Thirteenth Century Kabbalah," i 5: 393–442; Brill, *Thinking God*, 391–414; Boaz Huss, "Mysticism versus Philosophy in Kabbalistic literature," 125–135; Sara O. Heller-Wilensky, "The Dialectical Influence of Maimonides on Isaac ibn Latif and Early Spanish Kabbalah" (Hebrew).1: 289–306; Aviezer Ravitzky, "The God of the Philosophers and the God of the Kabbalists," 134–141; Adiel Zimran, "Philosophy, Tradition, and Esoterica in Isaac Ibn Latif's *Sha'ar ha-Shamayim*" (Hebrew); M. Idel, "Maimonides and Kabbalah," 31–81; Idel, "Maimonides in Nahmanides and his School, and Some Reflections,", 131–164, Idel, "Jewish Kabbalah and Platonism in the Middle Ages and Renaissance 319–353; and Idel, *Abraham Abulafia's Esotericism, Secrets and Doubts* and above, ch. 2.
949 See, e.g., Idel, *Enchanted Chains*, passim, especially 226–227.
950 See Gershom Scholem, *From Berlin to Jerusalem, Memories of My Youth*, tr. H. Zohn, (Paul Dry Books, Philadelphia, 2012), 11.
951 See my "George Steiner: the Prophet of Abstraction," reprinted in *Old Worlds, New Mirrors*, 52–78. Compare also to Wolfson's appropriation of Steiner in *Language, Eros, Being*, 117.

the Introduction.[952] With criticism of Enlightenment ideals, some of which themselves gradually dissipated, rejection of the intellectually-oriented religiosity re-emerged. Late eighteenth century Hasidism, and more recently the New Age renascence of an interest in Kabbalah and even more in Neo-Hasidism in the second part of the twentieth century represent a return to a greater interest in the body in general and to the female body in particular.[953]

It is ironic that the Kabbalists, primarily particularistic thinkers, whose interest in both the feminine and the body transcends that of most of the rabbis and Jewish philosophers, grafted some of their expositions concerning the divine Female onto certain important Greek philosophical themes, from both Aristotelian and Neoplatonic sources, which in their original contexts were quite indifferent to such topics as theosophy and divine Females. Although factors far removed from Kabbalah were most influential in the recent, post-Enlightenment shifts to adherence to some forms of mysticism, Kabbalah, nevertheless, contributed to them in a very modest way, and gradually, became more influential in the context of new forms of religious interests. This helps to explain the apotheosis of the *Shekhinah* in some feminist theologies in more recent decades,[954] and Her prominent place in various pieces of Hebrew literature in recent years.

The texts analyzed above, among others, are part of different, alternative religious traditions often explicitly critical of most of the philosophical ones, even when some philosophical elements have been amalgamated into Kabbalistic literature.[955] There is no great intellectual gain in reducing complex and sometimes contradictory texts, containing polyvalent symbols, to monolithic messages, or interpreting mythical religions, gravitating around performance and dynamic types of symbolism as if they are fraught with profound philosophical insights, derived from other speculative sources. Such undertakings in many cases represent an anachronistic retelling of recent European forms of speculative or older religious *imaginaire* in Christianity, as if they constitute the allegedly hidden, and thus far, unknown, contents of Kabbalah. A new shift has occurred: the

---

952 See Idel, "Maimonides and Kabbalah," 43–44; *Kabbalah: New Perspectives*, 252–253; and Garb, "Gender and Power in Kabbalah," 106–107.

953 See, e.g., the title of Abrams's book, *The Female Body of God* or the earlier collection of articles edited by H. Eilenberg-Schwartz, *People of the Body, Jews and Judaism from an Embodied Perspective*. This phenomenon is consonant with the recent phenomenon of "occult explosion" mentioned by Mircea Eliade, *Occultism, Witchcraft and Cultural Fashions*, 58–65.

954 See, e.g., the recent collection of studies edited by B. Huss, *Kabbalah and Contemporary Spiritual Revival*.

955 See, e.g., Idel, *Kabbalah & Eros*, 153–178, or *Kabbalah: New Perspectives*, 220–221. For the concept of philosophical religion in general as well as in Judaism, see Carlos Fraenkel, *Philosophical Religions from Plato to Spinoza*.

nineteenth and early twentieth-century transfer by Central European scholars in Jewish studies of intellectual categories – many of which ultimately derived from Greek philosophical origins – recurred, this time from Europe to the academy in United States, especially after World War II.[956]

In another irony, current scholarship on gender either omits the traditions and texts cited above or misunderstands them by interpreting them in light of the very same Greek philosophical traditions in European cultures[957] that most of the Kabbalists opposed.[958] Important as the Greek and Hellenistic philosophical themes are, they were absorbed into conceptual theosophical structures that were alien to those themes and thus dramatically changed their meanings.

In my opinion, without understanding most of the Kabbalistic projects as different ways of strengthening the relevance and the performance of rabbinic rituals, inspired by the centrality of national identity or the superior status of the sacred texts, one cannot do adequate justice to the meaning of the theosophical manner of thought.[959] Recent speculations about the existence of deep psychological structures in Kabbalah, or in its systems, which are informed by a monolithic androgynous phallocentrism, or any other type of monolithism,[960] are, therefore, new forms of theologization, which adapt Kabbalah to some modern intellectual fashions. In Elliot R. Wolfson's specific case, we may discern fidelity

---

956 See M. Idel, "Transfers of Categories: The Jewish-German Experience and Beyond," 15–43, especially 33–34.

957 In my opinion, resorting to rarely defined broad categories such as symbolism or contemplation, which have their source in general scholarship, can be misleading when trying to understand the Jewish authors of Kabbalistic and Hasidic texts. See Idel, *The German-Jewish Experience Revisited*, 24–27; Idel, *Old Worlds, New Mirrors*, 83–108; *Idel, Representing God*, 128–142, and above, nn. 63, 821. For problems related to scholarly descriptions of Hasidism as a contemplative type of mysticism see, for the time being, my "Modes of Cleaving to the Letters in the Teachings of Israel Baal Shem Tov: A Sample Analysis." Compare to Wolfson's unqualified views as to the centrality of symbolism in the Kabbalistic discourse in e.g., *Language, Eros, Being*, 6, 38–39.

958 See, e.g., Wolfson, "Beneath the Wings of the Great Eagle."

959 Abraham Abulafia's ecstatic Kabbalah and that of some of his followers, differ on these issues from most other Kabbalists. See my: *Abraham Abulafia's Esotericism*.

960 See, e.g., more recently the spiritual search of Haviva Pedaya, *Kabbalah and Psychoanalysis, An Inner Journey following the Jewish Mysticism* (Hebrew), 9, as formulated in the very opening statement of the book, where she confesses that she tries to describe, as I translate: "The pure, spiritual, Jewish path, that is separated from social, national and political circumstances" (Hebrew). Further on, she again refers to "the spiritual, Jewish path" in the singular. Does this uncontaminated tradition have something to do with her claims mentioned earlier, on p. 14? Elsewhere in the book (10), and in her more academic studies, however, she also uses plural forms for Kabbalah. This is one more case of conceptual fluidity.

to some totalizing clichés drawn from Luce Irigaray's special brand of feminism.[961] Her contention that all men have the same opinion on such a complex topic as the feminine is another monolithic view, which has been imposed on the kaleidoscopic and dynamic modes of thought found in Kabbalistic literature on many topics, including the *imaginaire* of the divine Female.[962]

In short, the surge of Kabbalistic and Hasidic discussions about the divine Female is related to a series of developments in these literatures, which include the attribution of the performance of rituals to the amendation of the Female to Her well-being or for the sake of Her elevation to higher sefirotic levels – a combination of the primacy of human performative acts with a dynamic vision of the supernal pleroma, which is the quintessence of the various schools in theosophical-theurgical Kabbalah. These enhancements are connected in many instances to the vision of the redemption of the people of Israel, as conditioned by Her redemption, or at least as symbolized by it. Those discussions thus represent an attempt at dealing with the history of the nation with theosophical, imaginary, tools. Last but not least, the more mundane emphasis on the centrality of procreation, a central topic in many Jewish schools and ways of life, a value that cannot be overemphasized, was understood here as dealing with the emergence of souls, attributed to the Female's sexual encounter with the Male.

All those events are perceived in terms of recurrent processes, and Kabbalistic theosophies are examples of process theologies which, in Kabbalah are quite dynamic ones and were put to work in order to promote the importance of those issues, and the more these theosophies developed, the greater the centrality of the Female became. For example, *Malkhut*, which symbolizes in many cases the people of Israel, was placed in the vicinity, or in direct relation, to the first *sefirah*, *Keter*, according to the circular type of theosophy, where they are sometimes depicted in diagrams on the same level. This was done, *inter alia*, by elaborating on ancient Jewish mythologoumena; for example, the view of the Jewish nation as the consort of God, mainly in biblical prophetic thought[963] and the vision of the nation as the wife of God in rabbinic literature[964] were adapted to the theosophi-

---

961 See, especially, Wolfson, *Language, Eros, Being* 86–87.

962 More on the kaleidoscopic and dynamic visions of the Female see in my "*Male and Female*," passim.

963 There are many studies on this topic. See, especially, Nelly Stienstra, *YHWH is the Husband of His People*; Moshe Greenberg, *The Anchor Bible, Ezekiel 1–20*, 55–58, 297–299; Tikva Frymer-Kensky, *Reading the Women of the Bible*, 335–337; Sanford Budick, *The Western Theory of Tradition*, 118–136; or André Neher, *Prophètes et prophéties, L'essence du prophétisme*, 223–231.

964 See *BT. Berakhot*, fol. 35b. See also David Hartman, *The Living Covenant, The Innovative Spirit in Traditional Judaism*, and Jacob Neusner, *Androgynous Judaism, Masculine and Feminine*

cal structures, which were enriched by philosophical themes, mainly Neoplatonic ones. Topics such as the specificities of individual identities, inner and spiritual growth, and individual perfections, which are very popular today and even the perfection of the theosophical system are relatively marginal in theosophical Kabbalah.[965] Some of these themes appear more frequently, however, in ecstatic Kabbalah and its Kabbalistic echoes and in eighteenth-century Hasidism, which sometimes reinterprets some of the components in theosophical systems into psychological terms.[966]

Kabbalists' perceptions of several negative aspects in the divine Female and women certainly played a role in theosophical forms of Kabbalah and in Judaism in general, and they deserve separate study.[967] Their presence should not detract attention, however, from the centrality of other issues that ranked high on the agenda of Kabbalists, Sabbateans, and Hasidic masters. Similarly, the occurrence of the "privileged" approaches discussed here should not diminish the importance of the negative attitudes.[968] Both should be analyzed seriously and properly presented in a balanced manner. There are no pure, unequivocal theories in the humanities, although there have been nostalgic or ideological attempts by those with a superficial acquaintance with the Kabbalah to reduce the complexity of phenomena to much simpler schemes. Only by renouncing or modifying them will it be possible to arrive at a balanced, scholarly view that will do justice to significant amounts of texts. The above examples of conceptual fluidity and complexity related to both the dynamic nature of the theosophies and the associative nature of Kabbalistic thought – a continuation of certain Midrashic trends – corroborate the proposed kaleidoscopic understanding of theosophical Kabbalah, with its "fugitive truths" precluding simple generalizations. The stability of the performative aspects provided sufficient room for inventiveness in the spiritual realm.

To summarize: the eminence of the Female in the theosophical scheme is not the result of a dramatic shift in the status of the divine Female qua a feminine power, or of some positive or negative fascination with the Feminine. In my opinion, the divine Female became and remained more important than it had

---

in the Dual Torah, and my *Kabbalah & Eros*, ch. 3; "The Triple Family," and *"Male and Female."* See also above, n. 25.

965 See my caveat in *Absorbing Perfections*, 98–99.

966 See, e.g., my *Hasidism: Between Ecstasy and Magic*, 227–238, and Ron Margolin, *The Human Temple: Religious Interiorization and the Inner Life in Early Hasidism* (Hebrew) and his *Inner Religion: The Phenomenology of Inner Religious Life and its Manifestations in Jewish Sources (From the Bible to Hasidic Texts)* (Hebrew), or Pedaya, *Kabbalah and Psychoanalysis.*

967 See, e.g., Scholem, *On the Mystical Shape of the Godhead*, 189–191 and Idel, *Kabbalah & Eros,*. 117–125.

968 See, e.g., Wolfson, "Constructions of the *Shekhinah*," 71–72.

been earlier in Judaism because in the theosophical literatures, She represented a more coordinated series of values, and because Kabbalists reordered certain basic concerns to conform to various multifunctional components of the theosophical structures. Values that had already been central in rabbinic Judaism long before the emergence of Kabbalah, such as the importance of the Jewish nation and its historical/mythical vicissitudes,[969] the importance of the Sabbath, the topic of procreation of Jewish souls, and finally, the echoes of mythologoumena about the hypostatic feminine powers in ancient and early medieval Jewish texts reinforced each other. The Kabbalists' approaches are very functionalist whereas a systematic interest in matters of gender, which can be described as intentionalist, is marginal.

The themes related to those issues and the divine Female have been variously fused and reinforced by the belief in an inclusive and dynamic type of kataphatic theology that could supply reasonable explanations for the different processes in which the multi-faceted image of the Female has been involved, not in Her precise gender *per se*. Kabbalistic theosophy and a Neoplatonic cyclical worldview – the latter concerned mainly with personal soteriology or cosmic processes – different as they are, have been put in service of what was considered to be crucial values in rabbinic Judaism. Theosophical forms of Kabbalah flowered in medieval rabbinic Judaism and were accepted in many Jewish traditional communities because they were consonant with a long series of important topics in rabbinic literature and with the contemporary situations of Jews. These factors both influenced its contents and ensured its wider reception in later years.

---

969 See, especially, my *Kabbalah & Eros*, ch. 3, and many cases in passages discussed above. This is one of the major differences between Jewish theosophical speculations and their reflection in Renaissance Christian Kabbalah.

Primary Sources

[Recent publication dates for some of the primary sources refer to the edition used for this work. Titles are in Hebrew unless otherwise indicated.]

Abrabanel, Isaac. *Yeshu'ot Meshiho*. Koenigsberg, 1861.

Abraham Yehoshu'a Heschel of Apta. *'Ohev Israel*. Zhitomir, 1863.

Abulafia, Abraham. *Gan Na'ul*. Ed. A. Gross. Jerusalem, 1999a.

Abulafia, Abraham. *'Imrei Shefer*. Ed. A. Gross. Jerusalem, 1999b.

Abulafia, Abraham. *'Otzar 'Eden Ganuz*. Ed. A. Gross. Jerusalem 2000.

Abulafia, Abraham. *Hayyei ha-Nefesh*. Ed. A. Gross. Jerusalem, 2001a.

Abulafia, Abraham. *Matzref la-Kesef*. Ed. A. Gross. Jerusalem, 2001b.

Abulafia, Abraham. *Sefer ha-'Ot*. In *Matzref la-Kesef*. Ed. A. Gross. Jerusalem, 2001c. See also under Jellinek.

Abulafia, Abraham. *Sefer Mafteah ha-Sefirot*. Ed. A. Gross. Jerusalem, 2001d.

Abulafia, Abraham. *Sefer 'Or ha-Sekhel*. Ed. A. Gross. Jerusalem, 2001e.

Abulafia, Abraham. *Shomer Mitzwah*. Ed. A. Gross. Jerusalem, 2001f.

Abulafia, Abraham. *Sitrei Torah*. Ed. A. Gross. Jerusalem, 2002.

Abulafia, Todros ben Joseph ha-Levi. *'Otzar ha-Kavod*. Warsaw, 1879.

Agrippa, Heinrich Cornelius of Nettesheim. *Declamatio de nobilitate et praecellentia foeminei sexus, Female Pre-eminence or the Dignity and the Excellency of That Sex above Male.* Trans. H. Care. London, 1670.

Aharon Kohen of Apta. *'Or ha-Ganuz la-Tzaddiqim*. Warsaw, 1887.

Al-Bataliausi, Muhamad ibn Sid. *Sefer ha-'Aggulot ha-Ra'yoniyyot*. Ed. D. Kaufmann. Budapest, 1880.

Alphabet of R. Akivah (Hebrew). In *Batei Midrashot*. Ed. Sh. A. and A. Wertheimer, Jerusalem: Mossad ha-Rav Kook, 1955.

Amudei ha-Qabbalah. Jerusalem, 2001.

Ashkenazi, Joseph ben Shalom. *Commentary to Sefer Yetzirah*. In *Sefer Yetzirah*. Jerusalem, 1965.

Axelrod, Abraham of Cologne. *Keter Shem Tov* (Hebrew). In *Auswahl Kabbalistischer Mystik*, vol. 1. Ed. Adoph Jellinek. Leipzig, 1853.

'Azaryah of Fano, Menahem. *Yonat 'Elem*. Lemberg, 1859.

'Azaryah of Fano, Menahem. *Ma'amar Me'ah Qeshitah*. Munkacz, 1892.

'Azaryah of Fano, Menahem. *Kanfei Yonah*. Ed. M. 'Atiyyah. Jerusalem, 1998.

Azikri, Eleazar. *Sefer Haredim*. Venice, 1597.

Azriel, [Rabbi Azriel of Gerona]. *Commentary on the Talmudic Aggadot*. Ed. Isaiah Tishby. Jerusalem: Mekizei Nirdamim, 1945.

Azulai, Abraham. *Hesed le-'Avraham*. Lemberg, 1863.

Azulai, Abraham. *'Or ha-Hammah*. Przemyslany, 1896.

Bakharakh, Naftali. *Sefer 'Emeq ha-Melekh*. [Amsterdam, 1648]. Repr. Benei Beraq, 1994.

The Book Bahir (Hebrew). Ed. D. Abrams. Los Angeles: Cherub Press, 1994.

Buzaglo, Shalom, *Hod Melekh*. In Buzaglo. *Penei Melekh*. London, 1773.

"Commentary on a Kabbalistic Song." In *Ma'or va-Shemesh*. edited by. Yehudah Qoriat. Leghorn, 1839.

Cordovero, Moshe. *'Elimah Rabbati*. Lemberg, 1881.

Cordovero, Moshe. *Shi'ur Qomah*. Warsaw, 1883.

https://doi.org/10.1515/9783110599800-014

Cordovero, Moshe. *Tefillah le-Moshe*. Premislany, 1891.

Cordovero, Moshe. *The Palm Tree of Deborah*. Trans. L. Jacobs. New York: Sepher-Hermon Press, 1960.

Cordovero, Moshe. *'Or Yaqar*. Jerusalem, 1964.

Cordovero, Moshe. *'Or Yaqar*, vol. 16, on *Ra'ya' Meheimna*. Jerusalem, 1989.

Cordovero, Moshe. *'Or Yaqar*, to *Tiqqunim*, Jerusalem, 6 volumes. Jerusalem, 1972–2009.

Cordovero, Moshe. *Sefer 'Elimah*. In *R. Moshe Cordovero, Ma'ayan 'Ein Ya'aqov*. Ed. B. Sack. Beer Sheva: Ben Gurion University Press, 2009.

David ben Yehudah he-Hasid. *The Book of Mirrors: Sefer Mar'ot ha-Zove'ot*. Ed. D. Ch. Matt. Chico: CA.: Scholars Press, 1982.

Dov Baer of Mezhirech. *'Or ha-'Emmet*. Zhitomir, 1900.

Dov Baer of Mezhirech. *Maggid Devarav le-Ya'akov*. Ed. R. Shatz-Uffenheimer. Jerusalem: Magnes, 1976.

Efrayyim of Sudylkov. *Degel Mahaneh 'Efrayyim*. Jerusalem, 1995.

Eibeschuetz, Jonathan. *And I come this day unto the Fountain*. Ed. P. Maciejko. Los Angeles: Cherub Press, 2014.

Eleazar of Worms. *Hilkhot Tefillah*. Ms. New York JTS 1885, fol. 19b.

Eleazar of Worms. *Perush ha-Roqeah 'al ha-Torah*. Ed. J. Klugemann. Benei Beraq, 1986.

Eleazar of Worms. *Commentary on Prayerbook*. Ed. M. and Y. A. Herschler. Jerusalem, 1992.

Eliashiv, Shlomo. *Lehem, Shevo ve-'Ahlema'*. Pietrkov, 1929.

Elijah ben Shlomo [Vilna Gaon]. *Commentary to Sifra' di-Tzeni'uta'*. Ed. Sh. Toledano. Jerusalem, 1986.

Enoch (Hebrew). Ed. H. Odeberg. Rpr., New York, 1973.

Epstein, Qalonimus Qalman. *Ma'or va-Shemesh*. Jerusalem, 1992.

Galante, Abraham. *Qol Bokhim*. Prague, 1621.

Gaster, Moses. "Das Shiur Komah." [1893]. repr in Gaster, *Studies and Texts in Folk-Lore, Magic, Medieval Romance, Hebrew Apocrypha and Samaritan Archeology*. London: Maggs Bros, 1925–1928. 2: 1330–1345.

Gerondi, Jacob ben Sheshet. *Meshiv Devarim Neḥokhim*. Ed. Y. A. Vajda. Jerusalem: Israel Academy of Science and the Humanities, 1968.

Goldreich, Amos. "*Sefer Me'eirat 'Einayim* by R. Isaac of Acre. A Critical Edition." Ph. D. diss., Hebrew University of Jerusalem, 1981.

Halperin, David, ed. *Miguel Cardoso, Selected Writings*. New York: Paulist Press, 2001.

Har'ar, Nathan ben Sa'adyah. *Sha'arei Tzedeq*. Ed. J. Porush. Jerusalem: Makhon Sha'arei Ziv, 1989.

Hayyim of Czernovitz. *Be'er Mayyim Hayyim*. Warsaw, 1938.

Hemdat Yamim. [anon.]. Constantinople, 1735.

Horowitz, Reuven ha-Levi. *Dudaim Ba-sode*. Lemberg, 1859.

Horowitz, Shabbatai Sheftel. *Shefa' Tal*. Hanau, 1612.

Ibn 'Arabi, *L'interprète des desirs*. Tran. M. Gloton. Paris: Albin Michel, 1996.

ibn Gabbai, Meir. *'Avodat ha-Qodesh*. Jerusalem, 1963.

ibn Tabul, Joseph. *Commentary to 'Idra' Rabba'*. In *Temirin*. Ed. Israel Weinstock. Jerusalem, 1982.

Ifargan, R. Jacob. *Sefer Minhat Yehudah*. Ed. M. Hallamish. Lod: 'Orot Yahadut ha-Magreb, 2001.

R. Isaac of Acre. *'Otzar Hayyim*. Ms. Moscow-Ginsburg 775.

Isaac Aizik ha-Kohen. *Berit Kehunat 'Olam*. Jerusalem, 1950.

Jacov Joseph of Polonnoye, *Toledot Ya'aqov Yosef*. Koretz, 1780.

Jacov Joseph of Polonnoye. *Tzafnat Pa'aneah*. Koretz, 1782.

Jellinek, A., ed. "Abraham Abulafia, *Sefer ha-Ot*": *Jubelschrift zum 70. Geburtstag des Prof. H. Graetz*. Breslau, 1887.

Joseph ben Shalom Ashkenazi. *Commentary to Sefer Yetzirah*. Jerusalem, 1961.

Joseph Hayyim ben Elijah. *Rav Pe'alim*. Jerusalem, 1905.

Karo, Joseph. *Maggid Meisharim*. Ed. Y. H. Bar Lev. Petah Tiqvah, 1990.

Kitvei ha-Ramban. Ed. Ch. D. Chavel. Jerusalem: Mossad ha-Rav Kook, 1964.

Kushnir-Oron, M., ed. *Sha'ar Ha-Razim, Todros ben Joseph Abulafia*. Jerusalem, Bialik Institute, 1989.

Lipshitz, Jacob Koppel. *Sha'arei Gan 'Eden*. Jerusalem, 1967.

Liqqutei Shikhehah u-Fe'ah. Ferrara, 1556. fol. 34b, and ms. New York, JTS 838 (1878), fol. 8b.

Liturgical Poems of R. Shime'on bar Yitzhaq. Ed. A. M. Habermann. Berlin, Jerusalem: Schocken, 1938.

Luria, Isaac. *Commentary to Sifra' di-Tzeniu'ta'* (Hebrew). In *Kabbalat ha-Ari*. Ed. J. Avivi. Jerusalem: Makhon Ben Zvi, 2008.

Luzzatto, Moshe Hayim. *Sefer ha-Kelalim*. Ed. Hayyim Friedlander. Bene Beraq, 1989.

Luzzatto, Moshe Hayim. *Qelah Pitehei Hokhmah*, no. 104. Warsaw, 1888.

Luzzatto, Moshe Hayim. *Quntres Kelalei Hathalat ha-Hokhmah*. Warsaw, 1893.

Luzzato, Moshe Hayim. *Da'at Tevunot*. Ed. Y. Toporowsky. Tel Aviv: Mahbarot le-Sifrut, 1970.

Luzzato, Moshe Hayim. *Qine'at H' Tzeva'ot*. In *Ginzei Ramhal*, vol. 2. Ed. H. Friedlander. Benei Beraq, 1980.

Luzzatto, Moshe Hayim. *'Otzrot ha-Ramhal*. Ed. H. Friedlander. Benei Beraq, 1986.

Luzzatto, Moshe Hayim. *Sha'arei ha-Ramhal*. Ed. H. Friedlander. Benei Beraq, 1989.

Luzzatto, Moshe Hayim. *'Adir ba-Marom ha-Shalem*. Ed. J. Spinner. Jerusalem, 1995.

Luzzatto, Moshe Hayim. *Tiqqunim Hadashim*, no. 44. Ed. J. Spiner. Jerusalem, 1996.

Luzzatto, Moshe Hayim. *'Iggerot Ramhal*. Ed. M. Chriqui. Jerusalem: Makhon Ramhal, 2001.

Ma'arekhet ha-'Elohut. Jerusalem, 2013.

Malka, Judah b. Nissim ibn, *Judeo-Arabic Commentary on the Pirqey Rabbi Eli'ezer, with A Hebrew Translation and Supercommentary by Isaac b. Samuel ibn Malka*. Ed. P. Fenton. Jerusalem, 1991.

Meir ibn Gabbai. *Derekh 'Emunah*. Ed. M. Schatz. Jerusalem, 1997.

Menahem Mendel of Shklov. *'Mayyim 'Adirim*. Jerusalem, 1987.

Menahem Mendel of Shklov. *Sefer Raza' de-Meheimanuta'*. In *Kitvei ha-RMM*. Ed. M. Stern, Jerusalem, 2001.

Moshe Hayyim 'Efraim of Sudylkov. *Degel Mahaneh 'Efraim*. Jerusalem, 1995.

Moshe of Kiev. *Shushan Sodot*, no. 526, fol. 84b. Koretz, 1784.

Nahmias, Yehoshu'a ben Shmuel. *Migdol Yeshu'ot*, Ed. R. Cohen. Jerusalem, 1998.

Nathan of Gaza. *Sefer ha-Beriy'ah*. Ms. Berlin, State University.

Nathan of Gaza. "The Treatise of the Menorah" (Hebrew). In *be-'Iqvot Mashiyah*. ed. G. Scholem. Jerusalem: Tarshish Books, 1944.

Nehemiah ben Shlomo. *Sefer ha-Hesheq* [*Commentary on the Seventy Names of the Angel of Presence*]. Ed. I. M. Epstein. Lemberg, 1865.

Ostropoler, Samson. *"Dan Yadin" Commentary on Sefer Karnayyim*, Amsterdam 1765.

Rabinovitch-Rubinstein, Tzadoq ha-Kohen of Lublin. *Peri Tzaddiq*. Lublin, 1922.

Rabinovitch-Rubinstein, Tzadoq ha-Kohen of Lublin. *Sefer Taqqanat ha-Shavim*. Benei Beraq, 1967.

Recanati, Menahem. *Commentary to the Pentateuch*. Jerusalem, 1961.

Sack, Bracha., ed. *R. Moshe Cordovero, Ma'ayan 'Eyin Ya'aqov*. Beer Sheva: Ben Gurion University Press, 2009.

Saruk, Israel. *Limmudei ha-'Atzilut*. Munkacz, 1897.

Sasportas, Jacob. *Tzitzat Novel Tzvi*. Eds. I. Tishby and Z. Schwartz. Jerusalem: Mossad Bialik, 1954.

Sefer ha-Peliyah. Premislany, 1883.

Sefer ha-Shem, Attributed to R. Moses de León. Ed. Michal Oron. Los Angeles: Cherub Press, 2010.

Sefer ha-Tzeruf. Ed. A. Gross. Jerusalem, 2004.

Sefer Sodei Razei Semukhim. [second edition]. Jerusalem: Kolel Sha'arei Qedushah u-Tefillah, 2001.

Shapira, Nathan of Jerusalem. *Sefer Mahaberet ha-Qodesh*. Koretz, 1783.

Sheshet, R. Jacob ben. *Sefer ha-'Emunah ve-ha-Bitahon*, ch. 8. In *Kitvei ha-Ramban*. Ed. Ch. D. Chavel. Jerusalem, Mossad ha-Rav Kook, 1964.

Shne'ur Zalman of Liadi. *Torah 'Or*. New York, 1985.

Tiqqunei Zohar. Ed. R. Margoliot. Jerusalem, 1978.

Toledano, J., ed. *Sefer ha-Malkhut*. Casablanca, 1930.

Tzemah, Jacob Hayyim. *'Adam Yashar*. Krakau, 1885.

Vital, Hayyim. *Sha'ar ha-Kavvanot*. Koretz, 1784.

Vital, Hayyim. *Peri 'Etz Hayyim*. Dubrowna, 1803.

Vital, Hayyim. *Sefer ha-Heziyonot*. Ed. A. Aescoli. Jerusalem: Mossad ha-Rav Kook, 1954.

Vital, Hayyim. *Sefer ha-Liqqutim*. Jerusalem, 1981.

Vital, Hayyim. *Liqqutim Hadashim*. Ed. D. Touitou. Jerusalem, 1985.

Vital, Hayyim. *Mevo' She'arim*. Jerusalem, 1988.

Vital, Hayyim. *Sha'ar Ma'amarei Rashby*. Jerusalem, 1988.

Weinberg, Abraham of Slonim. *Yesod ha-'Avodah*. Warsaw, 1892.

Wildman, Isaac Haver. *Berit Yitzhaq*. Warsaw, 1888.

Wildman, Isaac Haver. *Sefer Pithei She'arim*. Ed. Sinai. Tel Aviv, 1964.

Yalish, Jacob Tzevi. *Qehilat Ya'aqov*. Lemberg, 1870.

Yehudah ben Yaqar. *The Commentary to Prayers and Blessings* (Hebrew). Ed. Sh. Ashkenazi. Jerusalem, 1979.

Zioni, Menahem. *Commentary on the Pentateuch*. [Lemberg] Rpr. Jerusalem, 1964.

The Zohar, Pritzker Edition. Trans. and commentary Daniel C. Matt. Stanford: Stanford University Press, vols. 1–9. 2004–2016.

Bibliography

Abrams, Daniel. "'*The Book of Illumination*' of R. Jacob ben Jacob HaKohen, A Synoptic edition." Ph. D. diss., New York University, 1993.

Abrams, Daniel. "The Boundaries of the Divine Ontology: The Inclusion and Exclusion of Metatron in the Godhead." *Harvard Theological Review* 87, no. 3 (1994): 291–321.

Abrams, Daniel. "New Manuscripts to the 'Book of Secrets' Compiled by R. Shem Tov bar Simha and the Sources He Possessed" (Hebrew). *Asufot* 10 (1997a): 9–70.

Abrams, Daniel. *Sexual Symbolism and Merkavah Speculation in Medieval Germany*. Tübingen: Mohr, 1997b.

Abrams, Daniel. "Traces of the Lost Commentary to the Book of Creation by R. Jacob ben Jacob ha-Kohen" (Hebrew). *Kabbalah* 2 (1997c): 311–341.

Abrams, Daniel. *The Female Body of God in Kabbalistic Literature* (Hebrew). Jerusalem: Magnes Press, 2005.

Abrams, Daniel. "'A Light of Her Own': Minor Kabbalistic Traditions on the Ontology of the Divine Feminine." *Kabbalah* 15: (2006): 7–29.

Abrams, Daniel. "The Condensation of the Symbol 'Shekhinah' in the Manuscripts of the *Book Bahir*." *Kabbalah* 16 (2007): 7–82.

Abrams, Daniel. *Kabbalistic Manuscripts and Textual Theory: Methodologies of Textual Scholarship in the Study of Jewish Mysticism*. Jerusalem–Los Angeles: Magnes and Cherub presses, 2010a.

Abrams, Daniel. "The Virgin Mary as the Moon that Lacks the Sun: A Zoharic Polemic against the Veneration of Mary." *Kabbalah* 21 (2010b): 7–52.

Afterman, Adam. *The Intention of Prayers in Early Ecstatic Kabbalah* (Hebrew). Los Angeles: Cherub Press, 2004.

Afterman, Adam. "The Phylacteries Knot, The History of a Jewish Icon" (Hebrew). In *Myth Ritual, and Mysticism, Studies in Honor of Professor Gruenwald, [= Te'uda*, vol. 36]. Ed. G. Bohak, R. Margolin, and Y. Rosen-Zvi. Tel Aviv: Tel Aviv University Press, 2014. 441–480.

Ahituv, Shmuel. "The Countenance of YHWV" (Hebrew). In *Tehilah le-Moshe, Biblical and Judaic Studies in Honor of Moshe Greenberg*. Ed. M. Cogan, B.L. Eichler, and J. H. Tigai. Indiana: Eisenbraun, 1997. 3–11.

Ahituv, Sh. and E. Eshel, eds. *To YHWH of Teman and His Ashera* (Hebrew). Jerusalem: Ben Zvi Institute, 2015.

Altmann, Alexander. "Maimonides' Attitude toward Jewish Mysticism." *Studies in Jewish Thought*. Ed. A. Jospe. Detroit, 1981. 200–219.

Altmann, Alexander. "Notes on the Development of Rabbi Menahem Azaryah of Fano's Kabbalistic Doctrine." In *Studies in Jewish* Mysticism, *Philosophy, and Ethical Literature Presented to Isaiah Tishby*. Ed. J. Dan and J. Hacker. Jerusalem, 1986. 241–268.

Antonioli, Roland. Préface to *Heinrich Cornelius Agrippa, De nobilitate et praecellentia foeminei sexus*. Ed. Ch. Béné. Trans. O. Sauvage. Genève: Droz. 1990. 7–38.

Apetrei, Sarah. *Women, Feminism and Religion in Early Enlightenment England*. Cambridge: Cambridge University Press, 2010.

Ariel, David. *The Mystic Quest*. New York, 1988.

Asulin, Shifra. "The Double Construct of the Image of the *Shekhinah* in Ma'ayan 'Eyn Ya'aqov and its Relation to the '*Idra'* Literature." In *R. Moshe Cordovero, Ma'ayan 'Ein Ya'aqov, The Fourth Fountain of the Book 'Elimah*. Ed. B. Sack. Beer Sheva: Ben Gurion University Press, 2009.

https://doi.org/10.1515/9783110599800-015

Asulin, Shifra. "The Flaw and Its Correction: Impurity, the Moon and the *Shekhinah* – A Broad Inquiry into *Zohar* 3: 79 (*Aharei Mot*)." *Kabbalah* 22 (2010): 193–252.

Avivi, Joseph. "R. Menahem Azariah of Fano's Kabbalistic Writings" (Hebrew). *Sefunot* 4 (1989): 347–376.

Baer, Y. ed. *Seder 'Avodat Yisra'el*. Roedelheim, 1901.

Balentine, Samuel E. *The Hidden God, The Hiding of the Face of God in the Old Testament*. Oxford: Oxford University Press, 1983.

Basham, Diana. *The Trial of Woman, Feminism and the Occult Sciences in the Victorian Literature and Society*. London: Palgrave/McMillan, 1992.

Baumgarten, Eliezer. "Comments on Rav Naftali Bachrach's Usage of Pre-Lurianic Sources" (Hebrew). *AJS review* 37 (2013): 1–23.

Baumkehr, Clemens, ed. *Das pseudo-hermetische Buch der XXIV Philosophorum*. Muenster, 1937.

Beauvoir, Simone de. *The Second Sex*. New York: Bantam, 1970.

ben Shahar, Na'ama. "MS Nurenberg, Stadtbibliotek Cenr. V. App. 5: A Fresh Window on Mid-Thirteenth-Century Ashkenazi and French Tradition" (Hebrew). *Da'at* 82 (2016): 73–123.

ben-Shlomo, Joseph. *The Mystical Theology of Moses Cordovero* (Hebrew). Jerusalem: Mossad Bialik, 1965.

Benarroch, Jonatan. "'Piercing What Has Been Sealed' – The Blasphemer (Lev. 24: 10-16) and Toledot Yeshu: From the Homilies of the Zohar to R. Jonathan Eybeschutz's 'Va'avo haYom 'el ha'Ayin.'" In *R. Jonathan Eibeschütz 'And I Came this Day unto the Fountain.'* Ed. Paweł Maciejko. Los Angeles: Cherub Press, 2014. 243-277.

Benarroch, Jonathan. "An Edition of Early Versions of *Idra Zuta* and an Unknown Hebrew Translation from Ms. Vatican 226, copied in 1311" (Hebrew). *Kabbalah* 39 (2017): 157–247.

Benayahu, Meir. *Kitvei ha-Kabalah shel ha-Ramhal"* (Hebrew). Jerusalem: Defus Menachem, 1979.

Benayahu, Meir. "Rabbi Moshe Yonah, A Disciple of Luria and the First of those Who Copied His Doctrine" (Hebrew). In *Studies in Memory of the Rishon le-Zion*. Ed. M. Benayahu, Jerusalem: Yad ha-Rav Nissim, 1995.

Bindman, Yirmeyahu. *Rabbi Moshe Chaim Luzzatto: His Life and Works*. Lanham MD: Rowman & Littlefield Publishers, Inc., 2004.

Blickstein, Shlomo. "Between Philosophy and Mysticism: A Study of the Philosophical-Qabbalistic Writings of Joseph Giqatila (1248–c. 1322)." Ph. D. diss., Jewish Theological Seminary of America, 1984.

Bonfil, Reuven. "New Information Concerning Rabbi Menahem Azariah of Fano and his Age" (Hebrew). In *Peraqim be-Toledot ha-Hevrah ha-Yehudit bi-Yemei ha-Beinayim u-va-'Et ha-Hadashah (Jacob Katz Festschrift)*. Jerusalem: Merkaz Shazar, 1980. 98–135.

Bonfil, Reuven. "Halakhah, Kabbalah, and Society: Some Insights into Rabbi Menahem Azariah da Fano's Inner World." In *Jewish Thought in the Seventeenth Century*. Ed. I. Twersky, B. Septimus. Cambridge, MA: Harvard University Press, 1987. 39–61.

Brach, Jean-Pierre. "Son of the Son of God: The Feminine Messiah and Her Progeny according to Guillaume Postel (1510–1581)." In *Alternative Christs*. Ed. O. Hammer. Cambridge: Cambridge University Press, 2009.

Bréhier, Émile. *Les idées philosophiques et religieuses de Philon d'Alexandrie*. Paris: Vrin, 1925.

Brenner, Athalya. "The Hebrew God and His Female Complements." In *Reading Bibles, Writing Bodies: Identity and the Book*. Ed. T. K. Beal and D. M. Gunn. London, New York: Routledge 1966. 56–71.

Brill, Alan. *Thinking God: The Intellectual Mysticism and Spiritual Psychology of Rabbi Zadok of Lublin*. New York: Yeshiva University Press, 2002.

Buckley, Jorunn Jacobsen. *Female Fault and Fulfillment in Gnosticism*. North Carolina, London, 1986.

Budick, Sanford. *The Western Theory of Tradition*. New Haven, London: Yale University Press, 2000.

Busi, Giulio. *Qabbalah Visiva*. Torino: Einaudi, 2005.

Butler, Judith. *Gender Trouble: Feminism and the Subversion of Identity*. New York: Routledge, 1988.

Bynum, Caroline Walker. *Jesus as Mother, Studies in the Spirituality of the High Middle Ages*. Berkeley: University of California Press, 1984.

Cahana, Jonathan. "Dismantling Gender: Between Ancient Gnostic Ritual and Modern Queer BDSM." *Theology & Sexuality* 18 (2012): 60–75.

Carlebach, Elisheva. "Redemption and Persecution in the Eyes of Moses Hayim Luzzatto and His Circle." *Proceedings of the American Academy for Jewish Research* 54 (1987): 1–29.

Carlebach, Elisheva. *The Pursuit of Heresy: Rabbi Moses Hagiz and the Sabbatian Controversies*. New York: Columbia University Press, 1990.

Chajes, "In a Different Voice: The Non-Kabbalistic Women's Mysticism of Early Modern Jewish Culture" (Hebrew). *Zion* 67 (2002): 139–162.

Chajes, Jeffrey H. "He Said She Said: Hearing the Voices of the Pneumatic Early Modern Women." *Nashim* 10 (2005): 99–125.

Ciucu, Cristina. "The Metaphysical Foundations of the Sabbatean Messianism as reflected in Nathan of Gaza's *Sefer ha*-Beriah." In *Giacobbe e l'angelo. Figure ebraiche die radici delta modernita europea*. Ed. Emilia D'Antuono, I. Kajon, and P. Ricci Sindoni. Rome: Editrice Lithos, 2012.

Ciucu, Cristina. "Messie au fèminin: Mystique juive et messianisme aux XVIIe et XVIIe siecles." *Clio, Femme, genre, histoire: Judaisme[s] Genre et religion* 44 (2016): 63-93.

Cohen, Norman J. "*Shekhinta ba-Galuta*: A Midrashic Response to Destruction and Persecution." *Journal for the Study of Judaism* 13 (1982): 147–159.

Cole, Peter. *The Poetry of Kabbalah*. Trans. by Cole and co-edited with A. Dykman. New Haven: Yale University Press, 2012.

Copenhaven, Brian P. "Jewish Theologies of Space in the Scientific Revolution: Henry More, Joseph Raphson, Isaac Newton and Their Predecessors." *Annals of Science* 37 (1980): 489–548.

Corbin, Henry. *Alone with the Alone: Creative Imagination in the Sufism of Ibn 'Arabi*. Princeton: Princeton University Press, 1997.

Cousins, Ewert H. *Christ of the 21th Century*. Rockport, MA.: Element, 1982.

Cousins, Ewert H. "Male-Female Aspects of the Trinity in Christian Mysticism." In *Sexual Archetypes, East and West*. Ed. B. Gupta. New York: Paragon House, 1987. 37–50.

Culianu, Ioan Petru. "La 'passion' di Sophia nello Gnosticismo in Prospetiva storico-comparativa," and "La femme celeste et son ombre," reprinted in Petru, *Iter in Silvis*. Messina: Antonino Sfameti, 1981. 1: 1–14, 77–95.

Dan, Joseph. *The Esoteric Theology of Ashkenazi Hasidism* (Hebrew). Jerusalem: Mossad Bialik, 1968.

Dan, "The Emergence of Mystical Prayer." In *Studies in Jewish Mysticism*. Ed. J. Dan & F. Talmage. Cambridge, Mass. 1982. 85–120.

Devine, Luke. "How *Shekhinah* became the God(dess) of Jewish Feminism." *Feminist Theology* 23 (2014): 81–91.

Douglas, Mary. *Thinking in Circles*. New Haven: Yale University Press, 2006.

Ebstein, Michael. "The Circular Vision of Existence: From Ismā ʿīlī Writings to the Works of Ibn al-ʿArabī," *Shii Studies Review*, 2 (2018): 156–192.

Eichrodt, Walter. *Theology of the Old Testament*, Tran. A.J. Baker. London: SCM Press, 1972.

Eilenberg-Schwartz, H. *People of the Body, Jews and Judaism from an Embodied Perspective*. Albany: SUNY Press, 1992.

Eliade, Mircea. *Occultism, Witchcraft and Cultural Fashions*. Chicago: Chicago University Press, 1976.

Elior, Rachel. *The Theory of Divinity of Hasidut Habad, Second Generation*. Jerusalem: Magnes Press, 1982.

Elior, Rachel. *The Paradoxical Ascent to God, The Kabbalistic Theosophy of Habad Hasidism*. Trans. J. Green. Albany: SUNY Press, 1993.

Elqayam, Avraham. "Topics in the Commentary of Reuven Tzarfati to the *Book of Maʿarekhet ha-'Elohut*" (Hebrew). M.A. Thesis, Hebrew University of Jerusalem, 1987.

Elqayam, Avraham. "Between Referentialism and Performativism: Two Approaches in Understanding Symbol in *Maarekhet ha-Elohut*" (Hebrew). *Daʿat* 24 (1990): 5–40.

Elqayam, Avraham. "The Mystery of Faith in the Writings of Nathan of Gaza" (Hebrew). Ph. D. diss., The Hebrew University of Jerusalem, 1993.

Elqayam, Avraham. "'The Burden of Silence': Queen Esther as a Messianic Prototype of Fluid Identity in Sabbatean Mythopoesis" (Hebrew). In *Conceal the Outcasts, Jews with Hidden Identities*. Ed. A. Elqayam and Y. Kaplan. Jerusalem: Ben Zvi Institute, 2017.

Emerton, James A. "Yahweh and his 'Asherah': The Goddess or Her Symbol?" *Vetus Testamentum* 49 (1999): 315–337.

Faierstein, Morris N. "*Maggidim*, Spirits and Women in Rabbi Hayyim Vital's Book of Vision." In *Spirit Possession in Judaism, Cases and Contexts from Middle Ages to the Present.*, Ed. M. Goldish. Detroit: Wayne University Press, 2003. 186–196.

Faierstein, Morris N. "Women as Prophets and Visionaries in Medieval and Early Modern Judaism." In *Studies in Jewish Civilization: Women in Judaism*. Ed. L. J. Greenspoon, R.A. Simkins, and J. Axelrad Cahan. Omaha: Creighton University Press, 2004. 251–282.

Falk, Avner. "The Messiah and the *Qelippoth*: On the Mental Illness of Sabbatai Sevi." *Journal of Psychology and Judaism* 7, no. 1 (1982): 25–26.

Farber-Ginat, Assi, "The Concept of the Merkabah in the Thirteenth-Century Jewish Esotericism – 'Sod Ha-'Egoz and its Development." Ph. D. diss, Hebrew University of Jerusalem, 1986.

Fine, Lawrence. *Physician of the Soul, Healer of the Cosmos: Isaac Luria and His Kabbalistic Fellowship*. Palo Alto: Stanford University Press, 2003.

Fraenkel, Carlos. "The Problem of Anthropomorphism in a Hitherto Unknown Passage from Samuel ibn Tibbon's *Ma'amar Yiqqawu ha-Mayim* and in a Newly-discovered Letter by David ben Saul." *Jewish Studies Quarterly* 11 (2004): 83–126.

Fraenkel, Carlos. *Philosophical Religions from Plato to Spinoza*. Cambridge: Cambridge University Press, 2012.

Frymer-Kensky, Tikva. *In the Wake of the Goddess: Women, Culture and the Biblical Transformation of Pagan Myth*. New York: Free Press, 1992.

Frymer-Kensky, Tikva. *Reading the Women of the Bible*. New York: Schocken Books, 2012.

Gamlieli, Devorah ben David. *Psychoanalysis and Kabbalah: The Masculine and Feminine in Lurianic Kabbalah* (Hebrew). Los Angeles: Cherub Press, 2006.

Garb, Jonathan. "Gender and Power in Kabbalah, A Theoretical Investigation," *Kabbalah* 13 (2005): 79–107.

Garb, Jonathan. *Manifestations of Power in Jewish Mysticism* (Hebrew). Jerusalem: Magnes Press, 2005.

Garb, Jonathan. "Authentic Kabbalistic Writings of R. Moses Hayyim Luzzatto" (Hebrew). *Kabbalah* 25 (2011): 165–222.

Garb, Jonathan. *Kabbalist in the Eye of the Storm* (Hebrew). Tel Aviv: Tel Aviv University Press, 2014.

Garb, Jonathan. *Modern Kabbalah, as an Autonomous Domain of Research* (Hebrew). Los Angeles: Cherub Press, 2016.

Gilbert, Maurice. "L'éloge de la Sagesse (*Siracide* 24)." *Revue théologique de Louvain* 5, no. 3 (1974): 326–348.

Giller, Pinchas. *The Enlightened Will Shine. Symbolization and Theurgy in the Later Strata of the Zohar*. Albany: SUNY Press, 1993.

Ginsburg, Elliot. *Sabbath in Classical Kabbalah*. Albany: SUNY Press, 1990.

Ginzburg, Simon. *RaMHa"L u-Venei Doro: 'Osef 'Iggerot u-Te'udot* (Hebrew). Tel Aviv, 1937.

Goetschel, Roland. *R. Meir Ibn Gabbay; Le Discours de la Kabbale espagnole*. Leuven: Peeters, 1981.

Goldberg, Arnold L. *Untersuchungen ueber die Vorstellung von der Schekhinah in der Fruehen Rabbinischen Literatur*. Berlin: De Gruyter, 1969.

Goldreich, Amos. "Investigations in the Self-Understanding of the Author of Tiqqunei Zohar." In *Massu'ot, Studies in Kabbalistic* Literature *and* Jewish Philosophy in Memory of Prof. Ephraim Gottlieb (Hebrew). Ed. M. Oron and A. Goldreich. Jerusalem: Mossad Bialik. 1994.

Goldreich, Amos. *Automatic Writing in Zoharic Literature and Modernism* (Hebrew). Los Angeles: The Cherub Press, 2010.

Gottlieb, Efraim, *The Kabbalah in the Writings of R. Bahya ben Asher ibn Halawa* (Hebrew). Jerusalem: Kiriat Sefer, 1970.

Gottlieb, Efraim. *Studies in Kabbalah Literature* (Hebrew). Ed. J. Hacker. Tel Aviv: Tel Aviv University Press, 1976.

Gottlieb, Efraim. *The Hebrew Writings of the Author of Tiqqunei Zohar and Ra'aya Mehemna* (Hebrew). Jerusalem: The Israel Academy of Sciences, 2003.

Green, Arthur. *Tormented Master, A Life of Rabbi Nahman of Bratzlav*. Tuscaloosa: The University of Alabama Press, 1979.

Green, Arthur I. "Bride, Spouse, Daughter: Images of the Feminine in Classical Jewish Sources." In *On Being a Jewish Feminist: A Reader*, Ed. S. Heschel. New York: Schocken Books, 1983. 248–260.

Green, Arthur I. *Keter: The Crown of God in Early Jewish Mysticism*. Princeton: Princeton University Press, 1997.

Green, Arthur. "Kabbalistic Re-Vision: A Review Article of Elliot Wolfson's *Through a Speculum that Shines*." *History of Religion* 36 (1997): 265-274.

Greenberg, Moshe. *The Anchor Bible, Ezekiel 1-20*. New York, Doubleday, 1983.

Grossman, Avraham. *Pious and Rebellious, Jewish Women in Europe in the Middle Ages* (Hebrew). Jerusalem: Zalman Shazar Center, 2001.

Grossman, Avraham. *He Shall Rule over You? Medieval Jewish Sages on Women* (Hebrew). Jerusalem: Zalman Shazar Center, 2011.

Gruber, Mayer I. *The Motherhood of God and Other Studies*. Atlanta: Scholars Press, 1992.

Gruenwald, Ithamar. "God the 'stone-rock': myth, idolatry, and cultic fetishism in ancient Israel." *Journal of Religion* 76, no. 3 (1996): 428–449.

Gupta, Binah. Introduction to *Sexual Archetypes, East and West*. Ed. B. Gupta. New York: Paragon House, 1987.

Halbertal, Moshe. *By Way of Truth, Nahmanides and the Creation of Tradition* (Hebrew). Jerusalem: Shalom Hartman Institute, 2006.

Hallamish, Moshe. *Kabbalistic Customs of Shabbat* (Hebrew). Jerusalem: 'Orhot, 2006.

Halperin, David M. "Why is Diotima a Woman?" In *Before Sexuality, The Construction of Erotic Experience in the Ancient Greek World*. Ed. D.M. Halperin, J.J. Winkler, F. I. Zeitlin. Princeton, NJ: Princeton University Press, 1990.

Hansel, Joelle. *Moise Hayyim Luzzatto (1707–1746), Kabbale et philosophie*. Paris: Les Editions du Cerf, 2004.

Harries, Karsten. "The Infinite Sphere: Comments on the History of a Metaphor." *Journal of the History of Philosophy* 13 (1975): 5–15.

Hartman, Davidƿ *The Living Covenant, The Innovative Spirit in Traditional Judaism*. New York, London: The Free Press, 1985.

Heller-Wilensky, Sara O. "The Dialectical Influence of Maimonides on Isaac ibn Latif and Early Spanish Kabbala." (Hebrew).In *Shlomo Pines Jubilee Volume*. Ed. M. Idel, Z.W. Harvey, and E. Schweid. Jerusalem: Magnes Press, 1988. 1: 289–306.

Hellner-Eshed, Melila. "Of What Use is a Candle in Broad Daylight?" The Reinvention of a Myth. https://hartman.org.il/Fck_Uploads/file/havrutavol3LR.55-62.pdf.

Hellner-Eshed, Melila. "On Love and Creativity" (Hebrew). In *R. Moshe Cordovero, Ma'ayan 'Ein Ya'aqov*. Ed. B. Sack. Beer Sheva: Ben Gurion University Press, 2009. 161–188.

Hurowitz, Victor Avigdor. "Nursling, Advisor, Architect? אמון and the Role of Wisdom in Proverbs 8, 22–31." *Biblica* 80 (1999): 391–400.

Hurwitz, Siegmund. "Sabbatai Zwi, Zur Psychologie der haeretischen Kabbala." *Studien zur analytischen Psychologie C.G. Jungs, Festschrift zum 80. Geburtstag von C.G. Jung*. Zurich: Rascher Verlag, 1956. 2: 239–263.

Huss, Boaz. "Mysticism versus Philosophy in Kabbalistic literature." *Micrologus* 9 (2001): 125–135.

Huss, Boaz. "Holy Place, Holy Time, Holy Book: The Influence of the *Zohar* on Pilgrimage Rituals to Meron and the Lag-BaOmer Festival" (Hebrew). *Kabbalah* 7 (2002): 237–256.

Huss, Boaz. "Zoharic Communities in Safed" (Hebrew). In *Shefa' Tal: Studies in Jewish* Thought *and* Culture in Honor of Bracha Sack. Ed. Z. Gries, H. Kreisel, and B. Huss. Beer Sheva: Ben Gurion University Press, 2004. 149–169.

Huss, Boaz. *Kabbalah and Contemporary Spiritual Revival*. Beer Sheva: Ben Gurion University Press, 2011.

Idel, Moshe. *The Writings and the Doctrines of Abraham Abulafia* (Hebrew). Ph. D. diss., The Hebrew University of Jerusalem, 1976.

Idel, Moshe. "The Sources of the Circle Images in *Dialoghi d'Amore*" (Hebrew), *Iyyun* 28 (1978): 162–166.

Idel, Moshe. "An Unknown Commentary on Nahmanides's Secrets" (Hebrew). *Da'at* 2– 3 (1979): 121–126.

Idel, Moshe. "The Concept of the Torah in Heikhalot Literature and its Metamorphoses in Kabbalah" (Hebrew). *Jerusalem Studies in Jewish Thought* 1 (1980): 23–84.

Idel, Moshe. "The Attitude to Christianity in *Sefer ha-Meshiv*." *Immanuel* 12 (1981a): 77–95.

Idel, Moshe. "Prometheus in a Hebrew Garb" (Hebrew). *Eshkolot*, New Series 5–6 (1981b): 119–123.

Idel, Moshe. "Sefirot above Sefirot" (Hebrew). *Tarbiz* 51 (1982): 239–280.

Idel, Moshe. "Kabbalistic Material from R. David ben Yehudah he-Hasid's School" (Hebrew). *Jerusalem Studies in Jewish Thought* 2 (1983): 169–207.

Idel, Moshe. "Types of Redemptive Activities in Middle Ages" (Hebrew). In *Messianism and Eschatology*. Ed. Z. Baras. Jerusalem: Merkaz Shazar, 1984.

Idel, Moshe. *The Mystical Experience in Abraham Abulafia*. Trans. J. Chipman. Albany: SUNY Press, 1987.

Idel, Moshe. "Hermeticism and Judaism." In *Hermeticism and the Renaissance*. Ed. I. Merkel and A. Debus. Cranbury, New Jersey: Folger Books, 1988a.

Idel, Moshe. *Kabbalah: New Perspectives*. New Haven: Yale University Press, 1988b.

Idel, Moshe. *Studies in Ecstatic Kabbalah*. Albany: SUNY Press, 1988c.

Idel, Moshe. "Universalization and Integration: Two Conceptions of Mystical Union in Jewish Mysticism." In *Mystical Union and Monotheistic Faith: An Ecumenical Dialogue*. Ed. M. Idel and B. McGinn. New York and London: Macmillan Pub Co., 1989.

Idel, Moshe. "The Anthropology of Yohanan Alemanno: Sources and influences," *Annali di storia dell'esegesi* 7 (1990a): 93–112.

Idel, Moshe. "Maimonides and Kabbalah." In *Studies in Maimonides*. Ed. I. Twersky. Cambridge, MA.: Harvard University Press. 1990b. 31–81.

Idel, Moshe. "Kabbalism and Rabbinism; on G. Scholem's Phenomenology of Judaism." *Modern Judaism* 11 (1991): 281–296.

Idel, Moshe. "On the Concept of Zimzum in Kabbalah and Its Research" (Hebrew). In *Lurianic Kabbalah*. Ed. R. Elior, Y. Liebes. Jerusalem, 1992a.

Idel, Moshe. "Jewish Kabbalah and Platonism in the Middle Ages and Renaissance." In *Neoplatonism and Jewish Thought*. Ed. L. E. Goodman. Albany: SUNY Press, 1992b. 319–353.

Idel, Moshe. "Judah Muscato. A Late Renaissance Jewish Preacher." In *Preachers of the Italian Ghetto*. Ed. D. B. Ruderman. Berkeley: University of California Press, 1992c.

Idel, Moshe. "The Magical and Neoplatonic Interpretations of the Kabbalah in the Renaissance." In *Essential Papers on Jewish Culture in the Renaissance and Baroque Italy*. Ed. D. Ruderman. New York: New York University Press, 1992d. 107–169.

Idel, Moshe. "Prayer in Provencal Kabbalah" (Hebrew). *Tarbiz* 62 (1993): 265–286.

Idel, Moshe. "The Bride of God" (Hebrew). In *Local Goddesses*. Ed. D. Hershman. Jerusalem: Migdal David Museum, 1994. 44–46.

Idel, Moshe. *Hasidism: Between Ecstasy and Magic*. Albany: SUNY Press, 1995.

Idel, Moshe. "Gazing at the Head in Ashkenazi Hasidism." *Journal for Jewish Thought and Philosophy* 6, no.2 (1997): 265–300.

Idel, Moshe. "The Land of a Divine Vitality: Eretz Israel in Hasidic Thought." *The Land of Israel in Modern Jewish Thought* (Hebrew). Ed. A. Ravitzky. Jerusalem: 1998a. 256–275.

Idel, Moshe. *Messianic Mystics*. New Haven: Yale University Press, 1998b.

Idel, Moshe. "On Mobility, Individuals and Groups: Prolegomenon for a Sociological Approach to Sixteenth-Century Kabbalah." *Kabbalah* 3 (1998c). 145–176.

Idel, Moshe. *R. Menahem Recanati, the Kabbalist* (Hebrew). Jerusalem and Tel Aviv: Schocken, 1998d.

Idel, Moshe. "From Structure to Performance: On the Divine Body and Human Action in the Kabbalah (Hebrew). *Mishqafayim* 32 (1998e): 3–6.

Idel, Moshe. "Female Beauty: A Chapter in the History of Jewish Mysticism." In *Within Hasidic Circles, Studies in Hasidism in Memory of Mordecai Wilensky* (Hebrew). Ed. I. Etkes, D. Assaf, I. Bartal, and E. Reiner. Jerusalem: The Bialik Institute, 1999a. 317–334.

Idel, Moshe. "Kabbalah-Research: From Monochromatism to Polychromatism." *Studia Judaica* 7 (1999b): 27–32.

Idel, Moshe. "The Spouse and the Concubine, the Woman in Jewish Mysticism" (Hebrew). In *Barukh she-'Asani 'Ishah? The Woman in Judaism from the Bible to the Present Days*. Ed. D.Y. Ariel et alia. Tel Aviv: Yediyot Sefarim, 1999c. 141–157.

Idel, Moshe. "Eros in der Kabbalah: Zwischen Gegenwaertiger Physischer Realitaet und Idealen Metaphysischen Konstrukten." In *Kulturen des Eros*. Ed. D. Clemens and T. Schabert. Munich: Fink, 2001a. 59–102.

Idel, Moshe. "The Kabbalah's '"*Nishmat Eloha*:,' 1279–1279." *Me'ah She`arim, Studies in Medieval Jewish Spiritual Life in Memory of Isadore Twersky*. Ed. E. Fleisher, G. Blidstein, C. Horowitz, and B. Septimus. Jerusalem: Magnes Press, 2001b.

Idel, Moshe. *Absorbing Perfections: Kabbalah and Interpretation*. New Haven: Yale University Press, 2002.

Idel, Moshe. "Jewish Thinkers versus Christian Kabbalah." In *Christliche Kabbala*. Ed. W. Schmidt-Bigeman. Ostfildern: J. Thorbecke, 2003a.

Idel, Moshe. "Some Forms of Order in Kabbalah." *Daat* 50–52 (2003b): xxxi–lviii.

Idel, Moshe. "Italy in Safed, Safed in Italy, Toward an Interactive History of Sixteenth-Century Century Kabbalah." In *Cultural* Intermediaries, *Jewish Intellectuals in Early Modern Italy*. Ed. D. Ruderman, and G. Veltri. Philadelphia: Pennsylvania University Press, 2004a. 239–269.

Idel, Moshe. "Leviathan and Its Consort: From Talmudic to Kabbalistic Myth." In *Myths in Judaism: History,* Thought, *Literature* (Hebrew). Jerusalem: Merkaz Shazar, 2004b. 145–187.

Idel, Moshe. "*Nishmat Eloha*: The Divinity of the Soul in Nahmanides and His School" (Hebrew). In *Life as a Midrash, Perspectives in Jewish Psychology*. Ed. Sh. Arzy, M. Fachler, and B. Kahana. Tel Aviv: Yediyot Aharonot, 2004c. 338–380.

Idel, Moshe. "Sabbath: On Concepts of Time in Jewish Mysticism." In *Sabbath: Idea, History, Reality*. Ed. G. J. Blidstein. Beer Sheva: Ben Gurion University Press, 2004d.

Idel, Moshe. "On the Theologization of Kabbalah in Modern Scholarship." In *Religious* Apologetics – *Philosophical Argumentation*. Eds. Y. Schwartz and V. Krech. Tuebingen: Mohr, 2004e. 123–174.

Idel, Moshe. "Androgyny and Equality in the Theosophico-Theurgical Kabbalah." *Diogenes* 52, no. 4 (2005a): 27–38.

Idel, Moshe. *Ascensions on High in Jewish Mysticism: Pillars, Ladders, Lines*. Budapest, New York: CEU Press, 2005b.

Idel, Moshe. *Enchanted Chains, Techniques and Rituals in Jewish Mysticism*. Los Angeles: Cherub Press, 2005c.

Idel, Moshe. "On European Cultural Renaissances and Jewish Mysticism." *Kabbalah* 13 (2005d): 43–64.

Idel, Moshe. *Kabbalah & Eros*. New Haven: Yale University Press, 2005e.

Idel, Moshe. "R. Nehemiah ben Shlomo, the Prophet from Erfurt's Commentary on the Poem '*El Na' le-'Olam Tu'aratz*" (Hebrew). *Moreshet Israel* 2 (2005f): 1–36.

Idel, Moshe. "Some Forlorn Writings of a Forgotten Ashkenazi Prophet: R. Nehemiah ben Shlomo ha-Navi'." *Jewish Quarterly Review* 96 (2005g): 188–196.

Idel, Moshe. "The Anonymous Commentary on the Alfabet of Metatron – An Additional Treatise of R. Nehemiah ben Shlomo the Prophet" (Hebrew). *Tarbiz* 76 (2006a): 255–264.

Idel, Moshe. "From Italy to Germany and Back, On the Circulation of Jewish Esoteric Traditions." *Kabbalah* 14 (2006b): 47–94.

Idel, Moshe. "On R. Nehemiah ben Shlomo the Prophet's 'Commentaries on the Name of Forty-Two' and *Sefer ha-Hokhmah* Attributed to R. Eleazar of Worms" (Hebrew). *Kabbalah* 14 (2006c): 157–261.

Idel, Moshe. "Ashkenazi Esotericism and Kabbalah in Barcelona." *Hispania Judaica Bulletin* 5 (2007a): 69–113.

Idel, Moshe. *Ben, Sonship and Jewish Mysticism*. London and New York: Continuum, 2007b.

Idel, Moshe. "*'Adonay Sefatay Tiftah*: Models of Understanding Prayer in Early Hasidism," *Kabbalah* 18 (2008a): 7–111.

Idel, Moshe. "The Angelic World in a Human Shape" [1986]. repr. in Idel. *The Angelic World – Apotheosis and Theophany* (Hebrew). Tel Aviv: Yediot Sefarim, 2008b.

Idel, Moshe. "Incantations, Lists, and 'Gates of Sermons' in the Circle of Rabbi Nehemiah ben Shlomo the Prophet, and their Influences" (Hebrew). *Tarbiz* 77 (2008c): 476-554.

Idel, Moshe. "Kabbalah in Byzantium: A Preliminary Inquiry." *Kabbalah* 18 (2008d). 199–208.

Idel, Moshe. "On Angels in Biblical Exegesis in Thirteenth-Century Ashkenaz." In *Scriptural Exegesis, Shapes of Culture and Religious Imagination, Essays in Honour of Michael Fishbane*. Ed. D. A. Green and L. S. Lieber. Oxford: Clarendon Press, 2009a. 211–244.

Idel, Moshe. "The Image of Man above the *Sefirot:* R. David ben Yehuda he-Hasid's Theosophy of the Ten Supernal *Sahsahot* and its Reverberations." *Kabbalah* 20 (2009b): 181–212.

Idel, Moshe. "On Jerusalem as a Feminine and Sexual Hypostasis: from Late Antiquity Sources to Medieval Kabbalah." In *Memory, Humanity, and Meaning: Selected Essays in Honor of Andrei Pleşu's Sixtieth Anniversary*. Ed. M. Neamţu and B. Tátaru-Cazaban. Cluj: Zeta Press, 2009c.

Idel, Moshe. *Old Worlds, New Mirrors, On Jewish Mysticism and Twentieth-Century Thought*. Philadelphia: Pennsylvania University Press, 2009d.

Idel, Moshe "On the Performing Body in Theosophical-Theurgical Kabbalah: Some Preliminary Remarks." In *The Jewish Body, Corporeality, Society, and Identity in the Renaissance and Early Modern Period*. Ed. M. Diemling and G. Veltri. Leiden and Boston: Brill, 2009e.

Idel, Moshe. "Prayer, Ecstasy and Alien Thoughts in the Besht's Religious World (Hebrew). In *Let the Old Make Way for the New: Studies in the Social and Cultural History of Eastern European* Jewry, Presented to Immanuel Etkes, vol. 1: *Hasidism and the Musar Movement*. Ed. D. Assaf and A. Rapoport-Albert. Jerusalem: The Zalman Shazar Center, 2009f.

Idel, Moshe. "Maimonides in Nahmanides and his School, and Some Reflections." In *Between* Rashi *and* Maimonides. Ed. E. Kanarfogel and M. Sokolow. New York: Yeshivah University Press, 2010a, 131–164.

Idel, Moshe. "R. Joseph Karo and His Revelations: On the Apotheosis of the Feminine in Safedian Kabbalah." *Tiqwah Center Working Papers Series*, 05/10. New York: The Tiqwah Center for Law & Jewish Civilization, New York University, 2010b.

Idel, Moshe. "Revelation and the 'Crisis' of Tradition in Kabbalah: 1475–1575." In *Constructing Tradition, Means and Myths of Transmission in Western Esotericism*. Ed. A. B. Kilcher. Leiden: Brill, 2010c.

Idel, Moshe. "Ascensions, Gender and Pillars in Safedian Kabbalah," *Kabbalah* 25 (2011a): 57–86.

Idel, Moshe. *Kabbalah in Italy, 1280-1510, a Survey*. New Haven: Yale University Press, 2011b.

Idel, Moshe. "On *Magen David* and the Name *Taftafiah*: from Jewish Magic to Practical and Theoretical Kabbalah" (Hebrew). In *Ta Shma: Studies in Judaica in Memory of Israel M. Ta-Shma*. Eds. A. Reiner et al. Alon Shvut: Tevunot, 2011c. 1: 18–32.

Idel, Moshe. "Multiple Forms of Redemption in Kabbalah and Hasidism." *Jewish Quarterly Review* 101 (2011d): 57–65.

Idel, Moshe. "Mystical Redemption and Messianism in R. Israel Ba'al Shem Tov's Teachings. " *Kabbalah* 24 (2011e): 7–121.

Idel, Moshe. *Saturn's Jews, On the Witches' Sabbat and Sabbateanism*. London: Continuum, Jerusalem, 2011f.

Idel, Moshe. "*Sefer Yetzirah* and its Commentaries in the Writings of R. Abraham Abulafia, and the Remnants of R. Isaac Bedershi's Commentary and Their Impact" (Hebrew). *Tarbiz 79* (2011g): 383–466.

Idel, Moshe. "The Triple Family: Sources for the Feminine Perception of Deity in Early Kabbalah" (Hebrew). In *Tov Elem, Memory, Community & Gender in Medieval & Early Modern Jewish Societies, Essays in Honor of Robert Bonfil.* Ed. E. Baumgarten, A. Raz-Krakotzkin, R. Weinstein. Jerusalem, Mossad Bialik, 2011h. 91–110.

Idel, Moshe. "'In a Whisper': On Transmission of *Shi'ur Qomah* and Kabbalistic Secrets in Jewish Mysticism." *Rivista di storia e letteratura religiosa* 47, no. 3 (2011i) (Title of issue: *Il mantello di Elia. Tradizione, innovazione nella cabala*).

Idel, Moshe. "Androgynes: Reflections on the Study of Religions." *Labirinti della mente, Visione del mondo: Il lascito inttellectual di Elémire Zolla nel XXI secolo.* Ed. Grazia Marchianò. Tuscany, Italy: Società Bibliografica, 2012a. 17–48

Idel, Moshe. "Commentaries on the Secret of Impregnation in the Kabbalahs of Catalunia and their Significance for Understanding of the Beginning of Kabbalah and its Development" (Hebrew), *Da'at* 72 (2012): 5–49, and 73 (2012b): 5–44.

Idel, Moshe. "On the Identity of the Authors of the Ashkenazi Commentaries to the Poem *Ha-'Aderet ve-ha-'Emunah*, and on the Concepts of Theurgy and Glory in R. Eleazar of Worms" (Hebrew). *Kabbalah* 29 (2013a): 67–208.

Idel, Moshe. "Modes of Cleaving to the Letters in the Teachings of Israel Baal Shem Tov: A Sample Analysis." *Jewish History* 27 (2013b): 299–317.

Idel, Moshe. "The Changing Faces of God and Human Dignity in Judaism." In Moshe Idel, Representing God. Ed. Hava Tirosh-Samuelson, Aron W. Hughes. Boston: Brill, 2014. 103–121.

Idel, Moshe. "East European Hasidism: The Emergence of a Spiritual Movement." *Kabbalah* 32 (2014a): 35–61.

Idel, Moshe. "*Panim* – On Facial Re-Presentations in Jewish Thought." In *Moshe Idel, Representing God.* Ed. Hava Tirosh-Samuelson, Aron W. Hughes. Boston: Brill, 2014b. 71–102.

Idel, Moshe. "Archetypes and Androgynes at Eranos." *Spring* 92 (2015a): 193–221.

Idel, Moshe. "Conceptualizations of Tzimtzum in Baroque Italian Kabbalah." In *The Value of the Particular: Lessons from Judaism and the Modern Jewish Experience, Festschrift for Steven Katz, on the Occasion of His Seventieth Birthday.* Ed. M. Zank and I. Anderson. Leiden and Boston: Brill, 2015b. 28–54.

Idel, Moshe. "'Higher than Time' – Some Observations on Concepts of Time in Kabbalah and Hasidism." In *Time and Eternity in Jewish Mysticism*, Ed. B. Ogren. Leiden: Brill, 2015c. 185–197.

Idel, Moshe. "Symbols and Symbolopoiesis in Kabbalah." Ed. F. Buzzetta and M. A. Golfetto. *Schede Medievali* no. 53 (2015d): 197–247.

Idel, Moshe. "Transfers of Categories: The Jewish-German Experience and Beyond." In *The German-Jewish Experience Revisited.* Ed. S. E. Aschheim, V. Liska. Berlin: De Gruyter, 2015e, 15–43.

Idel, Moshe. "Visualization of Colors, 1: David ben Yehudah he-Hasid's Kabbalistic Diagram." *Ars Judaica* 11 (2015f): 31–54.

Idel, Moshe. "The Divine Female and the Mystique of the Moon: Three-Phases Gender-Theory in Theosophical Kabbalah." *Archaeus* 19/20 (2015/2016): 151–182.

Idel, Moshe. *Il male primordiale nella Qabbalah.* Trans. F. Lelli. Milano: Adelphi, 2016a.

Idel, Moshe. "Visualization of Colors, 2: Implications of David ben Yehudah he-Hasid's Diagram for the History of Kabbalah." *Ars Judaica* 12 (2016b): 39–51.

Idel, Moshe. "The Womb and the Infinite in the Kabbalah of R. Moshe Cordovero" (Hebrew). *Peamim* 146–147 (2017): 37–58.

Idel, Moshe. "On Gender Theories in R. Moshe Hayyim Luzzatto." In *The Path to Modernity, Festschrift Joseph Kaplan*. Ed. A. Bar-Levav and C. Stutzynski. Jerusalem, Merkaz Shazar, 2018a.

Idel, Moshe. *"Male and Female": Equality, Female's Theurgy and Eros, R. Moshe Cordovero's Dual Ontology*. Los Angeles: Cherub Press, 2018b, forthcoming.

Idel, Moshe. "R. Nehemiah ben Shelomo the Prophet's Commentary on Seventy Names of God and the Threefold Discourse" (Hebrew). In *Meir Benayahu Festschrift*. Ed. M. Bar Asher et al. Jerusalem: Ha-Yad Nissim, 2018c. 801–848.

Idel, Moshe. "Prophets and Their Impact in the High Middle Ages: A Subculture of Franco-German Jewry." *Regional Identities and Cultures of Medieval Jews*. Ed. J. Castano, T. Fishman, and E. Kanarfogel. London: Littman Library, 2018d. 285–337.

Idel, Moshe. *Secrets and Pearls: Abraham Abulafia's Esotericism*. Berlin: De Gruyter, Mouton, 2018e.

Idel, Moshe. "Some Observations on Gender Theories in Hasidism." In *Tamar Ross Festschrift*. Ed. R. Irshai and D. Schwartz. Ramat Gan: Bar Ilan University Press, 2018f.

Idel, Moshe. "Wedding Canopies for the Divine Couple in R. Moshe Cordovero's Kabbalah." In *Avidov Lipsker Festschrift*. Eds. Y. Schwartz et al. Ramat Gan: Bar Ilan University Press, 2018g. 83–104.

Idel, Moshe. *Abraham Abulafia's Esotericism, Secrets and Doubts*. Berlin: De Gruyter, 2019a.

Idel, Moshe. "On Gender Theories in R. Moshe Hayyim Luzzatto." In *Paths to Modernity: A Tribute to Yosef Kaplan*. Ed. Avriel Bar-Levav, Claude Stuchinsky Jerusalem: Zalman Shazar Center, 2019b.

Irigaray, Luce. Postface to *A Sex that is not One*. Trans. C. Porter, C. Burke. Ithaca, New York: Cornell University Press, 1985.

Jacobson, Yoram. "The Aspect of the 'Feminine' in the Lurianic Kabbalah." In *Gershom Scholem's Major Trends in Jewish Mysticism: 50 Years After*. Ed. P. Schaefer and J. Dan. Tübingen: J. C. B. Mohr, 1993.

Jacobson, Yoram. "The Problem of Evil and Its Sanctification in Kabbalistic Thought." In *The Problem of Evil and its Symbols in Jewish and Christian Tradition*. Ed. H. Graf Reventlow, Yair Hoffman. London, New York: T. & T. Clark, 2004. 97–123.

Jantzen, Grace M. *Power, Gender and Christian Mysticism*. Cambridge: Cambridge University Press, 1995.

Joel, Manuel. *Blicken die Religionsgeschichte*. Breslau, 1880.

Jung, Carl. *Memories, Dreams, Reflections*. Ed. Aniela Jaffé. Trans. Clara and Richard Winston. New York: Random House, 1961.

Jung-Kirsch Letters: The Correspondence of C.G. Jung and James Kirsch. Ed. A. Conrad Lammers. Trans. U. Egli, and A. Conrad Lammers. London-New York: Routledge, 2016.

Kadary, Yoed. "The Angelology of R. Moses Cordovero" (Hebrew). Ph. D. diss., Ben Gurion University, 2014.

Kanafogel, Ephraim. "Varieties of Belief in Medieval Ashkenaz: the Case of Anthropomorphism." In *Rabbinic Culture and Its Critics, Jewish Authority, Dissent, and Heresy in Medieval and Early Modern Times*. Ed. D. Frank and M. Goldish. Detroit: Wayne State University Press, 2008. 117–159.

Kaniel, Ruth Kara-Ivanov. *Holiness and Transgression: Mothers of the Messiah in the Jewish Myth* (Hebrew). Tel Aviv: Hakibutz haMeuchad, 2014.

Kaniel, Ruth Kara-Ivanov. *Holiness and Transgression, Mothers of the Messiah in the Jewish Myth.* Trans. E. D. Matansky, R. Kara-Ivanov Kaniel. Boston: Academic Studies Press, 2017.

Kaplan, Lawrence. "Faith, Rebellion, and Heresy in the Writings of Rabbi Azriel of Gerona." In *Faith: Jewish Perspectives.* Ed. A. Sagi and D. Schwartz. Boston: Academic Studies Press, 2013.

Katz, Steven. "Utterance and Ineffability." In *Neoplatonism and Jewish Thought.* Ed. L. E. Goodman. Albany: SUNY Press, 1992.

Kerenyi, Karl. *Eleusis: archetypal image of mother and daughter.* Princeton: Princeton University Press, 1991.

Kerenyi, Karl. *Athene, Virgin and Mother in Greek Religion.* Putnam, Conn.: Spring, 2008.

Kimelman, Reuven. *The Mystical Meaning of Lekhah Dodi and Kabbalat Shabbat* (Hebrew). Los Angeles: Cherub Press and Jerusalem: Magnes Press, 2003.

Klein, Viola. *The Feminine Character, History of an Ideology.* London: Routledge, 1989.

Knohl, Israel. *The Bible's Genetic Code* (Hebrew). Israel: Devir, 2008.

Knohl, Israel. "From the Birth of the Bible to the Birth of Theosophical Kabbalah" (Hebrew). *Kabbalah* 36 (2017): 193–225.

Koren, Sharon Faye. *Forsaken, The Menstruant in Medieval Jewish Mysticism.* Waltham, Brandeis University Press, 2011.

Koyre, Alexander. *From the Closed World to the Infinite Universe.* New York, 1958.

Kreisel, Howard "The Term *Kol* in Abraham Ibn Ezra: A Reappraisal." *Revue des études juives* 153 (1994): 29–66.

Kuntz, Marion Leathers. *Guillaume Postel: The Prophet of the Restitution of All Things, His Life and Thought.* The Hague: Nijhoff, 1981.

Kuntz, Marion Leathers. "Lodovico Domenichi, Guillaume Postel and the Biography of Giovanna Veronese." *Studi Veneziani* (NS) 16 (1988): 33–44.

Kuntz, Marion Leathers. "Guglielmo Postello e la 'Virgine Veneziana.' Appunti storici sulla vita spiritual dell'Ospedatello nel Cinquecento." *Centro Tedesco di Studi Veneziani Quaderni* 21 (Venezia) (1981): 3–24.

Lang, Bernhard. *Wisdom and the Book of Proverbs: A Hebrew Goddess Redefined* New York: Pilgrim, 1986.

Langermann, Y. Zvi. "MS. New York, JTSA Mic. 2497.". *Kabbalah* 1 (1996): 273–277.

Laurent, Jean-Pierre. "Un messianism à feminine." In *Féminité et spiritutalité.* Milan: Archè, 1995.

Lazar, Moshé. Amour Courtois et fin'amours dans la littérature du XIIe siècle. Paris: Klincksieck, 1964.

Lazzarini, Pietro. *Il Volto Santo di Lucca.* Ed. M. Pacini. Lucca: Fazzi, 1982.

Lenzi, Alan. "Proverbs 8: 22-31, Three Perspectives on its Composition." *Journal of Biblical Literature* 125 (2006): 687–714.

Liebes, Yehuda. "The Songs for the Sabbath Meals Written by the Holy Ari" (Hebrew). *Molad* 4 (1972): 540–555.

Liebes. Yehuda. "Sections of the Zoharic Lexicon" (Hebrew). Ph. D. diss, Hebrew University of Jerusalem, 1976.

Liebes, Yehuda "Mysticism and Reality: Towards a Portrait of the Martyr and Kabbalist R. Samson Ostropoler." In *Jewish Thought in the Seventeenth Century.* Ed. I. Twersky. Cambridge: Harvard University Press, 1987. 221–255.

Liebes, Yehuda. "Two Young Roes of a Doe. The Secret Sermon of Isaac Luria prior to his Death" (Hebrew). In *Jerusalem Studies in Jewish Thought* 10 (1992): 113–169.

Liebes, Yehuda. "On the Image, the Writings, and the Kabbalah of the Author of 'Emeq
    ha-Melekh" (Hebrew). Jerusalem Studies in Jewish Thought 11 (1993a): 101–137.
Liebes, Yehuda. Studies in the Zohar. Trans. A. Schwartz et al. Albany: SUNY Press, 1993b.
Liebes, Yehuda. "Myth vs. Symbol in the Zohar and Lurianic Kabbalah." In Essential Papers on
    Kabbalah. Ed. L. Fine. New York and London: New York University Press, 1995a. 212–242.
Liebes, Yehuda. On Sabbateanism and its Kabbalah (Hebrew). Jerusalem: Mossad Bialik, 1995b.
Liebes, Yehuda. Ars Poetica in Sefer Yetsirah. Jerusalem, Tel Aviv: Schocken, 2000.
Liebes, Yehuda. God's Story, Collected Essays on the Jewish Myth. Jerusalem: Carmel, 2008.
Liebes, Esther. "Cordovero and Luria" (Hebrew). In R. Moshe Cordovero, Ma'ayan 'Ein Ya'aqov.
    Ed. B. Sack. Beer Sheva: Ben Gurion University Press, 2009. 32–66.
Liebes, Yehuda. The Cult of the Dawn, The Attitude of the Zohar toward Idolatry (Hebrew).
    Jerusalem: Carmel, 2011.
Liebes, Yehuda, From Shabbetai Tsevi to the Gaon of Vilna, A Collection of Studies (Hebrew).
    Tel Aviv: Idra, 2017.
Liebes, Yehuda. "Shablonization and its Revival of Jewish Myth" (forthcoming) (Hebrew).
Livr, Amirah. The Oral Torah in the Writings of R. Tzadoq ha-Kohen of Lublin (Hebrew). Ph. D.
    diss., The Hebrew University of Jerusalem, 2007.
Lloyd, A. C. The Anatomy of Neoplatonism. Oxford: Clarendon and Oxford University Press, 1998.
Lloyd, G. E. R. Aristotle: the Growth and Structure of his Thought. Cambridge: Cambridge
    University Press, 1968.
Maciejko, Pawel. Sabbatean Heresy. Waltham: Brandeis University Press, 2017.
Magid, Shaul. "Conjugal Union, Mourning and Talmud Torah in R. Isaac Luria's Tikkun Hazot."
    Daat 36 (1996): XVII-XLV.
Magid, Shaul. From Metaphysics to Midrash, Myth, History, and the Interpretation of Scripture
    in Lurianic Kabbalah. Bloomington: Indiana University Press, 2008.
Magid, Shaul. "The Metaphysics of Malkhut: Malkhut as Eyn Sof in the Writings of Ya'aqov
    Koppel of Mezritch." Kabbalah 27 (2012): 245–267.
Mahnke, Dietrich. Unendliche Sphaere und Allmittelpunkt. Halle, 1937,
Mandelbom, Alexandra. "'Torat Ha-Mekifim': The Circular Model in Likutey Moharan of Rabbi
    Nachman of Breslov" (Hebrew). M.A. Thesis, Hebrew University of Jerusalem, 2017.
Margolin, Ron. The Human Temple: Religious Interiorization and the Inner Life in Early Hasidism
    (Hebrew). Jerusalem: Magnes Press, 2004.
Margolin, Ron. Inner Religion: The Phenomenology of Inner Religious Life and its Manifestations
    in Jewish Sources (From the Bible to Hasidic Texts) (Hebrew). Ramat Gan, Jerusalem:
    Bar Ilan University Press and Shalom Hartman Institute, 2011.
Mark, Zvi. Mysticism and Madness, The Religious Thought of Rabbi Nahman of Bratslav.
    Trans. Y. D. Shulman. London: Harman Institute, Continuum, 2009.
Mark, Zvi. The Revealed and Hidden Writings of Rabbi Nachman of Bratslav, the World of
    Revelation and Rectification. Trans. Y. D. Shulman. Oldenburg: De Gruyter, 2015.
McGinn, Bernard. The Flowering of Mysticism: Men and Women in the New Mysticism
    1200–1350. New York: Crossroad/Herder, 1998.
Menussi, Nil "'Arise from Dust': Feminist Theology in the Light of Hasidism." In The Two Great
    Lights, Woman's Equality in the Feminine from a Jewish Point of View (Hebrew).
    Ed. Z. Maor. Jerusalem: Makhon Binah le-'Ittim, 2006.
Meroz, Ronit. "Redemption in the Lurianic Teaching" (Hebrew). Ph. D. diss. The Hebrew
    University of Jerusalem, 1988.
Meroz, Ronit. 'On the Time and Place of Some Paragraphs of Sefer Ha-Bahir (Hebrew). Da'at 49
    (2002): 137–180.

Meroz, Ronit. "The Middle Eastern Origins of Kabbalah." *Journal for the Study of Sephardic and Mizrahi Jewry* (Feb. 2007a): 39–56 (http://sephardic.fiu.edu/journal/RonitMeroz. pdf).

Meroz, Ronit. "A Journey of Initiation in the Babylonian Layer of *Sefer ha-Bahir*." *Studia Hebraica* 7 (2007b): 17–33.

Meroz, Ronit. "The Archaeology of the Zohar – *Sifra Ditseni'uta* as a Sample Text." *Da'at* 82 (20016): 10–85.

Montagu, Ashley. *The Natural Superiority of Women, A noted anthropologist destroys the myth of male supremacy*. Walnut Creek, CA.: AlmaMira Press, 1999.

Mopsik, Charles. *Lettre sur la sainteté: Le secret de la relation entre l'homme et la femme dans la Cabbale*. Lagrasse: Verdier, 1986.

Mopsik, Charles. *Recherches autour de la lettre sur la sainteté, Sources, Textes, Influences*. Paris: Université Panthéon-Sorbonne, 1987.

Mopsik, Charles. "The Body of Engenderment in the Hebrew Bible, the Rabbinic Tradition and the Kabbalah." In Fragments for a History of the Human Body. Ed. M. Feher. New York: Zone Books, 1989.

Mopsik, Charles. *Les grands textes de la cabale, Les rites qui font Dieu*. Lagrasse: Verdier, 1993.

Mopsik, Charles. *Le secret du marriage de David et Betsabée*. Paris: L'Èclat, Combat, 1994.

Mopsik, Charles. "Maimonide et la cabale. Deux types de rencontre du judaisme avec la philosophie." In Mopsik, *Chemins de la cabale*. Tel Aviv-Paris: Éclat, 2004. 48–54.

Mopsik, Charles. *Sex of the Soul, The Vicissitudes of Sexual Difference in Kabbalah*. Ed. D. Abrams. Los Angeles: Cherub Press, 2005.

Morris, Leah. "*Neqqudat Zion, Sod Beit ha-Rehem*" (Hebrew). In *R. Moshe Cordovero, Ma'ayan 'Ein Ya'aqov*. Ed. B. Sack. Beer Sheva: Ben Gurion University Press, 2009. 112–147

Mottolese, Maurizio. *Bodily Rituals in Jewish Mysticism, the Intensification of Cultic Hand Gestures by Medieval Kabbalists*. Los Angeles: Cherub Press, 2016.

Muffs, Yohanan. *Love & Joy, Law, Language and Religion in Ancient Israel*. New York and Jerusalem: Jewish Theological Seminary, 1992.

Murphy, Ronald. *The Tree of Life: An Exploration of Biblical Wisdom Literature*. New York: Doubleday, ABRL, 1990.

Murphy, Ronald. "The Personification of Wisdom." In *Wisdom in Ancient Israel: Essays in Honor of J. A. Emerton*. Ed. J. Day, R. P. Gordon, and H. G. M. Williamson. Cambridge: Cambridge University Press, 1995. 222–233.

Myth, Religion, and Mother Right, Selected Writings of J. J. Bachofen. Tr. R. Manheim. Princeton: Princeton University Press, 1967.

Neher, André. *Prophètes et prophéties, L'essence du prophétisme*. Paris, Payot, 1995.

Neumann, Erich. *The Great Mother—An Analysis of the Archetype*. Trans. R. Manheim. New York, NY: Pantheon Books, 1954.

Neumann, Erich. *The Origins and History of Consciousness*. Trans. R. F. C. Hull. New York, NY: Harper Torchbooks, 1954.

Neumann, Erich. "Mystical Man." In *The Mystic Vision*. Ed. J. Campbell. Princeton: Princeton University Press, 1982.

Neumark, David. *Toledot ha-Filosofia be-Yisrael*. Jerusalem: rpr. Maqor, 1971.

Neusner, Jacob. *Androgynous Judaism, Masculine and Feminine in the Dual Torah*. Macon, Georgia: Mercer University Press, 1993.

Newman, Barbara. *Sister of Wisdom, St. Hildegard's Theology of the Feminine*. Berkeley, University of California Press, 1987.

Newman, Barbara. *From Virile Woman to WomanChrist*. Philadelphia: University of
    Pennsylvania Press, 1995.
Newman, Barbara. *God and the Goddesses, Vision, Poetry and Belief in the Middle Ages*.
    Philadelphia: University of Pennsylvania Press, 2003.
Newman, Barbara. "Gender." In *The Wiley-Blackwell Companion to Christian Mysticism*.
    Ed. J. A. Lamm. Blackwell, 2013.
Nini, Yehudah. "Sabbatean Messianism in Yemen" (Hebrew). *Pe'amim* 65 (1995): 5–17.
Oron, Michal. "Did R. Todros Abulafia ha-Levi write *Sefer Ma'arekhet ha-'Elohut*?" (Hebrew).
    Qiryat Sefer 51 (1976): 697–704.
Oron, Michal. "The Literature of Commentaries to the Ten *Sefirot*" (Hebrew). In *Studies in
    Jewish History Presented to Joseph Hacker*. Ed. Y. Ben-Naeh, et alia. Jerusalem: The
    Zalman Shazar Center, 2015. 212–229.
Pachter, Mordechai. "The Root of Faith is the Root of Heresy." In Pachter, *Roots of Faith and
    Devequt, Studies in the History of Kabbalistic Ideas*. Los Angeles: Cherub Press, 2004.
Pagels, Elaine. *The Gnostic Gospels*. New York: Vintage Books, 1981.
Patai, Raphael. *The Hebrew Goddess*. New York: Avon Books, 1978.
Pedaya, Haviva. "The Provencal Stratum in the Redaction of *Sefer ha-Bahir*" (Hebrew). *Shlomo
    Pines Jubilee Volume (= Jerusalem Studies in Jewish Thought*, vol. 9). Ed. Z. W. Harvey,
    M. Idel. Jerusalem: Hamakor Press, 1990. 2: 139–164.
Pedaya, Haviva. "Sabbath, Sabbatai, and the Diminution of Moon, – The Holy Conjunction,
    Sign and Image" (Hebrew). In *Myth in Judaism, Eshel Beer-Sheva*. Ed. H. Pedayah.
    Jerusalem: Mossad Bialik, 1996, 4: 143–191.
Pedaya, Haviva. *Vision and Speech, Models of Revelatory Experience in Jewish Mysticism*
    (Hebrew). Los Angeles: Cherub Press, 2002.
Pedaya, Haviva. *Nahmanides, Cyclical Time and Holy Text*. Tel Aviv: 'Am 'Oved, 2003.
Pedaya, Haviva. "The Great Mother: The Struggle between Nahmanides and the Zohar Circle."
    In *Temps i espais de la Girona jueva; actes del Simposi Internacional celebrat a Girona 23,
    24 i 25 de març de 2009*. Ed. Silvia Planas Marcé. Girona, 2011a.
Pedaya, Haviva. *Walking Through Trauma: Rituals of Movement in Jewish Myth, Mysticism,
    and History* (Hebrew). Tel Aviv: Resling, 2011b.
Pedaya, Haviva. *Kabbalah and Psychoanalysis, An Inner Journey following the Jewish Mysticism*
    (Hebrew). Tel Aviv: Yediyot Aharonot, 2015.
Pelikan, Jaroslav. *The Christian Tradition*. Chicago and London, 1971.
Penkower, Jordan S. *The Dates of Composition of the Zohar and the Book of Bahir, The History
    of Biblical Vocalization and Accentuation as a Tool for Dating Kabbalistic Works*.
    Los Angeles: Cherub Press, 2010.
Pépin, Jean. "Theories of Procession in Plotinus and the Gnostics." In *Neoplatonism and
    Gnosticism*. Ed. R.T. Wallis and J. Bregman. Albany: SUNNY Press, 1992.
Perlmuter, Moshe A. *Rabbi Jonathan Eibeschuetz and His Attitude towards Sabbatianism*
    (Hebrew). Jerusalem, Tel Aviv: Schocken, 1947.
Pessin, Sarah. "Loss, Presence and Gabirol's Desire: Medieval Jewish Philosophy and the
    Possibility of a Feminist Ground." In *Women and Gender in Jewish Philosophy*. Ed. Hava
    Tirosh-Samuelson. Bloomington: Indiana University Press, 2004. 27–50.
Pines, Shlomo. "Points of Similarity between the Exposition of the Doctrine of the Sephirot in
    the *Sepher Yetzirah* and a Text of the Pseudo Clementine Homilies: the Implications of
    this Resemblance." In Pines, *Studies in the History of Jewish Thought*, vol. 5. Jerusalem:
    Magnes Press, 1997.

Polen, Nehemia. "Miriam's Dance: Radical Egalitarianism in Hasidic Thought." *Modern Judaism* 12 (1992): 1–12.

Porat, Oded. "'Founding of the Circle': Rudiments of Esse and the Linguistic Creation in the Book 'Fountain of Wisdom' and its Related Treatises" (Hebrew). Ph.D. diss, Hebrew University of Jerusalem, 2012.

Poulet, Georges. *Les Metamorphoses du cercle*. Paris: Flammarion, 1981.

Rabil, Jr., Albert. *Henricus Cornelius Agrippa, Declamation on the Nobility and Preeminence of the Female Sex*. Chicago London: University of Chicago Press, 1996.

Rapoport-Albert, Ada. "On Women in Hasidism: S. A. Horodecky and the Maid of Ludmir Tradition." In *Jewish History: Essays in Honor of Chimen Abramsky*. Ed. A. Rapoport-Albert and S. Zipperstein. London: Peter Halban, 1988.

Rapoport-Albert, Ada. "On the Position of Women in Sabbatianism." In *Ha-Ḥalom ve-Shivero: The Sabbatean Movement and its Aftermath: Messianism Sabbatianism and Frankism*. Jerusalem: Mandel Institute for Jewish Studies, 2001. 1: 143–327.

Rapoport-Albert, Ada. *Women and the Messianic Heresy of Sabbetai Zevi, 1666–1816*. Oxford: Littman Library, 2011.

Ravitzky, Aviezer. "The God of the Philosophers and the God of the Kabbalists" [rpr.] In Ravitzky, *History and Faith. Studies in Jewish Philosophy*. Amsterdam, Gieben, 1986. 134–141.

Ravitzky, Aviezer. *Al Da'at ha-Maqom, Studies in the History of Jewish Philosophy* (Hebrew). Jerusalem: Keter, 1991.

Roi, Biti. "Women and Femininity: Images from the Kabbalistic Literature" (Hebrew). In *To be a Jewish Woman*. Ed. M. Shilo. Jerusalem: Urim, 2001.

Roi, Biti. "Lost and Found: the Evolution of Kabbalistic Interpretation from *Tiqquney ha- Zohar* to Rav Nachman of Breslav" (Hebrew). In *The Zoharic Story*. Ed. Y. Liebes, Y. Benarroch, and M. Hellner-Eshed. Jerusalem: Ben Zvi Institute and Magnes Press, 2017a. 654–694.

Roi, Biti. *Love of the Shekhina: Mysticism and Poetics in Tiqqunei ha-Zohar* (Hebrew). Ramat Gan: Bar Ilan University Press, 2017b.

Ross, Tamar. "A Response Article." In *The Two Great Lights, Woman's Equality in the Feminine from a Jewish Point of View* (Hebrew). Ed. Z. Maor. Jerusalem, 2006. 189–203.

Ringgren, Helmer. *Word and Wisdom: Studies in the Hypostatization of Divine Qualities and Functions in the Ancient Near East*. Lund, Sweden: Hakan Ohlssons Boktryckeri, 1947.

Ruether, Rosemary Radford. *Goddess and the Divine Feminine, A Western Religious History*. Berkeley, University of California Press, 2005.

Sack, Bracha. *The Kabbalah of R. Moshe Cordovero* (Hebrew). Beer Sheva: Ben Gurion University Press, 1995.

Sack, Bracha. *Shomer ha-Pardes, The Kabbalist Rabbi Sabbetai Sheftel Horowitz of Prague* (Hebrew). Beer Sheva: Ben Gurion University Press, 2002.

Sack, Bracha, ed. "The Secret of Thight, the Struggle between Good and Evil (Hebrew). In *From the Fountains of Sefer Elimah by R. Moshe Cordovero and Studies in his Kabbalah*. Ed. B. Sack. Beer Sheva: Ben Gurion University Press, 2013. 148–160.

Safrai, Uri. "The *Kavvanot* Homilies of R. Moses Jonah" (Hebrew). *Kabbalah* 38 (2017): 197–251.

Schäfer, Peter. *Mirror of His Beauty: Feminine Images of God from the Bible to the Early Kabbala*. Princeton: Princeton University Press, 2002.

Schlanger, Jacques E. "Sur le Rôle du 'Tout' dans la Création selon Ibn Gabirol." *Revue des études juives* 123 (1965): 125–135.

Schneider, Sarah Yehudit. *Kabbalistic Writings on the Nature of Masculine & Feminine*. Northvale, NJ: Jason Aronson, 2001 [Hebrew translation: Jerusalem, Reuven Mass, 2008].

Scholem, Gershom. "Eine unbekannte mystische Schrift des Moses de Leon." *MGWJ* [*Monats-schrift für die Geschichte und Wissenschaft des Judenthums*] 71 (1927): 109–123.

Scholem, Gershom. *The Kabbalot of R. Jacob and R. Isaac, the sons of R. Jacob ha-Kohen.* Jerusalem, 1927.

Scholem, Gershom. "Mafteah le-Perushim 'al 'Eser Sefirot" (Hebrew). *Qiryat Sefer* 10 (1933/1934): 498–515.

Scholem, Gershom, ed. *be-'Iqvot Mashiyah.* Jerusalem: Tarshish Books, 1944.

Scholem, Gershom. "On the Problems of *Sefer Ma'arekhet ha-'Elohut* and its Commentators." *Qiryat Sefer* 21 (1944/45): 284–295.

Scholem, Gershom. *Major Trends in Jewish Mysticism.* New York: Schocken Books, 1964.

Scholem, Gershom. *On Kabbalah and Its Symbolism.* Trans. R. Manheim. New York: Schocken Books, 1969.

Scholem, Gershom. *Sabbatai Sevi, the Mystical Messiah.* Trans. R. J. Z. Werblowsky. Princeton: Princeton University Press, 1973.

Scholem, Gershom. *Kabbalah.* Jerusalem: Keter, 1974a.

Scholem, Gershom. *Studies and Texts Concerning the History of Sabbateanism and Its Metamorphoses* (Hebrew). Jerusalem: Mossad Bialik, 1974b.

Scholem, Gershom. *Origins of the Kabbalah.* Trans. A. Arkush. Ed. R.J. Z. Werblowsky. Princeton: JPS, Princeton University Press, 1987.

Scholem, Gershom. *On the Mystical Shape of the Godhead.* Trans. J. Neugroschel. Ed. J. Chipman. New York: Schocken Books, 1991a.

Scholem, Gershom. *Researches in Sabbateanism* (Hebrew). Ed. Y. Liebes. Tel Aviv: 'Am 'Oved, 1991b.

Scholem, Gershom. *Studies in Kabbalah* vol. 1 (Hebrew). Ed. J. ben Shlomo, M. Idel. Tel Aviv: 'Am 'Oved, 1998.

Schwartzmann, Julia. "Gender Concepts of Medieval Jewish Thinkers and the Book of Proverbs." *Jewish Studies Quarterly* 7, no. 3 (2000): 183–202.

Schwartzman, Julia. "From Mystical Vision to Gender Equality Aspirations: A Hermeneutical Journey of Two Biblical Verses." *Journal of Jewish Studies* 66 (2015): 138–149.

Sed-Rajna, Gabrielle. *Azriel de Gerone, Commentaire sur la Liturgie Quotidienne.* Leiden: Brill, 1974.

Sed-Rajna, Gabrielle "L'influence de Jean Scot sur la doctrine du kabbaliste Azriel de Gerone," In *Jean Scot Erigene et l'histoire de la philosophie.* Paris, 1977.

Segol, Marla. "Genre as Argument in the *Sefer Yetsirah*: A New Look at Its Literary Structure." *Journal of the American Academy of Religion* 79 (2011): 961–990.

Shatil, Sharron. "The Doctrine of Secrets in *Emek ha-Melekh.*" *Jewish Studies Quarterly* 17 (2010): 358–395.

Smith, Mark S. "God Male and Female in the Old Testament: Yahveh and His 'Asherah.'" *Theological Studies* 48 (1987): 333–340.

Sobol, Neta. *Transgression of the Torah and the Rectification of God: The Theosophy of Idra Rabba' in the Zohar, and Its Unique Status in Thirteenth-Century Kabbalah.* Los Angeles: Cherub Press, 2017.

Sommer, Benjamin D. *A Prophet Reads Scripture: Allusions in Isaiah 40–66.* Stanford: Stanford University Press, 1998.

Stern, Joseph. *The Matter and Form of Maimonides's Guide.* Cambridge, MA.: Harvard University Press, 2013.

Stern, Samuel. "'The First in Thought is the Last in Action': the History of a Saying attributed to Aristotle." *Journal of Semitic Studies* 7, no. 2 (1962): 235–252.

Stienstra, Nelly. *YHWH is the Husband of His People*. Kampen: Pharos, 1993.

Stroumsa, Gedaliahu G. *Another Seed, Studies in Gnostic Mythology*. Leiden: Brill, 1984.

Stroumsa, Gedaliahu G. *Savoir et Salut*. Paris: Le Cerf, 1992.

Ta-Shma, Israel M. "Rabbeinu Dan Ashkenazi" (Hebrew). In *Studies in Jewish* Mysticism, *Philosophy and Ethical Literature Presented to Isaiah Tishby*. Jerusalem: Magnes Press, 1986. 385–394. [repr in Ta-Shma. *Knesset Meḥqarim*, Jerusalem: Magnes Press, 2004. 2: 157–166].

Ta-Shma, Israel M. *Ha-Nigle she-ba-nistar, The Halakhic Residue in the Zohar* (Hebrew). Tel Aviv: haKibbutz haMeuhad, 2001.

Tirosh-Samuelson, Hava. "Gender in Jewish Mysticism." *Jewish Mysticism and Kabbalah, New Insights and Scholarship*. Ed. Frederick E. Greenspahn. New York, London: New York University Press, 2011.

Tishby, Isaiah. "Passages from *Sefer Ma'arekhet ha-'Elohut* in *Sefer Tzioni*" (Hebrew). *Qiryat Sefer*19 (1942/1943): 55–57.

Tishby, Isaiah. *Netivei 'Emunah u-Minut* (Hebrew). Ramat Gan: Massada, 1964.

Tishby, Isaiah. *The Wisdom of the Zohar, An Anthology of Texts*. Trans. D. Goldstein. London, Washington: Littman Library, 1991.

Tishby, Isaiah. *Studies in Kabbalah and Its Branches* (Hebrew). Jerusalem: Magnes Press, 1993.

Tishby, Isaiah. *Messianic Mysticism: Moses Hayim Luzzatto and the Padua School*. Trans. M. Hoffman. Oxford and Portland: Littman Library, 2008.

Tubi, Joseph. *'Iunim be-Megillat Teiman* (Hebrew). Jerusalem, 1986.

Tworek, Wojciech. "Time and Gender in the Teachings of Shne'ur Zalman of Liadi." *Habad Hasidism, History, Thought, Image*. Ed. J. Meir, G. Sagiv. Jerusalem: The Zalman Shazar Center, 2016.

Tzemach, Adi. *Studies in the Work of Shlomo ibn–Gabirol, 'Yesh be-mo Yesh'* (Hebrew). Tel Aviv, 1985.

Uffenheimer, Rivka Schatz. *Hasidism as Mysticism: Quietistic Elements in Eighteenth-Century Hasidic Thought*. Trans. J. Chipman. Princeton–Jerusalem: Princeton University Press, 1993.

Urbach, Ephraim E. *The Sages, Their Concepts and Beliefs*. Trans. I. Abrahams. Jerusalem, 1979.

Vadet, Jean-Claude. *L'esprit Courtois et Orient, dans les cinq premiers siècles de l'Hegire*. Paris: Maisonneuve et Larose, 1968.

Vajda, Georges. *Le commentaire d'Ezra of Gérone sur le Cantique des cantiques*. Paris: Aubier-Montaigne, 1969.

Valabregue-Perry, Sandra. *Concealed and Revealed, 'Ein Sof' in Theosophic Kabbalah*. Los Angeles: Cherub Press, 2010.

Verman, Mark. "Kabbalah Refracted." *Shofar* 14 (1996): 123-130.

Vickers, Brian. "Analogy versus Identity: The Rejection of Occult Symbolism, 1580–1680." In *Occult & Scientific Mentalities in the Renaissance*. Ed. Brian Vickers. Cambridge, 1986. 95–163.

Vickers, Brian. "On the Function of Analogy in the Occult." în *Hermeticism and the Renaissance*. Ed. I. Merkel and A. Debus. Cranbury: Folger Books, 1988. 265–292.

Wachs, Ron. *The Secret of Unity, Unifications in the Kabbalistic and Hasidic Thought of R. Hayyim ben Solomon Tyrer of Czernowitz* (Hebrew). Los Angeles: Cherub Press, 2006.

Webster, Jane R. "*Sophia*: Engendering Wisdom in Proverbs, Ben Sira and Wisdom of Solomon." *Journal for the Study of Old Testament* 78 (1998): 63–79.

Weinfeld, Moshe "Feminine Features in the Imagery of God in Israel; the Sacred Marriage and the Sacred Tree." *Vetus Testamentum* (1996): 515–529.

Weinstein, Roni. "Abraham Yagel Gallico's Commentary on Woman of Valor." In *Tov* Elem, *Memory,* Community & Gender in Medieval & Early *Modern Jewish* Societies, *Essays in Honor of Robert Bonfil*. Ed. E. Baumgarten, A. Raz-Krakotzkin, and R. Weinstein. Jerusalem: Mossad Bialik, 2011a. 118–135.

Weinstein, Roni. *Kabbalah and Jewish Modernity* (Hebrew). Tel Aviv: Tel Aviv University Press, 2011b.

Weiss, Judith. *A Kabbalistic Christian Messiah in the Renaissance, Guillaume Postel and the Book of the Zohar* (Hebrew). Tel Aviv: Hakibbutz Hameuhad, 2016.

Weiss, Tzahi. *Cutting the Shoots, The Perception of the Shekhinah in the World of Early Kabbalah* (Hebrew). Jerusalem: Magnes Press, 2015.

Weissler, Chava. *Voices of the Matriarchs: Listening to the Prayers of Early Modern Jewish Women*. Boston: Beacon Press, 1998.

Werblowsky, Zwi. *Joseph Karo, Layer and Mystic*. Oxford: Oxford University Press, 1962.

Wind, Edgar. *Pagan Mysteries in the Renaissance*. New York, 1967.

Winston, David. *Logos and Mystical Theology in Philo of Alexandria*. Cincinnati: HUC Press, 1985.

Wirszubski, Chaim, "Francesco Giorgio's Commentary on Giovanni Pico's Kabbalistic Theses." *Journal of the Warburg and Courtauld Institutes* 37 (1974): 145–156.

Wirszubski, Chaim. *Between the Lines, Kabbalah, Christian Kabbalah and Sabbateanism* (Hebrew). Ed. M. Idel. Jerusalem: Magnes, 1990. 121–188.

Wisdom of Solomon. Trans. M. Hengel. In *The Messiah, Developments in Earliest* Judaism *and* Christianity. Ed. J.H. Charlesworth. Minneapolis 1992.

Wolfson, Elliot R. "Female Imaging of the Torah: From Literary Metaphor to Religious Symbol." In *From Ancient Israel to Modern Judaism, Intellect in Quest of Understanding – Essays in Honor of Marvin Fox*. Ed. Jacob Neusner, Ernest S. Frerichs, and Nahum Sarna. Atlanta, Georgia, 1990a. 2:271–307.

Wolfson, Elliot R. "God, the Demiurge and the Intellect: On the Usage of the Word *Kol* in Abraham ibn Ezra." *Revue des études juives* 149 (1990b): 77–111.

Wolfson, Elliot R. "Images of God's Feet." In *People of the Body,* Jews *and* Judaism from an Embodied Perspective. Ed. H. Eilberg-Schwartz. Albany: SUNY Press, 1992. 145–181.

Wolfson, Elliot R "The Tree that is All: Jewish-Christian Roots of the Kabbalistic Symbol in 'Sefer ha-Bahir.'" *Journal of Jewish Thought & Philosophy* 3, no. 1 (1993): 31–76.

Wolfson, Elliot R. *Through a Speculum that Shines, Vision and Imagination in Medieval Jewish Mysticism*. Princeton: Princeton University Press, 1994a.

Wolfson, Elliot R. "Woman: The Feminine as Other in Theosophic Kabbalah: Some Philosophical Observations on the Divine Androgyne." In *The Other in Jewish* Thought *and Identity,* Constructions *of Jewish* Culture *and* Identity. Ed. L. Silberstein and R. Cohn. New York: New York University Press, 1994b. 166–204.

Wolfson, Elliot R. *Along the Path*. Albany: SUNY Press, 1995a.

Wolfson, Elliot R. *Circle in the Square, Studies in the Use of Gender in Kabbalistic Symbolism*. Albany: SUNY Press, 1995b.

Wolfson, Elliot R. "Coronation of the Sabbath Bride: Kabbalistic Myth and the Ritual of Androgynisation." *The Journal of Jewish Thought and Philosophy* 6 (1997): 301–343.

Wolfson, Elliot R. "Tiqqun ha-Shekhinah, Redemption and the Overcoming of Gender Dimorphism in the Messianic Kabbalah of Moses Hayyim Luzatto." *History of Religions* 36 (1997): 289–332.

Wolfson, Elliot R. "Conceptions of Wisdom in Sefer ha-Bahir." *Poetics To-Day* 19, no.1 (1998): 147–176.

Wolfson, Elliot R. "Constructions of the *Shekhinah* in the Messianic Theosophy of Abraham Cardoso, with an Annotated Edition of *Derush ha-Shekhinah*." *Journal of Jewish Thought and Philosophy* 3 (1998a): 11–143.

Wolfson, Elliot R. "The Engenderment of Messianic Politics: Symbolic Significance of Sabbatai Sevi's Coronation." In *Toward the Millennium, Messianic Expectations from the Bible to Waco*. Ed. P. Schaefer and M. Cohen. Leiden: Brill, 1998b.

Wolfson, Elliot R. "Occultation of the Feminine and the Body of Secrecy in Medieval Kabbalah." In. *Rendering the Veil, Concealment and Secrecy in the History of Religions*. Ed. E. R. Wolfson. New York, London: Seven Bridges Press, 1999.

Wolfson, Elliot R. "Gender and Heresy in the Study of Kabbalah (Hebrew)." *Kabbalah* 6 (2001): 231–262.

Wolfson, Elliot R. "Beneath the Wings of the Great Eagle: Maimonides and thirteenth century Kabbalah." In *Moses* Maimonides *(1138-1204); His* Religious, *Scientific, and Philosophical "Wirkungsgeschichte" in Different Cultural Contexts*. Ed. G. K. Hasselhoff and O. Fraisse. Würzburg: Ergon Verlag, 2004. 209–237.

Wolfson, Elliot R. *Language, Eros, Being, Kabbalistic Hermeneutics and Poetic Imagination*. New York: Fordham University Press, 2005.

Wolfson, Elliot R. "The Impact of Maimonides' *Via Negativa* on Late Thirteenth Century Kabbalah." In *Maimonidean Studies*. Ed. A. Hyman. New York: Yeshivah University, 2008. 5: 393–442.

Wolfson, Elliot R. "Structure, Innovation, and Disremptive Temporality: The Use of Models to Study Continuity and Discontinuity in Kabbalistic Tradition." In *Essays in Honor of Moshe Idel*. Ed. S. and M. Frunza. Cluj-Napoca: ProvoPress, 2008.

Wolfson, Elliot R. *Open Secret*. New York: Columbia University Press, 2009.

Wolfson, Elliot R. *A Dream Interpreted within a Dream: Oneiropoiesis and the Prism of Imagination*. New York: Zone Books, 2011.

Wolfson, Elliot R. "Patriarchy and the Motherhood of God in Zoharic Kabbalah and Meister Eckhart." In *Envisioning Judaism: Studies in Honor of Peter Schaefer*. Ed. R. Boustan & alia. Tuebingen: Mohr/Siebeck, 2013. 2: 1049–1088.

Wolfson, Elliot R. "Interview." In *Elliot R. Wolfson, Poetic Thinking*. Ed. H. Tirosh-Samuelson and A. Agus. Leiden: Brill, 2015a.

Wolfson, Elliot R. "Retroactive Not Yet: Linear Circularity and Kabbalistic Temporality." In *Time and Eternity in Jewish Mysticism: That Which is Before and That Which is After*. Ed. B. Ogren. Leiden and Boston: Brill, 2015b. 37–48.

Yahalom, Joseph. *Priestly Palestinian Poetry, A Narrative Liturgy for the Day of Atonement* (Hebrew). Jerusalem: Magnes Press, 1997.

Yates, Frances A. *Giordano Bruno and the Hermetic Tradition*. London, 1964.

Yosha, Nissim. *Captivated by Messianic Agonies, Theology, Philosophy and Messianism in the thought of Abraham Miguel Cardoso* (Hebrew). Jerusalem: Ben Zvi Institute, 2015.

Zimran, Adiel. "Philosophy, Tradition, and Esoterica in Isaac Ibn Latif's *Sha'ar ha-Shamayim*." Ph. D. diss., Hebrew University of Jerusalem, 2016.

Zola, Elemire "The Archetype of the Supernal Lady from Ancient Arabia to Edwardian England." *Incognita* 1–2 (1990): 183–208.

Zola, Elemire. *I mistici dell'Occidente*. [second edition] Milano: Adelphi, 2003.

Zori, David. *Not in the Hands of Heaven, The Limit of Human Action in the Teachings of Early Hasidic Masters* (Hebrew). Jerusalem: Magnes Press, 2016.

Name Index

https://doi.org/10.1515/9783110599800-016

Subject Index

Adam 22, 37, 200
'Adam Qadmon 115n496, 141, 146
Agent Intellect 28, 78
'Akatriel 53, 54
Androcentric vii, 1, 3n4, 41, 100, 132, 138,
140n626, 153n698, 191, 198, 201, 204, 205
Androgyne 60, 64, 89n375, 93, 94, 106n456,
108, 123, 133, 196n884, 207, 217
Anthropomorphism 21, 56, 63n250,
82n345, 108
'Arikh 'anppin 106n458, 106, 109, 112,
113n483, 118, 166n764
Ashkenaz 18, 50, 52, 54–56, 57, 62n249, 63,
78, 102, 148–158, 191, 210
'Atarah/'Ateret (diadem) 8, 13, 25, 32, 33,
34, 38, 41, 43, 45, 68, 69, 70, 71, 96,
106, 119n512, 143, 148, 173, 174n803,
180, 184
– ascent of the 33, 52, 54, 126
– as encompassing 38, 49n168, 68
– on the head 33, 34, 49n168, 53n194, 59,
70n272, 106n456, 107, 113, 119n512, 123,
150, 151, 173
– and Keter 31n76, 33n86, 54, 56, 59, 70,
72, 123n530, 124, 210 (see also Keter
Malkhut)
'Ateret ha-Yesod 77n302, 109, 117, 173,
174n804
'Attiqa' 87, 107, 113, 115, 117n503, 133,
168, 170
'Attiq Yomin 106n455, 109, 114n488
'Attiqa' Qadisha' 104, 118, 126, 127, 128n564,
131, 136, 138n564, 165
Athena 6, 66, 85, 186, 200
Axial/pre-axial age 21–22, 50, 83, 85, 89,
105, 189, 193, 200n895, 212n938,
214, 215

Bahir, the Book 6n8, 12n20, 21–22, 29–30,
35n90, 37, 47n156, 157, 158, 48n165,
49n169, 50, 52, 54, 56–58, 63n251, 64,
70n282, 99n429, 148, 177n187, 183,
189, 190, 210
Binah ('Imma') 142–143, 170

Bride (Kallah) 6, 49, 53–55, 84–86, 121,
136–137, 159, 161n738, 172, 183, 203

Christian mysticism 15n30, 212n938
Chronos 129
Commandments 8, 12, 13n22, 16, 37, 53n194,
80, 162, 163, 179, 186, 211, 213n940
Configurations (Partzufin) 87, 90n383,
104n446, 105n452, 108, 109, 112,
114n489, 117n503, 118, 126–128,
142–143, 165n759, 166n764

Daughter 4, 5, 6, 13, 14, 21, 47–66, 79, 80,
81, 114–115, 120, 123n529, 128, 162, 162,
169, 181n832, 185, 192, 203
David 53, 173n802
Diagrams 7, 41, 72n302, 90, 94n403, 95,
111–112, 121, 218
Diotima 10
Du-partzufin 40, 41, 42, 45n153, 88, 90, 153,
179n822, 184

'Ein Sof, Infinite 46n133, 58n222, 64n257, 65,
72n297, 77, 82, 88–90, 91n386, 92–94,
95n407, 96, 99, 105n453, 106, 110,
114n489, 115, 116n501, 121n222, 124,
129, 131, 137, 138, 144–146, 154n701,
155, 156, 163n754, 164–166, 167n768,
168, 173, 174, 176, 177n814, 180
Electra complex 181
Equality viii, 12n21, 3, 19n44, 20, 29, 39,
46, 71, 72n297, 72n298, 84, 91, 92,
93, 94, 96, 109, 114n489, 126, 127,
140n627, 142n637, 150, 151–152, 156,
163, 191, 209
Eve, Havah 75n317, 181
Exile 8, 39, 81, 139
– exile of the Shekhinah 80n336, 81, 100,
142, 147, 154, 159, 168, 181, 191

Father 47–66
Female
– as action 31, 35–37, 42–44, 68, 70, 72,
73n306, 130, 137–139, 185–188, 200

https://doi.org/10.1515/9783110599800-017

CPSIA information can be obtained
at www.ICGtesting.com
Printed in the USA
LVHW092134191121
703921LV00003B/107